The Dynamics
of
Personal Adjustment

THE
DYNAMICS
OF
PERSONAL

ADJUSTMENT

GEORGE F. J. LEHNER

Director of the Psychological Clinic
University of California, Los Angeles

ELLA KUBE

Social Psychologist, Occidental College

NEW YORK   PRENTICE-HALL, INC.   1955

PRENTICE-HALL PSYCHOLOGY SERIES

Paul Meehl, Editor

Preface

We would not expect to cross the desert in a boat or the ocean in an automobile, but many of us fail to realize that it is just as unrealistic to expect inadequate behavior patterns to carry us satisfactorily through the journey of life. We tend to take ourselves and our behavior for granted. We tend to coast along, blind to the potentialities we are wasting, deaf to the danger signals manifest in our personalities, dumb in our inability to release the tensions we have suppressed.

The purpose of this book is to attempt to bring into sharper focus certain factors that may facilitate or hinder the journey— to offer suggestions concerning problems that may be encountered, solutions that may be discovered, goals that may be attained, personal relationships that may be established, and pleasures and satisfactions that may be enjoyed.

Contents of the book fall into four major areas. The first three chapters explain why it is important to understand ourselves and our associates and to achieve good mental health. These chapters call attention to the significance of social influences arising from interpersonal relations. They reveal how interesting variations in behavior occur as a result of cause-and-effect relationships. And they present a historical summary of man's views toward adjustment and maladjustment in himself and others, including a discussion of superstitions past and present.

Chapters 4 through 8 deal with the origin, nature, and development of our emotional and psychological needs, our reactions when these needs are frustrated or in conflict (involving the use and mis-use of psychological crutches and defense mechanisms),

v

and a brief consideration of the more severe behavior disturbances—the neuroses and functional psychoses.

The third part of the book, embracing chapters 9 through 14, discusses the dynamics of adjustment and the principles of mental health as related to the problems of family adjustments, school adjustments, social adjustments, job and career adjustments, psychosexual adjustments (before and after marriage), and adult living and old age adjustments. These chapters stress the fact that these basic adjustment problems do not confine themselves to a specific area or age level but span the entire life cycle. The book describes typical problems faced in each area, considers their origin and manner of solution, and emphasizes the fact that continual change must be expected—that each of us must continue to adjust and readjust throughout life, from birth to death.

Chapters 15 and 16 deal first with personal differences and their effect on personality development and adjustment. It is a fairly well accepted fact that no two people are alike, but, in the opinion of the authors, the significance of this fact as a factor in personal adjustment has not been sufficiently stressed. Here the significance of personal differences is emphasized, and the sources for such differences and the techniques for measuring them are discussed. This discussion leads to a consideration of the characteristics of good mental health and the goals of satisfactory personal adjustment *as related to our individual capacities and experiences.*

Chapter 17 discusses the resources and techniques that may be applied to the *process of improving personal adjustment;* an explanation of the meaning of psychotherapy, especially as a learning or re-learning process; and a description of the types of psychotherapeutic learning processes available.

Throughout the book the motivational and goal-directed aspects of behavior are stressed—i.e., that we do not merely act; we act with a purpose. An attempt is made not merely to describe behavior but to *explain* it, to reveal the inner workings, to interpret surface phenomena by exposing the deeper-lying dynamics. The expression "dynamics of adjustment" is intended to convey the multiple facets that operate to influence the relationships between needs, the blocking of these needs, the appearance, disappearance, and shifting of coping and defense mechanisms—the innumerable factors that determine the way in which each individual behaves. The expression implies learning and re-learning—especially in the area of social relations. It implies emphasis not on physiological structure but on psychological strain, not on physiological tonus but on psychological tension. Problems are viewed as a challenge to new learning. Since deviant behavior results from learning, just as does normal behavior, then re-learning may change deviant behavior into normal behavior.

What is a well-adjusted person? How can he remain well-adjusted? How can he reconcile his needs and his social relations? What do his characteristics reveal about himself? How can he handle his problems in order to achieve optimum adjustment—with or without special help? How can he best utilize his capacities and his experiences? These are some of the questions the book considers, from the viewpoint of both a clinical and a social psychologist, in an attempt to show the process of interaction between personal and social needs.

In this book we have tried to present material that we believe will be helpful to students taking courses in introductory psychology and to include, as well, certain ideas and concepts generally found only in more advanced courses and therefore lost to students who must limit the amount of time they can devote to the study of psychology. In discussing this material, we have attempted to avoid theoretical considerations and to stress, instead, the personal experiences of the student or general reader. It was our hope to eliminate technical terms without sacrificing the precision which they convey.

We want to express thanks to our respective wife and husband who have contributed to this book, not only through their general support and encouragement, but also because of their special skills—to Eleanor Lehner for her help in writing and editing, and to Kemper Nomland, Jr., for his help in the choice and preparation of the illustrative material. Our thanks also go to Wilbur Mangas, Coordinating Editor of Prentice-Hall, Inc., for his valuable assistance throughout the preparation of the book.

G.L.

E.K.

Contents

x CONTENTS

17 *Psychotherapy and Adjustment*   *441*

The Dynamics
of
Personal Adjustment

Understanding Ourselves and Our World

CHAPTER 1

- CHARACTERISTICS OF HUMAN ADJUSTMENT
- UNDERSTANDING OUR PERSONAL EXPERIENCES
- SOURCES OF UNDERSTANDING
- ESSENTIALS OF SCIENCE

Before we can understand *how* to adjust—to family, to business associates, to friends—we need to understand *why* it is necessary to adjust. In studying this *why* of adjustment we shall find the answers to three questions. We shall learn (1) to understand ourselves better, (2) to understand others better, and (3) to understand better the world around us. In other words, we need to study the adjustment processes in order to learn how to get along with other people, how to approach school, work or career problems, and how to recognize and resolve general emotional health problems. As long as we live we shall encounter problems that will demand some kind of adjustment, and a continuous procession of problems demands a continuous readiness on our part to adjust to them. We cannot avoid problems—we can only learn to handle them. And we shall be able to handle them only as we learn more about ourselves.

It is surprising that so many of us know more about cars and clothes and the like than we do about ourselves, about the conditions affecting our emotional ups and downs. Some people are most reluctant to take a close look at themselves—as though they were afraid of what they might see. Yet to take that close look is to take the first step toward recognizing our assets and liabilities for what they are. Such a realistic appraisal of self must be the beginning of an exploration in personal adjustment, and the purpose of this book is to provide a guide to such exploration.

Characteristics of Human Adjustment

As already indicated, adjustment is a universal, continuous process. Living organisms, from the simple, single-celled amoeba to complex multi-celled man, are constantly making adjustments of various kinds. These adjustments may concern the satisfaction of biological needs, such as hunger and thirst, or they may, at the human level, involve the fulfillment of psychological needs, such as our desire to belong, to receive love and affection, to gain approval or status, or to find an opportunity for creative self-expression.

When people ask (as they sometimes do), "Why should I adjust?" it usually means that they have confused the word "adjustment" with the word "conformity." The two words cannot be equated. Conformity is only one form of adjustment; and the quality of adjustment achieved by conforming may be good or bad, depending on the circumstances under which it occurs. To one person, for instance, *conforming* to the wishes that his parents cherish about his vocational plans may be the right way because these parental wishes correspond to his own wishes and abilities and because he has confidence in their judgment. To another, who finds himself in conflict with his parents and suppressed by their authority, conformity may mean surrender, leaving him in a state of uncertainty and doubt about himself and damaging his self-esteem. Still a third may not have the abilities necessary for the career his parents want him to enter, and conformity to their wishes in this case may well mean job failure.

Some people may ask the same question, "why adjust," because of the mistaken notion that adjustment is a one-way process. They believe that man is continually forced to adjust to his environment, but fail to realize that man also can shape his environment. Both man and his world are modifiable—whether the world be the physical or the social and psychological world. As our environment changes, we modify our behavior accordingly; and these modifications, in turn, affect the environment. Thus a process of constant interaction occurs.

From our interactions with other people stem some of the most significant experiences in our lives. Some of these people elicit our affection and trust; others arouse in us resentment, anger, jealousy, or rudeness; still others stimulate in us creative achievements that would never have found expression in the absence of social contacts. As Murphy [1] says:

> Affection and trust, belief in the unrealized potentialities of other human beings, calls into existence not only what is waiting to bud, but what never could otherwise be; and others, responding in their turn, lift those who reached out to them to a plane which they themselves could never have defined.

Neither the individual nor his world are static. Both change; both are being acted upon and shaped continually. To be sure, at times these changes are so small that an individual's efforts to adjust to them seem imperceptible. In fact, this apparent absence of changes, rather than the changes themselves, may constitute an adjustment problem. The individual becomes troubled

---

[1] Gardner Murphy, "Human Potentialities," *Journal of Social Issues,* Supplement Series, No. 7, 1953, 10.

by the sameness, the monotony of his life. He comes to look upon change and the adjustment thereto as a welcome relief from his drab, colorless existence. A person may feel that he could cope with the challenge of exciting and dramatic changes, but the monotony gets him down.

Hence both change and regularity or sameness demand adjustment. Always there is a dynamic relationship between the person and his world, and in this relationship lies the basis for the study we call the psychology of adjustment.

Understanding Our Personal Experiences

The process of adjustment, then, is characteristic of the life and development of each of us. Yet there are many of us who live out our lives without ever understanding ourselves and others, who are appalled and dismayed at the problems confronting us, and who, in our distress and anxiety, fall easy prey to the quack, the pseudo-psychologist, who appears on the scene ready with glib answers and solutions to all our problems.

This book is intended to help create and develop an understanding of human adjustment and to show how a knowledge of psychology can aid us in our daily living. We shall be primarily concerned with the adjustment of the normal person as he deals with everyday problems. Studying ways of adjusting to these problems, we shall discover the kind of information about ourselves that will facilitate better adjustment.

Such learning and insight may come about in several ways. It may occur, first of all, by becoming aware of our own behavior and our own problems. Where previously we muddled through somehow, we learn, perhaps for the first time, to look at ourselves. We begin to understand why certain values, goals, and ambitions are important to us, why some people are our friends and others are not, why certain events upset us while others make us happy, why we like what we like and don't like what we don't like. Why, in short, we are what we are and do what we do. In the process of looking at ourselves, we begin to appreciate increasingly our strong points and are willing to consider our weak points. We develop a certain objectivity about ourselves, enabling us to study ourselves more critically and dispassionately with a minimum of self-deception and camouflage.

Secondly, we may become aware of alternative ways of dealing with problems. While previously we may have failed in solving a problem mainly because we saw only one way out of it, we now see different possibilities, either because we have learned, directly, a new approach, or because we have learned to take into account more fully our own needs in relation to the situation. Thus a new approach to an old problem becomes possible.

Thirdly, we may become more fully aware of ourselves as a person-in-the-environment; we may realize that our social existence is one of interconnected, interdependent relationships. Therefore, in order to understand ourselves, we must also understand others, their effect on us and our effect on them.

Finally, we may learn that very few of us utilize our full potentialities and that, therefore, within ourselves we have many possibilities for more satisfying experiences. As Murphy [2] has stated:

> The realization of human potentialities, I suggest, lies in studying the directions in which human needs may be guided, with equal attention to the learning powers of the individual and the feasible directions of cultural evolution. Such study, I suggest, will give the esthetic satisfactions, the scientific satisfactions, and the interpersonal satisfactions a larger and larger place in the total way of life, and rather than achieving a goal, will define an ever widening theatre for the development of new potentialities.

Sources of Understanding

An intelligent inquiry into *what* is known must always concern itself also with the question of *how* it is known. What

---

[2] *Journal of Social Issues,* Supplement Series, No. 7, 1953, 19.

methods are used in arriving at certain findings? Is our information based on hearsay or on a careful investigation? Only if we know the methods by which knowledge is acquired can we evaluate it properly. For instance, somebody may tell us that the morale on a certain college campus or in a certain factory is poor. How did he arrive at this information? Did he interview a cross-section of the student body or the workers, or did he talk with a few articulate gripers? If the methods are inadequate, then the findings can be challenged.

Methods and techniques are also the tools by which we acquire further knowledge. In psychology, as in other fields, progress depends on the use and development of appropriate methods. Thus the intelligence tests constructed by Binet meant a great step forward in our study and our understanding of human intelligence.

Casual observations of our past experiences with certain people may have revealed to us some of their habits or attitudes that are so central to their personality that we may be able to predict quite accurately how they will behave in a particular situation. Knowing a few people of a certain cultural or national group well may enable us, occasionally, to generalize correctly about the whole group. Thus our limited observations may be excellent. Even so, such limited observations should be considered with caution, particularly if we try to generalize from them. At best they provide us with good hunches or—to put it in scientific terminology—with reasonable hypotheses. But these hypotheses must be checked and tested before they can be accepted as valid.

Methods appropriate for dealing with various problems will be discussed in detail in later chapters. Here we shall present only the essentials of a scientific approach to the study of human behavior in terms of which specific methods and specific investigations must be evaluated. We can distinguish five steps in scientific procedure.

The first of these, as already indicated, is the statement of the problem or the formulation of a hypothesis. This may be expressed either as a question or as an assertion of certain relation-

These are some of the methods of inquiry used in the study of human behavior. *(Top)* Psychologist giving a test to a child. *(Middle)* Laboratory Experiment. *(Bottom)* Public Opinion Poll.

(Top) Courtesy of Southern California Society for Mental Hygiene and Hal Adams, photographer. (Middle) Courtesy Laurence R. Cook, Occidental College. (Bottom) Courtesy Facts Consolidated, Los Angeles.

ships. Thus we might ask: What relationship is there between the marital happiness of parents and that of their children? Or we might state: Having a voice in decision-making in a work group increases the productivity of workers and makes them more satisfied with their jobs. An endless number of such problems and hypotheses could be presented. It is an essential requirement of a good hypothesis that it be of manageable size, i.e., that it be amenable to investigation. How many angels can dance on the point of a needle? is a question that does not lend itself to scientific inquiry; no procedure or plan can provide the answer to it. The relevance of such questions and hypotheses to our understanding of human behavior will vary greatly, depending on the experience, insight, and wisdom of the person formulating them. Cohen and Nagel [3] point this out when they say:

> . . . the ability to perceive in some brute experience the occasion for a problem, and especially a problem *whose solution has a bearing on the solution of other problems,* is not a common talent among men. . . . It is a mark of scientific genius to be sensitive to difficulties where less gifted people pass by untroubled by doubt. (Authors' italics).

Or, to put it another way: Scores of persons have been hit on the head by a falling apple, but only Newton, according to the legend, saw in the falling apple the secret of the law of gravity. Sometimes knowledge is advanced because an individual is able to break out of a traditional way of looking at certain phenomena and to formulate a new question or hypothesis.

The second step in scientific procedure is to develop a research design. Having formulated the question or hypothesis, we now plan how to collect the evidence to answer or support it. The type of research design chosen will depend upon the nature of the problem. For some problems controlled experimentation may

---

[3] M. R. Cohen and E. Nagel, *An Introduction to Logic and Scientific Method.* New York, Harcourt, Brace & Company, Inc., 1934, p. 200.

be possible. If we are interested in the effects of a specific movie dealing with gambling, we can set up a before-and-after experiment—i.e., we measure the attitudes of a group of people toward gambling before they see the movie and again after they have seen it. Changes in the attitudes of the group can be attributed,

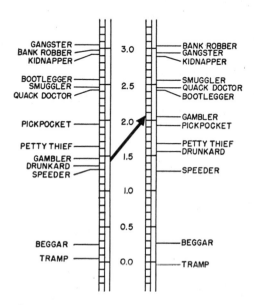

Ratings of crimes before and after seeing the movie "Streets of Chance." After seeing the movie, students ranked gambling a more serious crime. (From Ruth C. Peterson and L. L. Thurstone, Motion Pictures and the Social Attitudes of Children. New York, The Macmillan Company, 1933, p. 14.)

at least in part, to their having seen the movie. Or we can use experimental and control groups, showing the movie to the first but not to the second group and then having both answer an identical set of questions. Again the attitudes of both groups toward gambling will have been measured before we begin the experiment. If the group that saw the movie gives answers different from those of the group excluded from the showing, we can assume that the movie, not the questions asked, was responsible for the difference. With other problems, such an experimental plan may not be possible. If we wish, for instance, to determine the effects of maternal rejection of a child, we may have to get our evidence through intensive clinical case studies.

Third, the methods we use to collect our data have to be specified—i.e., whether we measure attitudes by questionnaires, by open-ended interviews, by projective tests, and so forth. In some studies, careful observation and recording of certain aspects of behavior may be most appropriate. Whatever methods are used, however, we must be sure that they are reliable and valid. By reliable, we mean that repeated measurement will give the same results; by valid, that our methods actually measure what we intend them to measure, that they yield relevant information about the things we are measuring. The conditions under which we make our measurements also must be stated. If we ask a person to answer a questionnaire and make him feel that a great deal is at stake for him in answering it, he will probably answer it differently than if we assured him that he was helping us in finding out whether the questionnaire was a useful one. Or, if we study competitive behavior among children on a playground, we must state whether competitive or cooperative behavior is encouraged by the adults in charge of the playground, what kinds of toys and games are available to the children and other characteristics of the situation that may influence the behavior of the children.

After the data have been collected, they are analyzed and the results are presented. The purpose of the analysis is to order the data in such a way that they give answers to the questions raised in the first step of our procedure. Sometimes these answers may disprove our hypothesis, but even negative results are valuable if they show us that this approach to the problem is not the correct one. In some cases the results may be ambiguous, indicating that a sharpening of the hypothesis or a refining of our methods may be necessary. Frequently, although the results obtained may provide a partial answer to our problem, other questions may be raised providing guides for further inquiries.

The fifth step is closely related to the preceding one. This step involves interpretations and conclusions. Interpretation essentially means relating the obtained evidence to a larger body of scientific knowledge and evaluating it in a theoretical framework. To refer again to the study of the movie on gambling: We are not content to state that this specific movie affects changes in attitudes toward gambling. If our general theoretical interest is in the factors determining attitude change, we want to compare our findings with the results from other studies on attitude change. Our findings may support what is already known about the conditions under which attitudes change, or they may add something new, making it necessary to modify previous interpretations and to reformulate theories. The conclusions, finally, are a summary statement of what the investigator has achieved.

Essentials of Science

Science involves observation—something must be observed by the scientific investigator. However, these observations differ from the random and casual observations that all of us make daily. They differ from them in that they are made systematically, with a definite question or hypothesis in mind, and they are planned in such a way that they can be repeated and thus verified by others. Most important, however, is the fact that the scientist does not stop with observation. He is not interested in a mere gathering of observable facts but attempts to relate them to other facts and to more basic laws. The essence of a scientific explanation is to relate a diversity of observed phenomena to underlying principles.

One person, for instance, may be hostile and belligerent, another shy and timid. But these different symptoms may arise from similar causes. Both may have been rejected as children. In order to understand their behavior, we must relate it to this experience, although our explanation is not complete until we have also explained why they reacted differently to the rejection.

On the other hand, the scientist must be on guard against assuming that the same factors determine certain events because

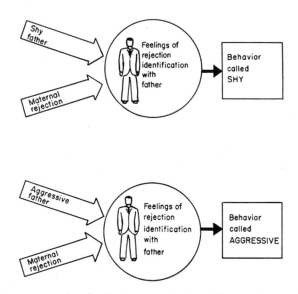

The experience of maternal rejection may lead to different forms of behavior, depending on other influences in the life-space of the child.

these events look similar. Thus a student may fail a college course because he is not interested in the subject matter, because he lacks either ability or necessary background information for it, or because of a severe conflict between him and the instructor.

A by-product of scientific explanation—and a test of its adequacy—is prediction. If our scientific explanation is correct, it will help us not only to account for and understand behavior, but also to predict what specific kind of behavior *will* occur under certain conditions.

Underlying all scientific explorations is the basic assumption of order—the belief that events do not occur haphazardly but only as a result of cause-and-effect relationships. Although most people readily accept this basic assumption to explain physical phenomena, they are skeptical about carrying it over into the area of human behavior. Many people ascribe their behavior to chance or accident and see no relationship between an act and an identifiable cause. But the fact that much of our behavior is puzzling to us and still unexplained is no reason to reject the idea of cause-and-effect.

Actually, it is more accurate to speak of causes and their effects. In a few very simple instances we may be able to identify *one* cause; but usually many underlying causative factors are present in a situation, particularly insofar as human behavior is concerned. A particular response r is not usually the consequence of a specific stimulus s but involves rather a whole grouping of stimuli, external to the organism and internal to it, which motivates behavior. The fact that we often give one name to a whole set of factors, such as rejection or over-protection, should not mislead us into thinking that we are dealing with one specific stimulus. Rejection or over-protection of a child denote a way of behaving toward him that pervades many of the social relations that are important to him. When we are dealing with pervasive influences of this kind, then it is often possible to predict certain trends of behavior. Thus over-protected children often become excessively dependent on their mother or rejected children unusually hostile as compared to other children. But these tendencies may be checked or arrested or even changed by other forces in the child's environment. Thus a warmly accepting grandmother whom the child sees fairly often may, to some extent, counterbalance the effects of the mother's rejection. Or an older sister or brother may help the over-protected child to develop some independence.

Awareness of the multiplicity of causes has brought about a considerable change in our attitude toward certain kinds of behavior not generally socially approved. For example, our attitudes toward alcoholics or alcoholism have changed as we have learned more about the many factors that cause a person to become an alcoholic. It is not merely "weak will" that makes it impossible for a person to stop drinking, or a matter of plain orneriness that makes an individual behave in an excessively hostile or aggressive manner. Such behavior is the natural consequence of many stimulating conditions.

One other point should be emphasized. In our attempt to identify causative factors, we are not interested in final or ultimate causes. The assumption of an ultimate cause does not help us to understand the behavior of the individual at a given time. In order to understand human behavior, we must observe carefully and describe accurately the dynamic forces affecting the individual at the moment of observation—his environment, his needs and goals, and his past experiences insofar as these are operating as determining influences in his present situation. The following chapters are offered in the hope of furthering such understanding.

For Additional Reading

Carroll, Herbert A., *Mental Hygiene—The Dynamics of Adjustment.* New York, Prentice-Hall, Inc., 1951.

Cohen, M. R. and E. Nagel, *An Introduction to Logic and Scientific Method.* New York, Harcourt, Brace & Company, Inc., 1934.

Evans, Jean, *Three Men. An Experiment in the Biography of Emotion.* New York, Alfred A. Knopf, Inc., 1954.

Jahoda, Marie, Morton Deutsch, and Stuart W. Cook, *Research Methods in Social Relations, Part I: Basic Processes.* New York, The Dryden Press, 1951.

Katz, Barney and George F. J. Lehner, *Mental Hygiene in Modern Living.* New York, The Ronald Press Company, 1953.

Langer, Walter C., *Psychology and Human Living.* New York, D. Appleton-Century Company, Inc., 1943.

Lehner, George F. J., *Explorations in Personal Adjustment: A Workbook.* New York, Prentice-Hall, Inc., 1949.

Murphy, Gardner, "Human Potentialities," *Journal of Social Issues,* Supplement Series, No. 7, 1953.

Overstreet, H. A., *The Mature Mind*. New York, W. W. Norton & Company, Inc., 1949.

Skinner, B. F., *Science and Human Behavior*. New York, The Macmillan Company, 1953.

White, Robert W., *Lives in Progress. A Study of the Natural Growth of Personality*. New York, The Dryden Press, 1952.

Social Influences
and Personal Adjustments

CHAPTER 2

- SOME BASIC PSYCHOLOGICAL PRINCIPLES
- STANDARDS OF ADJUSTMENT: SOCIAL NORMS

In order to understand why we act the way we do it is important to remember that our behavior, even such a simple act as smiling at another individual when passing him on the street, may be influenced by many factors. It is necessary, therefore, to study the factors that motivate us and to learn something about the social situations in which we function.

Some Basic Psychological Principles

In the first part of this chapter we shall set forth three principles that we shall follow in exploring the problems of adjustment. These principles involve the following concepts: (1) our life-space, (2) purposive or goal-directed behavior and behavior as a function of need and need-reduction, and (3) the importance of learning in our behavior.

The individual's life-space. The manner in which we behave must always be studied in relation to the environment in which we live. Our relationship to the environment, our perception of certain aspects of the world around us, our unconscious selection of the particular factors to which we shall react comprises what may be termed our "life-space." We use the term "life-space" here in preference to "environment" because we are not concerned with all aspects of environment but only with that portion that we experience directly and that therefore affects our behavior. Life-space denotes "the experienced totality of the individual, comprising a fluid yet indissoluble unity between the experiencing self and the experienced world without, and comprising not only the clearly conscious but also the half-conscious and unconscious dispositions and attitudes which color and give meaning to all that is experienced." [1]

Life-space refers to the environment as we perceive and experience it. A single social gathering, for instance, may have different meanings for the various persons present. To one, it may involve primarily an awareness of the opportunity for making business contacts. Another may look upon it as a chance to attract attention to himself, to be the life of the party. Still a third may feel extremely shy and be uncertain about how to converse with the person next to him. Thus the same social situation is experienced by some as an opportunity for enhancement, by others as a threat.

Another example of how different persons may vary in their reactions to a similar environment is seen in the contrasting behavior we often observe in children of the same family. Parents are frequently puzzled by the fact that their children are so different from one another, even though they have been raised by the same parents, lived in the same house, participated to a great extent in the same activities, heard the same discussions. The diversified personalities that emerge from these common experiences develop because of certain other factors that operate in such

---

[1] Murphy, *Journal of Social Issues,* Supplement Series, No. 7, 1953, 4.

The same situation calls forth different responses from different people: How to get across a puddle. (Courtesy Angus McDougall.)

a way as to provide each of the children with his own individual life-space—a life-space that his siblings cannot share. These factors include changes in the age and socio-economic conditions of the parents between the birth dates of each child, differences in amount of social stimulations available from earliest infancy (for example, the third born would have the attention not only of the parents, but also of the older children), and constitutional differences between the children as they might involve sensitivity to various kinds of stimulation. In short, the life-space of each child in the family is essentially different.

Basic to our understanding of the life-space of an individual is the fact that what we perceive in any given situation is influenced not only by the physical characteristics of that situation, but also by our needs, goals, and past experiences. It is these factors that cause one person's response to certain physical stimuli to be different from another person's. We perceive selectively and make selective responses to the many stimuli that impinge on us.

It is obvious, therefore, that we must consider the life-space of each individual in order to understand his behavior. For purposes of analysis, however, we may focus at times on physiological processes, at other times on psychological needs, or at still other times on the characteristics of a given social situation in which a person finds himself.

Purposive or goal-directed behavior and behavior as a function of need and need-reduction. As biological organisms, we all have needs that must be satisfied if we are to live. These needs have been variously called biological needs, tissue needs, and life-maintaining needs. They include hunger, thirst, the need for air, the need for rest, and so forth. Although we can postpone the satisfaction of these needs to some extent, they must be eventually satisfied if we are to survive.

These needs have their basis in man's biological make-up, but their expression and satisfaction is socially determined. Therefore, to understand what a person will do, how he will do it, and why he will do it, we need to know something not only about his bio-

When hunger remains unsatisfied, and the threat of hunger continues, this deprivation may disrupt the customary behavior of the individual; the person becomes preoccupied with food and "good manners" becomes a meaningless term for him. Here one of the subjects at the starvation experiments at the University of Minnesota licks his plate for the last trace of food. Most subjects saved bits of food to munch on in their quarters. (Courtesy Life Magazine.)

logical needs, but also about the social situations in which he has learned to satisfy these needs. Knowledge of the physiological state alone is not a reliable criterion for predicting behavior. The manner in which the same physiological need is satisfied and the objects chosen for need-satisfaction are different for different people. You, for example, have certain food preferences; or you

Behavior patterns are culturally determined. The Navajo mother cares for her child in one way; the Korean mother cares for hers in another. (Courtesy Southwest Museum, Los Angeles, and Unations.)

have "learned to like" some foods that at one time you found quite tasteless. But the foods you enjoy may be unpalatable to someone else. Let's take another example. Some people eat with chopsticks, some with forks, some with their fingers, depending on their cultural backgrounds. Techniques used for satisfying needs are culture-bound—i.e., they are learned.

In addition to the tissue needs, there are others that we call psychological or social needs or ego-needs. Within this category are the need to belong, the need for love and affection, the need for acceptance and recognition, and others. Although the satisfaction of someone's need for recognition may not be as necessary to his sheer physical survival as his need for food and drink, such a psychological need will, if allowed to remain unfulfilled, seriously affect his over-all well-being.

Psychological needs have a biological-social basis; they grow out of the early experiences of the child when his biological need-satisfaction is dependent on the attention and care of the mother or mother-substitute. Their development occurs in the setting of personal relations, at first with the mother and later extended to other persons. Psychological needs are characterized by certain emotional experiences that are conditioned by the close association with the satisfaction or frustration of physiological tensions. For instance, the young child soon learns that the mother provides not only food, but also attention and love, and before long he may value the attention and love more highly than he does the food. He has added the psychological hunger for affection to the biological hunger for food.

Behavior is a function of both biological and psychological needs, and of the objects and methods by which we satisfy these needs. Behavior, in being motivated by our needs, is purposive— i.e., it is directed toward the goals that will fulfill our needs. Behavior will vary depending on the strength and intensity of the needs, the nature of the goals, and the availability to us of socially approved outlets for satisfying our needs.

Our needs cannot always be satisfied immediately. External barriers may loom between us and the attainment of our goal. We may be hungry, but a traffic jam may delay us in getting home in time for dinner. Or other needs may be more pressing. We may be so intent on a conversation with a friend that we would rather continue it than rush off to eat. In some cases, the goal is set so far into the future that we must adjust to a long period of waiting. The young medical student, for example, must put in many years of study and work before he will be allowed to practice. The attainment of his final goal, the M.D., involves prolonged frustration that in this case is somewhat alleviated by a succession of subgoals, such as are involved in passing a series of courses or fulfilling other necessary requirements. If we can see ourselves progressing toward a goal, we can bear waiting to achieve it. In other instances, a person may be consistently thwarted in reaching a distant goal, no matter how hard he has worked toward it, and this frustration may result in strong emotional disturbances. At times, these may be so severe that they also affect the physical health of the person.

Needs, then, are internal tensions that we seek to resolve. The behavior sequence that they initiate ends when the need is satisfied or reduced. In many cases, the sequence from need to need-reduction is clearly understood. We are hungry; we eat; we are no longer hungry. After a certain length of time, the need will reappear and, most probably, we shall resort to the same sequence of behavior to satisfy it. However, in other cases, a person may not be so certain of the way to meet his needs. To begin with, he may not understand or be able to identify his needs. He may be aware only of a certain restlessness that drives him into various forms of trial-and-error behavior. One way of behaving may reduce his tensions and he is then likely to repeat it if his restlessness recurs. This is the case with a child who needs love, but who is unaware of the need or of ways to satisfy it. He may then resort to attention-getting behavior of various kinds that in many instances only invites further rejection rather than the love he so badly needs.

On the other hand, if you can identify your need, but have no idea what to do about it, other complications arise. This can happen when an adolescent awakens to an awareness of the sexual need, but finds all avenues of satisfaction closed to him by the dictums of our moral code. As a result of the restlessness created by this tension, he may discover masturbation, and if it aids in reducing his tension he may resort to it again when his restlessness returns. This masturbatory behavior, it should be noted here, may be "adjustive" from a physiological point of view, while being considered "maladjustive" from a social point of view. In general, the adjustive value of certain forms of behavior must be questioned if they create new problems for the individual.

In another sense the term "adjustive" refers to the solution of a problem while the term "maladjustive" indicates that only a symptom has been treated, leaving the core of the problem untouched. Adjustive and maladjustive behavior may both result in need-reduction. The difference is that maladjustive behavior does not really resolve the need. It is merely a temporary expedient and actually may impede complete satisfaction. The following example will illustrate this. A young man, new to a city, desperately seeks companionship. But he is awkward socially, and although he has had many opportunities to meet people he has been unable to establish any satisfactory relationships. He tries various ways of coping with his need, including denying it, saying that he does not really care for people. He spends an evening at home reading. The book is interesting, and he becomes so absorbed in it that for a while he is quite content. But his need is reduced only temporarily. Losing himself in his reading and withdrawing from all social situations prevents him from acquiring those social skills that would enable him to make friends and that would thus prevent the recurrence of this problem in the future.

The central position of learning. An organism's ability to learn is one of its most important and fundamental characteristics. Learning is the phenomenon upon which rests the entire superstructure of our complex mental activity and behavior. It is difficult to imagine what life would be like if we were incapable of learning. Even for biological organisms lower than man, learning plays a tremendously important role in their adjustment and total life processes.

Our total culture and civilization are the products and expressions of human learning. The books we read, the paintings we see, the music we hear, the skyscrapers we build, the airplanes we design and fly—all are the products of learning. To the extent that we benefit from these contributions we increase our own knowledge and ability by utilizing the learning and experiences of others. Education is the procedure whereby we use today the thoughts and ideas of those who preceded us. The ability of man to use that which other men have learned before him is one of the principal characteristics that distinguishes him from the other animals. A dog living today does not benefit from the fact that other dogs lived before him, but we, as human beings, can profit from the creativity of our predecessors. The basis of civilizations, their maintenance, and the utilization of their products by the individual rests on man's ability to learn, i.e., to change, to modify his behavior.

Man's ability to adapt in this way is essential to his continued existence. The learning process is the bridge between our innate behavior patterns and the requirements of our environment. Through the learning process we acquire not only what has been called "intellectual knowledge," but also a knowledge of various ways to behave—how to greet friends, express our interests, acquire new attitudes and feelings, approach peoples of different cultural and social backgrounds, react to anxieties and threats. We are not always aware that we are learning things because much of what we learn comes so easily, but the process is continuous nevertheless.

Many times we become aware that the old accepted ways we have learned for doing things are no longer appropriate to changed times and conditions. The old must then make way for the new. Sometimes we grow so "set" in our ways that we find it very hard to shake them off and learn new ones. But in the process of growth such new learning is essential, because patterns of behavior that are appropriate for one level of our development are not suitable for another. The adolescent, for instance, is allowed a certain degree of dependency, but if this dependent behavior continues into adulthood it becomes maladjustive.

Innate endowment may facilitate or limit what and how much we can learn, although few of us utilize our natural abilities to the limits. Similarly, social conditions may facilitate and direct learning or they may impede it. If parents and teachers encourage and reward a child's efforts to paint and model, it is probable that he will learn more readily than the child who is discouraged and told not to waste his time. In other instances, we have the necessary ability to learn more, but lack of motivation becomes the limiting factor.

Maladjusted, neurotic and psychotic individuals have, in one way or another, failed to learn the accepted methods for meeting the demands of their environment. Their symptoms are the evidence of their maladjustive reactions. The person with an anxiety neurosis, for example, reacts with fear and apprehension to all the various incidents that constitute his daily life, whereas the normal person fears only specific, really threatening situations. The neurotic person, therefore, is one who has "mislearned" and must be helped to re-learn if he is to make a satisfactory adjustment. This process of re-learning, involving primarily attitudes and feelings, is what we call psychotherapy. It will be discussed in detail in a later chapter.

Standards of Adjustment: Social Norms

The nature and function of social norms. At birth the child is relatively undifferentiated. He has a certain physiological structure and a nervous system that define the limits within which behavior can develop, but they do not specifically determine his personality. The singularity and the uniqueness of our personalities develop in the process of interaction that occurs between our potentialities and the environmental setting in which we are placed. Our potentialities become channeled, and thereby are made more specific, by the demands of our environment. Our behavior becomes trained in line with what is socially permissible. We must always view our development in the context of our social situation.

In most cases, we are born into and spend the early part of our lives within the family circle. The family is our main socializing agent during these years. The family determines largely the manner in which we shall satisfy our needs, and it sets the goals toward which we should aspire. Although each family is characterized by patterns of interpersonal relationships and behavior that are, in some respects, unique, it also reflects and expresses the characteristics of the social system of which it is a part.

The social system is a functioning concern when the child makes his entrance into it. Out of the infinite variety of possible ways of behavior, the social system has selected and given emphasis to certain forms. The family is the carrier of these selected forms of behavior, and the child is exposed from the beginning to a certain structure and selection of stimuli patterns. The standardized forms of behavior and the values that characterize each culture are called social norms.

Social norms provide frames of reference by which we orient ourselves to our social world. Social norms are communicated from one generation to the next, usually at first through the family to its new members, and are shared by most members of a given society. Some of the norms are rigidly enforced and transgressions against them are punished severely. Others, however, are more flexible and permissive. But in general these norms are means of social control by which society directs and regulates the behavior of its members. Norms imply expectancies and obligations.

In a complex society such as ours it is not easy to describe the content of the social norms. One reason for this difficulty is that the norms are not always explicitly stated. Often they are made articulate only in a crisis situation, and usually the negative norms —the forbidden behavior, the taboos—are more clearly expressed than the positive values. It is easier to define that which "thou shalt not do" than that which "thou shalt do." When a new theory, concept, or idea arises to challenge the established behavior of a social group, or when a certain individual's action disrupts its smooth functioning, the members mobilize to combat or to accommodate this innovation. In doing so they may be forced to reexamine and reconsider their positive values and approved forms of behavior. But as long as social life proceeds smoothly, few efforts are made to articulate and evaluate the social norms. This tendency to accentuate the negative also is reflected in the work of psychologists, sociologists, and historians. More books have been written about the negative aspects of society—about the deviant person, social disorganization, conflict and war—than have been written on the "normal," well-adjusted person, on the healthy development of a community, or on peaceful international cooperation.

The internalization of social norms. Although social norms vary for different societies, the process by which we learn them shows certain uniform characteristics. At first, the social norms are stimuli external to us. Some may remain so throughout our lives. Others, however, become internalized—that is, they become part of our mode of life and are no longer felt as a compulsion imposed from outside. If they are thus incorporated, we may express them in our behavior without being particularly aware of them or able to view them objectively. We can illustrate this process by referring to the manner in which a child learns to say "thank you." At first, he will probably say "thank you" only upon specific demand of the parent; a bit later he will say it only if the parent is present; but eventually he comes to internalize this social demand and to use the expression on his own without any parental pressure.

Because social norms become internalized, certain uniform behavior trends within one culture are sometimes mistakenly taken for innate human nature. When we compare these trends, however, to other cultures where other uniform behavior trends prevail, we see that they are learned.

The person who rejects or departs from the social norms, perhaps on the basis of a self-conscious, intellectual rebellion against them, may still experience feelings of guilt about his rebellious behavior. This may happen because his earlier feelings regarding the acceptance of the social norms may persist even though he consciously rejects the norms. This is often the case with people who are exposed to new ideas and theories that seriously challenge social attitudes that they have assimilated during childhood. Although they now feel these earlier teachings to be inappropriate or unsuitable, they have been emotionally involved with them for so long that they cannot violate them or the norms sanctioned by them without experiencing some feeling of guilt or anxiety.

Experimental demonstration of the influence of social norms. The adoption of shared social frames of reference has been dem-

onstrated experimentally by Sherif [2] in his studies of the autokinetic effect. The autokinetic effect is the phenomenon that causes
an individual to imagine that a stationary point of light in a dark
room is actually moving. At first the individual has no standards
by which to judge the apparent movement. After he has been exposed to the light a number of times, he judges about how far the
light appears to move within a certain range. This subjectively

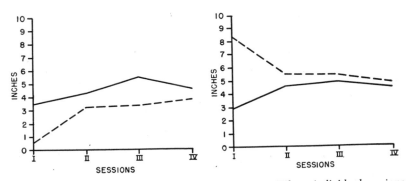

*Convergence of subjects' norms in a group situation. Where individual sessions
came first (Session I), divergent norms were established, giving rise to "funnel-
shaped" figures as a result of the convergence of the subjects' norms in the
subsequent group sessions (II, III, and IV). (From Muzafer Sherif, The Psychology of Social Norms. New York, Harper and Brothers, 1936, p. 102.)*

established standard serves as a guide for succeeding observations
and is peculiar to each individual. But if this person is exposed to
the same light stimulus in a group situation in which each member states his judgment, a shared norm or frame of reference develops. All members of the group now make their judgments of
the apparent movement within a restricted range peculiar to that
group. This holds true even if the person has previously, when
tested alone, established a personal norm different from the group
norm. Here then we see that group norms become effective determinants of perception and behavior, even superceding previously
established individual norms.

We have been dealing here with a new, highly ambiguous, un-

---

[2] Muzafer Sherif, *The Psychology of Social Norms*. New York, Harper and
Brothers, 1936.

structured situation. Very likely the individual has had no past experience in carefully observing a stationary light in a dark room and is not aware how subjective the apparent movement is. The results of Sherif's experiment, however, should not lead us into assuming that group or social norms always have a powerful, pervasive effect on the individual. Asch [3] has shown, in a different series of experiments, that individual norms derived from past experience may be strong enough to resist even unanimous social norms. These experiments are very significant because they indicate that the individual is not molded solely by social pressures. Although at times he may feel compelled to accept group opinions that conflict with his own, at other times he will resist group pressure.

Asch assembled a group of seven to nine students in a classroom and instructed them to match one of three lines to one standard line.

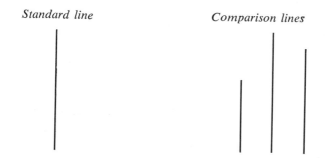

Standard line   *Comparison lines*

The differences in the comparison lines were great enough so that the matching presented no difficult perceptual problem. Asch had asked all members of the group except one to make unanimous errors of judgment in certain cases. The critical subject, i.e., the student who was not instructed in this way, was so seated in the group (i.e., behind it) as to observe in each instance the response of the majority.

The results showed that of 31 critical subjects tested, two-thirds gave correct responses independent of the majority trend; one-

[3] Solomon E. Asch, *Social Psychology.* New York, Prentice-Hall, Inc., 1952.

third made errors identical to those of the majority. In other words, two-thirds resisted the social pressure of the majority group; one-third yielded.

We are dealing here with a social group exposed to the same objective stimulus in which all persons are required to make judgments of perceptual relations. Only one correct judgment is possible in each case. (This is quite different from the *subjective* autokinetic judgment.) As far as the critical subject knew, all members of the group had been given the same instructions. Consequently, he would expect his answers to agree with the answers of the rest of the group. He is exposed to two main influences: his own perception and the judgments of the other members of the group. The conflict is created when he finds that his own perceptual judgment often is different from the judgment of the others. He cannot withdraw from the situation; he must take a stand.

Under these circumstances, some subjects conform to the group; others resist; but none is unaffected by the pressure of the group. Each critical subject is aware that his responses are different from those of the group and becomes concerned about his judgment. He pays closer attention to the perceptual stimulus; he becomes disturbed about his difference and begins to wonder if he is making some error, perhaps from having misunderstood the instructions or perhaps because of faulty vision. Most of the critical subjects reported in the discussion and in the interview that followed the experiment that they longed to be in agreement with the group, yet could not dismiss the evidence of their senses. The experiment also revealed that some individuals could withstand group pressure easier than others. The differences between those who yielded and those who resisted are described by Asch [4] as follows:

> The differences we have observed concern the ability of the person to relate himself independently to things or his steadiness in relation to reality under social opposition. Some were able to accept surprising stress and to endure social opposition without undue anxiety; others were quickly overwhelmed

---

[4] *Social Psychology,* p. 498.

and became narrowed in perception and feeling. Observation suggests at this point a broad hypothesis: that individual immunity to distortion by group pressure is a function of the person's relation to himself and others. Independence always requires some assertion of the self; at the least it needs the ability to acknowledge a shortcoming without loss of self-respect or ability to accept criticism without feeling rejected. It is therefore an expression of confidence about the self and its relation to others. Yielding on the other hand is a sign of lack of stability or confidence in these relations. It marks an inability to resist or reject others by an open assertion of one's dissident personal judgment. The independent person possesses certain sources of strength within himself that enable him to bear a brief ordeal, whereas the yielding person can find safety only by merging anonymously with the group. It would, however, be wrong to conclude that those who are not independent feel more deeply the need of close contact with others; the manner in which they are willing to achieve this closeness casts doubt on this assumption. These formulations are of course general, and will need to be replaced by more specific propositions.

Differences in extent of conformity to social norms. In the study by Asch, the extent to which a person yielded to or resisted group standards involved a choice between individual and group judgment. There are other instances in which the social norms are generally accepted, but the extent of conformity varies. Let us take traffic signals as an example. Drivers are expected to stop at a red light. Some will slow down and stop at the white line; some will drive over the white line; some will try to "beat the signal;" occasionally somebody may ignore it altogether. Furthermore, the extent to which a person will obey the signal may depend on whether there is a heavy or light flow of traffic or whether a policeman is on duty. Again, a person may merely pay lip service to the norms, observing them when it suits his conveniences, breaking them whenever he feels he can do so without having to suffer the consequences or whenever some other consideration appears to him to be more important. A student, for example, may openly express his distaste for anything dishonest, but will cheat on an exam rather than risk the disgrace that would attend his failing a course. In this case, the pressure to save face is stronger than the coercive effect of the norm against dishonesty.

Social norms in conflict and their relation to deviant behavior. In a certain sense our culture is divided against itself. In early childhood, for example, we are taught Christian concepts of brotherly love, charity, and fellowship. But we soon find these ideals clashing head-on with our cultural emphasis on intense individual competition. In school, at play, at work, in sports, we are continually trying to get ahead of someone else. We are encouraged to do better than the other fellow, to compete with him successfully, to win. Competition is often interpreted as an attempt to destroy the competitor rather than to cooperate with him. As a result, many of us become hostile toward others and become overanxious and distraught if we feel we are failing or falling behind in the struggle.

Or, take another example. A culture must appear to be consistent to its members—that is, it must provide the means by which the wants and desires it creates can be satisfied. But in a society like ours, where the "good life" is often identified with material abundance, with "getting ahead," with financial success, where the rich are conspicuously rich, where wants are created by producers and distributors, the majority of the people cannot satisfy the wants created by their culture. This gap between level of aspiration and level of achievement, between what people want and what they have or can reasonably expect to have, makes for widespread discontent and restlessness. If this gap becomes too great, the social norms that regulate the methods by which wants are satisfied will break down. In such a situation people may feel compelled to violate socially approved ways of behaving in order to better their position. The effect of conflicting norms on individual behavior is described in various novels, such as John Marquand's *Point of No Return* or Cameron Hawley's *Executive Suite.*

Under ordinary circumstances the conflicting nature of many of our norms may not be apparent to us. Even though they are always present, they may not be perceived by the individual as conflicting. Only when they are so perceived can a change in the existing system of values and beliefs be initiated.

Individual and social problems. Some social norms are temporary and merely incidental to the functioning of society; others are more enduring and vitally important to the functioning of society. Fashions and fads, for example, are patterns of behavior that alternate very quickly, are superficial, and have an irrational and intense satisfaction. High-school students especially are subject to swiftly changing fads in clothes and dance steps, or in manners of dress and decorative accessories. On the other hand, religion has flourished in some form throughout human history because it answers certain basic questions that man has felt a need to answer—questions about the nature of God, the nature and destiny of man, and the nature of the universe. Out of these religious needs and practices have come many social institutions. Later we shall discuss how different types of religious organizations fulfill the needs of different individuals.

The social norms govern a great part of human behavior in every society. However, within the range of permissible behavior established by the norms, there is scope for individual expression. We are allowed some leeway in choosing our own way of doing things without having to run the risk of incurring social disapproval or punishment. Deviant behavior, however, is behavior that goes beyond the limits of this permissible behavior, thus creating individual and social problems. Such deviant behavior constitutes an individual or a social problem according to the following characteristics: (1) whether it is a problem to the individual but not to others, (2) whether it is a problem to others but not to the individual, and (3) whether it is a problem both to the individual and to others.[5]

---

[5] Edwin M. Lemert, *Social Pathology.* New York, McGraw-Hill Book Company, Inc., 1951.

An individual problem exists when your behavior is unsatisfactory and disturbing to you, requiring you to make a new adjustment. Parenthetically, it should be noted that the term "problem person," which the layman often uses, is misleading because it implies something inborn in a person that leads him into trouble. This meaning is avoided when we speak instead of a "person with a problem." If you worry about your inadequacy, if you are unhappy about your social awkwardness, or if you feel generally anxious, you have an individual problem. You may talk about your problem to your friends; you may even, in some instances, seek professional psychiatric help. But your problem usually remains a part of your private world, and does not intrude upon the attention of the public and become a matter of community concern.

At the social level, a problem exists when a large number of the people in a community believe that the behavior of a certain individual threatens the social norms. In this case, they may take steps jointly to modify, correct, or change the behavior in question.

This second type of problem arises when the individual causing this community concern has made an adjustment that he finds personally satisfying but of which a substantial section of the community disapproves. Homosexuality is an example of this type of problem. The social stigma that attaches to homosexuality in our society is severe, but often the homosexual, by carefully observing all other social conventions and by deliberately hiding his tendencies, appears to be no different from anybody else. In some cases, such camouflage may generate guilt feelings, but it does not become a problem to the homosexual unless he is found out.

The third type of problem, where both the individual and the society are involved, may be illustrated by the following brief case presentation.

Ruth is a young married woman. She lives with her husband and her two children in moderately comfortable circumstances. She sought psychological help because she could not control her compulsion to steal. She said that she was quite able to buy the things she stole, but once she got inside a store she could not refrain from taking things without paying for them. She was greatly upset by this, not so much because she was afraid of what might happen to her personally, but because, if she were caught and her deeds made public, her children and their friends would hear about it. As a result, her children might be ostracized in school and in the neighborhood. Her kleptomaniac tendency was clearly a problem both to herself and to society.

Some of the major social problems—mental illness, family disorganization, and sexual deviation—will be discussed in subsequent chapters.

For Additional Reading

Asch, Solomon E., *Social Psychology.* New York, Prentice-Hall, Inc., 1952.

Berrien, F. K., *Comments and Cases on Human Relations.* New York, Harper and Brothers, 1951.

Gillin, J., *et al., A Science of Social Man.* New York, The Macmillan Company, 1954.

Hochbaum, Godfrey M., "The Relation between Group Members' Self-Confidence and their Reactions to Group Pressures to Uniformity," *American Sociological Review,* Vol. 19, 1954, 678-687.

Honigmann, John H., *Culture and Personality.* New York, Harper and Brothers, 1954.

Kluckhohn, Clyde and Henry A. Murray, eds., *Personality in Nature, Society, and Culture,* 2nd rev. cd. New York, Alfred A. Knopf, Inc., 1953.

Lemert, Edwin M., *Social Pathology.* New York, McGraw-Hill Book Company, Inc., 1951.

Lewin, Kurt, *A Dynamic Theory of Personality.* New York, McGraw-Hill Book Company, Inc., 1935.

Maier, Norman R. F., *Principles of Human Relations.* New York, John Wiley & Sons, Inc., 1952.

Murphy, Gardner, "Human Potentialities," *Journal of Social Issues,* Supplement Series, No. 7, 1953.

———, *Personality: A Biosocial Approach to Origins and Structure.* New York, Harper and Brothers, 1947.

Newcomb, Theodore M. and Eugene L. Hartley, eds., *Readings in Social Psychology.* New York, Henry Holt & Company, 1947.

Plant, James S., *Personality and the Cultural Pattern.* New York, Oxford University Press, 1937.

Sherif, Muzafer, *The Psychology of Social Norms.* New York, Harper and Brothers, 1936.

Man's Views
of Himself and
His World

CHAPTER 3

Throughout the long period of his existence, man has always sought explanations, has striven to erect systems of thought that would aid him in understanding more about himself, about the nature of some final reality (called by various names, such as God or Spirit) and about the universe. He has found it necessary to make the universe meaningful to himself. But more than curiosity or intellectual restlessness has motivated man's quest for understanding, namely, his need to feel secure. Appearing often as a helpless creature, driven and tossed by forces that seemed beyond his power to control, man has tried to relate the unknown to the known and has gathered these explanations into systems that have taken values and beliefs out of the realm of the abstract and endowed them with the reality of personal meaning. Thus man has provided himself with explanations that often became a faith. These explanations, often myths, relate man to nature. With these explanations and myth-systems man is at home in his world; he feels secure.

41

Whether these explanations are correct or incorrect is irrelevant insofar as such feelings of security are concerned. Primitive man believed that evil spirits caused volcanic eruptions and epileptic seizures. We prefer a more scientific explanation. But both explanations serve the same function psychologically. They represent man's search for security, his yearning for meaningful answers to the riddle of his life. In his eagerness for an answer, man frequently accepts explanations today that tomorrow he finds incorrect and inadequate as he discovers more about himself and the world in which he lives. (As we saw in Chapter 1, it is sometimes very difficult for a person to replace an old, accepted, but incorrect view with a newer, more correct one. It is against such resistance that new discoveries or ideas usually have to struggle.)

We evaluate systems of explanations or beliefs by examining them in the light of two questions. First: to what extent have the explanations been validated scientifically? The more positive their scientific validation, the more enduring they are, the more they provide us with reliable guides for further exploration and understanding. Second: how does the theory function in society? What is the value of this theory in relation to other different theories? What are the social implications and consequences of the different theories? Theories, it must be remembered, influence behavior; they have consequences; they lead to action. Suppose we take as an example some theories we may hold concerning the causes of crime and delinquency. One person may believe that crime and delinquency are the result of certain innate fixed characteristics with which a person is born, that these characteristics lead him into criminality no matter what his personal experiences may have been. If we accept this view, then all we can do with the person born to be a criminal is either to lock him up or destroy him. Such a view provides no hope for preventing a person from becoming a criminal, or of changing him if he is one.

Another view might hold that criminal behavior is a result of childhood experiences and environmental forces to which the person was exposed as he grew up. This view emphasizes that the

criminal is the product of environment, not heredity. The acceptance of this view would affect our attitudes and actions in a
manner quite different from the other view. In this case we
should conclude that control of the environment in relation to a
particular person might help to prevent criminal behavior on his
part, or change him if he is given the necessary help.

Because of their significant effect upon behavior we shall review here some of the beliefs that man has held, or holds today,
concerning his world and his place in it.

Beliefs That Have Influenced Man's Behavior

Magic and the spirit theory. Magic is linked with the
earliest records of man's existence, and its use and appeal have
continued unabated in all societies down to the present day. To
quote Dr. Castiglioni, a medical historian:

> Magic has existed at all times, among all peoples, and in
> all forms: imitative and contagious, fantastic and speculative
> magic; state magic and religious magic, white and black,
> mystic and diabolic, alchemistic and natural, medical, spirit-
> istic, and scientific.[1]

Ancient man developed the spirit theory to account for all
natural phenomena. The spirit theory ascribed human-like qualities, a personal life-force or spirit, to everything that moved or
seemed to be a potential source of danger. These spirits controlled
clouds, pushed rocks, created rain, drove the sun across the sky,
and rustled the leaves on the trees. But these spirits were very
transitory; no one could tell when they might appear or disappear; and to try to predict events on the basis of past performance
was well-nigh impossible.

Primitive man extended the spirit theory to account for human
behavior as well. If a person behaved well—was guilty of no sins

---

[1] Arturo Castiglioni, *Adventures of the Mind.* New York, Alfred A. Knopf,
Inc., 1946.

or transgressions against the tribal mores—it was a sign that he was inhabited by good spirits. Elaborate prayers, incantations, rituals and sacrifices were offered up to patronize good spirits and to insure their remaining among the people. But erratic, unsocial behavior indicated that evil spirits had gained the upper hand; this was the signal for initiating extreme measures designed to purge the afflicted person of his curse. These measures took the form of bloodletting, boring holes in the skull, whipping, dunking, exposing the person to fire, and coating his body with foul-smelling concoctions.

Good and bad spirits might inhabit the same body at different times or even at the same time. In the latter instance there might occur a tremendous struggle between the "good" and "evil" spirits for control of the individual thus occupied.

However, not all persons who acted strangely or unnaturally were believed to be possessed by evil spirits. The healer or prophet, who derived inspiration from trances, epileptic seizures, hypnosis, somnambulism, and a wide variety of other psychological phenomena was considered specially blessed and holy. In ancient Egypt, lunatics and imbeciles were looked up to as saints, and people would travel great distances to hear them speak and make predictions about the future.

Primitive man felt himself to be very close to other animals and often believed that at one time or another during his lifetime he actually assumed the form of an animal. *Lycanthropes* was the name assigned to an animal form assumed by a human. In some parts of Europe this belief persists even today. During the Middle Ages, lycanthropes were called werewolves. The person transformed into a werewolf was considered to be in league with the devil. But to primitive man lycanthropes could be either good or evil, depending on the kind of animal involved and the purpose of the transformation.

The beginning of science. According to Taylor,[2] science had its beginnings with man's first attempts to use fire, flint, and metal

[2] Sherwood F. Taylor, *The March of Mind.* New York. The Macmillan Company, 1939.

and to fashion and apply such devices and techniques as the wheel, basket-making, pottery, weapons, clothing, houses, and boats.

Around 4000 B.C. craftsmanship improved, especially in Egypt and Mesopotamia, and learned practitioners—physicians, architects, mathematicians, astronomers, and diviners—began to appear on the scene. But science as a coherent body of tested hypotheses did not actually come into being much before the seventeenth century.

Curiously enough, although belief in magic usually precedes the development of organized religions (historically speaking), magic is, in a sense, more closely allied to science than to religion. In many instances the primitive magician or diviner did not depend upon the intervention of a god or other spiritual power to aid him in his work, but attempted directly through his rites and practices to bring about a desired effect. He tried to influence certain circumstances by representing or creating similar events—a hunting dance, for instance, to insure success in the hunt, or voodoo pinsticking to exterminate an enemy. When procedures such as these failed, the magician probably felt that he was to blame for applying his assumed "laws" incorrectly. These laws, of course, were not based on accurate observations, but arose instead out of a person's wish to accomplish something beyond his own physical power. But failure led to more accurate observations and new trial-and-error efforts at control, and thus better information and understanding. The idea that material phenomena are not influenced by what we wish was not fully grasped by science until the seventeenth century. Such wishful, or artistic, thinking can be seen in children—and many adults.

It is interesting to note at this point that those who lack training in the scientific method often cannot distinguish between fact and fantasy. (This can also work in reverse—a scientist, though trained in the scientific method, when venturing into the field of politics, may be unable to differentiate between subjective beliefs and objective facts.) In contrast to the average lay person, who tends to adhere to suppositions and opinions that he has accepted without proper investigation, a scientifically trained person is likely to regard with healthy skepticism everything that he hears, sees, and reads. Although he may appear infuriatingly undecisive at times, he is more likely to arrive at workable solutions of everyday problems than the non-scientist, because he does not limit his field of action to one specific, rigid, narrow course. He realizes that every event arises from a multiplicity of causes, all interacting in a complex, dynamic manner. In Chapter 1, the role of this multiplicity of causes in human behavior was discussed.

The confusing of fact and fantasy is illustrated by Krech and Crutchfield [3] in the example of a man who treasures his own toenail clippings for fear they will fall into the hands of another person who might then harm him. And he may not regard this belief as any different from the belief that if he eats a poisonous fruit he will die. Or the farmer who plants his potato crop in the moonlight might consider this precaution no more peculiar than rotation of crops. He may believe both to be valid—he may have observed the poorness of his neighbor's crop and remember that his neighbor planted in the daytime.

The rise of religion. Religion has often been closely interwoven with magic. Early religions attempted to combat belief in magic by replacing superstition with simple, definite explanations. These explanations usually centered around one or more deities who were believed to be the origin and cause of everything—natural or supernatural. Men continually sought to curry the favor of these gods and enlisted their aid and support whenever danger threatened. The gods were also consulted about the cause and significance of all that happened. Usually they represented a noble breed, exemplifying honor, trust, sincerity and all other attributes of ideal social behavior. Sometimes, however, they were regarded as very much like ordinary humans (anthropomorphic), possessing all the foibles and weaknesses of man.

---

[3] D. Krech and R. S. Crutchfield, *Theory and Problems of Social Psychology.* New York, McGraw-Hill Book Company, Inc., 1948, p. 170.

The role the gods played in the creation of the world has provided interesting material for man to speculate about. All manner of explanations have evolved, each supported by mythology and legend or "popular belief," and each entailing a complex pattern of worship and ritual grounded in the mores—those obligatory customs whose observance was considered vital to the welfare of the group. Strangely enough, this interest in deities soon led to scientific investigation of a sort. When people began to speculate about broad issues they often found themselves reducing their arguments to specific details, and these specific details lent themselves to direct observation. In observation—and in checking and rechecking the details—we have the basis of science.

Man's view of the world in ancient Egypt, early Greece, and Rome. A better appreciation of the views we hold today about the world in which we live, and about the nature of man and his relation to the world, can be gained by a brief summary of how man in earliest times viewed himself and the world. Egyptian priests, for example, taught that the sun, moon, and stars possessed intelligence and that these exerted a direct influence upon the destinies of men. Here we see the beginnings of astrology, a pseudo-science that has persisted over two thousand years and has many ardent devotees even today. In Egypt, public astrologists almost always were consulted during times of personal stress and grave national emergency—a practice also followed by Hitler in our modern times. These men were considered the source of all wisdom and sometimes were raised to an almost god-like status. In addition to practicing astrology, the Egyptians worshipped certain sacred animals that they associated with deities. Among the most revered creatures were the bull, dog, hawk, wolf, cat, goat, and crocodile. The penalty for wilfully killing one of these animals was immediate death. At one time a severe famine struck Egypt, and many people turned to cannibalism to save themselves—but the sacred animals were not touched.[4]

---

[4] William J. Fielding, *Strange Superstitions and Magical Practices.* Philadelphia, The Blakiston Company, 1945.

Magic was a favorite study among learned Egyptians and the early Greeks. Its practitioners would spend long hours weaving elaborate, systematic defenses for their practices and theories. This exaggerated absorption was responsible for hatching forth all kinds of nostrums and fads, including, for example, a popular delusion that coral was a preventive against evil spirits. This led to the decorative use and popularization of coral in necklaces and bracelets.

Primitive man's belief in spirits was slightly changed in the thinking of the early Greeks and Romans by the substitution of gods for spirits. These gods, like the spirits, were vested with all kinds of power and were believed to be responsible for the appearance and control of various natural phenomena. Thus the sun, for example, became a fiery chariot driven across the sky by Apollo and his sacred horses. As we recall from our study of ancient history, an almost endless list of gods was created to help explain the phenomena that man observed. While these gods were believed to have many powers, some control was also believed to reside in man. Men were believed able to evaluate, to judge, and to choose—to control their actions and destinies. From this premise Plato and Aristotle developed a doctrine of man's "free will." The work of these philosophers also led to the emphasis on logical reasoning and argument. Beginning with certain premises and assumptions, they were able to elaborate complex logical and consistent arguments to explain their view of the world and man's role in it. Error in their logical systems was inevitable, however, because of the incorrect premises with which they started. This was due mainly to the fact that no effort had yet been made to subject these premises to careful observation or experimental verification. Views of man and the world were elaborated by armchair philosophizing and not by controlled observation and careful checking of hypotheses and hunches. Often the theories of men like Plato and Aristotle came to be regarded as the ultimate truth by virtue of the eminence these men enjoyed. This blind acceptance of the views of Plato or Aristotle served effectively to discourage the exploration of new or conflicting ideas. The danger of thus accepting ideas merely on the basis of "authority," rather than demanding carefully documented verification will be further discussed later.

No field of scientific inquiry was outside the realm of the inquisitive Greeks. Aristotle, one of the leaders of this intellectual quest, founded logics and ethics and made great contributions to natural science—in fact, he is often called the first biologist. Aristotle bestrode the intellectual life of his day like a colossus and his influence persisted down through the first 15 centuries of Christianity. He was "The Philosopher" of Dante, and his statement of a scientific "fact" was considered the best proof of its truth. Actually, much of what Aristotle had accomplished represented but starting points along the way to greater knowledge and understanding, but the aura and reverence, the stamp of authority that surrounded his words held men enthralled, blinding them to the need for further investigation, observation, and experimentation. His "intellectual empire" was to last down to the Italian Renaissance and German Reformation.

The rise of medicine. From 500 B.C. to 200 A.D. great progress was made in medicine. In this field one man stood out from all others—the Greek, Hippocrates. For our purposes it is interesting to note that Hippocrates believed that mental abnormality was caused by disease or brain injury, a theory that ran counter to the generally accepted view that the brain was nothing but a huge tear gland, having no relationship to mental illness. Hippocrates also stated that there was no true normality-abnormality dichotomy, that abnormality was a matter of degree, a fact that generally was overlooked until the waning decades of the nineteenth century. Hippocrates and his followers attacked not only the primitive belief that illness was caused by spirit visitation, but also the treatment of the sick by the ordeals of bloodletting, dunkings, and the like. Instead, Hippocrates recommended medical treatment involving good nursing, wholesome food, fresh air, and rest.

Of course, not all the contributions the early Greeks made to medicine were reliable and authoritative. They believed, for example, that a harmonious blending of the four bodily liquids—phlegm, blood, and yellow and black bile—was a condition necessary for health.

Many other advances were made during the Greek and Roman civilizations, but they are beyond the scope of this discussion, which attempts only the briefest of sketches. For example, Asclepiades, who practiced medicine in Rome around 100 B.C., advocated psychotherapy (catharsis) and musical and occupational therapy for the mentally unbalanced. Suffice it to say that the fire of interest for natural science was replaced again by an intense devotion to religion and mystical philosophy in the period 300 to 900 A.D.

The medieval period. From about 300 to 900 A.D., religion was a subject and object of learning, and scientific development came to a virtual standstill. Cassiodorus (490–580 A.D.), an Italian monk, statesman, and scholar, compiled a bulky encyclopedia of the knowledge of his time, but before 1170, generally speaking, the only universities were monasteries and cathedrals, and scholars had access only to a very small segment of the early discoveries and speculations.

The scholastic learning of the thirteenth century (exemplified by such men as Roger Bacon, Albertus Magnus, and Thomas Aquinas) was more extensive but not more scientific than that found in the preceding ages. Highlights of the scholastic revival were Aquinas' reconciliation of Christianity and Aristotle and Roger Bacon's condemnation of the scholars of the period for depending on unsound authority, yielding to established customs, seriously considering public opinion as valid, and concealing their ignorance by pretending knowledge. That he, himself, was guilty of some of these practices in no way invalidated his criticism, which is still relevant today.

Medicine during the medieval period was still based primarily upon the authority of Galen, the great Roman physician who died about 205 A.D. His theory of disease was drawn from Aristotle and stressed the four humors already mentioned. Not until the

Renaissance did Paracelsus (1493–1541), the famous Swiss physician, alchemist, and mystic, revolt against ancient authority in medicine and proclaim himself superior to the great physicians of antiquity. He attacked the philosophy and science of Aristotle. He publicly burned the works of Avecinna (980–1037), the follower of Galen, and the works of Galen himself, and advocated a new medicine—a strange mixture of the physical and the occult. All things, claimed Paracelsus, had a spirit; these spirits could influence man and vice-versa. He believed that diseases were caused by external spiritual influence, or by the failure of the stomach to separate poisonous from wholesome foods. He encouraged alchemists to develop new medicines rather than to spend their days trying to make gold out of baser metals. Paracelsus, incidentally, received most of his surgical training and techniques from gypsies, barbers, and executioners.

We see here that during the medieval period disease was still believed to be the work of the devil and magic the best way to effect a cure. Man's continued dependence on authority rather than on personal observations and experimentations perpetuated for centuries the same errors of belief, thereby preventing any progress toward a better appreciation of the cause and effect relationships really operating in the world.

The Renaissance and the Reformation. The Renaissance first flowered in Italy and then spread throughout Europe. It was an age of great political, social, and intellectual ferment. The eager curiosity and limitless ambitions of men who were shaking themselves free of the bondage of ecclesiastical authority opened up new vistas. And as the Renaissance spread throughout Europe, the impact of the new ideas it was spawning culminated in the Protestant Reformation.

The whole period of the Renaissance and Reformation contained a curious mixture of the medieval and the modern. The years that witnessed the crumbling of corporate medieval society also saw a revival of the medieval belief in occult sciences. The witchcraft mania flared up anew. Within the space of two hun-

Matthew Hopkins, Witch Finder Generall, frontispiece in The Discovery of Witches: In Answer to Severall Queries, Lately Delivered by the Judges of Assize for the County of Norfolk. And now published by Matthew Hopkins, Witch Finder. London, 1647. *(Courtesy The Huntington Library, San Marino, California.)*

dred years in England, 30,000 suspected witches were put to death. One particularly odious example of the newly found social function of ferreting out witches and bringing them to justice concerns Matthew Hopkins, an English lawyer, who conferred upon himself the title of "Witch finder General." Having procured some kind of license, he tortured his suspects so that they would confess to the most improbable or impossible offences. Such confessions were followed quickly by the death penalty.

On the Continent, the witch hunt was equally intense. "At Toulouse, the seat of the Inquisition, 400 persons were put to death for sorcery at a single execution. Remy, a judge of Nancy, boasted that he had put to death 800 witches in sixteen years. . . . In the province of Como, Italy, 1000 persons were executed in a single year. So great was the severity of the Inquisitors in that country that it finally created a popular rebellion." [5]

By the middle of the seventeenth century, the witch hunt mania had penetrated to all levels of society. Every misfortune that beset individuals, groups, or nations, was attributed to witches or warlocks.

The modern period. The rapid strides that science made during the middle and late seventeenth century owed much to the work of two men, Galileo and Francis Bacon. It was Galileo (1564–1642) who gave the world one of the earliest examples of the scientific method—the systematic and controlled testing of hypothesis. It was Bacon (1561–1626) who roundly criticized the existing knowledge of his time and emphasized that the object of knowledge was not to find some abstract, metaphysical "truth" but to give man power and control over the forces of nature, including himself. Bacon rebelled against the authority of Aristotle and attacked the kind of speculative philosophy that began with preconceived ideas or premises. He built a system of thought purely through abstract reasoning, without recourse to direct observation or verification.

Bacon proposed that a system of knowledge about the physical world—a system to be called natural science—be established by the method of induction rather than by supposition or recourse

---

[5] Fielding, *Strange Superstitions and Magical Practices,* p. 138.

to an "authority," magical, theological, or otherwise. Induction is a process of reasoning from particulars to generals. The particular premises, however, provide only evidence for the conclusions; they make the conclusion probable on the basis of the evidence, but not certain. During the seventeenth and eighteenth centuries, scientists began to turn away from Baconian procedures and to build a picture of the universe as governed by unvarying laws, allowing less and less leeway for supernatural intervention. Preconceived ideas were excluded, and a theory, to be acceptable, had to predict results that could be verified experimentally. The business of pursuing knowledge irrespective of the seeker's hopes, fears, and prejudices was becoming established. Philosophers began to speculate about a universe conforming to natural law, and they rejected authority as the ground for accepting any belief. Modern science, rejecting Bacon's method, has become hypothetico-deductive rather than inductive. Hypotheses are set up and specific consequences are deduced and then tested and verified.

Views about Human Behavior

The brief historical summary just presented concerning man's views about the world in which he lived has a parallel in his views about human behavior. These were similarly animistic and speculative, accepted without question from "authorities" who had made certain assumptions about the "nature" of man. An historical summary of man's views concerning normal and abnormal behavior may be characterized briefly as follows.

1. The demonological view, in which, as previously stated, man's behavior was thought to emanate from the good or evil spirits who occupied and possessed him.
2. The theological view, in which man's behavior was related to his alliance with either "God" or the "Devil"—a view essentially similar to the previous one with the exception that theologi-

The demonological view of human behavior. (Top) A demon's flight from the body of a possessed woman. (Bottom) A fit of demoniac fury with twisting of bodily members.

(Courtesy, The Huntington Library, San Marino, California.)

cal systems replaced magical spirits as the basis for interpreting "good" and "evil."

3. The naturalistic view, which regarded man's behavior as governed by cause-and-effect relationships that could originate in various areas, as follows:

a. *Organic basis*—stressing the bodily or physiological basis of behavior and ascribing abnormal behavior to organic pathology, especially of the brain;

b. *Functional basis*—stressing the significance of environmental stimulation and ascribing abnormal behavior to environmental situations that place the person in a conflict situation that prevents him from solving his problems satisfactorily;

c. *Organic-functional basis*—stressing the fact that biological and environmental factors must both be taken into consideration if we are to understand human behavior and its deviations.

The naturalistic view, as will be apparent from our subsequent discussion, applies the scientific method to the study of human behavior and considers such behavior as part of the same cause-and-effect operation that governs our entire world. Though the cause-and-effect relationship may involve different factors in the animate world (which encompasses human [or animal] behavior) than in the inanimate, the former are just as surely "determined" as are phenomena in the physical world.

Magic Today

This is an age of worship at the altar of science. There are relatively few among us who know in detail what science is, but almost all of us are in favor of it. Indeed, for some the word "science" has taken on magical qualities. One of the surest ways of gaining support and widespread approval of almost any project is to suggest that it is a *scientific* attempt to do something or other. "Science" is one of the key virtue words of twentieth-century American society. This phenomenon helps to explain the strange fascination that astrology, palmistry, and other so-called "sciences" hold for many Americans. In other words, we still find with us today much old-fashioned magic masquerading under the label of science.

Astrology and some related occult sciences. The early Babylonians, Egyptians, Greeks, and Romans made no distinction between astrology and astronomy. Not until the Middle Ages did astrology emerge as a single, elaborate, systematized theory. Briefly described, the medieval astrologer divided a globe longitudinally into 12 sections, each one representing a specific "house of heaven." The sun, moon, and all the stars passed through each

Astrology. Woodcut from Jacob Rueff, De Conceptu et Generatione Hominis, *1554, showing a woman, seated on a birth stool, attended by three midwives. At the window in the background, an astrologer is casting the horoscope of the child about to be born. (Courtesy The Library of Congress.)*

of these houses every 24 hours. An individual's character, personality, indeed his entire future could thus be determined by the house in which he was born, that is, by the position of the sun, stars, and the moon at the moment of his birth. It would follow from this that all people born in the same part of the world at the same time should all have the same future. The obvious discrepancy between this idea and simple observed facts did not seem to bother the medieval astrologist any more than it bothers the modern astrologist. Only when it was discovered that the earth was not the center of the universe was popular faith in astrology shaken.

To keep step with the changing times, astrologists, many of whom sincerely believe in their work, began to describe their "system" in terms of accepted neurological, physiological, or psychological terms. The use of such terminology, however incorrect, serves to impress the unwary. The use of such specialized terminology has led certain astrologists to label themselves as bio-astrologists, bio-psychophysic astrologists, glandular astrologists, natal astrologists, sexual astrologists, and radix astrologists. A review of the articles provided as reference at the end of this chapter indicates that there are at least twenty-five thousand astrologists working full or part time to supply the demands of the millions of persons who wish to guide their lives by the dictates of an astrologist. The number of fortune tellers, including astrologists, working in the United States is estimated to be about eighty thousand. The Better Business Bureau estimates that Americans spend over $200,000,000 annually for astrological services. There are about 20 astrological associations, at least 5 leading astrology magazines with a total circulation of approximately 1,000,000, and about 2,500 daily and weekly newspapers carrying astrological features.

H. F. Pringle, who made rather extensive investigations years ago, found such a tremendous amount of evidence against astrology and such complete rejection of it by men of science that he felt it only fair to give the Astrologers Guild a chance to defend itself. He asked the president of the Guild to choose four of his most able astrologers and to send them to the office of *Good Housekeeping*, the magazine for which Pringle did the article, where they would be placed in separate rooms and asked to give astrological readings for the same two subjects. All records were to be published verbatim no matter how they came out. Although the president of the Guild seemed to think that this was a good plan, no astrologers were ever sent to participate in the experiment in spite of repeated requests. Nor did any others throughout the country volunteer.

A group oi scientists were questioned some years ago concerning their views about astrology. The following excerpt clearly indicates the general opinion held by men of science:

> Psychologists find no evidence that astrology is of any value whatsoever as an indicator of past, present or future trends . . . (or that) social events can be foretold by divinations of the stars. . . . A considerable section of the American public (has faith) in a magical practice that has no shred of justification in scientific fact. The principal reason why people turn to astrology and to kindred superstitions is that they lack in their own lives the resources necessary to solve personal problems confronting them. . . . They yield to the pleasant suggestion that a golden key (to their difficulties) is at hand. . . . Faith in astrology or in any other occult practice is harmful in so far as it encourages an unwholesome flight from the persistent problems of life . . . it does no good to turn to magic and mystery in order to escape misery . . . men's destinies are shaped by their own actions in this world. . . . Our fates rest not in the stars, but in ourselves.[6]

Astrology, used as a psychological crutch by persons in need of support, is an opiate, and there are no harmless opiates. It is an escapist device that may weaken a person's ability to adjust to the continuous demands and problems of daily living.

Another pseudo-science similar to astrology is phrenology. Phrenology holds that the protrusions or bumps on a person's head

---

[6] B. J. Bok and M. W. Mayall, "Scientists Look at Astrology," *Scientific Monthly*, Vol. 52, 1941, 244.

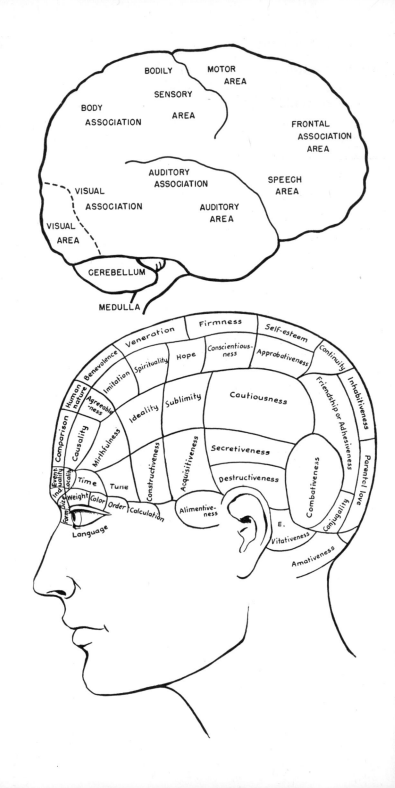

may be taken as indicators of his personality or character. According to this "bumpology," the shape of a person's head might indicate such characteristics as combativeness, congeniality, jealousy, discretion, envy, ambition, honesty, and so forth.

There is no evidence that the mind consists of a large number of different emotional, esthetic, or intellectual faculties and traits localized in specific areas of the cortex, or that the degree of development of the cortex in any way reflects the strength of the trait, or that the development of the cortex can in any way be determined from the outer surface of the skull. The cerebral localization found from a careful study of the cortex is of an entirely different kind.

It should be noted, further, that most of these terms do not refer to actual *behavior,* but rather to *evaluations* or *judgments* made about one person's behavior by another person. For example, to characterize a person as "ambitious" tells us nothing about his specific behavior but only presents an evaluation of his behavior in the opinion of the person using the term. It may, in fact, tell us more about the person who uses the term than about the one to whom it is applied.

Another pseudo-science similar to phrenology is physiognomy. While phrenology is concerned with the bumps on the head, physiognomy uses the shape of the face and its parts as an indicator of psychological traits. Here the *assumption* is made that psychological traits are reflected in the face. Thus we find claims that a certain kind of chin denotes strength or weakness, that the set of the eyes indicates honesty or deceit, or that the lips reveal sensitivity or grossness. We are aware, of course, that a sorrowful face may appear different from a joyful one, but this difference stems from behavior, not from personality or character.

Localization of functions in the brain: science vs. phrenology. (Top) Scientifically established localization of functions. (Bottom) Phrenologist's map of the brain. (Drawing at top is adapted from Clifford T. Morgan, Physiological Psychology. *New York, McGraw-Hill Book Company, Inc., 1943, p. 16. Drawing at bottom is adapted from Spurzheim.)*

Through the centuries man has tried to divine temperament and character from outward appearances, especially from facial features. Here are woodcuts from a book by Barthélemy Coclès, La Physiognomie Naturelle et la Chiromance, *Rouen, 1697, showing (top) foreheads of irascible, cruel, and covetous men and (bottom) hair of a very proud and of a very timid person. (Courtesy The Huntington Library, San Marino, California.)*

The claims of palmists, graphologists, or mediums and occultists of various kinds are equally unreliable.

What about the predictions these persons make? "But," you often hear someone say, "astrology (or phrenology) is accurate; the astrologist (or phrenologist) *can* predict the future." A mistaken sense of the predictive accuracy of these systems arises from the following techniques, employed by their practitioners in order to imbue their pronouncements with the appearance of authenticity and accuracy: (1) They employ broad generalizations that are true of everyone to some extent. (2) They flatter their visitors until they are ready to believe anything. (3) They give contradictory information in the same statement. For example, the astrologist might say, "You are generous but careful to spend wisely." Obviously most of us like to think we spend wisely, and where this is not the case, we like to think we are generous. (4) These persons have developed the "fishing" technique into a fine art. With gentle and unobtrusive probing, prying, and observing, they are able to get twice as much information from a client as they give back. (5) They draw analogies between superficial or nonrelated resemblances. For example, a graphologist will say that the person who makes an open "L" is "generous" while the person who makes a tight "L" is tight and stingy. Or that the open "L" means "honesty," equating "honesty" with "openness."

Quack psychologists. Quack psychologists are persons who have assumed the label of psychologist without the necessary training and qualifications. It is not known exactly how many unqualified people using this label are busily engaged in tampering with personality disorders throughout the country, but a recent investigation of private clinicians in Los Angeles suggests the extent in one state, at least. Shoben [7] sent questionnaires to 88 individuals who listed themselves as Clinical Psychologists in the classified section of the Los Angeles Telephone Directory. A letter sent with the questionnaire indicated that the university was overloaded with persons requesting psychological assistance, and that it was necessary to build up a referral list. The clinicians were invited to send in information about the services they offered together with their academic background and formal training so that they might be placed on the list. If the questionnaires were not returned, Shoben tried to telephone or visit the clinicians in

---

[7] E. J. Shoben, Jr., "Private Clinicians in Los Angeles," *American Psychologist,* Vol 3, 1948, 127-132.

order to get the information personally. In all, he received 53 replies out of the 88 requests. He believed that many, if not all, of the 35 who did not reply were trying to hide their lack of qualifications. Here are his results:

Services offered	Per cent of total
(1) Counseling and Psychotherapy	94
(2) Vocational Guidance	49
(3) Speech Correction	13
(4) Remedial Reading	13
(5) Industrial Personnel Consulting	23
(6) Diagnostic Testing	38

Type of psychotherapy employed	Per cent of total
(1) Psychoanalytic	18
(2) Hypnosis	14
(3) Spiritual Philosophy	12
(4) Jungian Analysis	12
(5) Non-Directive Counseling	12
(6) Program of Action	10
(7) General Semantics	10
(8) Courses in Personality Development	8
(9) Diet Therapy	6
(10) Play Therapy	6
(11) Relaxation	6
(12) Courses in Public Speaking	4
(13) Group Therapy	4
(14) Dream Analysis	4
(15) Astrology	4
(16) Narcosynthesis	4
(17) Numerology	2
(18) Common Horse Sense	2
(19) Not Stated	10

In addition, Shoben reported these observations:

1. Although 17 reported having Ph.D.'s, only six had taken their degrees in psychology. Others received them in religion, education, philosophy, literature and law, and only three had spe-

cific training in the clinical area. These three are the only ones out of the entire 53 who replied who could qualify as certified psychologists by present American Psychological Association standards.

2. Fees ranged from $3 to $25 an hour, with a mean of $9 and a median of $10.

3. Only one of seven speech correctionists reported having had any specialized training in this area, and none of the remedial reading practitioners reported any special training.

4. Only one of the 12 persons who listed industrial personnel work reported special training, and this man was not a psychologist but an ex-naval engineer who had done vocational counseling in the service.

5. Psychological tests were not used at all by 45 per cent of the clinicians.

As a general rule, the pseudo-psychologist has had no academic training, or at most has taken a few correspondence courses or been enrolled in so-called diploma mills. Some of these "schools" mail lessons to students for $50 a subject, and no academic prerequisites of any kind are necessary to qualify a person for a fake degree such as "Doctor of Psychology" (Ps.D.) or for the degree of Doctor of Metapsychics, in which case the person may list himself as M.D.

D. E. Lawson [8] has drawn up a list of common differences between the legitimate and the fraudulent psychologists. The fraudulent psychologist generally shows the following characteristics: (1) a suave, oily manner, (2) knows all the answers immediately, (3) boasts about his diplomas, (4) quotes a price for his "treatment," which he frequently requests in advance, (5) may criticize other professionals, by way of building up his own reputation, (6) may use mystic language and symbols in order to impress his client.

The legitimate psychologist, on the other hand, tends to show the following characteristics: (1) suggests that the patient

---

[8] D. E. Lawson, "Psychologists: Professional or Charlatan," *Hygeia*, Vol. 21, October 1943, 718-719.

undergo a medical examination by a qualified M.D.; (2) asks questions, administers tests, attempts to obtain all relevant information; (3) does not jump to conclusions; (4) cooperates with other professionals in obtaining and giving information; (5) uses understandable language; (6) does not boast or advertise (other than the ethically accepted listings in the telephone directories, and so forth); (7) does not propose to "strengthen" any mental faculties (for example, has no memory exercises, or "will" exercises); (8) does not use such terms as vibrations, soul-substance, spirit world, personal power, invisible forces, life force, character reading, getting in tune, extrasensory powers, messages, or personal destiny; (9) does not predict the future except in the limited sense of a prognosis, which is generally given as a tentative hypothesis; (10) does not attempt to keep his clients emotionally dependent on him but makes every possible effort to break dependence as quickly and as gently as possible.

Because of situations such as these just described, efforts are being made in a good many of the states to obtain certification or licensing laws that would prevent abuse by unqualified "psychologists" and help the public to differentiate between the trained psychologists and the quacks. There are at present about 13,000 psychologists who qualify, through education, experience, and character, for membership in the American Psychological Association. Professional clinical psychologists, to mention just one specialty, have an educational training of eight years (minimum) of college work for their Ph.D., including an internship of supervised experience in hospitals or clinics. The American Psychological Association has a professional specialty examining board that awards diplomas to qualified clinical psychologists (about 1200 such diplomas had been issued up to 1954).

The need for legal and educational controls over the various psychological quacks who prey on the gullibility of persons in trouble is all the more important today because these fraudulent practitioners now have at their disposal various media of mass communication that enable them to reach not only hundreds, but thousands or millions. Many of us are familiar with the various programs on radio and television that offer glib advice and snap judgments to persons in difficulties, advice that probably does more harm than good. Advice given by newspaper columns, magazine articles, radio or television, can obviously not be based on a careful analysis of a particular person's unique problem. Yet without such a careful analysis no realistic appraisal of the problem is possible—let alone a solution.

Superstitious beliefs. In the preceding pages we have seen how primitive man was engulfed in mystery, with little or no understanding of cause-and-effect relationships as they functioned in his behavior or in the world around him. By now we have made significant progress toward gaining control over physical forces by studying them scientifically, but we have shown considerable lag in gaining understanding and control over ourselves, either individually or collectively. Many persons seem reluctant to apply the scientific method to a careful study of their own behavior, apparently preferring preconceived fantasy to authentic fact.

We must recognize the fact that superstitions did not disappear with the Dark Ages. We must stop regarding superstition as merely the unfounded belief of someone else. We must wake up to the fact that many of our own beliefs are completely lacking in validity, especially our beliefs about why we behave the way we do. The examples of superstitious beliefs in our own behavior are almost endless. The following are but a few.

1. Today, instead of blaming an occurrence on a spirit, we attribute it to "good or bad luck." Some of us attempt to court "Lady Luck" by wearing special charms, just as did primitive man. We still have "wishbones," carry around a rabbit's foot, nail horseshoes above doors, and give mystic credence to the "power" of a certain number. Thirteen is still considered by many an "unlucky number" (since Jesus sat down with his disciples and was betrayed). This is carried so far that in many hotels one finds no thirteenth floor, the number going from twelve to fourteen. The mystic 3 also gets a great deal of attention. Many games are built around the number (3 strikes, you're out), many religious prac-

Superstitions today. A mountain congregation installed corner windows in its church in the belief that the devil would thus be prevented from gaining entrance. In the photo on the right, a farmer hangs a horseshoe over his barn door for good luck. (Courtesy Acme Roto Service and American Stock Photos.)

tices employ it, and many believe that a drowning man who goes down for the third time does so for the last time. Similarly, seven years of bad luck are believed to follow the breaking of a mirror (because it was once believed that the "soul" was reflected there).

2. The term "human nature" is frequently used as a concept to explain behavior. But even a cursory study of behavior of persons in diffcrent cultures, or even of various persons in our own culture, should convince us that so-called "human nature" is really not very "natural," or uniform, or fixed, or dependable and predictable. There is no justification for "explaining" something we may do, or shrugging off responsibility by vague references to "human nature—that's what made me do it."

3. Wishful thinking, thinking guided by what we wish to believe rather than what the facts suggest, is a popular method of attempting to handle a situation. Many of us seem to believe what we want to believe regardless of any evidence to the contrary. We arrive at a conclusion on the basis of our feelings and then avoid facing the facts for fear they might disturb our con-

clusion. Usually we reinforce such conclusions by assertion, not by verification. It is an interesting psychological phenomenon that the person who is least secure about the conclusions he has accepted ready-made (or on the basis of his wishful thinking) is the one who proclaims them the most vociferously and with the least tolerance for the conflicting opinions of others. The word "thobbing" has been coined by Ward [9] to describe such thinking, the process of thinking out the opinion that pleases us and believing it.

4. Legendary lore of old is the basis for many of the days we celebrate today—St. Valentine's Day, Hallowe'en, May Day, for example. Many practices associated with ecclesiastical days are actually folk customs preserved from pre-Christian times. Cleaning the slate at New Year's and making New Year's resolutions is a hold-over from the early English custom of cleaning chimneys so that "good luck" of the new year could descend.

We cannot pride ourselves on our modern enlightenment. Although superstition recedes before the spread of knowledge, it does so very slowly. Change itself is a constant condition of living, but many of us try to insulate ourselves against it. When a new idea contradicts one of our sacred or valued beliefs, we resist it with all the power at our command. Yet intelligent living and solving of personal and social problems cannot transpire in psychological rigidity or even in a state of perpetual doubt. We must think, not "thob," our way through problems if we are to live effectively, always realizing that sometimes our pet philosophies and most cherished beliefs will be at variance with reality. Even the obvious is not always right. In the appreciation of change lies the hope of progress. In the appreciation of the need to learn *continuously,* regardless of age, lies the source of good mental health.

For Additional Reading

"Astrology has 3,000,000 followers," *Life,* Vol. 21, December 30, 1946, 45-50.

[9] Henshaw Ward, *Thobbing—A Seat at the Circus of Intellect.* Indianapolis, The Bobbs-Merrill Company, 1926.

Baker, John N., "The Great Sky-reading Swindle," *Scientific Digest,* Vol. 16, 1944, 78-79.

Bok, B. J. and M. W. Mayall, "Scientists Look at Astrology," *Scientific Monthly,* Vol. 52, 1941, 233-244.

Castiglioni, Arturo, *Adventures of the Mind.* New York, Alfred A. Knopf, Inc., 1946.

Cohen, M. R., *Reason and Nature.* Glencoe, Ill., The Free Press, 1953.

————, and E. Nagel, *An Introduction to Logic and Scientific Method.* New York, Harcourt, Brace and Company, Inc., 1934.

Fielding, William J., *Strange Superstitions and Magical Practices.* Philadelphia, The Blakiston Company, 1945.

Gross, Mary E., "Read My Palm, Please," *Catholic World,* Vol. 161, 1945, 426-428.

Hollingworth, H. L., *Abnormal Psychology.* New York, The Ronald Press Company, 1930.

Jastrow, Joseph, *Wish and Wisdom.* New York, D. Appleton-Century Company, 1935.

Krech, D. and R. S. Crutchfield, *Theory and Problems of Social Psychology.* New York, McGraw-Hill Book Company, Inc., 1948.

Langer, Walter C., *Psychology and Human Living.* New York, D. Appleton-Century Company, 1943.

Lawson, Douglas E., "Psychologists: Professional or Charlatan," *Hygeia,* Vol. 21, 1943, 718-719.

McDonald, A. H., ed., *The Encyclopedia Americana,* Vol. II. Chicago, Americana Corp., 1948, pp. 452-453.

Meyer, Adolph E., "Astrology Racket," *American Mercury,* Vol. 60, 1945, 81-85.

O'Mere, Gene, "The Astrology Racket," *American Mercury,* Vol. 60, 1945, 765.

Pringle, H. F., "What Do You Think of Astrology?" *Good Housekeeping,* Vol. 3, November 1940, 28-29.

Reichenbach, Hans, *Experience and Prediction—An Analysis of the Foundations and the Structure of Knowledge.* Chicago, University of Chicago Press, 1949.

Rhine, J. B., *The Reach of the Mind.* New York, William Sloane Associates, 1947.

Seligmann, Kurt, *The Mirror of Magic.* New York, Pantheon Books, Inc., 1948.

Shoben, Edward J., Jr., "Private Clinicians in Los Angeles," *American Psychologist,* Vol. 3, 1948, 127-132.

Skinner, B. F., *Science and Human Behavior.* New York, The Macmillan Company, 1953.

Steiner, Lee R., *Where Do People Take Their Troubles?* Boston, Houghton Mifflin Company, 1945.

Taylor, Sherwood F., *The March of Mind.* New York, The Macmillan Company, 1939.

Valentine, Willard L., *Experimental Foundations of General Psychology.* New York, Farrar & Rinehart, 1941.

"What To Do About Astrology?" *Scientific American,* Vol. 165, 1941, 243.

Ward, Henshaw, *Thobbing—a Seat at the Circus of Intellect.* Indianapolis, The Bobbs-Merrill Company, 1926.

"Will I Succeed?" *Time,* Vol. 47, March 25, 1946, 23.

Willoughby, R. R., "Magic and Cognate Phenomena: An Hypothesis," in Carl Murchison, ed., *Handbook of Social Psychology.* Worcester, Mass., Clark University Press, 1935, pp. 461-516.

Woodbury, Clarence, "Star Salesman," *American Magazine,* Vol. 131, 1941, 46-48.

Personal Needs
—Their Nature and
Development

CHAPTER 4

- The nature and strength of needs
- Goals and satisfaction of needs
- How we reach our goals
- The development of psychological needs

In Chapter 2, we saw that behavior occurs in response to needs. We also distinguished two kinds of needs—psychological and biological—and noted that our main problem as individuals was to satisfy adequately our needs for food, water, and air—our biological needs—and also our needs for recognition and security—our psychological needs. What is considered adequate satisfaction will vary, of course, for different individuals and in different cultures. Therefore, to understand behavior fully, we must consider not only the various needs of an individual, but also the goals toward which he aspires in order to satisfy his needs, and the social norms that govern how he will proceed to these goals. In this chapter we shall discuss more fully the nature and development of needs, and in Chapter 5, the ways in which a person's efforts to satisfy his needs may be thwarted, and the effect such frustration has on behavior.

The Nature and Strength of Needs

Frequently several needs clamor for satisfaction at the same time and may influence how we react to a situation. Suppose we decide to dine out with friends. Obviously, this will satisfy our craving for food. But suppose also that we wish to impress our friends. We choose an expensive night club rather than the local diner. Both a biological need and a social need, then, influence our behavior in this situation.

We go to much greater lengths to satisfy a strong need than a weak one. If, above anything else, you want to finish college, you will be willing to struggle to overcome many more obstacles—financial difficulties, parental disapproval—than the person who cares little for a college education. An explorer, driven by curi-

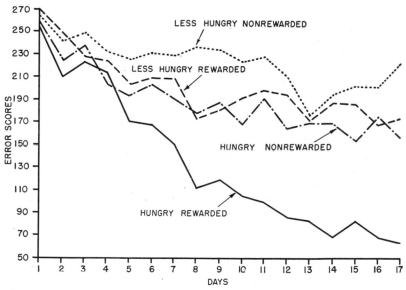

The strength of the need and the nature of the reward influence behavior. The graph shows the effect of reward and non-reward on the maze learning of hungry and less hungry rats. (From E. C. Tolman and C. H. Honzik, "Degrees of Hunger, Reward and Non-reward and Maze Learning in Rats," University of California Publications, Vol. 4, No. 16, 1930, 246.)

osity or a desire for fame, will willingly accept hardships that would prove too much for a person not so motivated.

Experiments with animals placed in an obstruction box have demonstrated clearly how differences in strength of need affect behavior. Let's reconstruct one of those experiments here. At one end of the box we place a piece of cheese and at the other our experimental animal, say a small mouse. Between the mouse and the cheese we place an electrically charged grid. If we feed the mouse just prior to placing him in the box, he will show only a perfunctory interest in the cheese. But if we do not feed him, if he is ravenously hungry, he will bend all his efforts to get the cheese, even risking contact with the charged grid, until he succeeds or falls victim to exhaustion. It is obviously impossible to perform this same kind of experiment with humans, but many valuable experimental studies of human behavior related to needs have been made, and we shall refer to some of them throughout the book.

Needs influence not only our overt behavior, but also our perceptions, our awareness of things. We do not perceive everything around us; we perceive only those things that are associated with the satisfaction of our particular need of the moment. A woman out shopping for a new hat, for example, is "hat conscious," she sees all hats.

A number of experiments have been conducted to show how needs influence perception when the environmental stimuli are not clearly defined. In one of these tests [1] a group of college students was asked to interpret meaningless drawings, ambiguous drawings of food articles, and drawings of various household articles. Each subject was tested once a week at various periods ranging from one, three, six, and nine hours after eating. The results show that the students who went without food for the longest periods tended to perceive the largest number of food responses in the ambiguous figures, although beyond a certain length of

---

[1] R. Levine, I. Chein, and G. Murphy, "The Relation of Intensity of a Need to the Amount of Perceptual Distortion," *Journal of Psychology*, Vol. 13, 1942, 283-293.

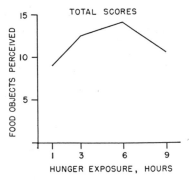

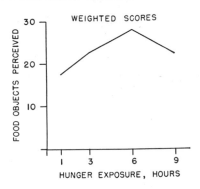

Effect of hunger on perception. The average number of ambiguous objects that college students perceived as food objects increased with the number of hours since they last ate, up to six hours. When the scores were weighted for the different time intervals in terms of "strong" and "weak" food responses, the relationships among the scores for the different time intervals were essentially the same. (From R. Levine, I. Chein, and G. Murphy, "The Relation of Intensity of a Need to the Amount of Perceptual Distortion," Journal of Psychology, Vol. 13, 1942, 291.)

privation a decrease occurred in the number of food responses perceived. The authors of the experiment suggest two possible processes that could account for the results: (1) an autistic process (that is, wish-fulfilling fantasy), which leads to an increased number of perceived food objects as the period of privation increases; and (2) a reality process (that is, reactions based on the factual situation), which results in an increasing necessity to find some means of satisfying the hunger need. As the period of deprivation increases, the reality process takes precedence over the autistic process, because the pictures do not really satisfy the need for food.

Goals and the Satisfaction of Needs

To understand our behavior, we must know what goals we seek. Certain goals are acceptable to us; others are not. And among those that are acceptable, we prefer some to others. We learn to choose from among different goals on the basis of personal utility. Those goals that have satisfied our needs in the past we retain; others we discard. Thus our behavior becomes selective.

It is possible, of course, that our needs may change, and with the change in needs comes a change in goals to satisfy them. We probably all know of persons who at one time believed that the most important need was to make money and who chose their work accordingly, only to find that their devotion to satisfying the need to make money left certain other needs unsatisfied, their social or educational needs, for example. Thus we find many businessmen returning to school to pursue an education in a field that interests them, or to make social contacts denied them in their business.

How We Reach Our Goals

As a child grows up, he learns not only that certain goals are more satisfactory than others, but also the ways or techniques for obtaining these goals. If you are hungry and know what food you want, you still must acquire it. As we have already indicated, some methods of obtaining our goals are socially approved, others are not. In our society, we buy our food at a store or raise it ourselves, but we are forbidden to steal it. And the goals themselves differ in different cultures. Within any given society, however, the manner in which needs are satisfied—goals are reached—often becomes highly stereotyped. We develop personal, characteristic ways of achieving our goals. Thus a child who has found that an aggressive, demanding attitude toward his mother will get him what he wants may use this same approach with others. Another child who is punished for being forward and aggressive may develop a submissive attitude in all his social relationships. A child learns also to employ different techniques to meet different situations.

The Development of Psychological Needs

Psychological needs have a biological-social basis—that is, they grow out of the early experiences of the child; they are conditioned by the satisfaction or frustration of physiological needs; and they develop in a context of interpersonal relationships, at first with the mother and later with other persons.

We derive our evidence concerning the effect of infantile experiences on the later personality development of the individual from three main sources: (1) clinical material, (2) experimental findings, and (3) anthropological data. The first of these is the oldest and was initiated and given impetus by Freud, who maintained that the emotional problems of the adult had to be understood in terms of his childhood experiences. Clinical procedures involve using such techniques as free association and dream analysis in order to reconstruct the developmental history of the adult, thus uncovering in his past experience clues to his present problems.

Another approach would be to make clinical observations of infants from birth, watching especially for reactions that might be related to later personality disorders, and following the development of these children over a long period of time.

The experimental approach to personality problems involves the experimental control of the life histories of organisms, and since this is difficult with human beings, this type of research is confined mainly to animals.

The anthropological approach involves comparing the infant and child-training practice and the personality structure of adults in different cultures. With these research techniques data has been obtained that is discussed below, supporting two conclusions concerning the influence of early experiences upon personality development:

(1) The satisfaction or frustration of biological needs has consequences not only in terms of physical growth, but also in terms of psychological development.

(2) If a child's psychological needs are left unsatisfied for long his physical development may be impaired, even if his biological needs are apparently satisfied, e.g., if the child receives enough and the right kind of food, drink, sleep, and the like.

Let us examine some evidence supporting these conclusions.

Three decades ago a disease known as marasmus was responsible for about half of the deaths of babies under a year old. Marasmus, meaning "wasting away," was found in well-to-do homes as often as among poor families. The careful study of this condition, undertaken by physicians and social workers, showed that in almost every instance infants suffering from the disease had received very little "mothering." The afflicted babies were wasting away as though starved by lack of adequate psychological care. This emotional hunger gradually affected their physical health, first the elimination process, then their breathing and circulatory systems.

Just what is involved in this process of mothering? Ribble,[2] who has made clinical observations of many infants over a long period of time, lists three types of sensory experiences that enhance the satisfaction a child derives from his emotional attachment to his mother. The first of these involves the sense of touch. The infant derives his first pleasurable sensations—as indicated by disappearance of activity and muscular tension—from sucking. The child who is breast-fed enjoys very close contact with his mother. Even the bottle-fed baby usually is cradled closely by his mother. Thus an infant's first contact with the outside world involves food, sucking, and a mother figure.

The second of the sensory experiences from which the child derives satisfaction is kinesthetic—that is, it stems from being held and fondled and moved about. This manifests itself in im-

---

[2] Margaret A. Ribble, "Infantile Experiences in Relation to Personality Development," in: J. McV. Hunt, ed., *Personality and Behavior Disorders*, Vol. 2. New York, The Ronald Press Company, 1944, pp. 621-651.

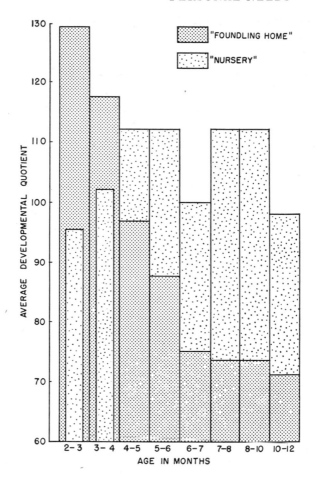

Comparison of development in "Nursery" and "Foundlinghome." The two institutions were similar in all respects except one—the amount of emotional interchange offered to the children. In the nursery, the children were raised by their own mothers, in the foundlinghome by overworked nursing personnel from the third month on, with one nurse taking care of from eight to twelve children. The developmental quotient represents the total of the development of six sectors of personality—mastery of perception, of bodily functions, of social relations, of memory and imitation, of manipulative ability, and of intelligence. The response to the mothering in the nursery and to the lack of mothering in the foundlinghome expresses itself in striking differences in the developmental quotient. (From Rene A. Spitz, "The Role of Ecological Factors in Emotional Development in Infancy," Child Development, *Vol. 20, 1949, 148.)*

proved breathing, and, when observed over a long period of time, in improved digestion.

The third sensory factor is the sound of the mother's voice. When the mother speaks softly to the child or sings to it, the child is soothed.

All these sensory experiences arise from the presence of another person, the mother or mother substitute, and form the basis for the emotional attachment of the child to the mother. If such mothering is interrupted or withdrawn, or if the mother oscillates between tender care and neglect, the child may show increasing muscular tension and disturbances in breathing.

If the mother provides skillful psychological mothering of the newborn child, she facilitates the process by which the child's emotional, sensory, and perceptive processes are developed and integrated. The mother's prolonged care for the child is also the basis for the socialization of the child, the process whereby the biological organism becomes a social being.

However, we do not yet have the final word on the relationship between childhood experiences and personality development. On the basis of an extensive survey of the books and journal articles dealing with infant care and personality, Orlansky [3] came to different conclusions. He states that the social sciences have failed to prove that childhood experiences influence character development, and he rejects the idea that specific nursing disciplines have a specific, invariant, psychological impact upon the child. He feels that Ribble's statements about mothering are exaggerated, and cites studies that contradict her claims.

Dennis [4] studied a set of twins who were separated from one another by a screen and who received only minimum care for seven months. He concluded that normal behavioral development can occur in infants who have had only minimum social stimulation during their first year of life, and feels that the behavior of

[3] Harold Orlansky, "Infant Care and Personality," *Psychological Bulletin*, Vol. 46, 1949, 1-48.

[4] Wayne Dennis, "Infant Reaction to Restraint," *Transactions of the New York Academy of Science*, Vol. 2, 1940, 202-218.

the adult in relation to the child may in many respects not be as important as some persons believe it is.

Anthropological studies and cultures other than our own have shown that children who are restricted or denied some of the sensory stimulation that Ribble considers important nevertheless have grown up to be healthy and well-adjusted persons.

But even if the particular kind of care that the child has received is not necessarily or in a predictable way related to his physical and psychological health, the constancy of care a child receives does influence his over-all well-being. If there is a sudden change, the infant may have difficulty adjusting to it because the behavior he has learned is inadequate to meet the new situation. For instance, Orlansky points out that children who are restrained —swaddled or tied to a board—do not become frustrated. But if the child has been allowed to move about freely for some time, any attempt to reimpose the restraint will frustrate him.

In the last few years, the effects of infantile nursing and feeding experiences on adult behavior have been investigated experimentally in animals. In one such experiment, the effects of infantile feeding frustration on adult hoarding in rats was investigated by Hunt.[5] Using split litters to control heredity, he submitted halves of two litters to a controlled feeding schedule of fifteen days, beginning at the 24th day of life, and halves of another two litters to the same schedule, beginning at the 32nd day of life. The control animals from all litters were allowed to feed freely. At the end of these two 15-day periods, all animals were allowed to feed freely for five months, after which the adult animals were restricted to one feeding a day for five days. Hunt then measured the amount of hoarding and found that those rats that had been frustrated in infancy beginning at the 24th day hoarded approximately two and a half times as many food pellets as their litter-mate controls. But those that were frustrated beginning at the 32nd day hoarded about the same amount as their litter-mate

---

[5] J. McV. Hunt, "The Effects of Infant-feeding Frustration upon Adult Hoarding in the Albino Rat," *Journal of Abnormal and Social Psychology*, Vol. 36, 1941, 338-360.

control. The traces of the infantile experience did endure into adulthood in the group whose feeding had been restricted at infancy or at the 24th day. Hunt maintains that the hunger aroused in the group whose feeding was controlled at the 24th day of life was so strong that it set off a conditioned stimulus leading to a hunger anxiety that prompted them to hoard more food than their mates whose feeding was not controlled. The group whose feeding was controlled beginning with the 32nd day of life did not hoard as much as the group whose feeding was controlled at the 24th day because the 32-day group was older and better developed than the 24-day group, and they found the controlled feeding schedule less severe—i.e., it failed to fix the traces of their infantile deprivation.

It appears from this study, then, that certain infantile experiences affect adult behavior, and the time at which such experiences occur is related to the effect that they have. This last point is an important one for us to consider. As the child grows older, and as his personality becomes more differentiated, an experience that would have caused him great anxiety as an infant may now only frustrate or annoy him temporarily. The adolescent or adult has developed a higher "frustration tolerance" (see Chapter 5), partly because of his greater differentiation, partly because he has learned to adjust to changing situations. The following case study shows rather strikingly how childhood deprivation can affect an adult's behavior:

James R, 43 years of age, was in the truck-farming business in which income was seasonal, fluctuating between a very high and a very low income. During times of high income he would provide his wife with enough money to meet the needs for herself and their four children, although even when he made a great deal of money he was always very careful. He was extremely anxious to "put away" as much money each month as he possibly could. In fact, it was almost an obsession with him that money be saved, even when his income was low.

At times when his income was too low to cover the necessary

household expenses he would refuse to dip into his savings. This was a main source of conflict between him and his wife, for she found herself unable to purchase enough food or clothes needed by the children. The husband's refusal to take money from his savings led to quarreling and hard feelings between husband and wife and to emotional disturbances in the children.

The husband had additional "quirks" of behavior as shown in his tendency to hoard things. The wife, for example, would be looking for canned goods on her kitchen shelves and suddenly discover some cheese that had been hidden away. Or she would discover half a box of raisins on the top shelf of the broom closet. When confronting her husband with these findings, he would at first attempt to rationalize this hoarding behavior by saying that he wanted to surprise her, or to keep something in reserve in case they should suddenly run out of food. James R was also unable to throw anything away. He saved old clothes and had worn-out shoes, hats, gloves and so on, around the house; he saved such things as wire, string, nails, hairpins, etc.

The childhood of James R, it is interesting to note, was as follows:

He was one of 12 children born to parents who were extremely poor farmers in Canada. The father and mother, even with the help of their children, were able to make only a bare living off the land no matter how hard they worked. The house in which they lived was only a shack of three rooms; overcrowding was painful and no privacy was possible. There was never enough food available to satisfy all of them, and James R has said that he can hardly remember a time as a child when he was not hungry.

The clothes that he had as a child were not better than his food; they consisted of rags, and James remembers his extreme embarrassment when he started to school and noticed that not all children dressed as poorly as he did. James is now a "finicky" dresser.

James R studied hard at school, working his way through high school and college.

Apparently the deprivation during infancy and childhood experiénced by James R had some effect on the hoarding behavior shown by him as an adult.

Clinical as well as experimental studies also indicate that an infant must be able to satisfy his needs for sucking.

Levy's [6] experiments with puppies illustrate the importance of sucking and point up the problems that arise when the urge is not satisfied. In a litter of six puppies, two of the puppies were fed by their mother. The other puppies were fed by bottle. Two of the bottle-fed puppies were given milk and water through nipples pierced with a *moderately* large hole. Their feeding time consumed about five minutes. The other two puppies were fed through nipples having a *very large* hole. They consumed all their liquid in about two minutes. Within a few weeks, Levy observed that the two breast-fed puppies thrived well and engaged in *no* sucking activity except when feeding. The second two fed through the *moderately* large nipple engaged in *frequent* sucking activities on various objects and showed more restlessness than the two breast-fed puppies. The two puppies fed by the *very large* nipple engaged in almost continuous sucking activities and were restless almost all the time, even in their sleep. They were irritable and combative and did not play and socialize with the other four puppies. These last two also lost weight even though they received the same amount of nourishment as the second two.

These results indicate two needs: (1) the need for food as such, and (2) the need to have food presented in such a way as to satisfy the urge to suck. The findings show that not only is it important that physical needs be satisfied, but also that such needs be satisfied in certain ways. In a study on bottle-fed infants, Levy [7] found that those who were fed through a large-holed nipple invariably sucked their thumbs. When a smaller hole was substituted, however, the thumb-sucking stopped; the infant's urge was satisfied. This conclusion was also confirmed by Ribble, who

[6] D. M. Levy, "Experiments on the Sucking Reflex and Social Behavior In Dogs," *American Journal of Orthopsychiatry*, Vol. 4, 1934, 203-224.

[7] D. M. Levy, "Finger Sucking and Accessory Movement in Early Infancy," *American Journal of Psychiatry*, Vol. 7, 1928, 881-918.

found no thumb-sucking among babies who had been allowed to suck freely, except when illness interfered or when the child received insufficient mothering of other sorts. If a child's sucking routine was interrupted suddenly, he would suck his thumb to compensate.

Ribble also noticed, as did Levy with his puppies, excessive restlessness among some children who were deprived of adequate nursing. But other infants, she notes, became increasingly lethargic and a few stopped sucking entirely and had to be tube-fed.

The satisfaction or frustration of the sucking urge also affects the weaning period. If the sucking urge has been satisfied completely, children will give it up spontaneously and no weaning will be necessary. But if a child has not been able to satisfy his sucking needs, weaning will be quite difficult. The child probably will regard the whole weaning process as a further frustration. Since the sucking need varies in different children, we cannot set a definite date at which weaning should be begun.

Although some researchers have found a direct bearing between feeding experiences and behavioral and psychological characteristics, Orlansky [8] points out that this does not necessarily indicate a causal relationship. In reviewing studies dealing with specific forms of feeding practices he found a great many contradictions. Concerning breast feeding, which is considered superior to bottle feeding by Ribble and others, a well-controlled study by Faber and Sutton [9] showed that artificial feeding need be in no way inferior to breast feeding in promoting the biological and emotional well-being of the infant. And length of breast feeding showed no definite correlation to a child's over-all physical and psychological health. Some studies did show that children who were breast-fed for long periods presented signs of overprotection and children who were breast-fed for short periods showed symptoms of rejection; but other studies found no such correlation.

---

[8] *Psychological Bulletin*, Vol. 46, 1-48.
[9] H. K. Faber and T. L. Sutton, "A Statistical Comparison of Breast-Fed and Bottle-Fed Babies During the First Year," *American Journal of Diseases in Childhood*, Vol. 40, 1930, 1163-1176.

The manner in which the child is given the food probably is less important than the feelings and attitudes the mother displays toward the child as she feeds him.

Modern practice favors feeding by demand rather than by schedule. Advocates of the demand practice assert that feeding the child in response to the clock rather than in response to his needs will injure or warp his personality development. However, such claims are not supported by experimental evidence. Orlansky found only two studies covering this subject, the findings of one contradicting the conclusions of the other.

Nor is there concrete evidence on the effects of early and late weaning. Some authorities believe that early weaning causes a child to become pessimistic or sadistic, late weaning to make him self-assured and optimistic. These claims are based mainly on psychoanalytic theory and no empirical studies appear to prove this claim. We may assume, however, that when weaning disrupts a satisfactory experience that the child has been enjoying since infancy—especially nursing—it can become a source of frustration. This is in line with our earlier comment concerning the constancy and continuity of care.

As to thumb-sucking, we have cited some studies that showed that thumb-sucking arises when an infant is denied adequate nursing, i.e., is deprived of the opportunity to satisfy his sucking urge. But again Orlansky raises the red flag of caution. He points out that this is not necessarily nor always the case, and offers the proof that some infants in primitive societies suck their thumbs even though they are nursed almost continuously, that is, on demand.

The picture is similar in regard to toilet-training. Psychoanalysts particularly have emphasized the important effect of toilet training on later personality characteristics, but again there is little evidence to back up the assertion. Sometimes a mother will begin toilet-training her children while they are still very young, solely to inflate her own pride, to let others know how "advanced" her children are. But the child may be unable to meet his mother's demands, and the whole process of elimination will become fraught with anxiety for him. And parents who are irrationally prudish and self-conscious when toilet-training their children often infect them with these same attitudes, attitudes that may color the youngster's whole attitude toward sex.

One of the significant things a child learns while he is being toilet-trained is to postpone relief of a physiological need. A youngster's ability to postpone immediate satisfaction of physiological and psychological needs is a significant step in his passage from childhood to adulthood. But if he is pushed too fast, he will grow anxious, hostile, guilty. Individual differences in rate of growth and development must be considered by the parents in any training procedures.

Freudians maintain that children who are toilet-trained too early become acquisitive, tend to hoard, and develop a mania for orderliness. However, Orlansky points out that these are merely traits that middle-class parents cultivate in their children and are to be understood mainly in terms of our culture.

What conclusions, therefore, can we draw about the importance of early experiences on personality development? There are two main difficulties inherent in the clinical case material:

(1) Our theoretical orientation directs attention to certain aspects of early experience that we believe are significant.

(2) We assume that the infant or the young child interprets his experiences in the same way that we as adults see them. Perhaps we are making an adult interpretation of such experiences, an interpretation that is foreign to the child. Certainly we should be cautious about drawing definite conclusions from clinical case studies, although they are valuable in providing us with to-be-tested hypotheses.

In commenting on this research, Orlansky makes two points: (1) That a specific discipline, whatever its nature, does not exert a specific, invariant psychological influence upon a child. The effects of a specific discipline or training procedure upon the child can only be ascertained from a study that includes consideration of the parent's attitudes toward the child, the child's capacities and development, and the total social and familial situation in which personality develops. (2) The rigidity with which character structure in the adult is determined during the first year or two has probably been exaggerated. The normal infant has such a wide range of experiences subsequent to the first year or two of his life that they "confirm or deny" the personality of the growing infant, depending on whether the subsequent experiences perpetuate or modify the early situation in which the infant was reared.

We should also note, in connection with this last consideration, that the personality of the one- or two-year-old child is relatively plastic and susceptible to change. Lewin [10] has pointed out that the various interests of the one-year-old are not as differentiated as are the adult's; few are more or less important or pressing than others. His personality is still being changed or shaped by new experiences. Maladjusted behavior, such as temper tantrums and excessive hostility toward other children, often disappear when the child is transferred into a social situation that gives him the opportunity to satisfy needs that previously had frustrated him.

The change in a child's behavior when transferred from one social setting to another may be remarkable. The little boy who in nursery school kicks, spits, has temper tantrums, and bites his fingernails, may, when he comes to kindergarten, find a new situation, a new teacher, and a new approach by his teacher to the problems that he shows. His need for attention, if handled with affection and understanding by his new teacher, may soon lead to the disappearance of the behavior found so distractive by others in the nursery school.

A child's physical needs are satisfied within the setting of interpersonal relationships—that is, *somebody* has to attend to his needs if he is to survive. In our culture, this person is usually the mother. When a child is satisfied, he smiles, sleeps contentedly, is not restless. He associates his mother's voice, touch, her very image and presence with the satisfaction of his needs.

At first, feeding is a totally undifferentiated experience for the

---

[10] Kurt Lewin, *A Dynamic Theory of Personality. Selected Papers.* New York and London, McGraw-Hill Book Company, Inc., 1935.

infant. But gradually, as the child develops, he differentiates between his physiological needs and his needs for protection and love. These psychological needs, arising out of an undifferentiated whole and having been strongly conditioned by physiological needs, persist. They stem from the child's early experiences; they are learned and they are characterized by certain attitudes and feelings and are based on interpersonal relations.

Although infancy is his period of greatest helplessness, the child depends on others for many years beyond infancy. From others he gradually learns certain skills by which to satisfy physiological needs, but these skills are only a small fraction of the total he must acquire. Others will initiate him into a highly complex world of physical objects, of social relationships, and of group behavior. Frank [11] comments on this situation by pointing out that the young child born into our society has to struggle with complicated and cumulative customs of thousands of years in order to fit and conform to the social requirements that face him. The social group thus, through the parents, imposes upon the child a heavy task for learning many things, a task for which parents and teachers must provide endless patience and sympathetic understanding. A small child, for example, may make many errors concerning private property, as a result of which parents and others frequently punish him and accuse him with shouts of "thief" or "liar" or other terrifying characterizations. Out of these experiences in learning what is demanded of him, a child comes to acquire attitudes and feelings not only about the problems that confront him, but also about ways in which to handle these problems. Thus he may come to approach problems and learning situations with timidity, or anxiety, or be intensely concerned with getting the better of everyone in all situations.

As the child grows older, his psychological needs become more evident. The development of speech, both in terms of understanding of the other person and in communicating his needs to him,

---

[11] Lawrence K. Frank, "The Fundamental Needs of the Child," in E. Hartley, H. G. Birch, and R. Hartley, eds., *Outside Readings in Psychology*. New York, Thomas Y. Crowell Company, 1950.

enables him to satisfy some of his needs at the symbolic level, through encouragement, praise, sympathy, and instruction. He differentiates other persons more clearly and, as his social horizon broadens, he comes to expect certain things of them, just as he does of his mother. He learns to regard others, as he does his mother, as his source of gratification or frustration, to anticipate their presence with pleasure, fear, or anxiety.

If his relationship with his parents has been warm and affectionate, he will expect his contacts with others to be likewise. If he has been rejected or dominated by his parents, he will expect others to bully him and order him about. Thus, the parent-child relationship is highly important, but it does not inalterably fix the child's personality. Human personality and behavior are flexible and can be modified. A child who has been rejected by his parents may receive love and attention from a grandmother, or perhaps a teacher. The child who can differentiate among persons does not automatically become a "problem" when certain people reject or ignore him. His personality is determined not only by his early associations with his parents, but also by his continuing experiences with others. Some of these will re-enforce his early experiences, others will modify or perhaps negate them.

We must consider one further aspect of the developmental process in order to understand the importance of a child's relationships with others—the self-concept. The self-concept develops out of the child's social interaction with others, with parents and friends. One of the chief duties of parents is to help the child build a sound and satisfying self-conception. By giving him a feeling of belonging, by accepting him, parents give their child the self-confidence and security he needs to adjust to others and to meet new situations easily.

We may say, then, that psychological needs have a biological-social basis. They grow out of the early experiences of the child and are characterized by certain feelings and attitudes that are conditioned by the satisfaction or frustration of physiological needs. They develop in a context of interpersonal relationships, first with a mother or a mother-substitute and later with other persons. The satisfaction or frustration of such psychological needs is an important factor in the personality development of the child. Although early experiences are important, subsequent ones may greatly change or re-enforce the earlier ones. In understanding the effects of such experiences, we must take into account not so much specific disciplines, but primarily parental attitudes and the meaning that a given culture attaches to certain forms of behavior, as well as individual differences among children.

For Additional Reading

Anderson, John E., *The Psychology of Development and Personal Adjustment.* New York, Henry Holt & Company, Inc., 1949.

Dennis, Wayne, "Infant Reaction to Restraint," *Transactions of the New York Academy of Science,* Vol. 2, 1940, 202-218.

English, O. Spurgeon and Gerald H. J. Pearson, *Emotional Problems of Living. Avoiding the Neurotic Patterns.* New York, W. W. Norton & Company, Inc., 1945.

Faber, H. K. and T. L. Sutton, "A Statistical Comparison of Breast-fed and Bottle-fed Babies During the First Year," *American Journal of Diseases in Childhood,* Vol. 40, 1930, 1163-1176.

Frank, Lawrence K., "The Fundamental Needs of the Child," in E. Hartley, H. G. Birch, and R. Hartley, eds., *Outside Readings in Psychology.* New York, Thomas Y. Crowell Company, 1950.

Hunt, J. McV., ed., *Personality and the Behavior Disorders,* 2 Vols. New York, The Ronald Press Company, 1944.

Katz, Barney, *How to be a Better Parent.* New York, The Ronald Press Company, 1954.

Levine, R., I. Chein, and G. Murphy, "The Relation of Intensity of a Need to the Amount of Perceptual Distortion," *Journal of Psychology,* Vol. 13, 1942, 283-293.

Levy, D. M., "Experiments on the Sucking Reflex and Social Behavior in Dogs," *American Journal of Orthopsychiatry,* Vol. 4, 1934, 203-224.

Lewin, Kurt, *A Dynamic Theory of Personality. Selected Papers.* New York and London, McGraw-Hill Book Company, Inc., 1935.

Orlansky, Harold, "Infant Care and Personality," *Psychological Bulletin,* Vol. 46, 1949, 1-48.

Ribble, Margaret A., "Infantile Experiences in Relation to Personality Development," in, Hunt, *Personality and Behavior Disorders,* Vol. 2, pp. 621-651.

Ruch, Floyd L., *Psychology and Life,* 4th ed. Chicago, Scott, Foresman and Company, 1953.

Symonds, Percival M., *The Dynamics of Parent-Child Relationships.* New York, Columbia University, 1949.

Young, Kimball, *Personality and Problems of Adjustment.* New York, Appleton-Century-Crofts, Inc., 1952.

Wawerka, A., "What It Is Like to Starve. A Doctor Tells the Story," *Our Nation's Children,* Federal Security Agency, Social Security Administration, U. S. Children's Bureau, May 1947.

Personal Needs
and Adjustments to
Frustration

CHAPTER 5

- SOURCES OF FRUSTRATION
- HOW WE REACT TO FRUSTRATION
- FRUSTRATION TOLERANCE
- THE POSITIVE VALUE OF FRUSTRATION

A need, once aroused, causes activity until it is satisfied. The tension accompanying the need makes us anxious and distraught, keeps us busy seeking ways to satisfy it, forces us to learn and to adjust. If we have established adequate patterns of behavior for satisfying our needs, we lessen our adjustment problems. But if we are thwarted or frustrated in our attempts to satisfy our needs, problems and conflicts arise.

Sources of Frustration

Frustration stems from the following sources:

1. Obstacles in the physical environment may prevent our reaching a goal. We may be driving to keep an important appointment, for example, only to discover that the road over which we must travel has been washed out. The child in his playpen who

wants to be free, and the man in prison who wants to be free, both find the physical environment restrictive and frustrating.

2. Our biological limitations are another source of frustration. An athlete may suffer a crippling injury that forces him to the sidelines. A girl may be so unattractive that she is never invited out. In the latter instance frustration springs from the fact that beauty is highly regarded in our culture, although what is considered physically attractive in one culture may not be so regarded in another.

3. The complexity of our psychological make-up is a third source of frustration. Thus we may be faced with the necessity of satisfying two or more needs simultaneously, but in caring for one

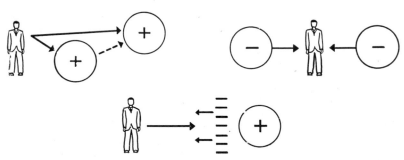

Sources of frustration. Frustration may occur because we have to choose between two goals, both of them attractive, but one near at hand, the other remote. Choosing the near one does not necessarily mean giving up the remote one, but may lead to considerable delay in reaching the remote one. Frustration may occur because we are faced with two demands, both negative, such as having to finish a difficult task or being punished for failing to finish it. Frustration also may occur if in order to reach a desirable goal we have to accomplish negative tasks, i.e., tasks that are of no interest to us.

we postpone or prevent satisfaction of the others. The young man who wants to marry a girl of whom his parents disapprove and also retain the affection of his parents may have to make a choice between one or the other.

4. Our social environment is a fourth source of frustration. Although social factors are present in the other three sources of frustration that we have just discussed, we refer here specifically to the conflicting mores and taboos, the opposing regulations and

laws of a society that sometimes thwart us. As we have seen already in Chapter 2, cultural values often conflict. We Americans place great stress on getting ahead, on beating the other fellow, on advancing relentlessly. But we also stress love and cooperation with our fellow man. Thus a conflict emerges between competition and cooperation.

How We React to Frustration

Individual differences in responding to frustration. People respond to frustrations in many different ways. Let us take as an example two people trying to solve a mathematical problem. One may throw down his pencil in disgust after but a few minutes' work because the answer did not come to him immediately. But the other may continue puzzling over the problem until he has solved it. Moreover, although we have described these different approaches here as applying only to a temporary situation—the solving of a mathematical problem—these approaches may persist and come to characterize our future behavior. Having failed to solve the problem in the first instance, we may avoid all such problems in the future, or, if we are forced to meet them, we may defend against the possibility of future failures by saying: "I am just no good at mathematics." As a result, we shall never develop the skills necessary to meet this type of problem—or perhaps any other problems, for that matter. If we learn to stick with a problem until we solve it, we acquire confidence and skills that will make our success in dealing with future problems much more likely.

It sometimes happens that we try to solve all our problems on the basis of a single approach, merely because this approach has proved successful in dealing with certain problems in the past. But this tendency can boomerang. When a new problem arises, the old approach may be inadequate to cope with it and we become disturbed, then anxious, finally dismayed at our apparent helplessness. Thorstein Veblen has spoken of the "trained incapacity" of persons who become so used to following one method that they fail to see others that may be better. They lose their flexibility. The following well-known problem illustrates this same tendency.

It is possible to draw four straight lines that will pass through all the nine dots in the figure without lifting the pencil from the paper. Try to think this out without drawing the lines. Then, if necessary, make a copy of the figure and try drawing the actual lines.

```
        .    .    .


        .    .    .


        .    .    .
```

Usually we see this figure only as a square and attempt the solution within this framework. To solve the problem we need to change our set and abandon our framework of a square, permitting the lines to go beyond the square. After your attempt to solve this problem, check the answer at the bottom of page 108.

What we have said here about non-personal problems applies to interpersonal and personal problems as well. The person who does not get along well with other people, who does not make friends easily, may withdraw from all social contacts as the easiest way out of his problem, rather than explore new possibilities. In order to preserve his self-esteem, he probably will say that he does not care for other people and prefers to be alone, or that what he values most is truth, and people just don't like to hear the truth. He may, by way of compensation, pride himself on what he calls his "forthrightness" or "honesty" without ever facing up to the possibility that his behavior might better be described as "rude" or "tactless." By thus rationalizing, he convinces himself that his liabilities really are virtues.

We may show the same lack of ingenuity in solving personal problems. We may, for example, have poor work habits that make it difficult for us to do well in school or on the job. All too often we try one or two approaches to such problems, and if they don't work we give up as though we had exhausted a wide range of various possibilities.

Disruptive effects of frustration. Rarely are we able to satisfy immediately each of our needs as it arises. As we have already noted, many needs may arise simultaneously and often we must postpone satisfaction of some to care for others. And others may not be of the type that can be handled quickly and easily. Usually a time lapse occurs between the time we first become conscious of the need and the time it takes us to satisfy it. And this time lapse can lead to frustration.

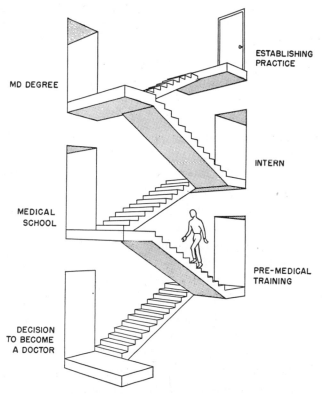

Delay in reaching a goal is made tolerable if there are clearly defined and successfully achieved sub-goals marking the path toward the goal.

Not all forms of frustration pose problems for the individual. Some of our needs can be satisfied only in the distant future. The college freshman who wants to become a doctor knows that his goal is distant and that he must work many years, perhaps experience many deprivations, before he will reach it. But he will not become discouraged if he is conscious of making some progress toward his goal and if he takes his difficulties philosophically, sees them as the sort of thing that happens to most people. But he will become deeply troubled if he feels that he is not succeeding, if this frustration persists and threatens to ruin his future. Tensions may appear that he will be unable to handle.

Our responses to such tensions vary greatly. If effective alternatives are at hand, our tensions may dissolve, but if there seem to be no alternatives, or if we have tried a few and found them wanting, our mounting anxiety and tension may inhibit our ability to see still other avenues of relief, or may lead us to take a course we might not ordinarily consider, one contrary to our own best interests.

The frustration-aggression hypothesis. Some persons believe that frustration is the source of all aggressive behavior. Undoubtedly frustration is an important factor in causing aggressive behavior, but though frustration *may be* responsible for aggressive acts, it does not *necessarily* lead to aggression. Frequently persons will assume the inevitability of the frustration-aggression sequence merely to give themselves an excuse for being aggressive. We may respond to frustration in many different ways, some maladaptive, others constructive.

One of the factors that determines the overt expression of aggression (by aggression here we mean a response whose goal is injury to the person at whom the behavior is directed) is the amount of punishment the person expects to receive for indulging in such non-approved behavior. The mores of our society brand aggression as unacceptable when it occurs in certain situations or in regard to certain individuals. If a person chooses to flaunt the mores, he runs the risk not only of being punished, but also of burdening himself with guilt feelings. A child who is chafing under home discipline may want to strike out at his parents. But the social norms tabooing such behavior are strong; the older child is aware of this and realizes that the punishment that would follow such an act would be swift and sure. Perhaps just the thought of wanting to injure his parents would make him feel guilty. The question of direct expression of aggression is a serious problem for modern man in many of his daily activities.

Complexity and variability of responses to frustration. Because of the complexity of the human organism, and the fact that reactions to frustration may be so varied and may be either overt or implicit, it is perhaps better to think of the frustration-aggression hypothesis as referring to the fact that frustration *inclines* a person toward a number of different responses, one of which is some form of aggression.

In a study by Allport, Bruner, and Jandorf [1] of the life histories of refugees from Nazi Germany, the authors were especially concerned with the question: What responses appear under conditions of extreme frustration? Their data brought to light a great diversity of responses that failed to fit into the already established categories of aggression or displaced aggression. The authors proposed instead the following nine-fold classification:

(1) *Resignation and other defeat reactions.* Not infrequently subjects reported giving up their struggle against the Nazis because they saw no hope of winning. They yielded to the circumstances in a completely submissive way although this yielding was in most cases accompanied by feelings of defeat and depression.

(2) *Adoption of temporary frames of reference.* This sometimes took the form of faith in the underground movement, or hope of emigration, or temporarily conforming to hated activities.

(3) *Heightened In-Group feelings.* Often there was a strength-

---

[1] Gordon W. Allport, J. S. Bruner, and E. M. Jandorf, "Personality Under Social Catastrophe. Ninety Life Histories of the Nazi Revolution," in Clyde Kluckhohn and Henry A. Murray, eds., *Personality in Nature, Society and Culture,* 2nd rev. ed. New York, Alfred A. Knopf, Inc., 1953, pp. 436-455.

102 PERSONAL NEEDS

ening of ties within already established groups—within a family, for example, which had been persecuted.

(4) *Shifts in level of aspiration.* Often subjects reported a lowering in their level of aspiration with reference to occupational and community status.

(5) *Regression and fantasy.* The case material indicates that some people fell victim to a type of emotional exhaustion that produced in them an intense desire for sleep. Others sought refuge and withdrawal from the horrors of the day by resorting to daydreams and living in a world of fantasy.

(6) *Conformity to the regime.* Many of the refugees reported that they had bent to the demands of their masters in order to avoid further frustration and punishment, especially after they had tried other methods of dealing with the situation and found them to be futile.

(7) *Changes in philosophy of life.* Many become increasingly fatalistic, especially after they had tried other ways of dealing with the situation and found them to be futile.

(8) *Planning and direct action.* As the subjects realized the extent of the threats to themselves, they developed many ingenious and realistic plans to overcome these threats.

(9) *Aggression and displaced aggression.* The threat of severe punishment deterred most subjects from direct aggression, but many, in their imagination, plotted aggressively against their captors, or expressed their hostility secretly among friends.

Thus we see that aggression and displaced aggression are by no means the only responses people displayed to extreme frustration. Different persons react to frustration in different ways, depending on their personality characteristics. Nor are all conceivable alternatives of behavior equally available to all individuals.

Expression of hostility as catharsis. Many authorities maintain the expression of hostility serves to release a person's pent-up feelings, reduces aggression, and thereby constitutes a beneficial catharsis. It is quite possible, however, that under certain circumstances, expression of hostility increases rather than reduces aggressiveness. The catharsis theory neglects the person against whom the hostility is directed. Our own emotions do not exist apart from the emotions and attitudes of others, and since the objects of our hostility are human beings, they may become hostile in turn because of our hostility toward them. We all know that if we attack someone, either verbally or physically, that the most immediate reaction to this attack is usually a counterattack.

In certain other instances, we may not release our aggressions for fear of harming others, or perhaps because we may fear the violence of the expression of our own feelings.

Frustration Tolerance

Individual differences in frustration tolerance. Frustration tolerance refers to the individual's ability to endure delay, thwarting, or conflict without resorting to maladaptive behavior or suffering personality disorganization.

We differ not only in our responses to frustration, but also in our degree of frustration tolerance. Some of us are always "in a stew about something," always complaining that life is against us. Others take difficulties in their stride. Next time you have the opportunity, observe how different people react toward a flat tire, for example, or to some other similar mishap. One person will complain and fret at the enforced delay; another will pitch right in to get the tire fixed or the obstruction removed as soon as possible; still another will welcome the brief opportunity to stretch his legs.

Factors influencing frustration tolerance. In order to understand individual differences in frustration tolerance we need to consider the relation of the event to the person. The same event may have quite different *meanings* for different individuals. For you, an examination failure may be annoying, but no more. To another student, however, who is struggling to keep a scholarship, the failure may mean a great deal more and have far-reaching effects on his work and life. In one case, failing an examination may mean merely the loss of that course from the schedule, while for another person the failure may be interpreted as a sign of personal inferior mental ability against which the person may react ego-defensively. The distinction in meaning of a frustrating situation for a person as merely annoying vs threatening has been stressed by Rosenzweig,[2] who speaks of need-persistive and ego-defensive reactions to frustration, and by Maslow,[3] who insists that it is important to distinguish between deprivation and threat in understanding the individual's reaction to frustration.

In need-persistive reactions to frustration, our interest is centered on the obstacle to be overcome; we are problem- or goal-oriented. In this type of frustration, relatively little tension is aroused beyond that related to overcoming the obstacle. The example of the flat tire, mentioned above, and the efforts to repair it in order to continue the trip, is an example of a need-persistive reaction to frustration.

In ego-defensive reactions, however, we see the frustrating obstacle as a personal threat, and we respond defensively and become very anxious. A remark that casts a reflection on our dancing ability or on our intelligence, may cause us to become frustrated and to resort to ego-defensive reactions. The need-persistive reactions are more limited in aim than the ego-defensive ones. In the former, only a segmental need—a need for more money, for example—is frustrated; but in the latter, the total personality may be involved, such as in trying to gain emotional security or social acceptance.

In order to test this distinction, Rosenzweig carried out an experiment in which two groups of subjects were given a series of jigsaw puzzle pictures to solve. To the first group, the puzzles were presented informally and the participants were told that their work would help the experimenter in classifying the puzzles for future use. To the second group, the puzzles were presented as an

---

    [2] S. Rosenzweig, "Need-Persistive and Ego-Defensive Reactions to Frustration as Demonstrated by an Experiment on Repression," *Psychological Review,* Vol. 48, 1941, 347-349.
    [3] A. H. Maslow, "Deprivation, Threat and Frustration," *Psychological Review,* Vol. 48, 1941, 364-366.

intelligence test and in a much more formal atmosphere. Both groups were permitted to finish half of the puzzles but were stopped mid-way through the remaining half. After that, they were asked to name all the puzzles, both those they had finished and those they had not finished. The hypothesis guiding the experiment was this:

> Under the informal conditions the unfinished tasks would be better recalled than the finished ones because need-persistive reactions alone would be operative and would make for easier recall of tasks with which undischarged tension was associated. On the other hand, subjects in the formal group were expected to recall finished tasks more frequently because with the arousal of pride and accompanying ego-defense in case of failure, the individuals' needs for inviolacy would take precedence over the task-tension making for the recall of the unfinished tasks. The experimental data substantiated this hypothesis.

Similarly, Maslow points out that a goal objective may have two meanings for an individual, an intrinsic meaning and a symbolic one. Thus, a child who is refused an ice cream cone may regard this merely as a case of simple denial. But a second child who is denied an ice cream cone may interpret his mother's refusal as a sign that she no longer loves him. For him, the ice cream cone has a symbolic psychological value as well as an intrinsic one. Maslow questions whether the two kinds of deprivations or frustrations should even be called by the same name, since their effects on behavior are quite different. It is only when the goal object is endowed with psychological values, when it represents a level of prestige, is important to the feelings of the person, that being deprived of it will have the bad effects ordinarily attributed to frustration in general.

In order to understand an individual's frustration tolerance in a given situation, then, we must know the value and symbolic meaning that the goal object has for him.

A frustrating situation also will have varying significance for us depending on whether we feel that it is caused by some external force over which we have little or no control, or whether we feel that we have, through our own actions, helped to bring it about. The student who comes late to class probably feels more at ease about his tardiness if he can attribute it to flooded roads rather than to oversleeping. If the cause of a frustrating event can be assigned to an external force for which we are not responsible, we do not feel guilty about it.

Often our frustration tolerance will depend on what we regard to be the cause of the frustrating situation. This, in turn, will determine the direction of our responses. Rosenzweig, studying this direction of reaction, distinguished between extrapunitive, intrapunitive, and impunitive individuals.

The extrapunitive individual avoids blaming himself. If he breaks a vase, it was slippery, or his wife put it too close to the edge of the table. His characteristic emotional response is one of anger and indignation, but directed at some other person. On the other hand, the intrapunitive person tends to blame himself. If he breaks a vase, he apologizes for his clumsiness, is humiliated and feels guilty, and may offer to make good the damage. An impunitive person treats the situation impersonally, blaming neither himself nor others. He feels "It couldn't be helped," or "That's life."

Frustration tolerance varies not only for different individuals with reference to the same event, but also may vary within a given individual at different times. A person's frustration tolerance may be much lower when he is fatigued than when he is rested. On the other hand, fatigue may be a symptom of a low frustration tolerance. Such fatigue may result not from physical factors associated with energy output on the job, but rather from emotional tension generated by frustration arising from and related to the work. For example, a person doing his job may be more fatigued by the tension aroused by competing with his equals, or maintaining a position of subordination to his superiors, or because advancement may not have come as rapidly as he has hoped, than by the effort expended. Low tolerance for these factors may thus lead to

Rosenzweig Picture-Frustration Test. The first four items in a series of situations that the test covers. The subjects are instructed to write in the blank box the very first answer that comes to mind. (Reproduced, by permission, from the Rosenzweig Picture-Frustration Study, copyright, 1948.)

fatigue. It is not so much the work we do as how we feel about the work that often makes us tired.

The Positive Value of Frustration

Although frustrating experiences can be disruptive, they also have value. In many cases frustration is a prerequisite for learning and for psychological growth. In meeting frustrations, in developing techniques and skills to overcome obstacles, we learn, our personalities develop, and we adjust to our problems. The important point to consider is whether the child—or adult—possesses enough resources to handle frustration without becoming unduly upset. If a person becomes too distraught, he may begin to rationalize his shortcomings or he may withdraw completely instead of trying to find ways to handle his problems. It is important to remember this in setting tasks for children so that the task is within their ability to perform adequately without their being overwhelmed by the emotion of frustration.

The development of a higher level of frustration tolerance may be aided by certain conditions. For frustrations to be least disruptive, the person, especially the child, must feel secure and wanted. He should be given tasks to perform at which he can persevere and succeed. He should be helped to realize what he is capable and what he is incapable of doing. Thus, by making the child wanted and secure, by helping him to succeed, and by making him aware of his abilities and shortcomings, we can nurture within him the proper development of frustration tolerance. The person who can face frustration as not ego-threatening is able to forego immediate satisfaction without being seriously upset and to con-

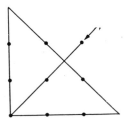

trol his emotional behavior so that it is in proportion to the frustrating experience that elicited it. This requires a problem-orientation, rather than a self-orientation.

For Additional Reading

Allport, Gordon W., J. S. Bruner, and E. M. Jandorf, "Personality Under Social Catastrophe. Ninety Life-Histories of the Nazi Revolution," in Clyde Kluckhohn and Henry A. Murray, eds., *Personality in Nature, Society and Culture*, 2nd rev. ed. New York, Alfred A. Knopf, Inc., 1953, pp. 436-455.

Cameron, Norman, *The Psychology of Behavior Disorders*. Boston, Houghton Mifflin Company, 1947.

Dollard, J., L. W. Doob, N. Miller, O. H. Mowrer, and Robert R. Sears, *Frustration and Aggression*. New Haven, Yale University Press, 1939.

Krech, David and Richard S. Crutchfield, *Theory and Problems of Social Psychology*. New York, McGraw-Hill Book Company, Inc., 1948.

Lewin, Kurt, *A Dynamic Theory of Personality. Selected Papers*. New York and London, McGraw-Hill Book Company, Inc., 1935.

Maier, Norman R. F., *Frustration—The Study of Behavior Without a Goal*. New York, McGraw-Hill Book Company, Inc., 1949.

Maslow, A. H., "Deprivation, Threat and Frustration," *Psychological Review*, Vol. 48, 1941, 364-366.

Morlan, George K., "A Note on the Frustration-Aggression Theories of Dollard and his Associates," *Psychological Review*, Vol. 56, 1949, 1-8.

Rosenzweig, Saul, "An Outline of Frustration Theory," in J. McV. Hunt, ed., *Personality and the Behavior Disorders*, Vol. I. New York, The Ronald Press Company, 1944.

————, "Need-Persistive and Ego-Defensive Reactions to Frustration as Demonstrated by an Experiment on Repression," *Psychological Review*, Vol. 48, 1941, 347-349.

————, "Types of Reaction to Frustration," *Journal of Abnormal and Social Psychology*, Vol. 29, 1934, 298-300.

Sargent, S. S., "Reaction to Frustration—A Critique and Hypothesis," *Psychological Review*, Vol. 55, 1948, 108-113.

Seleye, H., "Experimental Evidence Supporting the Concept of 'Adaptation Energy,'" *American Journal of Physiology*, Vol. 123, 1938, 758-765.

Adjustment
and the Defense
Mechanisms

CHAPTER 6

- TYPES OF DEFENSE MECHANISMS
- GENERAL PRINCIPLES CONCERNING THE NATURE AND FUNCTION OF DEFENSE MECHANISMS

Inadequately satisfied needs give birth to additional or secondary needs—face-saving needs, so to speak. The individual who has failed to satisfy a need, or who feels that such failure is imminent, suddenly finds it urgently necessary to produce some sort of an explanation for—or defense against—that failure. He feels a need to justify his failure, in his own eyes as well as in the eyes of his associates. Usually, when this occurs, the individual is totally unaware of the psychological mechanics that are prompting his reactions.

Defense mechanisms is the name given to the reactions that result when the emphasis shifts in this manner, i.e., when the attempt to satisfy the original need is abandoned in favor of an attempt to avoid the discomforts of failure. In this chapter we shall discuss the major defense mechanisms, their nature and function, and their value for adjustment.

Types of Defense Mechanisms

Chart Number 1 shows how the human organism, beset by frustration, threat of self devaluation, and anxiety, while en-

CHART 1

HOW INDIVIDUAL RESORTS TO VARIOUS DEFENSES THAT LEAD TO SUB-GOALS
WHEN FRUSTRATED IN ATTEMPTS TO REACH MAIN GOAL

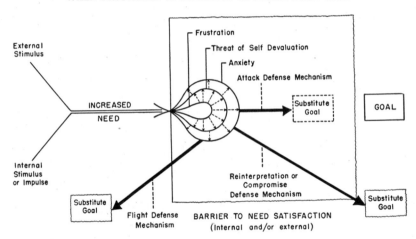

gaged in the pursuit of a goal, tends to resort to various defenses that cause him to veer off in the direction of substitute goals. The amount of discrepancy between the original goal and the substitute goal varies according to the type of defense mechanism selected by the individual involved.

Chart Number 2 indicates the various types of defense mechanisms from which the individual may make this unconscious selection. These defense mechanisms can be grouped under three headings: *attack, reinterpretation or compromise,* and *flight.* However, as the diagram indicates, there is considerable overlapping, and several different defenses may involve any one of these three approaches. Some defense mechanisms lead the individual to in-

CHART 2

Adjustment Approaches of Defense Mechanisms

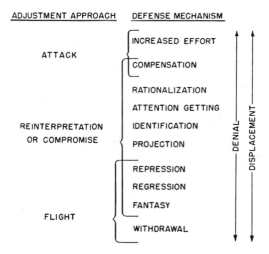

crease his efforts to attain his goal, to attack the undertaking in a more efficient manner. Other defense mechanisms permit the individual to run away from the painful situation. Still others suggest the possibility of effecting a compromise or of reinterpreting the goal. A detailed discussion of the defenses listed in the diagram follows.

Denial. Every time we overlook or ignore the unpleasant we are employing the mechanism of denial. It prompts us to turn away from shocking scenes of catastrophe. It blinds us to the defects and shortcomings of loved ones. The habitual liar lies in order to deceive not only his associates but also himself. The proverbs "Love is blind," and "None are so blind as those who will not see," are common cultural acknowledgments of the presence and operation of denial.

Denial desensitizes the individual to his handicaps and therefore fosters a mistaken self-esteem. Denial sometimes occurs in pure form, as in the examples above. But elements of denial can be detected in all the defense mechanisms, since all of them tend to blot out that part of reality that threatens self-esteem. Because it helps to avoid traumatic stress and to relieve the cumulative irritations of petty annoyance, denial offers a tempting refuge. But the individual who denies his problems in order to indulge in the luxury of this retreat is at the same time denying himself the opportunity to understand and to conquer his problems.

Displacement. Displacement, like denial, is common to all defense mechanisms. This is due to the face-saving elements it affords—face-saving being the prime objective of the defense mechanisms.

When we substitute a non-threatening situation in place of a threatening one, we are employing displacement. If a worker submits meekly to a tyrannical boss whom he detests, and then releases his pent-up hatred by mistreating a subordinate worker, or a friend, or a member of his own family, he is resorting to displacement. He is taking the safe way out. The timid boy who plays court to an unattractive girl, because he fears that the beautiful girl whom he secretly admires would reject him if he approached her, is using displacement in order to safeguard himself against embarrassment and shame. This method can be applied to any emotion, to any desire or fantasy. Such substitutions permit the individual to maintain satisfactory relationships with his fellows and, even more important, to preserve a good opinion of himself.

Displacement provides an outlet for emotions and minimizes the possibility of outward conflict. But it creates substitute areas of conflict and maladjustment within, thereby making discovery and resolution of the real problem even more difficult.

Increased effort and work. The individual who has failed to solve a certain problem or satisfy a certain need often finds his efforts and attention drawn back to this problem or need again and again. As the problem recurs he may redouble his efforts; new approaches may occur to him. Possibly he may eventually come up with a solution of sorts. Such persistence may seem to indicate a mature approach. But if he continues to seek a solution even after it becomes apparent that the problem is too big for him to cope with, if he fails to recognize that the problem is beyond his handling, then his behavior is unrealistic and maladjustive. An extreme situation of this kind is illustrated by the following case:

Bert F. was determined to become a great chemist regardless of the social and financial handicaps that stood in his way. Through intense effort he had done fairly well in high school, but when he entered college it soon became clear that he lacked the ability to achieve his aim. He had to leave college. Withdrawing from all social contacts, he shut himself up in a room and rarely ventured out. He spent his time working out fantastic chemical formulae that bore no relation to established knowledge in the field but in which he was completely absorbed. His father finally had him admitted to the hospital, where he was diagnosed as a schizophrenic.

For another individual, frustrated and disturbed by a problem, work may become a means of temporary escape with beneficial effects. One student states that often when she is upset by an emotional problem she feels a strong inclination to work. Usually she is able to keep working for hours and to accomplish a great deal. When she stops, she discovers that she feels all right again. In this case, the student, by busying herself with something unrelated to her problem, especially something that she could do successfully, eased her nervous tensions. Later, when she thought about the disturbance again, it had lost its intense, immediate significance. She could view it in a calmer mood and from a new perspective.

We should note, however, that some people develop a neurotic, maladjusted dependence on work. Work becomes an end in itself, an escapist device to which such people invariably turn to avoid meeting their problems.

Compensation. If a person finds that a physical or social defect prevents him from satisfying his needs in one way, he may attempt to overcome the obstacle by emphasizing or developing other traits and abilities in which he can excel and that will serve to divert attention from his deficiency. The crippled, unsightly Toulouse-Lautrec became a great painter whose friendship was valued by many. The sickly boy who cannot compete successfully in athletics may find satisfaction in scholastic achievement. The child of low intelligence who cannot keep up with his class may still gain the praise of his teachers by an attentive and cooperative attitude.

Another person, anxious to avoid as much competition as possible, will attempt to cultivate unusual abilities where they can excel for lack of a rival. He may, for example, develop the ability to break strong iron bars over his knees or with his teeth. Although the value of such a talent is questionable, it serves its purpose insofar as the individual is concerned. It gives him a chance to excel and to draw attention to himself.

Compensatory behavior, then, may produce peculiar skills of little social value, or it may lead to great creative achievements.

Parents who wish to satisfy their own ambitions through their children are seeking indirect compensation. A father whose youthful dreams of a medical career were frustrated by lack of money may try to satisfy his ambition by urging his son to become a physician. A mother whose marriage was unhappy may try to compensate by arranging a brilliant marriage for her daughter. Although such compensation sometimes brings satisfaction to the parents, it may seriously frustrate the children.

Rationalization. When an individual's self-esteem is disturbed or threatened, he frequently resorts to rationalization. The person who rationalizes gives plausible, socially acceptable, or "good" reasons for his actions and beliefs in order to avoid acknowledging the "real" reasons, which he regards as unworthy or improper —or which may not even be apparent to him. There are many forms of rationalization. Perhaps the best known is the "sour grapes" reaction, derived from the story of the fox who wanted a certain bunch of grapes but discovered that they hung too high for him to reach, whereupon he declared, "I did not want them anyhow. They are sour." This same attitude was manifested by

Dick when he missed out on a job he had tried very hard to get. Instead of acknowledging his failure he began to belittle the job. He said that he really did not want the job in the first place, that it did not pay enough, that it required too much work and too much time. These are all rationalizations, because if he had really felt that way about the job he would not have applied for it, worked for it, waited to be promoted to it.

Or consider the following case of a young man whose girl left him. Tom and Betty went together for a year. They enjoyed one another's company, were almost inseparable. But then something happened, and Betty discarded Tom in favor of Bob. So what did Tom do? Although before the breakup Tom had raved about Betty to all his friends, he suddenly discovered, after she had left him, that there were a thousand things wrong with her. This was his way of protecting himself. He was not mature enough emotionally to acknowledge defeat and to give the other fellow credit for winning his girl.

Sometimes we rationalize in reverse. Instead of trying to convince ourselves and others that we did not actually want the thing we were after, we talk ourselves into believing that our present situation really is best for us, that we are completely satisfied and wish for nothing more. This "sweet lemon" mechanism applies to anyone who insists that his life is just what he wants, no matter how poor and humble it may be. If he misses a promotion he insists he doesn't care. His present job suits him fine.

Another rather common form of rationalization is to blame other things or other people for frustrations or failures for which we alone are responsible. We kick the chair that caused us to stumble; we blame the tools for our poor workmanship, or the tennis racket when we miss the ball. We neglect to prepare for an exam, then try to excuse our failure by saying that the teacher has a grudge against us. Sometimes we use prejudice to help explain our failure. This is called scapegoating. If our business fails or if we lose an important sale we accuse our Jewish, Italian, or Irish competitors of shady dealings. And, finally, some of us adopt a fatalistic attitude, attributing everything that befalls us to "the Lord's will."

The person who rationalizes is not deliberately lying. As a child he has learned that certain motives are acceptable and others are not, and in accounting for his behavior he selects the acceptable motives. Furthermore, he learns to accept his own explanations and thus deceives not only others, but also himself.

In giving "good" reasons rather than "real" reasons for our behavior we do not, as a rule, invent a factor that did not enter into our behavior at all. Rather we select and overemphasize one of the factors that led us to act as we did. Since human motivation is always complex, it is usually not difficult to find at least one acceptable motive for our actions.

Sometimes we are blind to inconsistencies in our own behavior even when they are quite apparent to our associates. This is illustrated by the man who one day criticizes others for "showing off" and the next day goes out and buys a car that is really too expensive for him, explaining that he needs dependable transportation in his business. His associates know that a less expensive car would have served his purposes just as well.

Such a person is not aware of contradictions in his behavior. He believes his motives are valid. He has erected "logic-tight compartments;" segments of his behavior are walled off from one another, and he is not aware of any lack of consistency among them, since each one taken separately has internal logical coherence.

Let us look at another example. Some people will answer "yes" to the question, "Are all groups of people equal?" But they will say "no" when asked if Negroes and whites are equal. Logically, a yes answer to the first question implies a yes answer to the second, but pervasive stereotypes, i.e., highly simplified pictures that people have formed about a group of other people, function as rationalizations and prevent many from noting the logical error in their responses. Similar contrasts, as we have noted in Chapter 2, often can be observed between expressed attitudes and the actual behavior of an individual. The relative frequency of such inconsistencies springs in large degree from the fact that the culture itself exposes the individual to contradictory value systems.

Rationalization is important psychologically because it helps us to maintain our self-respect and self-confidence. In everyday affairs we have neither the time nor the inclination to track down and explain all our motives. Rationalizations provide protection against anxiety and failure.

But rationalizations may be harmful if carried to an extreme. First, if we refuse to accept responsibility for our failures we shall never be able to overcome them. Second, rationalizations may in time shade into delusions. If we consistently blame others for whatever goes wrong in our lives we may become completely dissociated from reality and develop delusions of persecution. The following case study illustrates the development of such a delusion:

William B. started off well in business, but after a few years something began to go wrong. As his business declined he blamed various circumstances for his difficulties. He also regarded his business associates and competitors with increasing suspicion. Eventually the business failed. After a while he opened a new business venture but it also failed. His suspicion of his associates increased. He began to believe that they were trying to destroy him as well as his business. He avoided all contact with them, fearing, for example, that if he ate lunch or dinner with them they would try to poison his food. His delusions finally became so marked that he was admitted to a hospital for the mentally ill.

Delusions may also take the form of delusions of grandeur in which a person believes himself to be a great person, unassailable and without blame.

Attention-getting behavior. In a culture that stresses competition and getting ahead, a certain amount of attention-getting behavior is inevitable. The person who cannot distinguish himself by socially approved means is likely to resort to subtle substitutes. The child who refuses to eat, for instance, becomes the central figure in a prolonged tussle of parental pleading and coaxing, a situation that serves to enforce the youngster's own sense of importance. Another child may deliberately disobey his parents' instructions because he would rather be punished than ignored.

Such resistant or negative behavior is common in early childhood and may be considered a part of normal development. Whether it develops into adjustive or maladjustive behavior depends on the motivation behind it and the results it achieves. Negative behavior enables the child to assert himself and achieve partial independence, but it can also signify intense hostility toward others—a hostility that punishment will serve only to intensify.

Resistance to demands may become a habitual mode of response. Prohibition of an act may enhance the desire to perform it. Even adults sometimes take a view opposed to one that is expressed because some compulsion forbids them to agree with anyone. In their minds the act of agreeing is identified with submission and subservience—which may be the way the parents made this person feel as a child when they demanded agreement.

Some persons feign sickness in order to get attention. The child who feels that his sick brother is getting more than his share of attention may start complaining about various imagined ills of his own. The neglected wife or mother or old person may conjure up all manner of ailments and become overly concerned about health in an effort to get more attention.

Certain forms of delinquent behavior also serve as attention-getting mechanisms. Lying and stealing, although they undoubtedly have other contributory factors, are means of drawing attention to oneself.

Identification. An individual who has been unable to achieve his own goal may derive satisfaction and enhance his self-esteem by identifying himself with the achievements of others. One of the most common forms of identification is hero-worship, seen in the case of the adolescent boy who avidly follows the exploits of his football idol and basks in the reflected glory of his gridiron accomplishments. His hero may live next door, or may be some-body he has never met personally, or may even be a fictional character.

Identification plays an important role in the socialization of the child. By identifying with his mother or father the child not only finds security, but also learns to accept the demands his parents make on him. In their play children emulate their parents; in association with other children they talk about what their

Identification. In their play, these two small girls are playing the role of mothers. Many traits, ranging in importance from mannerisms to moral and social attitudes, are learned by children through imitating parental qualities. (Courtesy the Los Angeles Mirror.)

father or big brother can do, boosting their own status by referring glowingly to the prestige of their family. Not only the
children, but also adults often identify themselves with recognized
prestige groups, especially when approaching a new situation.
The girl who transfers to another college mentions her membership in a well-known sorority; a man making new business contacts points out casually but intentionally that he is an active
member in a service club.

The individual identifies not only with specific persons, but
also with certain groups. He joins a club and it becomes *his* club.
He speaks of *his* school, *his* state, and *his* country. The achievements of his group become his achievements, and he becomes
upset when any slurring remark or attack is made against the
group. Strong ego-involvement characterizes the identification
process.

Identification also enters into a great many imaginative activities. Many people derive intense satisfaction from identifying
themselves with the characters in the books they read and the
plays or movies they see.

Whether or not identification plays a constructive role in the
development of an individual depends on a number of factors.
(1) In his adjustment to society it will make a great difference
whether a person models himself after a gangster or a saint, after
a Hitler or a Ghandi, after a poet or a mechanic. (2) The example set by his hero or model may give direction and impetus to
a person's own activities. (3) In extreme cases of identification,
such as occur in paranoia, an individual loses all sense of distinction between himself and the person with whom he identifies
and actually believes himself to be a famous king or statesman, a
persecuted saint, a great scientist.

Projection. Most of us harbor certain feelings or tendencies
that we are unwilling to recognize or accept. Hostility toward
parents or children, jealousy toward husband or wife, envy of a
friend's success, probably all these have been felt at one time or
another by almost everyone. If the individual regards such feel-

ings as a sign of depravity, or if they recur persistently and burden him with a feeling of guilt, he may try to deal with them by projecting them onto others.

This does not mean that he *consciously* assigns to others those qualities that he cannot tolerate in himself. Like other defense mechanisms, projection is an unconscious process. The first step in this process is repression. The individual pushes the disturbing elements out of his consciousness. But repression, as we have already seen, does not resolve the conflicts and tensions that the situation or incident has created. Further defense mechanisms are thus called into play. One of these—projection—occurs when an individual succeeds in attributing to other persons or groups of persons qualities and emotions that he cannot accept in himself. We say that he externalizes his inner conflicts. This, obviously, may have serious consequences for the other person, and in this sense projection differs from the other defense mechanisms we have discussed. The individual who daydreams or withdraws impairs his relationships with others; he may even withdraw as a form of revenge on the person from whom he withdraws. But he does not necessarily develop an image of the other person as wicked or immoral, hostile or aggressive, as he does in projection. In a study of anti-Semitism, Ackerman and Jahoda [1] found that the mechanism of projection permeates the entire personality structure of the anti-Semite. He projects onto the Jew whatever weaknesses or disturbing impulses he fears in himself.

The same process operates with respect to prejudice against other groups, and the often contradictory nature of accusations against others becomes understandable when we realize that in the process of projection many different qualities that the individual finds disturbing in himself can be attributed to others.

We should note one further consequence of the projection process. After a person has transferred his unacceptable or undesirable emotions or attitudes to another person or group, he is free to launch an attack, to direct suspicion toward the other

---

[1] Nathan W. Ackerman and Marie Jahoda, *Anti-Semitism and Emotional Disorder*. New York, Harper and Brothers, 1950, p. 56.

person or group through inuendo, gossip, or slander. He feels amply justified in withholding certain privileges from individuals or from members of a group, denying them equal opportunity and segregating or ostracizing them because of their alleged characteristics.

Thus the projective mechanism gives an individual the satisfaction of defending virtue by attacking evil or weakness in others. He places himself in a position of righteousness, of moral vigilance, which helps to allay any additional doubts he may have about himself.

Although projection usually operates in the way just described, we should note that unacceptable qualities are not the only ones projected. In a more inclusive sense, the use of the term may be illustrated by reference to projective techniques. These are utilized by the psychologist to gain insight into an individual's personality. The basic assumption is that the individual will project his own feelings, attitudes, and values into his responses to a projective test. Projective tests are discussed in detail in Chapter 15.

Apart from such tests, the mechanism of projection operates in our interpretations of another person's motivations or impressions of what an experience means to him. We draw our conclusions about his reactions by projecting onto him our own motivations and experiences. This tendency corresponds to the creative artist's projection of himself into that which he creates—that is, he externalizes his emotions and desires and needs into the characters of his play or novel or painting.

Projection characterizes some extreme forms of personality disorganization. The persecution delusions of the paranoic, for example, stem from his tendency to project onto other persons his own dangerous tendencies.

Repression and forgetting. We are all somewhat forgetful. We forget the phone number of a friend, the name of an acquaintance, the title of a book. Indeed, it would be a dubious advantage if we did remember everything that happened to us, the relevant as well as the irrelevant, the wrong solutions or answers along with the correct ones. Selective forgetting often is a positive factor in enabling us to adjust adequately. For example, forgetting inappropriate motor responses in driving a car makes our driving more efficient. But certain types of forgetting—particularly those that affect our social relationships—can seriously handicap our adjustment. The person who consistently forgets the names of persons he has met—or perhaps does not even remember that he has met them—or who forgets a dinner date or a business appointment, may find that his embarrassing memory lapses are causing his friends to reject him and to exclude him from their social plans. Forgetting is a dynamic process; that is, we forget or remember experiences in accordance with our needs. The act of dismissing unpleasant memories from consciousness (repression) protects us against experiences that threaten or disturb our self-concept.

Experimental studies show that repression occurs among normal people as well as among the mentally ill. Most of these studies have found that pleasant experiences are recalled more often than unpleasant ones. In extreme cases of repression a condition known as dissociation may be present. By dissociation a person erases fear, guilt, or other strong emotions from his mind. He may completely forget certain highly disturbing events, although his intellectual processes are otherwise intact. The nature of this event may be revealed through hypnosis.

Repression may result from frustration of needs and from painful experiences associated with such frustration. Behavior associated with strong social taboos is the type most frequently repressed. A large proportion of our anxieties and repressions are associated with sex. If repression reduced the strength of the sex need we might consider it an aid to adjustment. But repression does not reduce the need, nor satisfy the sex drive; it merely inhibits the sexual responses. Repression also inhibits the desire to seek needed advice and assistance.

Repression interferes with adjustment because even after the originai incident has been "forgotten" the tensions and emotional disturbances associated with it remain. Some unforeseen occurrence—a chance meeting, an accidental discovery of a long-lost letter—will bring back the memory of the incident and evoke the original emotional response. Such a situation is quite different from our recalling, humorously and objectively, "our most embarrassing moment." The question of repression will be discussed further in Chapter 7.

Regression (and retrogression). Regression occurs when a person reverts to previous levels of behavior. Often when a new baby arrives in a family an older child reverts to infantile behavior. He may begin to crawl or wet himself again, even though he has long since learned to walk and use the toilet. Regressive behavior may occur at any age level and is characteristic of many forms of maladjustive behavior.

Prolonged homesickness is one form of regressive behavior. It is understandable that we should miss old friends and old surroundings when we move from one place to another. But when homesickness continues to the extent that adjustment to a new environment becomes impossible, it is a form of maladjustive behavior. Sometimes the homesick person becomes physically ill and must return to his former home.

Such homesickness and other forms of regressive behavior are especially likely to occur in persons who have been overprotected and overindulged. Another factor contributing to regressive behavior is the fact that we usually recall pleasant experiences and forget the unpleasant, thus making the past appear much more attractive than it actually was.

Where regressive behavior centers around a particular object or person, we assume that a strong fixation has occurred—an overly strong attachment that causes the person to remain at a certain level of development. He may be so devoted to his mother and so accustomed to her way of doing things that he finds it impossible to establish a satisfactory love-relationship with another woman. Or, if he has grown beyond the mother complex, he may return to it when he cannot adequately cope with his present life-situation.

Fixation may take the form of habit-fixation—i.e., an individual may regress to a way of behaving that proved successful in the past. A forty-year-old woman who throws herself on the floor and cries uncontrollably when things go wrong is clearly manifesting regressive behavior.

To avoid confusion, remember that by regression we do not mean the tendency to act in a way that past experience has demonstrated to be satisfactory in meeting such a situation as now presents itself. Such a procedure is the essence of the learning process. But when a person reverts to behavior that clearly belongs to a more immature level of development, then he has regressed.

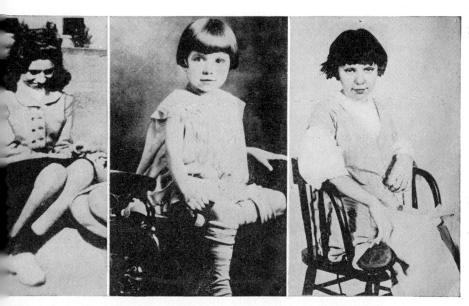

Regression. Regression is a withdrawing type of defense in that the individual does not face up to his difficulties directly, but instead retreats to an inferior type of adjustment—the helplessness and irresponsibility of an earlier age, for example. (Courtesy Dr. Jules H. Masserman, Dr. John Romano, and the W. B. Saunders Company.)

An extreme case of regressive behavior has been reported by Masserman.[2]

The mother of a seventeen-year-old girl complained that the girl's behavior had become increasingly destructive and irrational during the past few months. Her general behavior was very childish, she spoke in simple sentences, giggled a great deal, and had to be fed and cleaned as if she were an infant. Her history showed a highly unstable family background. When she was four years old her parents began to have violent quarrels, and when she was seven they separated. The mother was given custody of the child, a factor that further upset the child because she was greatly attached to her father. She became increasingly sullen and withdrawn, tendencies that were further accentuated by another violent encounter between her parents some years later. After that she refused to go to school, and while her mother was at work she would destroy the clothes her mother made for her and create complete disorder in the house. At one such time she found a photo of herself as a five-year-old. It showed her with a baby bob and, because of poor lighting, without eyebrows. Immediately she cut her hair, shaved off her eyebrows, and began to imitate the expressions and posture of the photographed child. These actions, together with the childish behavior described earlier, gave a clear picture of regression to a time that she remembered as a relatively happy one.

The occurrence of regression in frustrated children was demonstrated experimentally by Barker, Dembo and Lewin.[3] Each child's general level of constructiveness was determined by studying him closely for a half-hour period, during which he was free to play with various toys. Following this, the children were shown some beautiful new play materials. But after they had inspected them for a few moments they were led back to their old play equipment and the new toys were locked behind a wire

[2] Jules H. Masserman, *Principles of Dynamic Psychiatry*. Philadelphia: W. B. Saunders Company, 1946, p. 64.

[3] R. G. Barker, T. Dembo, and K. Lewin, "Frustration and Regression: An Experiment with Young Children," *University of Iowa Studies in Child Welfare*, Vol. 18, No. 1, 1941.

mesh. Then the children were again carefully observed in the familiar play situation in which their constructiveness had already been scored. Following their frustration—being exposed to tempting new toys but not being allowed to play with them—a striking regression in their level of constructiveness occurred, averaging 14 months for the group of 30 children. Only five of the children did not show regressive behavior.

Fantasy and daydreaming. Through fantasy and daydreaming we attain satisfactions that are denied us in real life. In our imaginations we sweep away the restrictions and frustrations that normally thwart us and manipulate objects and people as we please. We see ourselves as the conquering hero, the life of the

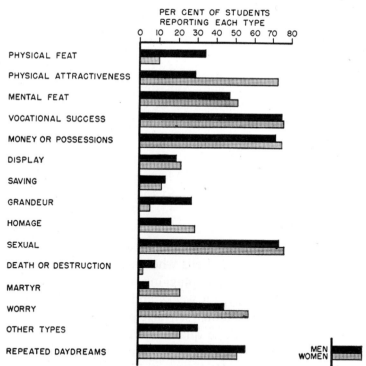

Daydreaming among normal people. Responses to a questionnaire, answered by 64 men, mostly students of engineering, and 131 women, about evenly divided in the practical arts and the fine arts, concerning the kind of daydreams that they have frequently. (Based on data from L. F. Shaffer, The Psychology of Adjustment. Boston, Houghton Mifflin Company, 1936, p. 194.)

party, the adored lover, the successful and respected businessman, the brilliant lawyer who helps the poor and oppressed, the
artist whose paintings receive world-wide acclaim.

Whether fantasy and daydreaming are adjustive or maladjustive depends on their intensity and extent. Often they afford a
necessary opportunity to relax, to withdraw temporarily from the
bustle of everyday living and to attack our problems from a new
perspective. Sometimes they provide an outlet that enables us to
make careful, useful plans. Today's daydreams may become tomorrow's accomplishments.

Frequently it is difficult to draw the line between daydreaming
and creative imaginative thought. The novelist, for example,
often finds it necessary to assume the identity of his characters,
to try to imagine their thoughts and experience their moods, in
order to write realistically about them. The artist daydreams
about the things he wants to put on canvas.

But we reach the danger point when our world of daydreaming and make-believe becomes consistently more satisfying than
our everyday experiences. Because we can ignore our usual obligations and manipulate events as we wish, we can attain, in our
imaginary experiences, complete success and ideal relationships
with others. Compared to our daydreams our real-life experiences then seem disappointing. When we transfer our high expectancies and idealized notions to the real world we see our
hopes dashed and our wishes blighted. In such a situation, adjustment to everyday living can become very difficult.

Or we may resort to daydreams to escape from our problems.
Take the case of Langford Wells who wanted to write a famous
novel. Writing a novel means plugging away minute by minute,
hour by hour, day by day, for weeks and months and sometimes
years. This takes tremendous self-discipline and perseverance.
Langford Wells lacked these qualities and did not get his novel
written. Failing to attain the satisfaction of a job well done, he
resorted to daydreaming. He imagined himself as having already
done the job. Daydreaming about his finished novel was much
easier than actually writing it. For Langford Wells daydreaming

was an opiate, a mental crutch that enabled him to see himself as a success when he really was a failure.

There are also ready-made daydreams into which we may escape when our problems become too unbearable. The student who is baffled or bored with his assignments can go to the movies, which offer excitement and make no demands upon him. By doing so he falls further and further behind in his work, thereby inviting the necessity to lose himself more and more in ready-made daydreams.

Not all daydreams are pleasant. Some produce anxiety and guilt, as may be the case when a person has vivid daydreams of sexual experiences that he rejects in his everyday life. Others produce self-pity; in them the person may assume the role of a martyr, suffering for others, being hurt by others, and picturing himself as a heroic person who makes sacrifices for others. Still others may have a nightmarish quality. Children who have been incessantly warned by their parents against certain dangers— playing with matches, for example—may develop neurotic fears and imagine themselves constantly threatened by fire.

For those who daydream a great deal, the daydreams— whether pleasant or unpleasant—may be repetitive and stereotyped, with the same theme and the same routine recurring again and again; or they may become highly elaborate and intricate.

As mentioned previously, we reach the danger point when our daydreams become more satisfying than our everyday experiences. Some people lose all contact with the real world—i.e., they become psychotic. They develop hallucinations. They believe they hear voices. They profess to see and to feel the touch of persons who are invisible to everyone else. They develop delusions of grandeur, regarding themselves as emperors or saints.

Daydreams and fantasies, then, may operate in many different ways, affecting our adjustment variously, depending on the extent to which we use them and the importance they assume for us. All of us have spent time daydreaming; and perhaps the success of such plays as "Harvey," which introduced an imaginary rabbit who made life more interesting for Ellwood P. Dowd and his associates, can be traced to the fact that many of us have at times felt the world of daydreams and fantasy to be more satisfying than everyday existence.

Withdrawal. Often we find it necessary to withdraw from social contacts and from various pressures to which we are exposed. Such periods of withdrawal give us the opportunity to reevaluate our problems, ideas, and relationships. The person who is too closely involved in a situation may find it difficult to make a wise, dispassionate decision. Under such conditions it is helpful to withdraw for a while. After a good night's rest, he may see the situation more clearly and approach it more effectively.

Withdrawal may take various forms. The person who feels inadequate in social situations may become submissive and shy, withdrawing from contacts whenever possible, preferring solitude

Withdrawal. Withdrawal is a defense mechanism to which many individuals resort when they feel thwarted. A person who withdraws retreats from the situation in which he experiences adjustive difficulty. (Courtesy Coronet Films.)

to sociability, observing rather than participating in the activities around him.

Frequently the shy, retiring individual escapes detection. The teacher or parent is more likely to notice—and perhaps criticize —aggressive children than the quiet children who cause less "trouble." Yet if a tendency to withdraw becomes pronounced it may indicate a serious maladjustment.

The person who is reserved and formal in his dealings with others may also be manifesting symptoms of withdrawing. His cloak of aloofness serves as a screen to conceal deep-seated feelings of inferiority. He keeps others at a distance for fear that they may come to share his own low opinion of himself. His acquaintances, therefore, can never feel that they really know him. Such a person has no confidence either in himself or in others.

The person who withdraws constantly is often anxious and fearful. If he has felt threatened and insecure at some time—at home, in school, at a social gathering—he may persistently feel the possibility of having to face such a situation again. He generalizes from one situation to others and responds to such future situations by avoiding them. He may shun persons who threaten his security and shy away from various tasks he feels he cannot accomplish. Sometimes a traumatic experience, i.e., an unexpected incident which comes as a shock to the person, may initiate such behavior, although it is more likely that a previous tendency to withdraw is accentuated by the traumatic event.

If a woman is suddenly deserted by the man she expected to marry, the event is likely to be traumatic. If her friends also know of it, the element of wounded pride is added. She may withdraw from all social engagements, not only in order to be alone with her grief, but also to avoid having to face the pity of her friends. Her disappointment makes her bitter, and although she may reject sympathy by insisting that she has forgotten the man and does not wish to hear him mentioned again, the hurt persists. Her withdrawing tendencies may lead to the development of additional defense mechanisms. Her reluctance to face her friends may be rationalized into a claim that social gatherings are a waste of time, that she would rather spend her time at home reading. She may resort to daydreaming in which she indulges in the satisfaction of imagining that the man begs her to take him back, a request that she haughtily refuses. Withdrawing, rationalizing, daydreaming—all function to guard her against future exposure to the same frustrating experience, the same repeated failure.

The withdrawing tendency may also be illustrated by a person who is afraid that no one will want to hire him. He keeps reading newspaper ads and consulting his friends about promising openings but is always a little late in applying for the job. His delay is a form of withdrawal. By applying a day or two late he does not expose himself to the possibility of being refused the job. In this sense the effects of withdrawal are similar to those of rationalization—i.e., the real problem is not faced and therefore cannot be resolved.

Some persons avoid the problems and conflicts of everyday life by withdrawing into illness. They may not deliberately make themselves ill, but they do become especially sensitized to certain physical disturbances that other people would scarcely notice.

Apathy and lack of interest also may be symptoms of withdrawal. Some people, in order to justify their withdrawing, profess a lack of interest in others. Lack of interest becomes an additional protective mechanism. Withdrawal in its most acute form is seen in schizophrenia, a severe mental disorder (discussed later) characterized by a pronounced loss of interest in external affairs and by emotional apathy and seclusiveness.

What we popularly describe as narrow-mindedness also is a form of withdrawal. The narrow-minded individual is unwilling to expose himself to ideas contrary to his own. He dismisses as "propaganda" anything that opposes his own prejudices. He avoids opinions that threaten his own. He withdraws from contacts with people who disagree with him. To some extent this is true of all of us. We are all selective in what we read and listen to. But when this selectivity becomes so pronounced as to blur our conception of reality, then it is maladjustive.

General Principles Concerning the Nature and Function of Defense Mechanisms

As rules of thumb for solving limited and petty problems, the defense mechanisms free us from some stress. But they produce, at best, an automatic, rigid reaction. Problems arising from deep-seated personality disorders must be handled cautiously, with flexibility and insight. Applying defense mechanisms to such problems is about as useful as binding an ankle in an effort to relieve a fractured arm.

Defense mechanisms contribute to a distorted conception of the nature of adjustment problems, which leads, in turn, to an attempt to solve them by methods that do not logically apply. If important but unpleasant facts are ignored; if emotions, thoughts and persons intimately related to the frustration of some need are replaced by less threatening substitutes; if flattering reasons for doing things replace the true reasons; if important consequences of behavior are conveniently overlooked; if qualities and impulses we fear in ourselves are too readily attributed to others —then the microscope of psychotherapy must be used to expose the core of problems buried so deeply beneath layers of unconscious deception.

By its very nature the defense mechanism is immediately concerned with *relieving anxiety,* not in satisfying the need or frustration that produced the anxiety. It treats the symptom or byproduct. It does not treat the cause. Consequently, satisfaction of the original need is either neglected or only partly accomplished. This produces an accumulation of unrelieved tension and dissatisfaction regarding the original need. In the long run, tensions associated with unrelieved needs will create more anxiety, preparing the way for wider and less discriminate use of defense mechanisms in a relentless cycle.

As unrelieved tension of unsatisfied original needs accumulates, as dependence on defense mechanisms increases, the individual often realizes that his own inadequacy must lie at the base of his difficulties.

From the foregoing descriptions of various defense mechanisms, certain general principles concerning their nature and function can be summarized:

1. An individual uses defense mechanisms to cope with frustrations he encounters in the course of his development. They are *learned* forms of behavior.

2. Defense mechanisms serve to protect the individual from threats to his security.

3. Everyone has suffered frustration at some point in his life. Whether defense mechanisms are adjustive or maladjustive depends on the extent to which the individual utilizes them. Occasional daydreaming or withdrawal can be a source of relaxation and strength, but when these tendencies lose their temporary nature and become permanently more satisfying than reality they lead to maladjustment.

4. The individual who can maintain some flexibility in his approach to problems will be able, in general, to deal more adequately with frustration and conflict than the person who tries to solve all his problems on the basis of a single approach.

5. Defense mechanisms cease to be adjustive when:

  a. our imagined world becomes consistently more satisfying than our real world;
  b. they obscure the real nature of the problem confronting us and the source of our conflicts;
  c. they lead to cumulative maladaptions, i.e., when a person who has failed to obtain a job says that he did not want the job anyhow ("sour grapes" mechanism), when he next blames others for his failure (scapegoating), and when he then starts to daydream about being a successful businessman without actually making any effort to become one.

6. And finally, defense mechanisms become maladjustive when they prevent an individual from making an objective anal-

ysis of himself in relation to his problem and blind him to the possibility of alternative courses of action.

For Additional Reading

Barker, R., T. Dembo, and Kurt Lewin, "Frustration and Regression: An Experiment With Young Children," *University of Iowa Studies in Child Welfare,* Vol. 18, No. 1, 1941, 1-314.

Cameron, Norman, *The Psychology of Behavior Disorders.* Boston, Houghton Mifflin Company, 1947.

Cantril, Hadley, *Gauging Public Opinion.* Princeton, Princeton University Press, 1944.

Carroll, Herbert A., *Mental Hygiene—the Dynamics of Adjustment.* New York, Prentice-Hall, Inc., 1951.

Cole, Luella, *Attaining Maturity.* New York, Rinehart & Company, Inc., 1944.

James, William, *The Principles of Psychology,* Vol. 1. New York, Henry Holt & Company, Inc., 1890.

Keister, M. E. and R. Updegraff, "A Study of Children's Reactions to Failure and an Experimental Attempt to Modify Them," in T. M. Newcomb and E. L. Hartley, eds., *Readings in Social Psychology.* New York, Henry Holt & Company, Inc., 1947.

Kraines, S. H. and E. S. Thetford, *Managing Your Mind.* New York, The Macmillan Company, 1947.

Lewin, Kurt, "Time Perspective and Morale," in G. Watson, ed., *Civilian Morale.* Boston, Houghton Mifflin Company, 1942, pp. 48-70.

Masserman, Jules H., *Principles of Dynamic Psychiatry.* Philadelphia, W. B. Saunders Company, 1946.

May, Rollo, *The Meaning of Anxiety.* New York, The Ronald Press Company, 1950.

McKinney, Fred, *The Psychology of Personal Adjustment,* 2nd ed. New York, John Wiley & Sons, Inc., 1949.

Murphy, Gardner, *Personality. A Biosocial Approach to Origins and Structure.* New York, Harper and Brothers, 1947.

————, L. B. Murphy, and T. M. Newcomb, *Experimental Social Psychology,* rev. ed. New York, Harper and Brothers, 1937.

Richards, T. W., *Modern Clinical Psychology.* New York, McGraw-Hill Book Company, Inc., 1946.

Ruch, Floyd B., *Psychology and Life,* 4th ed. Chicago, Scott, Foresman and Company, 1953.

Saul, Leon J., *Emotional Maturity.* Philadelphia, J. B. Lippincott Company, 1947.

Shaffer, Laurence Frederic, *The Psychology of Adjustment. An Objective Approach to Mental Hygiene.* Boston, Houghton Mifflin Company, 1936.

Symonds, P. M., *The Dynamics of Human Adjustment.* New York, D. Appleton-Century Company, 1946.

Adjustment
and the Neuroses

CHAPTER 7

Cultural norms, as we have noted already in Chapter 2, define patterns of behavior for groups and individuals within a society. Usually, however, the norms make some allowance for deviant behavior so that an individual may choose his own way of doing things without fear of social disapproval or punishment. The allowance permitted may vary greatly from one culture to another and also within a given culture at various periods of time. If, however, the individual steps beyond the bounds of permissive behavior, we call his behavior abnormal. This means that there is no single standard of normal for all mankind. Abnormal behavior, whether neurotic or psychotic, can be understood only within its cultural context. It is well to keep in mind this relativity of standards by which any behavior is judged as normal or abnormal. The adjustment process, or adjustment difficulties, such as neuroses, involve a relationship between the person and his environment.

Let's look a bit closer at this relationship between environment and neurosis. There are approximately 8,000,000 psychoneurotics in the United States, more than the number of persons suffering from any other single disease. A neurotic, broadly described, is a person who is unable to adjust to the many varied situations he is called upon to face. We live in a dynamic, fluid, ever-changing society, one that is constantly posing new issues and problems for the individual, one that is constantly making demands on a person's ability to adjust. Hence, as a society grows more complex, as people are called upon to adjust to an ever-increasing number of new and perplexing situations, we may expect the rate of neuroses to rise.

Before we go further let us emphasize that the difference between the neurotic and the normal person is mainly a difference of degree and not of kind. Or to put it another way, the neurotic shows *more* or *less* of the behavior that characterizes all of us. Thus, while the normal person may fear a specific event at a specific time, the neurotic may fear most things most of the time. An understanding of neurotic behavior, therefore, often leads to a better understanding of normal behavior.

Contrast Between Neuroses and Psychoses

Mental disorders usually are divided into two main categories: neuroses (also called psychoneuroses) and psychoses.

The psychoses are serious behavior disorders that render a patient unable to care for himself and/or dangerous to himself and to others. Psychotics require medical and frequently institutional care. The following chapter will discuss the psychoses.

The neuroses, on the other hand, make an individual less personable or sociable, but they do not necessarily prevent him from participating in ordinary, daily activities. The neuroses are a group of behavior disorders that spring from a person's inability to adapt to stress and conflict.

The neurotic individual is aware, to some extent, of his difficulties. He may be aware of some of his symptoms, his difficulties, although not aware of the causes. The psychotic is not aware of his difficulties. The psychotic's total personality is affected; the neurotic, instead, shows disturbances in certain specific areas, such as his inability to control his feelings, or his lack of control over compulsive acts, such as stealing (called kleptomania), or certain thoughts and feelings, such as phobia of closed places (called claustrophobia).

In terms of psychiatric criteria, we can differentiate the neuroses from the psychoses in several ways.

1. No organic basis can be detected in neurosis. This does not necessarily mean that the neurotic person is free from organic disease, but any such disease from which he may be suffering is irrelevant as far as his neurosis is concerned.

2. Unlike the psychotic, there is no consistent and lasting deterioration of the neurotic's intellectual functions.

3. The neurotic's experiences and mood changes are less sudden than those of the psychotic and more related to specific changes in the environment.

4. The neurotic suffers no persistent distortion of external reality, such as hallucinations and delusions. Although the neurotic may withdraw from social relations to some extent, he does not lose contact with reality as does the psychotic.

More specifically, the following symptoms characterize the behavior of the neurotic.

1. Anxiety, which reveals itself in various physiological or psychological symptoms, such as ulcers, or in various abnormal fears, such as phobias.

2. Use of various psychological defenses (such as depression, obsession or phobia) and extensive reliance on such defense mechanisms as repression, projection, and rationalization in an automatic, unconscious attempt to control anxiety.

3. Symbolic bodily expressions, such as hysterical or psychosomatic functions.

4. Indications (revealed through studies of his life history) that the victim has manifested periodic or constant maladjustment, in varying degrees, since early childhood—or even from infancy.

We see thus that neurotic symptoms may express themselves in physiological symptoms, such as ulcers, headaches, allergies, or even functional blindness, deafness, or paralysis. Or they may express themselves psychologically through distortions in behavior, such as in phobias, compulsions, or other bizarre behavior.

Classification and Description of the Neuroses

The various neuroses represent different reactions through which the neurotic tries to deal with his anxiety. On the basis of the particular pattern of symptoms (a symptom is a single item of behavior) or syndrome (a syndrome is a combination or pattern of symptoms that occur together and are the distinguishing feature of a particular disorder), the neuroses fit into different categories. These categories differ somewhat with different authorities but generally include the following:

1. Anxiety reactions
2. Dissociative reactions
3. Conversion reactions
4. Phobic reactions
5. Obsessive compulsive reactions
6. Depressive reactions
7. Hypochondriacal and neurasthenic reactions

We shall now consider briefly the distinguishing characteristics of the behavior disturbances found under each of these headings.

Anxiety reactions. Anxiety disorders are quite common. Many authorities believe that anxiety is the common core from which all neurotic behavior arises.

The person suffering from an anxiety neurosis is seized with sudden attacks of intense fear, which, at least in the beginning, cannot be traced to any particular cause; it is a "free-floating" fear. Physiologically, the same symptoms we associate with real fear appear: this involves a kind of paralysis of the musculature, palpitation of the heart, profuse sweating, sense of pressure in the head, dryness in the mouth, and in certain cases relaxation of the sphincters.

As time goes on, one symptom, such as dizziness or faintness, may become more pronounced than the others. And, as already mentioned, the attacks may become chronic, inducing a feeling of panic, emotional breakdown, suicidal ideas, and even temporary mental confusion and disorientation.

Anxiety in these reactions is *not* as effectively controlled by any specific psychological defense mechanisms as it is in other psychoneurotic reactions.

Anxiety stems from various causes, most of which are related to the discrepancies between an individual's level of achievement and the goals and rewards a society regards as desirable. Thus, an individual who is a member of a society that stresses material wealth and status may become anxious, worried, and distraught if he fails to make a lot of money and to improve his social position. This will be true especially if his close friends and associates expect him to achieve these goals. Cultural mores that forbid extra-marital sexual relations also may cause a person to worry and grow anxious as his needs for sexual expression come into conflict with the standards of society. The need to express aggressiveness or hostility may also be a source of anxiety when such expression is stifled by cultural restrictions or threatening consequences. This is often the case with a child in relation to his parents. Indeed, any demands with which the individual feels he cannot cope or that are in conflict with his needs can be sources of anxiety.

Dissociative reactions. The dissociative reactions, often classified as a form of conversion hysteria, are neurotic attempts to

escape inner conflict and anxiety by repressing, forgetting, blocking off, or dissociating from usual awareness certain unwelcome
ideas, feelings, or drives. The dissociative reactions include amnesia, fugue, and multiple-personality disorders.

The amnesia victim cannot remember certain episodes or periods of his life. The shock of seeing a fatal accident may, for
example, blot out all traces of the event from his memory. An
attack of amnesia may vanish after a day or week or may persist
for a period of years.

A fugue is quite similar in certain respects to an attack of
amnesia. The fugue victim forgets his identity and runs away
from familiar surroundings, "coming to" later in some distant
place, dazed, confused, and unable to remember how he got
there. His memory lapse may continue for several days, weeks,
or even months, during which time he will be unable to recall
his past. When he recovers, he will recall the past; the period of
the fugue however may remain a blank.

From fugues it is but a step to multiple personality. Cases of
dual or multiple personality are rare, Dr. Jekyll and Mr. Hyde
notwithstanding. Ordinarily everyone of us plays several different roles during the course of a day. A man may assume the role
of husband, father, employer, philanthropist, or sportsman, all
in a day and act quite differently in each role. But he recognizes
himself as a unified, integrated personality no matter how diverse
his roles may be. In the case of multiple personality, however,
this integration is missing. The individual is unable to reconcile
the character traits of one personality, of one role he assumes,
with another, and frequently is unable to recall—or to recall only
dimly—the acts and thoughts of the other personality.

In cases of amnesia, fugue, and multiple personality, the individual erases unwelcome ideas, feelings, or drives from his consciousness. The amnesia victim forgets unpleasant and disturbing
events; a fugue victim flees into a different life and forgets his
past; a multiple personality dissociates functions, characteristics,
and roles.

Dissociative reactions are usually found in emotionally immature persons who want to escape from an anxiety-producing situation but do not dare to try. Generally this type of person rejects the conscious desire to run away because he considers it too cowardly or immoral. The resulting neurotic adjustment is a repression or dissociation of that part of experience that he cannot bring himself to face.

Conversion reactions (conversion hysterics). In the conversion reactions, often classified as conversion hysterias, an underlying emotional conflict is "converted." By some unfathomable process, this overwhelming and uncontrollable emotion is transformed into an actual physical handicap. The victim may go blind or deaf, become paralyzed, or develop a tic or tremor for no organic reason that is discernible. The physical symptoms may appear where no organic pathology ever existed, or they may retain the characteristics of an illness after the organic cause of the illness has passed. In the latter case the patient unconsciously exploits a symptom suggested by the illness. When this occurs, it is often difficult to distinguish the hysterical conversion reaction from deliberate malingering.

Conversion reactions fall into three categories: hysterical sensory disturbances, hysterical paralyses, and hysterical motor disturbances.

In hysterical sensory disturbances the function of one or more of the senses is impaired. The victim may become blind or lose his sense of smell. Sometimes the sense of touch is affected, resulting in the notion that the skin is tingling or crawling.

Hysterical paralyses may involve partial or complete loss of the voice, paralysis of one or more limbs, or even paralysis of half the body.

Motor disturbances involve loss of muscular control. Tics, tremors, involuntary posturing, and catalepsy belong in this category.

Like other neurotic symptoms, the conversion reactions lack organic basis. These symptoms serve merely to lessen feelings of anxiety and are usually symbolic of underlying mental conflict.

These reactions usually meet the immediate needs of the patient, allowing him to make a short-range, neurotic adjustment.

Phobic reactions. Phobias are unwarranted fears; a person with a phobia realizes his fear is groundless, but is still unable to rid himself of it. A girl, for example, who has a panic reaction when a feather comes out of a pillow, may recognize this as an irrational fear, that is, as a phobia, but still not be able to rid herself of the intense emotional reaction to feathers. A person with a phobic disorder often feels that he is compelled to think or act in a certain manner "against his will," as the layman might say. All of us are familiar with the more common phobias— claustrophobia, the fear of confined spaces; agoraphobia, fear of open spaces; mysophobia, fear of contamination; acrophobia, fear of high places, and so on. A person may also develop phobias about blood, germs, animals, and an almost endless variety of other things.

In phobic reactions the person has learned to use fear of specific objects or situations as a shield to prevent or avoid an anxiety-producing situation. The object that terrorizes the phobic may bear only a symbolic relationship to the object or situation that originally produced anxiety. The adult who as a child was attacked by a bulldog may now be terrorized by all kinds and sizes of dogs, cats, furry animals, and even birds and fur pieces. This shift of fear reaction from one stimulus object to another is one example of displacement. In this case the displacement may be due to simple generalization or irradiation of the original fear-evoking stimulus. What the person consciously fears depends on the form and direction of the displacement, and these are determined by the person's psychological needs. The highly moral woman's morbid fear of syphilis may serve to satisfy her need for high self-esteem by displacing her real (but unacceptable) source of anxiety—sexually promiscuous impulses. Simultaneously, her fear of syphilis helps her to avoid situations in which she might give vent to unacceptable impulses.

The foregoing example illustrates another common aspect of

phobic reactions. The source of danger may be internal as well as external. What is "dangerous" in a given situation may be the phobic's own impulse or desire in response to a specific stimulus or its symbolic surrogate—an unconscious desire or impulse that he has repressed because it is unacceptable to him. Thus a person's abnormal fear of knives may represent a repressed urge to commit suicide.

The phobic reactions may be divided into simple and complex types.

The simple phobic reactions may be directly learned from bad examples—as a phobic parent may teach a child to fear insects, dark, or lightning. Or they may be persistent, maladaptive responses to an originally terrifying object or situation.

The complex phobic reactions are an attempt to prevent or avoid strong anxiety by repressing the fear of the actual internal or external danger and displacing that fear to some part or symbolic representative of the danger. The neurotic then can avoid having to face the real cause of anxiety by fleeing the camouflaged symbol.

Obsessive compulsive reactions. The central characteristic of the obsessive compulsive reaction is a persistent repetition of an unwanted and often symbolic thought or act.

Obsessions are characterized by the persistent recurrence of certain undesired and disquieting thoughts. Constant worry about death or finances, for example, may become an obsession. When an obsession becomes so strong that it begins to interfere with a person's work, study, or rest, then it is abnormal. Obsessions may involve a persistent idea that the person may harm himself or someone else, as in the case of the woman who couldn't help thinking that she might step in front of an oncoming car on the street. Sometimes obsessions involve thoughts about sexual activities, as in the case of the man who continually kept thinking he might engage in homosexual activities.

Compulsions are acts that an individual performs without knowing the reason why. One of the most common forms is the hand-washing compulsion, in which a person feels compelled to wash his hands over and over again, even though they are perfectly clean. Other examples of compulsions are kleptomania, or the compulsion to steal, and pyromania, or the compulsion to set fires. Often a person will not even try to explain or justify his compulsions, beyond saying that he simply cannot help himself. This is illustrated by the case of the young woman who took small items from store counters. She said that her husband could well afford to buy the things that she had stolen, and that she lived in fear that she might be found out and thus disgrace herself, her husband, and her two children. Yet she was unable to resist the temptation to steal.

Phobias, obsessions, and compulsions may occur alone or in combination. The person who has a phobia about contamination, for example, may unconsciously fall victim to the hand-washing compulsion. And phobias may be complicated by obsessions. The person may find himself haunted by thoughts of a particular object or situation he fears, and become just as distraught as if he were actually meeting the object or situation face to face.

The victim of a phobia is compelled to experience exaggerated, illogical fear when exposed to certain stimuli. In the obsessive compulsive reaction, persistent repetition of the maladaptive emotion, thought, or act is the central characteristic.

What is the reason for such symptoms? They are an attempt on the part of the individual to protect himself against stress and anxiety by displacing his fears or guilt feelings onto some object, act, or thought. The hand-washing compulsion, for example, may indicate a deep-seated fear that the person has sinned, or been "dirty," and needs therefore to atone for his sins through this symbolic cleansing act. By concentrating on the symbol, rather than the pent-up emotion behind it, the person avoids having to face disturbing facts. The symbol becomes an outlet for releasing tensions and controlling anxiety.

Freud maintained that obsessive and compulsive behavior represented a person's desire to defend his ego against the memory of sexual aggression (in fantasy or in actuality) early in life.

Other writers have emphasized the conflict between desire and fear as a basic cause of obsessive and compulsive behavior; that is, the individual feels a strong biological or psychological need, the satisfaction of which is threatened. Although conflict between opposing needs or between biological needs and social approval occurs and produces tension in the lives of many individuals, an abnormal amount of tension is produced in those situations in which the satisfaction of one drive constantly prevents the satisfaction of another. Phobias, obsessions, and compulsions represent an individual's attempt to reduce these tensions.

Dorcus and Shaffer [1] point out that erratic disciplining of a child by its parents may constitute an important predisposing factor. If the child is not taught the differences between acceptable and unacceptable behavior, if the same act brings reward at one time and punishment at another, he will grow apprehensive and insecure. Since approval or disapproval seems to depend on the changing moods of his parents rather than on his own behavior, the child will not learn which behavior is most effective in handling this problem. This leads to anxiety, and the anxiety in turn to such symptoms as those just mentioned.

Neurotic depressive reactions. In the neurotic depressive reactions the person tries to reduce acute anxiety by pronounced and prolonged depression and self-depreciation. The term neurotic depressive reaction is synonymous with reactive depression and must be differentiated from the more severe psychotic forms found in involutional melancholic and manic-depressive reactions. This will be discussed in more detail in the next chapter.

Neurotic depressive reactions are marked by feelings of guilt and ambivalence. Thus the neurotically depressed soldier, whose life was spared in combat while his best friend was killed, is troubled by such feelings. He feels that it is wrong for him to enjoy life, since his friend cannot be alive to enjoy it with him. On occasions he may even feel responsible for the death of his friend. The extent and degree of the depression depends on the

---

[1] Roy M. Dorcus and G. Wilson Shaffer, *Textbook of Abnormal Psychology,* 4th ed. Baltimore, The Williams and Wilkins Company, 1950.

person's predisposition to feelings of inadequacy, the extent to which he regards the world as unfriendly and hostile, the objective severity of his traumatic experience, and the degree of ambivalence associated with that experience. In these cases the urge to suicide is often present. There is also evidence that the individual uses his depression to attract sympathetic support.

Hypochondriacal and neurasthenic reactions. In hypochondria and neurasthenia the individual is excessively preoccupied with his physical condition—the way he *feels*. In hypochondria he feels sick and in neurasthenia he feels tired.

The complaints of a hypochondriac run the whole gamut of man's ills—indigestion, stomach aches, heart or lung trouble, glandular ailments, urinary disturbances, sore muscles, and others in almost endless variety. He spends much of his spare time in doctors' offices or poring over popular medical books and journals looking for remedies. Many seem to "enjoy poor health" and like to tell others about their symptoms, their operations, their tribulations, and their expenses in trying to find relief. Often they become the unwary dupes of quacks.

The chief symptom of neurasthenia is an exaggerated feeling of fatigue, which explains why neurasthenia is often called the fatigue neurosis. A neurasthenic complains of exhaustion and a feeling of general weakness. He feels mentally and physically inadequate, and often complains that he cannot concentrate. Difficulties that appear small to others may upset him completely. He is very irritable and this irritability may give way to emotional exhaustion, accompanied by feelings of depression. Sometimes, without any specific organic basis, he may develop specific physiological symptoms, such as headaches, backaches, numbness in various parts of the body. Often the neurasthenic will lose all sexual vigor, becoming virtually impotent. Neurasthenia is often difficult to diagnose because many of its symptoms may have their origin in some temporary or chronic physical condition. Physical condition, however, serves mainly as a "psychological excuse" to develop the other symptoms found in the neurasthenic picture.

Case studies of neurasthenics reveal that the symptoms of pronounced fatigue rarely arise from overwork or from other forms of strenuous mental or physical work. Rather, the fatigue seems to be of an emotional or mental variety, arising from a person's inability to resolve a long series of emotional difficulties. Neurasthenic symptoms, like other symptoms in neuroses, serve an important function for the person. They may be a form of ego protection against the admission of inadequacy, or failure, in many different areas.

The main differences between the neurasthenic and the hypochondriac is that the former complains of bodily fatigue, disorder and "all over" discomfort while the latter tends to focus his complaints upon a specific organ or function of his body. Instead of being tired all over, he has a heart that doesn't work right, or a kidney that won't let him function adequately. Both, however, share the characteristic of abnormal concern about their own well-being. "Poor health" serves important psychological functions for both of them.

The various forms of hysterical reactions just described, like other neurotic behavior described earlier, represent attempts by the individual to handle his conflicts. Why one person will handle his problem by developing an amnesia, another a fugue, and another dissociation, is difficult to answer specifically. In general, one may say that the neurotic symptoms a person develops have been evolving along with his other characteristics throughout his entire life. Individual differences contributing to this development will be discussed in detail in Chapter 15.

Genesis of Neurotic Behavior

We have pointed out previously that the difference between normal and neurotic behavior is one of degree; the same dynamic processes that operate in normal behavior can be observed in neurotic persons, and vice versa. If we are to understand personality problems we must take into account the same general set of factors regardless of whether we are dealing with normal or deviant behavior. These factors involve: (1) heredity; (2) the individual's background and relevant experiences—his relationships with others in childhood and adolescence, the frustrations and deprivations he has experienced and their impact on his personality, the way in which he perceives his roles, the extent to which he has accepted the values of his culture, the nature of his adaptive responses, especially the skills he has developed to use in solving problems; (3) the social environment in which he lives—its stability or instability, the economic demands and pressures it exerts on the individual, its degree of restraint or freedom, the absence or presence of conflicting cultural mores; and (4) the situation or situations that cause neurotic behavior.

None of these factors by themselves cause neuroses, although in certain cases the influence of one may stand out more clearly than the influence of another. It is a combination of factors that causes the neuroses, just as it is a combination of factors that causes all other forms of behavior. Let us now turn to a consideration of these factors as they function in neurotic behavior.

Heredity. The influence of heredity on neurotic behavior is difficult to evaluate because it is almost impossible to differentiate between a person's inherited characteristics and those he acquires very early in life. For example, the attempt to link mental illness with heredity by tracing the incidence of mental disorders in a person's family usually fails because, even if the incidence is high, we cannot tell whether the person inherited predisposing characteristics or whether he acquired them through close and frequent contact with afflicted members of the family.

Background of relevant experiences. Whether inherited or acquired, there appear to be in the life histories of neurotic persons certain characteristics, certain reaction tendencies, indicating that the development of neuroses was likely. For example, life histories of chronic complainers often reveal a deep fear of some disease from early childhood on. Actual illness may center that person's attention on certain symptoms that become the focus of neurotic complaints long after the illness has been cured. In psychasthenia, the obsessive and compulsive dispositions appear to be found in such predisposing characteristics as unusual scrupulousness and exactitude, an overconcern in being precise, in being orderly, in being clean, in being on time, and in adhering strictly and often irrationally to certain rules and regulations.

Life histories of neurotics also generally show a background of conflict and unhappiness and of inability to solve problems. We should remember, however, that their difficulties and conflicts as such do not cause neurotic behavior; such difficulties occur in the lives of everybody. It is the manner in which a person approaches his problems, his resourcefulness, his way of perceiving and evaluating his problems that are the decisive elements in inclining someone toward normal or neurotic forms of adjustment.

The social environment. The neurotic usually is anxious and insecure in his dealings with other people, a condition that generally can be traced to childhood experiences. The individual who has been rejected as a child seeks love as much as or more than others. He wants to love and to be loved, but he is afraid lest he be rejected again. This approach-avoidance conflict, that is, the desire to approach a person and at the same time the fear of approaching him, appears to be a basic problem in the social conflict of the neurotic person.

As the child grows up he develops new needs. These must be satisfied in socially acceptable ways, and often this involves a delay in their gratification, and help from others. But if help and guidance are not forthcoming, the child's world becomes threatening, hostile, dangerous. The basic conflict in such cases is between the needs of the individual and the demands of society that the needs be satisfied in certain prescribed ways and at certain specified times.

Maladjustive ways of dealing with such conflicts may develop early in life, and since they do reduce tension to a certain extent (although they do not resolve the conflict), they persist and become preferred ways of responding. Even so, the individual may carry on his daily activities fairly well as long as no new disturbances crop up. But if a sudden storm appears—a quarrel between husband and wife, a financial problem, an accident—the person may develop neurotic symptoms. War neuroses are good examples of individuals breaking down under unexpected stresses and pressures.

Situations that produce neurotic behavior. Although most of our knowledge of abnormal behavior comes from studying the case histories of mentally ill persons, a significant contribution has been made through experiments inducing abnormal behavior in animals. Pavlov, the famous Russian physiologist, produced what he called "experimental neuroses" in a dog, and other investigators have extended his work. In the Pavlovian conditioning studies, the problem involved determining the extent to which the animal could discriminate between two patterns that were made increasingly similar. The procedure was as follows: The animal was trained to give a certain response to a circle, but to withhold this response when confronted with an ellipse. After the animal had learned to discriminate between these patterns, they were altered so that the circle became more and more like the ellipse and the ellipse more and more like the circle, until finally the animal was unable to differentiate and his response habits broke down. A conflict was aroused between two contradictory kinds of response because the animal, no longer being able to discriminate, was stimulated to express and withhold his response at the same time. In the experimental neurosis thus produced, many symptoms similar to those observed in human patients, such as variations in heart beat and peculiar fears, could be noted.

Norman Maier in his experimental studies [2] has shown that if a white rat is confronted with an insoluble problem it will develop certain highly stereotyped and rigid response patterns. Such an insoluble problem exists, for example, when the rat is confronted with two different cards, behind one of which it receives food, and

---

[2] Norman R. F. Maier, "Experimentally Induced Abnormal Behavior," *The Scientific Monthly*, Vol. 67, 1948, 210-216.

Experimentally induced abnormal behavior. At top, rat on the jumping platform is confronted with discriminating cards. The platform behind the large screen is the feeding station that the rat reaches if it strikes the unlocked card. The net near the bottom of the picture catches the rat when the rat jumps against the punishment card, which is locked in place.

At bottom, rat jumps to the punishment card, which is placed on the side of its right-position fixation. The rat's strong tendency to jump to the right makes it impossible for him to jump to the open window on the left in which food is exposed. Before jumping to the punishment card, this rat sniffed toward the food and then quickly jumped to the right.

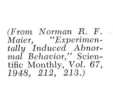

(From Norman R. F. Maier, "Experimentally Induced Abnormal Behavior," Scientific Monthly, Vol. 67, 1948, 212, 213.)

behind the other an electric shock. If after learning to respond correctly, the animal is subjected to a situation in which the food and the shock appear indiscriminately behind just one card and then another, it no longer understands what to do to get the reward and avoid the punishment. (This is similar to the situation of the child who at times is punished and at other times not punished for the same behavior.)

Under these circumstances, the rat develops a certain response preference; it may, for example, always jump to the card on the right side even though this response leads at times to food and at other times to punishment. The animal's response, in other words, becomes compulsive. Furthermore, these compulsive responses, learned under highly frustrating conditions, are very difficult to change. Even if the experiment is changed so that the animal can solve the problem again, it will continue to behave as it did during the period of stress. These compulsive responses and this stereotyped rigid behavior of the animal represent abnormal fixations; just as in the case of the human being whose compulsion represents an abnormal fixation.

This rigid behavior is one of the differences between abnormal and normal behavior in animals. Animals that were rewarded while learning to make a particular response learned new responses when the conditions of the experiment were changed. Maier calls this motivation-induced behavior in contrast to the frustration-induced behavior described in the preceding paragraph. Since these two kinds of behavior closely parallel the differences between normal and neurotic behavior as we have described them, we present the following table developed by Maier showing the contrasting characteristics.

Characteristics of Motivated and Frustrated Behavior [3]

Motivation-induced	*Frustration-instigated*
Goal-oriented	Not directed toward a goal
Tensions reduced when goal is reached	Tensions reduced when behavior is expressed, but increased if behavior leads to more frustration

[3] *The Scientific Monthly,* Vol. 67, 1948, 215.

Characteristics of Motivated and Frustrated Behavior

Motivation-induced	Frustration-instigated
Punishment deters action	Punishment aggravates state of frustration
Behavior shows variability and resourcefulness in a problem situation	Behavior is stereotyped and rigid
Behavior is constructive	Behavior is nonconstructive or destructive
Behavior reflects choices influenced by consequences	Behavior is compulsive
Learning proceeds and makes for development and maturity	Learning is blocked and behavior regresses

When it comes to applying these principles to human behavior, Maier points out that we must direct our therapy toward the source of frustration that is causing neurotic behavior. Punishing a ten-year-old child who wets his bed does not help him correct the habit. Rather, punishment may aggravate the habit by increasing the youngster's frustration. Here are Maier's exact words on the subject:

> The child that regresses may feel rejected. Punishment makes him feel more rejected. On the other hand, love and understanding reduce the state of frustration. It then follows that a child is most likely to be cured if he is given treatment that reduces the frustration, and this is frequently what the practicing psychiatrist recommends. He suggests love and attention because they work. Nevertheless, from a motivational point of view, rewarding a bad response with love should strengthen it. Yet both aggressive and regressive behaviors are reduced when treated with love and understanding.[4]

---

[4] *The Scientific Monthly,* Vol. 67, 1948, 215.

The Function of Neurotic Behavior
in the Life of the Individual

The function of neuroses in our life may be highlighted by indicating the difference between hysteria and malingering. In discussing conversion hysterias, we pointed out that it is sometimes difficult to differentiate between hysteria and malingering. Although the symptoms may be similar, in malingering the individual makes a conscious attempt to simulate physical symptoms whereas in hysteria the person makes no conscious effort. The motivation in hysteria and in other forms of neurotic behavior lies at the unconscious level. Neurotic behavior patterns are unconscious attempts to deal with conflict situations. The malingerer is aware that he is attempting to get out of a conflict situation by developing a symptom; the neurotic is not.

Neurotic behavior is an expression of conflict within the individual, but it does not resolve the conflict. What function then does neurotic behavior perform? It reduces tension, at least temporarily. The guilt-ridden individual who develops a hand-washing compulsion does not actually free himself from his guilt feelings, but the symbolic act of washing his hands does reduce for the time being the tensions his guilt generates. The person who is afraid to face his problems does not solve them by developing hysterical blindness, but he does relieve himself temporarily of the responsibility of dealing with them.

Although it reduces tension temporarily, neurotic behavior may, at the same time, aggravate the underlying causes of the tension. A person who does not get along well with other people may alienate them further by compulsive or obsessive behavior. The rigidity that marks his every response to a situation makes it difficult for him to learn the new, more acceptable ways of behavior. An inability to learn from experience has been emphasized as one of the main characteristics of people suffering from serious psychological disorders. The neurotic in one sense of the word brings into the present too much of the past even when it is not relevant to the problems he encounters.

Although neurotic behavior prevents a person from making more satisfactory adjustments, it also seems to inhibit the development of more serious psychotic disorders, probably by reducing tension through the neurotic symptoms. Various estimates indicate that only about 10 per cent of neurotics have been found to develop psychoses.

We shall more readily understand the tension-reducing function of the neuroses if we consider for a moment the restlessness and anxiety that we all experience when anticipating an important event in our lives. If we are expecting a visit from a close friend whom we have not seen for a long time, if we are waiting for an appointment that may lead to our securing a better job, if we have only three or four hours left before taking an important examination, we are likely to become increasingly anxious. In order to calm ourselves, we may read, sew, or turn to any activity, useful or not, that will help to pass the time and to keep us occupied. These activities reduce our tension or "nervousness," but they do not affect the outcome of the event that created tension.

In addition to its general tension-reducing function, neurotic behavior may serve other, more specific, purposes for the individual. Neurotic complaints protect the individual from having to face problems that are beyond his ability to handle. The neurasthenic or the hypochondriac shifts responsibility for his failure or inadequacy to some cause over which he cannot be expected to have any control. Consequently, others cannot blame him for his inadequacy, and he can maintain his self-respect.

From what we have said, we see that neurotic tendencies lie latent in all of us and that whether we become neurotic or not depends on several interrelated factors, such as (1) the experiences or problems confronting us, (2) our sensitivity or responsiveness to these experiences, and (3) our adaptability or ability to handle the experiences. Put another way, whether any one "breaks" or not depends on *what happens, how he reacts to it, and what he can do about it.* This means that an evaluation of these three factors is essential to the understanding of any given individual. One person may react deeply to disturbing experiences and yet avoid becoming neurotic because he has adequate ways of handling the situation. Another may break under less trying circumstances because he lacks the techniques for controlling his mental and emotional reactions. (The basis for these individual differences in sensitivity is in itself a complex and interesting problem.)

We may summarize this discussion briefly by saying that *environmental changes, acting upon an organism with a certain receptivity, will evoke certain reactions, depending on what facilities (innate or learned) the organism has at its disposal for adjusting to the stimuli.* An understanding of this whole process should dispel any tendency to regard neurotic behavior (in ourselves or in others) with shame or disgust. Anyone can develop a neurosis. Neuroses appear in the highest educational and social levels as often as in the lowest. Psychological aid need no longer be sought surreptitiously with feelings about "what will people think." Cause and effect relationships operate in neurotic behavior just as surely and completely as in any other behavior, although the causes and motives leading to the symptoms may at times appear obscure.

For Additional Reading

Coleman, James C., *Abnormal Psychology of Modern Life*. Chicago, Scott, Foresman and Company, 1950

Committee on Nomenclature and Statistics of the American Psychiatric Association, *Diagnostic and Statistical Manual of Mental Disorders*. Washington, D. C., American Psychiatric Association Mental Hospital Service, 1952.

Dollard, John and Neal E. Miller, *Personality and Psychotherapy—An Analysis in Terms of Learning, Thinking and Culture*. New York, McGraw-Hill Book Company, Inc., 1950.

Dorcus, Roy M., "The Psychoses and the Psychoneuroses," in L. A. Pennington and I. A. Berg, eds., *An Introduction to Clinical Psychology*. New York, The Ronald Press Company, 1948.

———— and G. Wilson Shaffer, *Textbook of Abnormal Psychology*, 3rd ed. Baltimore, The Williams and Wilkins Company, 1945.

Fenichel, O., *The Psychoanalytic Theory of Neuroses*. New York, W. W. Norton & Company, Inc., 1945.

Horney, Karen, *The Neurotic Personality of Our Time*. New York, W. W. Norton & Company, Inc., 1937.

Katz, Barney and George F. J. Lehner, *Mental Hygiene in Modern Living*. New York, The Ronald Press Company, 1953.

Kraines, S. H., *The Therapy of the Neuroses and Psychoses*, 2nd rev. ed. Philadelphia, Lea and Febiger, 1943.

Landis, C. and M. M. Bolles, *Textbook of Abnormal Psychology*. New York, The Macmillan Company, 1946.

Leonard, W. E. C., *The Locomotive-God*. New York, The Century Company, 1927.

Maier, Norman R. F., "Experimentally Induced Abnormal Behavior," *The Scientific Monthly*, Vol. 67, 1948, 210-216.

Malamud, William, "The Psychoneuroses," in J. McV. Hunt, ed., *Personality and the Behavior Disorders*, Vol. II. New York, The Ronald Press Company, 1944, pp. 833-860.

Maslow, A. H., *Motivation and Personality*. New York, Harper and Brothers, 1954.

———— and Bela Mittelmann, *Principles of Abnormal Psychology*, rev. ed. New York, Harper and Brothers, 1951.

May, Rollo, *The Meaning of Anxiety*. New York, The Ronald Press Company, 1950.

White, Robert W., *The Abnormal Personality*. New York, The Ronald Press Company, 1948.

Young, Kimball, *Personality and Problems of Adjustment*, 2nd ed. New York, Appleton-Century-Crofts, Inc., 1952.

Adjustment
and the Psychoses

CHAPTER 8

- MAIN CHARACTERISTICS OF PSYCHOTIC BEHAVIOR
- CLASSIFICATION AND DESCRIPTION OF THE PSYCHOSES
- GENESIS AND DYNAMICS OF PSYCHOTIC BEHAVIOR

In addition to the approximately 8,000,000 persons in the United States who suffer from *neuroses,* around 750,000 to 1,000,000 more persons suffer from *psychoses,* the most severe type of mental disorder. Each year approximately 130,000 psychotics are admitted into mental institutions in this country. This includes only first admissions, not those who have been released and are returning. And not all psychotics end up in hospitals; many are cared for at home or in other institutions that do not classify them as psychotic.

In this chapter we shall summarize briefly the main characteristics of psychotic behavior and present a classification and description of the major psychoses.

"Madness" print by the eighteenth-century English painter and engraver, William Hogarth. (Courtesy The Huntington Library, San Marino, California.)

Main Characteristics of Psychotic Behavior

The major differences between the neuroses and the psychoses were outlined in Chapter 7. Let us review briefly the main characteristics of the psychoses. Although each psychosis has its particular symptoms (syndromes), all psychoses have certain characteristics in common. First of all, the patient's total personality is involved, and he usually is unable to take care of himself. Also, the victim's mental faculties begin to deteriorate. His mind wanders; his speech becomes incoherent and rambling. The patient becomes extremely moody, either very morose or highly elated, or sometimes depressed one minute and happy the next. The psychotic person, unlike the neurotic, does not realize there is anything wrong with him. He has lost all contact with reality. He is inclined to distort what goes on around him. He misinterprets other people's behavior, misconstrues an offer of help as a threat to his safety, grows suspicious and furtive, believes everyone is against him, alienates friends and associates.

Classification and Description of the Psychoses

The psychoses are usually classified as either functional or organic. The *functional* psychoses are those behavior disorders for which we find no detectable organic basis; they originate in the mind, i.e., are *psychogenic*. Schizophrenia, paranoia, and manic-depressive or affective disorders are examples of functional psychoses. The *organic* psychoses are accompanied by physiological and neurological disorders that affect the brain and bring on severe behavior disturbances. Infectious diseases, brain tumors, head injuries, toxins, epilepsy, and other organic injuries or dysfunctions can lead to organic psychoses. The psychoses that sometimes accompany old age, such as senility or other effects of hardening of the arteries, are also classified as organic psychoses.

The functional psychoses

SCHIZOPHRENIA. Schizophrenia, which often appears in adolescence or early adulthood, is a psychosis of disorganization that affects a person's thinking and acting. As the name indicates, the schizophrenic person is "split" from the world. He moves only in his own private world, out of touch with reality and other people. The schizophrenic usually suffers from delusions. He ascribes all his difficulties to the malice or interference of other persons and believes that his behavior is influenced by magical or mysterious agents, by strange "powers" and "forces." He also sometimes claims that he can hear voices that tell him how to act or what to do. Frequently the schizophrenic is indifferent and apathetic, but his mood may change suddenly and inexplicably. He may turn on, even attack, a person he previously trusted and loved. Often the schizophrenic's mannerisms are stereotyped or ritualistic, as in the case of the patient who could never sit down without first turning around three times. At times the patient appears to shut himself off from all mental or emotional contact with others, as though he is indifferent to or unaware of their physical presence. He may sit alone for hours, rigid, motionless, refusing to talk to anyone who approaches him.

Schizophrenia has been divided into four subgroups: (1) simple, (2) hebephrenic, (3) catatonic, and (4) paranoid. In each of these groups certain characteristics predominate, although sometimes the symptoms of one type may appear in other types. Also, a patient may pass from one subgroup to another in the course of an illness.

A person afflicted with *simple* schizophrenia is unconcerned, apathetic, and unable to get along. Usually, the patient is not subject to emotional outbursts or to hallucinations and delusions. If he does suffer from hallucinations and delusions, the patient is generally very secretive about them and they can be discovered only by careful investigation.

In *hebephrenic* schizophrenia, the patient appears silly, laughs and giggles without any apparent reason, and experiences pleasant hallucinations. But his delusions cause him to become suddenly hostile and aggressive.

In *catatonic* schizophrenia, motor disorders predominate rather than intellectual or emotional disturbances. The patient may be overactive or listless, excitable or torpid. He may sit motionless or he may assume odd positions, such as standing on one foot or curling himself up into a ball. And once he takes up a position or posture, he will resist anyone's efforts to make him change it.

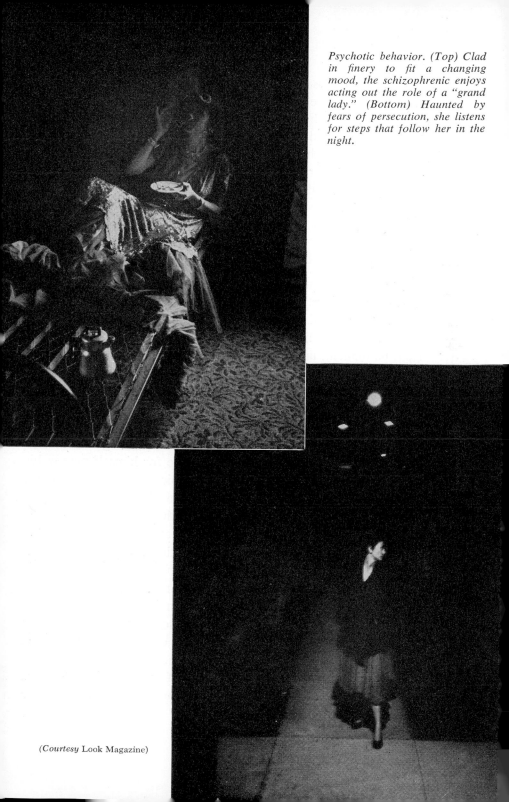

Psychotic behavior. (Top) Clad in finery to fit a changing mood, the schizophrenic enjoys acting out the role of a "grand lady." (Bottom) Haunted by fears of persecution, she listens for steps that follow her in the night.

He also may refuse to speak to anyone. Yet in spite of his apparent indifference to others, he seems to be aware of what is going on around him because he can recall later much of what has happened. And he may suddenly become much more normal.

The *paranoid* schizophrenic suffers from a persecution complex and delusions of grandeur. He sees himself constantly threatened by all kinds of evils. Or he may believe himself to be a famous historical, religious, or political figure. These delusions are usually transitory and temporary—they change often and come and go quickly. As the illness progresses, the patient may become increasingly suspicious and apathetic.

PARANOIA. Paranoic disorders, which often develop between the ages of 35 to 55 years, are characterized by suspicions that become more and more numerous and finally develop into a whole system of highly organized delusions. The highly organized, permanent, and systematic nature of the delusions differentiates paranoia from the paranoid *tendency* in certain schizophrenics.

Paranoic delusions are based partly on incorrect interpretations of events and partly on false premises. If his original premise is fairly reasonable, the paranoic can sound quite logical and consistent, can make a very convincing case for himself among his friends and acquaintances. The paranoic nature of his claims often becomes apparent only after prolonged contact and conversation with him have demonstrated that the evidence upon which he bases his conclusions is very meager and that he is unwilling even to consider any alternative explanations.

Another reason for his ability to convince others that he is rational and objective is that his appearance and actions seem quite normal. The characteristic delusional system appears to be isolated from the rest of the patient's personality pattern. It seems that his contact with reality is broken at one point only and that this gap is filled by the delusional system.

The delusion usually takes the form of a persecution complex. The patient is convinced that others are out to hurt him or to

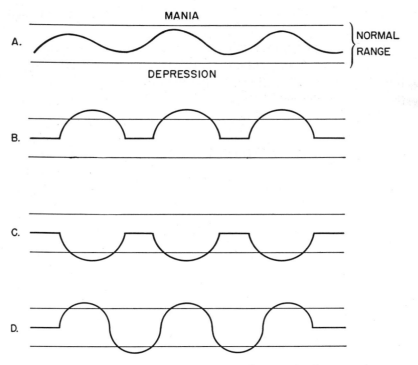

Manic-depressive psychoses. Changes of mood occur in the normal person (A), but in the psychotic the swings in moods go beyond the normal limits. Different sequences are shown in (B)—recurrent mania; in (C)—recurrent depression; and in (D)—circular type.

interfere with his life. Being markedly egocentric and suspicious, he builds up in his delusions a private world, or pseudo-world, which replaces the normal world that others inhabit. A woman may develop the delusion, for example, that others are trying to poison her, or to control her thoughts by "special waves" from another world. A man or a woman may see himself as a new religious savior, and this viewpoint may color all his attitudes toward his associates.

Since the patient shows little additional mental deterioration, he often develops clear and logical plans for warding off the persecutions or affronts of others. Such plans may even involve a decision to kill his "enemy," which indicates the danger in such delusions.

THE MANIC-DEPRESSIVE PSYCHOSES. In the manic-depressive psychoses, disturbances of emotion or feeling predominate, rather than intellectual distortions. In the *manic phase,* we can observe three major characteristics—elation, flight of ideas, and great activity. The patient is extremely happy; he feels well and is optimistic. He laughs frequently and may try to cheer others. At the same time, he is easily distracted; his mind and conversation wander haphazardly. The manic is always on the go—talking to others, organizing parties, arranging furniture. But his thoughts, feelings, and activities are unstable. If he meets interference or if

Delusions. A paranoid patient has elaborated on a photograph of sunspots. By giving the spots human features, he can fit them into his magic system of delusions. (Courtesy of H. Lehmann, M.D., Montreal, Verdun Protestant Hospital, and Ayerst, McKenna and Harrison, Ltd.)

someone contradicts him, he becomes irritable and suspicious. At times he has wild delusions; he thinks of himself as an emissary of God, a great military genius, a famous political figure. Occasionally he has hallucinations. He hears voices, voices that advise him about his role as God's special disciple, for example, voices that flatter him and that inspire him. Usually the manic suffers from rapid heart action and high blood pressure, induced by his ceaseless exertion and activity. He may lose a great deal of weight and, because of his overexcitement, may be unable to sleep.

On the basis of the intensity of reaction, three varieties of manic behavior may be distinguished: *hypomania, acute mania,* and *delirious mania.* As the manic condition intensifies, the patient's speech becomes increasingly incoherent, his moods more unstable, his restlessness more extreme. The patient suffering from delirious mania lacks all insight and loses his sense of shame. His speech becomes heavily obscene; he may expose himself and make open sexual advances to others. He may lose weight rapidly and become physically exhausted.

The *depressive phase* of manic-depressive psychosis is characterized by despondency, impaired reasoning ability, and slowness of movement, called psychomotor retardation. The patient feels hopeless and sad, his future seems black. He is indifferent to other people. Nothing cheers him. Frequently he ponders suicide. He labors long and hard over problems, and thinking requires a tremendous effort on his part. His speech is slow and hesitant; he resists any sort of activity, moves slowly, if at all, and often sits in the same place for long periods of time. Physiologically, his bodily processes slow down perceptibly. Menstruation may stop, constipation, loss of appetite, and loss of weight also may follow the onset of the depressive phase.

The manic patient usually has a high opinion of himself, but his depressive counterpart is plagued by all manner and form of guilt feelings. He may harbor the delusion that he has committed an unpardonable sin, a delusion that has been nourished by hallucinations, by voices that speak to him accusingly of his crimes and faults.

Four varieties of the depressive phase may be distinguished, depending on the degree of intensity of the symptoms: (1) the mild form, (2) simple retardation, (3) acute depression, and (4) depressive stupor. In general, as the depression increases, the danger of suicide also increases. In extreme depression—depressive stupor—the patient becomes so apathetic that he must be fed. He feels increasingly guilty, bemoans his worthlessness, and condemns himself unceasingly.

In some cases of affective disorders, only the manic stage is present; in others only the depressive phase; in still others, i.e., in the *mixed or circular* type, there is an alternation between the two extremes, frequently with an intervening period of normalcy.

INVOLUTIONAL MELANCHOLIA. Another affective or emotional disturbance is involutional melancholia. This depression or melancholia generally occurs around the time of the involutional or change-of-life period, ranging from about 40 to 55 years for women and 50 to 65 years in men. The involutional melancholic becomes depressed, agitated, and restless. Mild delusions about persecution beset him. He becomes excessively concerned with bodily functions; begins to feel worthless, hopeless, guilty, much like the depressive. He may even contemplate suicide.

Although physiological and endocrine changes accompanying the change-of-life may contribute to the onset of the disturbance, it is generally believed that the major causes of involutional melancholia are psychological, not physiological. Otherwise, of course, all persons undergoing change-of-life should experience the symptoms mentioned above—but they do not.

What are some of these psychological factors? The older person feels himself slowing down, his life has been lived, he is no longer important. The world is passing him by. Former opportunities cannot be recaptured. (See Chapter 14.) The melancholia, in other words, may be a reaction to the stress and strain resulting from these factors and to the anxiety produced by such stress.

The organic psychoses

Organic psychoses are responsible for about 40 to 45 per cent of all first admissions to mental hospitals in this country. Organic psychoses may stem from a wide variety of causes, but damage or injury to the brain or other parts of the central nervous system is always involved. The chief symptoms of the organic psychoses are (1) impairment of intellectual functions; (2) emotional instability, shown by general irritability or violent mood swings without apparent cause; and (3) inappropriate behavior and changes in general conduct, including lack of interest in personal appearance, neglect of responsibilities, and anti-social behavior.

The organic psychoses that we shall take up here are:

1. Psychoses associated with infectious diseases, especially general paresis;

2. Psychoses associated with toxins, especially the alcoholic psychoses;

3. Psychoses associated with head injuries;

4. Psychoses associated with old age.

PSYCHOSES ASSOCIATED WITH INFECTIOUS DISEASES, ESPE-CIALLY GENERAL PARESIS. The organic cause of general paresis is syphilitic damage of the brain tissue; however, syphilis does not necessarily result in psychosis. It has been estimated that only 2 per cent of the people who contract syphilis ever develop paresis. The first mental symptoms usually appear from five to twenty-five years after the initial infection, and unless the patient receives treatment, are followed by almost certain death.

A tell-tale sign of paresis in its early stages is the absence or sluggishness of certain reflexes, such as the pupillary reflex. Also, the victim's lips, tongue and hand may tremble. Other definite changes may be detected either by a Wassermann test of the blood or by chemical changes of the spinal fluid.

As the spirochetes, the corkscrew-like microorganisms that cause syphilis, progress with their deadly work, the patient's intellectual faculties fail, especially his memory and particularly his memory for recent events. Eventually delusions take hold of him. He claims to be Napoleon, Babe Ruth, or President of the United States. Some patients, after a while, become very depressed. They seem to realize, intermittently at least, that their powers are declining. Others, however, become very benign and contented. Sometimes the victim's mood changes swiftly, very much like the manic-depressive.

PSYCHOSES ASSOCIATED WITH TOXINS, ESPECIALLY THE ALCOHOLIC PSYCHOSES. Some psychologists believe that every kind of addiction, whatever the intoxicant involved, represents a person's attempt to escape from anxiety, frustration, or unbearable conflict. There are various forms of *toxic psychoses* caused by infection or poisoning. The most insidious of these toxins, and socially the most consequential, is alcohol. Alcohol is relatively cheap and easy to obtain. It acts as a depressant, making the drinker forget his pressing worries and relieving him of burdensome inhibitions. Sometimes alcohol makes an ordinarily boastful person very contrite and repentant, or turns an ordinarily modest person into a roaring braggart. Such attitudes may represent deeply hidden desires or compulsions. When they well to the surface, they reveal the person as entirely different from what he has appeared to be.

The best known of the alcoholic reactions is *delirium tremens.* It typically occurs in people who have been heavy drinkers for many years.

The delirium patient is acutely ill. He is confused, is unable to respond to outside stimuli, and has vivid and frightening hallucinations, usually of rats, snakes, and other small animals. The most striking symptom, which gives its name to the condition, is a severe trembling of the hands, face, and tongue. The patient often has high fever, a rapid and weak heartbeat, a coated tongue, and sometimes suffers convulsive seizures. The delirium typically lasts from three to six days and is usually followed by a deep sleep. The death rate as a result of heart failure or exhaustion is as high as 10 to 15 per cent.

Another frequent after-effect of chronic alcoholism is *Korsakow's psychosis,* named after a Russian psychiatrist who first described it. Its most characteristic mental symptom is loss of memory for recent events. The patient fills out the vexing gaps in his memory by improvising stories. Other symptoms include a painful inflammation of the nerve trunks, loss of feeling in certain skin areas, and wrist drop (the patient is unable to raise his hand).

Korsakow's syndrome is a definite vitamin deficiency disorder (deficiency of the "B"-complex) and the patient usually receives heavy injections of vitamins. But a complete cure is rare; some memory defects usually remain. These defects have to be considered as symptoms of psychological deterioration, for postmortem studies of the brains of persons who have died in the course of Korsakow's psychosis reveal no gross organic lesions.

The symptom picture for the chronic alcoholic varies, but he usually is emotionally numb and lacks intellectual or mental vigor. The alcoholic seems unable to control his reactions; he is moved to tears, laughter, or anger at the slightest provocation. He is apt to boast a lot, he seems always on the point of realizing his dreams of glory. He may be affable and charming with strangers, only to be abusive toward his family and close associates. His judgment, his memory, and his capacity to work show unmistakable signs of deterioration. In the later stages of the disease, organic complications, such as gastritis, cirrhosis of the liver, heart disease, and nephritis often appear.

Most of the personality changes caused by chronic alcoholism are considered to be permanent. The cures effected in sanitaria and mental hospitals are usually far from complete. The patient may attain relief from his most disturbing physical symptoms, but he seldom, if ever, regains his former mental ability.

PSYCHOSES ASSOCIATED WITH HEAD INJURIES. *Head injuries,* or more precisely, *brain injuries,* may lead to various personality disturbances, depending to a great extent on what part of the brain is damaged. Most of these injuries are caused by blows to the head resulting from accidents, notably traffic accidents, and from war. In fact, many important discoveries concerning brain damage have resulted from studies of war-caused head injuries.

A person who has suffered a brain injury may exhibit many different symptoms. He may be temporarily dazed, or he may lose consciousness for several days, may become nauseous, vomit, develop severe headaches or dizziness. Quite frequently the victim becomes delirious upon regaining consciousness. Finally, he may lose all sense of time and place and suffer from hallucinations.

The study of brain injuries points out the intimate interweaving of psychological and biological factors in human behavior. Individuals sustaining apparently identical damages may develop entirely different symptoms. Psychologists and psychiatrists are increasingly inclined to relate a patient's symptoms to the way he acted and behaved before he was injured. The patient who shows a severe depressive psychotic reaction may have been already despondent before the accident occurred. The patient who becomes morbidly dependent after the acute phase of the psychosis has passed probably lacked self-reliance even before his accident. One study shows that even chronic headaches as an after-effect of brain injury seem to be more closely related to the personality of the victim than to the extent and the location of the organic damage. Many symptoms of brain injury can probably be interpreted as efforts by the patient to cope with the limitations and restrictions his injury imposes upon him.

PSYCHOSES ASSOCIATED WITH OLD AGE. Certain mental or behavior disturbances may accompany the physiological changes that come with age. Some of these disturbances are so severe that we can classify them as psychotic. As more people live to an advanced age, the problem of senile psychoses becomes increasingly important.

The biological changes associated with aging, similar to the organic damages discussed previously, are usually not in themselves sufficient to explain the changes that occur in the behavior of older people. Not all elderly people fall victim to mental disturbances. The factors of aging are accessory causes of mental disturbances rather than sole causes. What then are the real causes? The answer here, as in the case of involutional melancholia, lies in certain psychological problems that confront the aging persons. Some of these, briefly considered, are as follows. (See Chapter 14 for a more extended discussion of the problems of the aged.)

1. Fear of dependence and uselessness. As a person ages, he begins to fear retirement, unemployment, financial insecurity, loss of mental keenness and manual skill, and the possibility of having to rely on children for support.

2. Fear of illness. As we get older, failing health often becomes a problem. We no longer see or hear as well as we used to, our reflexes slow down, strength begins to ebb, and such things as digestion and circulation grow sluggish.

3. Fear of isolation. Closely related to fear of illness is fear of isolation, which may result from illness. The unpleasant specter of invalidism also walks step by step with the aged, threatening to shut them off completely from their already shrinking social contacts. The loss or death of friends, of spouse, of colleagues on the job—all emphasize the older person's feeling of isolation and the imminence of personal death.

These, then, are some of the main psychological factors that may pose problems for an old person, that may lead to psychoses. The symptoms that herald the approach of a psychosis are often similar to those mentioned for involutional melancholia (which is in a sense part of the senile psychoses). The person may be depressed and sometimes highly irritable. He may insist upon doing things only in a certain way and this rigidity may manifest itself in other ways also. His interests may narrow. Books or magazines or newspapers that formerly used to charm and interest him now lose all their appeal. His conversation becomes more and more cluttered with past recollections, often highly glamorized. "In the good old days, when I was young . . ." becomes his refrain for introducing his views and for rejecting changes and progress. Such a person can be most difficult to live with. Younger people may

find him boring, intolerant, "funny." And if they allow their feelings to show through, the older person may begin to feel that he
is not wanted.

It is extremely unfortunate, of course, that we have not yet
worked out a plan to utilize the experience and wisdom of our old
people. Perhaps in the future, with increasing attention being
given to the problems of the aged, we may find a solution that will
make old age a less threatening, foreboding period than it is
today.

Other organic behavior disturbances

EPILEPSY. Epileptics were once considered to be inhabited by
malignant spirits who surreptitiously entered the brain of the sufferer in order to cause malicious havoc. The human body was
seized (epilepsy means "seize upon") by supernatural powers.
Some psychotics suffer epileptic seizures, but only a very few
epileptics develop psychoses or require hospitalization.

There are three main types of epileptic seizure. The most
dramatic is the *grand mal* attack. The victim loses consciousness,
his entire body jerks frenziedly, his arms and legs thrash wildly,
his face grows bluish, his lips foam. The second variety, *petit
mal,* is less severe. The sufferer loses consciousness, but only for
a moment. During the attack, the victim may stand rigidly, or he
may manifest no noticeable change of behavior. The seizure may
be so transient that the patient and those around him may be
unaware that it occurred at all. Sometimes even medically trained
personnel cannot tell when an attack has occurred. The third
variety, the least common of the three, is usually called a *psychomotor* attack. During a psychomotor attack, the patient
blacks out, although, as in petit mal attacks, he may continue to
perform routine tasks. Sometimes, however, a psychomotor attack victim may become very violent. He may mutilate himself
or suddenly assault an unsuspecting bystander. He might even
unwittingly commit murder. When the attack has passed, the

patient will have no recollection of what happened during the seizure.

Potential causes for epileptic convulsions may include brain injuries, brain tumors, hardening of the arteries of the brain, gunshot wounds in the head, and brain hemorrhages.

Opinions vary about the effect of epilepsy on *personality*. Some contend that a distinctive epileptic personality type exists, a person who is eccentric, supersensitive, emotionally shallow, and rigid. Others claim that the personality of most epileptics is essentially normal and that the personality disturbances that occur are the result of the continuous seizures since early childhood.

PSYCHOSES ASSOCIATED WITH GLANDULAR DISTURBANCES. The endocrine disorders afford another illustration of the way both organic and psychological factors may influence behavior. The endocrine glands secrete directly into the blood stream and thus affect the nutrition of all nerve cells. The interactions of the different glands are far from simple, but it is possible to trace specific behavior disorders to certain parts of the endocrine system.

The most easily traced and most thoroughly explored disorders are those that stem from thyroid disturbances. One of these is *hypothyroidism,* underactivity of the thyroid during childhood. Hypothyroidism leads to cretinism, a form of feeblemindedness.

The first sign of thyroid deficiency in a hitherto normal adult is called *myxedema.* The patient becomes dull and listless, his mental faculties begin to fail, he feels tired all the time, and he moves as though he were carrying a heavy burden. In addition, his face swells and becomes puffy, his skin looks coarse and dry, his pulse slows down, and his general bodily chemistry is affected.

Overactivity of the thyroid is called *hyperthyroidism.* The patient's goiter enlarges and protrudes and his eyes begin to bulge. His pulse and basal metabolism quickens, in direct contrast to the myxedemic patient. He becomes emotionally oversensitive and irritable, cannot relax or sleep, loses weight, and becomes anxious and distraught. Finally, the patient may suffer hallucinations that magnify his excitement and his fears.

Genesis and Dynamics of Psychotic Behavior

The causes of psychotic behavior are probably as diverse as the forms it assumes. Heredity, constitutional predisposition, faulty parent-child relations, social disintegration, psychological frustration, endocrine dysfunction, and brain infections can all be included among the multitude of causes or antecedent conditions whose interaction is related to the onset of the disorder. Let us discuss briefly the most important of these *pathogenic,* or psychosis producing, agents.

Biological causes of functional psychosis. It has been known for a long time that mental disease tends to run in families. For this reason some persons believe, and legends have often suggested, that mental illness is hereditary, and various statistical investigations have seemed to substantiate this belief. But critics of the hereditary theory have pointed out that the statistical evidence is far from clear-cut, since members of the same family "inherit" not only their genes, but also their social environment. Furthermore, the statistics themselves are open to question. Many people are reluctant to divulge information that might reveal the "disgrace" of familial insanity.

The hereditary hypothesis, somewhat modified, is revived today in the *constitutional* view, which postulates a relation between organic or bodily predisposition and personality and behavior of the person. Psychological research seems to indicate that new-born infants have certain consistent reaction tendencies, and some psychologists believe that these reaction patterns are congenital. But no conclusive evidence has yet been advanced that links functional psychoses to well-defined organic or physical factors.

Social causes of functional psychosis. Some psychologists and many social scientists stress the relationship between social disorganization and mental disease. Two sociologists [1] have shown that the incidence of mental illness is highest in certain urban areas, such as slums, and that there is a regular decrease from the center to the outskirts of the city. The statistical figures for the different sections are strikingly stable, in spite of the continuous flux of residents. Furthermore, a kind of sociological patterning for specific categories of mental disease seems to prevail. For example, the rate of incidence of paranoid schizophrenia was highest in the rooming-house district, whereas catatonic schizophrenia seemed to seek out the first-generation immigrant neighborhoods.

Again, one is not justified in concluding that social disintegration "causes" mental disease. The relationship might also work the other way around in that mentally stricken people are socially downgraded and pushed by the social maelstrom toward the dumpyard districts. But however that may be, the social conditions appear to be important determining factors.

Psychological causes of functional psychosis. The importance of psychological factors in the genesis of psychotic behavior has been stressed particularly by the psychoanalysts.

All psychologically oriented clinicians more or less agree that a clash between the individual and his social environment, as first embodied in the parent-child relationship, may be instrumental in preparing the ground for later psychotic reactions. The defense mechanisms evolved in the various forms of psychoses may be different, but their origin can often be traced to early childhood and to the consequence of parental rejection of one kind or another. The child who is rejected feels inferior, insecure, and is unable to get along well with other people. His emotional starvation is a serious psychological handicap that may lead to exaggerated maladjustive behavior.

Yet the fact remains that some children do succeed in surmounting seemingly unconquerable handicaps, whereas others are shattered by relatively mild frustration and disappointments.

---

[1] R. E. L. Faris and H. W. Dunham, *Mental Disorders in Urban Areas.* Chicago, University of Chicago Press, 1939.

This fact has led certain clinicians to assume that physical or constitutional inadequacies must initiate the difficulty. But so far they have been unable to isolate definite body defects or to trace convincingly the links in the causal chain.

Psychological determiners in the organic psychoses. Although we speak of organic psychoses, we should emphasize that the "same" infectious or toxic psychoses can be associated with a wide range of behavioral symptoms. It is almost as if the organic disease were merely a kind of trigger to set off a variety of different symptoms in different persons. It is natural, then, to ask why a patient develops one set of symptoms rather than another.

Furthermore, we must note that severe organic lesions of the nervous system do not necessarily lead to behavior disorders. As a matter of fact, when behavior disorders do occur, many clinicians now seek to explain them in terms of adjustment difficulties that may have preceded the organic damage. More and more they come to look on the organic lesion as the precipitating factor, rather than the cause, of the psychotic behavior. They are therefore not surprised when, as happens frequently, the apparent removal of the organic trouble does not also automatically clear up the behavior disorder.

It would seem, thus, that psychotic behavior, like behavior described for the defense mechanisms and the neuroses, serves a purpose for the patient.

For Additional Reading

Alexander, F. and H. Ross, *Dynamic Psychiatry.* Chicago, University of Chicago Press, 1952.

Brody, E. B. and F. C. Redlich, *Psychotherapy With Schizophrenics.* New York, International University Press, 1950.

Bychowski, G., *Psychotherapy of Psychosis.* New York, Grune and Stratton, 1952.

Cameron, N. A. and A. Margaret, *Behavior Pathology.* Boston, Houghton Mifflin Company, 1951.

Coleman, J. C., *Abnormal Psychology and Modern Life.* Chicago, Scott, Foresman and Company, 1950.

Conklin, E. S., *Abnormal Psychology.* New York, Henry Holt & Company, Inc., 1951.

Culpin, M., *Mental Abnormalities, Facts and Theories.* New York, Longmans, Green & Company, 1950.

Dorcus, R. M. and G. W. Shaffer, *Abnormal Psychology,* 4th ed. Baltimore, Williams and Wilkins Co., 1950.

Fischer, S., *Principles of General Psychopathology.* New York, Philosophical Library, Inc., 1950.

Fitzgerald, O. W., *Personality and Psychosis.* Baltimore, Williams and Wilkins Company, 1951.

Goldhamer, H. and A. Marshall, *Psychosis and Civilization.* Glencoe, Illinois, The Free Press, 1953.

Landis, C. and M. M. Bolles, *Textbook of Abnormal Psychology.* New York, The Macmillan Company, 1950.

Maslow, A. H. and B. Mittleman, *Principles of Abnormal Psychology.* New York, Harper and Brothers, 1951.

Noyes, A. P., *Modern Clinical Psychiatry,* 4th ed. Philadelphia, W. B. Saunders Company, 1953.

O'Kelly, L. I., *Introduction to Psychopathology.* New York, Prentice-Hall, Inc., 1949.

Perry, J. W., *Self in Psychotic Process.* Berkeley, University of California Press, 1953.

Schilder, P., *Introduction to a Psychoanalytic Psychiatry.* New York, International University Press, 1951.

Shaffer, G. W. and R. S. Lazarus, *Fundamental Concepts in Clinical Psychology.* New York, McGraw-Hill Book Company, Inc., 1952.

Strecker, E., *A Basic Psychiatry.* New York, Random House, Inc., 1952.

Sullivan, H. S., *Interpersonal Theory of Psychiatry.* New York, W. W. Norton & Company, Inc., 1953.

Taylor, W., *Dynamic and Abnormal Psychology.* New York, American Book Company, 1954.

Thorpe, L. P. and B. Katz, *The Psychology of Abnormal Behavior.* New York, The Ronald Press Company, 1948.

Family
Adjustments

CHAPTER 9

- ROLES AND STATUS
- FUNCTIONS OF THE FAMILY
- DYNAMICS OF FAMILY INTERACTION
- FAMILY ADJUSTMENT

The family is probably the oldest social institution known to man. Although its specific form has changed—and will continue to change—it has been, in most cultures, the basic unit of social order. This social unit, based on marriage, consists as a minimum of the parents and their children, but may include others. In Western culture, the large family that included grandparents, parents, and children, as well as an aunt or uncle or cousin, has almost disappeared, and the small family unit has taken its place. The role and status of members of the family also have changed, and some of the functions once performed by the family have been delegated to other groups in the society. At the same time, other functions have been receiving stronger emphasis. Finally, people's attitudes and values toward marriage and family life have changed along with family functions.

Roles and Status

The role and status assigned to family members and the functions performed by the family provide a framework for comparing different families and for assessing changes in the American family.[1] In discussing psychological trends in American family relationships, Marmor[2] points out that one of the significant changes that has taken place in this country since the turn of the century has been "a gradual shift in the equilibrium of intra-familial relationships—a shift from patriarchal authoritarianism to what might be termed democratic equalitarianism." Although the father continues to be, in most instances, the chief provider, he no longer occupies an exclusive position of authority. Decisions now are jointly made and control is shared between husband and wife, with children also having a voice in family affairs.

In a recent study[3] of urban communities, which included questions concerning decision-making in the family, only 25 to 30 per cent of the persons interviewed said that the father made the decisions in the family when they were a child, but almost 50 per cent named the mother as the person making major decisions in the family. In 20 per cent of the cases, mother and father played an equal role. When they were asked if the children had any say in family affairs, about half of them said "yes."

Family forms differ according to location of authority. In the *patriarchal* family, the father is the ultimate authority; his word is almost law to wife and children. The mother or grandmother controls a *matriarchal* family, although the father may retain his position of chief provider. In the *adult-centered* family, all major

---

[1] Howard Becker and Reuben Hill, eds., *Family, Marriage, and Parenthood.* Boston, D. C. Heath & Company, 1948.

[2] Judd Marmor, "Psychological Trends in American Family Relationships," in *Marriage and Family Living*, Vol. 13, No. 4, 1951, 145-147.

[3] Scott Greer and Ella Kube, *Social Participation in Urban Communities.* Unpublished MS, 1954.

decisions are made jointly by husband and wife, and many tasks, such as the training of children, are jointly shared. In the *democratic* family, as noted above, decisions and responsibilities are shared by all members.[4]

We may illustrate diagramatically the decision-making process in these four types of family as follows:

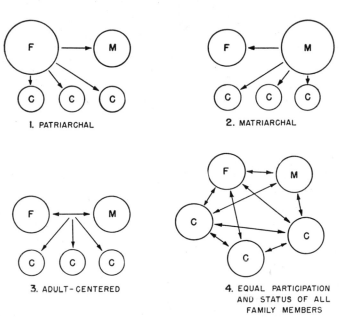

Decision-making in four types of family. The status of each member of the family differs and is perceived as being different by other members of the family. The arrows indicate the direction of influence.

One or another of these family types may be characteristic of any given culture, but all four may be found in American society. Within each formal structure, deviations are possible and permitted to some extent. Although the formal structure gives us some indication of status relationships within the group, it does not necessarily indicate the location of authority. The father may

---

[4] Reuben Hill, *Families under Stress. Adjustment to the Crises of War Separation and Reunion.* New York, Harper and Brothers, 1949.

be the nominal head of the family, but the actual reins of control may be firmly held by the mother or perhaps by an older son.

Although one particular family type may be predominant in a culture, subcultural variations, or exceptions within the culture, may occur. Warner, Dollard, Allison Davis and other students of the family have traced the development of well-established, class-typed family patterns that revealed quite distinctive differences, e.g., in child-training. Even within a homogeneous cultural group no two families are exactly alike, because cultural norms alone do not determine such factors as intelligence, health, and temperament.

Functions of the Family

Many social scientists have spent long hours compiling lists of the various functions the family has performed in the past, is performing now, or ought to be performing. In some societies most functions concerned with satisfying a person's needs were performed within the family; in others, only certain of these functions were carried out by the family, the remainder being delegated to appropriate groups within the society. From all these lists we may identify eight major functions: (1) Reproduction, (2) Protection and care of the child, (3) Socialization of the child, (4) Education of the child, (5) Conferment of status, (6) Economic production and consumption of family goods and services, (7) Recreation, and (8) Satisfaction of psychological needs (emotional security).[5] To what extent are these functions performed by the contemporary American family?

Reproduction. Although births occur outside the legal family, by far the largest number of children are born into legally recognized family groups. Approximately 96 per cent of the children in this country are born to married couples, substantiating the importance of the family's reproductive function. The reproduc-

---

[5] Becker and Hill, eds., *Family, Marriage and Parenthood*, p. 779; Robert F. Winch, *The Modern Family*. New York, Henry Holt & Company, Inc., 1952.

tive function has been modified, however, as is seen by the declining birth rate in some countries and especially among some
groups, the variations in birth rate for different socio-economic
groups, and the decrease in family size with increase in urbaniza-
tion.

Protection and care of the child. Protection and care of the
child has remained largely within the family home. Only 2 per
cent of the children in this country are brought up in foster
homes or institutions. In a survey of variations in family patterns,
Kluckhohn [6] has pointed out that the care of children is a universal function in all families. The specific form in which this
function is carried out varies, but the basic function itself is a
constant. Child care is a universal family function because the
infant is born helpless and for a long period after birth requires
constant care and attention in order to survive.

Although the American family continues to assume major responsibility for the care of children, other groups in the society
also help if the responsibility is beyond a certain family's power,
ability, or desire. These non-family agencies work (1) by providing homes for children whose own families cannot or will not,
for various reasons, provide one for them, and (2) by helping
parents to care for their children more effectively. Since 1912,
the U. S. Children's Bureau has been concerned with all aspects
of child life and has made available to parents a flood of bro-
chures, pamphlets, and booklets containing proved and valuable
advice on child care. The World Health Organization is attempting to do the same thing on an international scale.

The concern of persons and groups outside the immediate
family for child care and health is not exclusively a modern phenomenon. The medicine man, the mid-wife, the priest were called
upon in many societies to help avert dangers confronting the
child. But the extensive planning in which the local community,

---

[6] Clyde Kluckhohn, "Variations in the Human Family," in *The Family in a
Democratic Society,* Anniversary Papers of the Community Service Society of
New York. New York, Columbia University Press, 1949, pp. 3-11.

the county, the state, and the nation join hands is of fairly recent origin, emphasized mostly within the past 25 years.

Socialization of the child. In every society, the family has been and continues to be the fundamental institution for the socialization of the child, i.e., for transmitting to the child the basic values and mores of the culture. Socialization in different kinds of families varies because the content of the culture that is to be transmitted varies and because different methods are employed in carrying out the socialization process. Among the Zuñi Indians of the southwestern United States, personal crises, such as birth, death, marriage, and divorce are minimized and the child is trained for individual submission. The Mundugumor child of New Guinea, on the other hand, grows up in an atmosphere of violence and is expected to be aggressive and combative. Students of family life in our own country have noted marked differences in the process of socialization among middle-class and working-class families. In general, middle-class children are socialized more slowly than working-class children, the latter being pushed more rapidly into adult roles than the former, because of economic pressures and less parental protection. A summary of these class differences in child training is given in the following chart, taken from Bennett and Tumin.[7]

Class Differences in Socialization Patterns

Child training and child behavior in the middle class	*Child training and child behavior in a lower-class slum family*
1. "Slow" socialization; child not pushed toward adult roles. Much parental shielding of child from world.	1. "Fast" socialization; child pushed into adult roles rapidly, owing to economic pressures and less parental protection.
2. Child encouraged in later years to "succeed," often to "do better" than father in achieve-	2. Same goals often present, but played down. More acceptance of fact that child will prob-

[7] Reprinted from *Social Life* by John W. Bennett and Melvin M. Tumin, by permission of Alfred A. Knopf, Inc. Copyright 1948 by Alfred A. Knopf, Inc., pp. 668-671.

ment and status. Child-training methods in general develop a desire in child for achievement.

3. Parents habitually stress conformity to group norms as well as individualistic achievement. Success of child often measured against neighborhood paragon. Child often unsure of what standards he must adopt.

4. Sexual roles distinct: Boys should be "masculine but gentlemanly;" "sissy" stigma fairly strong; varies by age group. Girls should be "feminine" and attractive to boys. Variation with respect to issue of equal education, right to earn own living, etc.

5. Training teaches the virtue of competition and cooperation in the "fair play" sense ("get ahead, but do it fairly"). Playing down of aggressive methods and of aggression in general, at least in overt forms. Middle-class child in school with lower-class pupils is often labeled "sissy." Middle-class child gangs compete, but do not follow regular aggressive pattern.

6. Training methods use parental love systematically as a reward for obedience and achievement, thus stimulating anxiety. Guilt on part of parents arises, and sympathy characteristically and inconsistently follows severe

ably follow status of father. Training methods do not usually develop desire for achievement.

3. Much less stress on conformity. Group norms less rigid, more informal. No "living up to the Joneses" pattern. Rare stress on measuring up to standard set by neighbor child. Child freer to set own standards.

4. Sexual roles distinct, but different: Boys should be hypermasculine, aggressive, anti-gentlemanly. "Sissy" stigma very pronounced. Girls should be feminine, but also greater aggressiveness is accepted. More acceptance of right of girl to earn own living, etc.

5. Training teaches the virtue of aggressive defense and attack-as-defense. Aggression in general less tabooed, more accepted. "Fair play" unstressed or absent in home, but child encounters it in school. Leads to conflict with school authorities, who are middle-class-minded. Lower-class child gangs very aggressive and combative.

6. Training methods do not use love as reward systematically. Rewards more usually in material sphere. "Obedience" not stressed beyond basic adjustment to somewhat informal family routine. Love more freely given.

Class Differences in Socialization Patterns

Child training and child behavior in the middle class

Child training and child behavior in a lower-class slum family

withholding of love, breeding further anxiety.

Hostility between parents and child more readily accepted. System probably less anxiety-producing.

7. Sibling rivalries usually intense; center around competition for parental love and attention.

7. Sibling rivalries probably equally intense, but are more open and aggressive. Center on competition in social relationships outside family to some extent.

8. Family and home environment more complex in material sense; more restrictions required to maintain routine and order.

8. Family and home environment simpler, fewer restrictions required.

9. Punishment inconsistent. Parents tend to have much guilt over punishment, and do not sustain practices. More emphasis on "humanitarian" treatment of child, although alternating with severe punishment. Child learns more complex and variable patterns of love and hostility. *Situational* punishment stressed ("go-stand in the corner and feel ashamed").

9. Punishment, like love, given more freely and more consistently. Child learns simpler, more clearcut patterns of love and hostility. *Physical* punishment stressed.

10. Considerable restriction and repression of organic functions of body. Elimination viewed as "dirty"; toilet training early and rigid (usually earlier than physical maturation of child can assimilate). Sex tabooed; intro-

10. Less restriction and repression of organic pleasures and functions. Partly due to such physical factors as more crowded living conditions, partly due to more relaxed attitudes. Earlier exposure to sexual functions,

duction to sexual knowledge occurs late in childhood. Whole system introduces anxieties and tensions over organic functions.

11. Routinized feeding of child in infancy; carries over into later childhood in form of a rigid three-meals-a-day system. Children in general show more anxieties of a basic sort over food.

12. Children's fears seem to center in symbolic areas (as in the fear of not being loved, of not living up to the neighborhood paragon, or to parents' goals for child).

13. Training in the use of language stresses the symbolic expression of i d e a s . Literacy stressed greatly, because it is a large factor in "success."

often within home. Children permitted to "get dirty;" fewer taboos on dirt; more likely to be seen as a practical rather than a moral issue. Probably less anxiety-producing. Some conflicts with school authorities over system.

11. Feeding not routinized in infancy; rigid meal schedules not adhered to later. Family tends to "eat when there's food." Anxieties over food more realistic—based on hunger.

12. Fears seem to center in environmental areas (as in the fear of going hungry, being dispossessed, and the like). Some symbolic fears develop in school, when awareness of deprivation develops.

13. Training in the use of language stresses emotional expression (e.g. profanity), and in utilitarian control over environment, rather than in the expression of ideas. Literacy n o t stressed. Leads to school difficulties.

Sometimes, within a culture, the accepted methods for socializing children become modified over a period of time. Most of us are aware, for example, how recommended methods regarding the care and training of children have changed during the last four decades. As the conception of the child's basic nature was altered during that period, ideas about how the child should be raised were modified accordingly. At the beginning of this period, the child was assumed to possess dangerous impulses and an essentially sinful nature against which the mother was advised to wage a constant battle. By 1945, however, this concept had disappeared and the baby had come to be regarded as almost completely pure and harmless. As a result, the infant has benefited. He is no longer treated like a demon. The following two quotations [8] regarding masturbation provide a dramatic example of this change. In 1914: "Masturbation 'must be eradicated . . . The child should have his feet tied to opposite sides of the crib so that he cannot rub his thighs together; his nightgown sleeves should be pinned to the bed so that he cannot touch himself.' " But in 1942: " 'Babies want to handle and investigate everything that they can see and reach. When the baby discovers his genital organs he will play with them . . . A wise mother will not be concerned about this. See that he has a toy to play with and he will not need to use his body as a plaything.' "

Many methods are used in the process of socialization, some direct, some indirect. A child may be taught culturally approved habits directly by his parents or he may learn them indirectly, by the more subtle method of being praised when he obeys, by being punished when he rebels. Reward and punishment may take various forms. Some of the methods used reinforce one another; others are contradictory and leave the child uncertain and anxious.

As in the case of child care and protection, the function of socialization is not strictly confined to the family. The church and school play an important role in a child's socialization, and all persons with whom the child comes in contact for any length of time affect his socialization to some extent.

Education of the child. The extensive system of public and private education in this country furnishes ample evidence that the education of the child is not confined to the family. The process of socialization is, of course, an educative process, but fairly little formal education takes place within the family. Winch [9] has pointed out that formal schooling becomes necessary when the

---

[8] Martha Wolfenstein, "The Emergence of Fun Morality," *The Journal of Social Issues,* Vol. 7, No. 4, 1951, 16-17.

[9] Winch, *The Modern Family.*

parent generation is unable to transmit the basic skills (reading, writing, arithmetic, and vocational education) to the following generation. This is certainly true in the highly complex society that exists in the United States. Where formal education is concerned, perhaps the most important thing the family can do is to transmit to its children an attitude that is receptive and sympathetic to such education. Parents who only talk about "all the rubbish that children are taught in school these days" are not likely to instill in their children the desire to learn and to take advantage of their educational opportunities.

Conferment of status. Every person not only has a certain status within his family, but also, through the family, a certain rank and position in the society he inhabits. General behavior and manners, dress, and speech habits reflect different socio-economic levels in our society and often determine the individual's relationship to other members of society. The kind of neighborhood in which he lives, the church he attends, the play-groups to which he belongs, all help to confer a certain status upon him. The matter of "position" in society attains significance for the individual by the time he reaches adolescence. If he finds that the status of his own family is lower than that of most of his friends, he will grow dissatisfied and perhaps fall prey to severe conflicts.

Economic function of the family. The modern urban family is not a self-sufficient economic unit. Many of the goods and services needed by the family are supplied from outside the home. It is no longer economically advantageous for members of the family to stay together and to work together, as is the case in relatively isolated rural communities. The usual pattern in the urban family is for the husband to be the provider, although an increasing number of women now work outside the home.

Whether it produces the goods it requires or buys them from others, the modern family is expected to assume the responsibility for meeting its own minimum economic needs. But if for some plausible reason the family is unable to provide for its own necessities, other groups, such as governmental relief agencies or charitable organizations, step in and provide aid, the amount depending on the family's circumstances.

Recreation. It is evident in our culture, where so much commercial entertainment is available and where personal mobility (through widespread ownership of cars) is so high, that a great deal of recreation is pursued outside the home. Facilities for recreation are provided mainly by other than family groups. Some of these may bring the whole family together, such as picnic parks; others meet the recreational needs of various age groups; and some may encourage family recreation *at home,* such as television and the increased interest in do-it-yourself projects.

Satisfaction of psychological needs. A lament frequently overheard nowadays is that outside agencies have taken over too many of the functions that once belonged exclusively to the family. Some people have attacked public education on the ground that it is "usurping" the functions of the home. The underlying assumption seems to be that as fewer and fewer functions come to be performed in the home, family life will inevitably disintegrate.

However, the picture is not nearly so dark as some would paint it. The fact that the family is no longer a self-sufficient economic and social unit, for example, means that it has been relieved of many dreary and time-consuming tasks and can therefore turn its attention to other tasks that it can handle more effectively.

One of the most important of these "other tasks" is the satisfaction of psychological needs. The family is in a unique position to fulfill the need for affection and love, for acceptance and recognition, for belonging, for all that contributes to the emotional security of its members.

Children as well as adults need affection and love and emotional security. The family that can fulfill these needs is a cohesive family. The question might well be raised: Why should the individual look for emotional security in the family? The need for emotional security implies that the individual feels threatened or is bewildered and distraught. It is almost inevitable, as we have seen in Chapter 5, that a person living in these times will feel threatened, anxious, at sea. Almost daily he encounters a disparity between real and ideal culture patterns, finds himself in the midst of situations in which old ways of behaving no longer apply. In order to alleviate and reduce the tensions such situations spawn, the individual turns to the intimate family circle in which he feels a sense of belonging and of love. This does not mean that the family always fulfills this function adequately. When the family fails, it fails, at least in part, because it happens to be in a stage of transition at the particular time. During a transition period, the infiltration of outside influences demands that new ways of behaving be learned and this requires great flexibility on the part of all the members of the family. In order to understand better the processes involved in this family adjustment and the satisfaction of these psychological needs, we turn now to a consideration of the dynamics of family interaction, focusing first on the interaction between husband and wife and secondly on the relationships between parents and children.

Dynamics of Family Interaction

Although a family reflects the mores, values, and behavior patterns of the particular culture in which it exists, no two families are exactly alike. Each family pattern derives from the interaction of the distinctive personalities involved. In the course of its existence, the family is changing constantly. New members are born into it, others die or simply leave. And changes in the behavior of each member affect the behavior of the others.

Interaction between husband and wife. The interaction and adjustment that occurs between husband and wife is determined, in the beginning, by the hopes that each partner builds up before the marriage. How does the girl look upon her future husband? How does the boy expect his future wife to behave?

The courtship period frequently arouses hopes in one party

that the other party cannot possibly fulfill in married life. Re-inforced by movies and "true stories," a romantic rather than a realistic perception of the other person is built up. This romantic picture involves an over-idealized picture of the prospective mate, a sort of dream-world hero or heroine, who is expected to be constantly loving and lovable, loyal, devoted, and above all, highly thrilling in a romantic way. The "best behavior" of court-ship, as shown by some persons, is expected to continue through-out marriage. Unfortunately, an approach to marriage with these expectations leads all too frequently to severe disappointments, not because there is necessarily anything "wrong" with the wife or husband but because the mate's expectations were incorrect. To expect too much, whether in marriage or otherwise, is to in-vite disappointment. An unwarranted, idealized generalization about the desirability of the prospective mate inevitably arises if the other person sees him or her only in certain favorable situa-tions, and on best behavior.

Courtship should not necessarily follow the romantic tradition. It should be a period of getting to know and learning to adjust to one another. Many of the marriages that took place during World War II failed because the couples concerned rushed into them blindly after having known one another but a very short time. Although additional factors, such as background, age, fi-nances, and the like, have to be taken into consideration, the length of the courtship and engagement period definitely in-fluences the success or failure of a marriage.

In one study, Ernest W. Burgess,[10] an authority on family matters, queried 1,000 engaged couples on the factors they con-sidered most important in marriage. From their replies, he came to the following conclusion. The factor first in importance was economic security. Many of the couples interviewed were sure that both would have to work for at least a year or two until the furnishings for the house had been bought. After that, if they

[10] Ernest W. Burgess, "What the Family Faces in the Light of a Study of 1,000 Couples," in L. F. Wood and J. W. Mullen, eds., *What the American Family Faces*. Chicago, The Eugene Hugh Publishers, Inc., 1943.

were fortunate, the wife might give up her outside work and have children. The second factor, closely related to the first, concerned a higher standard of living. The young people in this study felt that they must attain a certain standard of living. They had to have a refrigerator and a car, for example, before they could think of having a child. A third factor emerging from the interviews implied that each new couple felt that they were on their own in marriage. The pattern set by parents and grandparents was not necessarily to be taken as a guide; they did not look to their parents for advice. Finally, the thing most of the couples looked for in marriage was companionship. Burgess assumed from these interviews that the romantic love concept was waning. "There is in this generation much less of the idealization that tended to blind the person to the imperfections of the others."

A good mutual understanding before marriage will not always guarantee that we shall be able to anticipate and predict what the other person will do, nor will it insulate us from all disappointment. It will, however, give us confidence in the other person, confidence that whatever problems arise can be worked out together. Tied in with this confidence is the readiness and willingness to build a mutually satisfying relationship.

When individuals marry, they enter into a new relationship, yet in many respects they bring to it the same behavior, needs, and attitudes that have characterized their former relationships. The woman who has always been dominant is not likely to become suddenly submissive after she marries. The man who has always been inept at his job is not likely to become suddenly a model employee. In many instances, the couple will continue to act and believe as they did before they were married, and the persistence of these traits, habits, and attitudes may play an important part in the success or failure of the marriage.

On the other hand, although a person's past experiences do affect the marriage, new ways of behaving can be learned and new roles assumed. New demands may bring out qualities in a person that previously had lain dormant.

As the marriage relationship develops, either frictions and

crises or increasing cooperation and enjoyment may result. Husband and wife may become aware of differences that they previously failed to recognize. These differences may become sources of irritation and conflict, or they may be handled in a manner that will help to enrich the marriage relation. A wife may disagree with her husband about personal habits, financial matters, religion, morality, friends, in-laws, or raising children. None of these differences, however, need necessarily lead to conflict. The

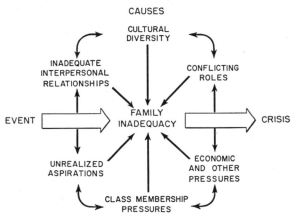

Causes of family inadequacy. (From Reuben Hill, Families under Stress. *New York, Harper and Brothers, 1946, p. 106.)*

attitude with which both partners approach them is the decisive factor. If either or both partners take an attitude of "I know I am right," the chances that they will reach a satisfactory solution are very slim. But if each makes an honest effort to understand the other person's point of view and is willing to compromise minor points, the differences probably can be ironed out.

What factors are closely related to marital happiness? There has been a good deal of research in this area, both in sociology and in psychology, more than we could possibly cover here. Instead, we shall concern ourselves with the major findings of one of the pioneers in the field, the psychologist Lewis M. Terman.

Terman's study [11] was based on a sample of 792 married couples who came from urban- and semi-urban middle-class and upper-middle-class backgrounds in California. He collected from them information concerning (1) certain personality characteristics, (2) background factors, and (3) factors having to do with sexual adjustment in marriage. In order to relate these factors to marital happiness, Terman had to compile a kind of happiness index. This index was based on information regarding (1) common interests; (2) average amount of agreement or disagreement between spouses in ten different fields, such as family finances, matters of recreation, religion, in-laws, and the like; (3) customary methods of settling disagreements; (4) regret over marriage; (5) choice of spouse if life were to be lived over again; (6) contemplation of separation or divorce; (7) subjective estimates of happiness; (8) direct admission of unhappiness; and (9) a complaint score based on domestic grievances.

The personality schedule the couples filled out contained 233 items dealing with interests, attitudes, likes and dislikes, habitual response patterns, and specific opinions about what constituted the ideal marriage. By noting the individual items that differentiated persons with a high and low happiness score, Terman derived descriptive composite personality pictures of the happily and unhappily married individuals. These are not the exact likeness of any one individual but represent the patterns that are more characteristic of the one group than of the contrasting group. The personality pictures of the happily married women and men will serve as illustrative examples:

> Happily married women, as a group, are characterized by kindly attitudes toward others and by the expectation of kindly attitudes in return. They do not easily take offense and are not unduly concerned about the impressions they make upon others. They do not look upon social relationships as rivalry situations. They are cooperative, do not object to subordinate roles, and are not annoyed by advice

---

[11] Lewis M. Terman, *Psychological Factors in Marital Happiness.* New York, McGraw-Hill Book Co., Inc., 1938.

from others. Missionary and ministering attitudes are frequently evidenced in their responses. They enjoy activities that bring educational or pleasurable opportunities to others and like to do things for the dependent or underprivileged. They are methodical and painstaking in their work, attentive to detail, and careful in regard to money. In religion, morals, and politics they tend to be conservative and conventional. Their expressed attitudes imply a quiet self-assurance and a decidedly optimistic outlook upon life.[12]

Happily married men show evidence of an even and stable emotional tone. Their most characteristic reaction to others is that of cooperation. This is reflected in their attitudes toward business superiors, with whom they work well; in their attitude toward women, which reflects equalitarian ideals; and in their benevolent attitudes toward inferiors and underprivileged. In a gathering of people they tend to be unselfconscious and somewhat extroverted. As compared with U (unhappy husbands), they show superior initiative, a greater tendency to take responsibility, and greater willingness to give close attention to detail in their daily work. They like methodical procedures and methodical people. In money matters they are saving and cautious. Conservative attitudes are strongly characteristic of them. They usually have a favorable attitude toward religion and strongly uphold the sex mores and other social conventions.[13]

The background factors included (a) general factors, such as occupation, family income, presence or absence of children, present age of respondent, length of marriage, age at marriage, age difference between spouses, amount of schooling, relative mental ability of spouses, place where spouses first met, how long and how well they knew each other before marriage, and how long they were engaged; (b) factors pertaining to the families of the spouses, such as marital happiness of the parents, sibling relationships, parent-child conflicts, the Oedipus complex, childhood happiness, home discipline, punishment, and religious training;

---

[12] Terman, *Psychological Factors in Marital Happiness*, pp. 145-146.
[13] *Ibid.*, p. 155.

and (c) factors relating to sex education and sex attitudes, such as rated adequacy of sex education, sources of early sex information, age when subjects learned about conception, attitude of parents toward the child's sex curiosity, premarital attitude of the subjects themselves toward sex, adolescent petting, association with opposite sex while in high school, desire to be of the opposite sex, history of sex shock, and age of first menstruation.

The ten items on this list of background factors that Terman found to be most predictive of marital happiness were these:

1. Superior happiness of parents
2. Childhood happiness
3. Lack of conflict with mother
4. Home discipline that was firm, not harsh
5. Strong attachment to mother
6. Strong attachment to father
7. Lack of conflict with father
8. Parental frankness about matters of sex
9. Infrequency and mildness of childhood punishment
10. Premarital attitude toward sex that was free from disgust or aversion.

It is also interesting to note those factors that were either totally uncorrelated with happiness scores or that showed very small correlations. These included family income, occupation, presence or absence of children, amount of religious training, birth order, number of opposite-sex siblings, adolescent popularity, and spouse differences in age and schooling.

The results, insofar as they deal with sex and marital happiness, are especially significant, since it has often been claimed that sexual adequacy or inadequacy are the major determinants of success in marriage. The factors of specific sexual adjustments that were included are these: frequency of intercourse (both actual and preferred), relative ardor of the spouses, refusal of intercourse, the orgasm, duration of the sex act, desire for extramarital intercourse, homosexual attraction, wife's response to first intercourse, contraceptive practices, wife's rhythm of sexual desire, and sexual complaints of each spouse against the other. Of these factors, two show a marked correlation with happiness scores, namely, the wife's orgasm adequacy and the husband-wife difference in strength of sex drive. Wives who said they never experienced an orgasm were unhappier than wives who said that they always did. However, adequacy in this respect does not guarantee marital happiness. Equality or near equality in the strength of the husband's and wife's sex drives—as measured by the ratio of actual and preferred number of copulations per month and the husband's and wife's ratings of their relative ardor —contribute to marital happiness. As the difference in ardor increases between husband and wife, the happiness scores of both drop significantly.

In summarizing the relative importance of sexual and psychological compatibility, Terman states:

> Our data do not confirm the view so often heard that the key to happiness in marriage is nearly always to be found in sexual compatibility. They indicate, instead, that the influence of the sexual factors is at most no greater than that of the combined personality and background factors, and that it is probably less. The problem is complicated by the fact that the testimony of husband and wife regarding their sexual compatibility is influenced by their psychological compatibility. Couples who are psychologically well mated are likely to show a surprising tolerance for the things that are not satisfactory in their sexual relationships. The psychologically ill-mated show no such tolerance but instead are prone to exaggeration in their reports on sexual maladjustment. The two sexual factors of genuine importance are wife's orgasm adequacy and relative strength of sex drive in the two spouses.[14]

These studies, however, do have certain limitations. Waller and Hill,[15] for example, point out that:

---

[14] Terman, *Psychological Factors in Marital Happiness,* p. 376.

[15] Willard Waller and Reuben Hill, *The Family. A Dynamic Interpretation,* rev. ed. New York, The Dryden Press, 1951, p. 353.

1. The criteria used tend to "stack the cards" in favor of conventionality and conservatism.

2. Factors associated with success in marriage are often not confirmed by other studies.

3. The factors, if valid, probably hold only for the early years of marriage.

4. The findings apply mainly to the white, urban, middle class from which data were drawn.

5. Probably 75 per cent of the factors that make for marital success are left unaccounted for.

The same two authorities have suggested that a marriage can be judged successful in proportion as the following criteria are fulfilled:

1. Love is fixed firmly on the mate. In a successful marriage, each mate must continue to be the principal love object of the other.

2. A spirit of compromise exists and an honest effort is made to understand one another's viewpoints, thus minimizing conflict, stabilizing the relationship, and yet leaving it open to constant change and revision.

3. Shared experiences, giving common purposes, joint participation, common memories, and other forms of solidarity.

4. The roles of spouses are compatible and complementary, and each role is satisfactory to both.

5. The marriage gives to both a sense of security and belonging.

6. The marriage furnishes a wholesome background for rearing children.

7. Psychological needs of both are met.

8. Economic problems are under control.

9. Freedom for self-development and self-expression for both without threatening the relationship.[16]

---

[16] *Ibid.*, pp. 368-369.

Family Adjustment

Parent-child relationships. Statistics indicate that the number of divorces become less in direct proportion to the number of children in the family, and that three times as many couples without children separate as do couples with one child. From this, it would appear that children add a stabilizing element to the family group. However, a few qualifications are necessary. First, social and economic pressures may operate against a divorce, even when ties of affection among the members of the family are weak. Second, a marriage already on the rocks is not likely to be saved because of the arrival of a child. Third, perhaps the happily married are the ones, mainly, who desire to have children.

Even in happy marriages, children may cause considerable strain. Although such tensions may be resolved rather easily, the arrival of any new member in any small group makes readjustment necessary. The family group has the advantage that it can make some preparation for this readjustment. It knows months ahead that a new member will be added, and in conversation and in action it can anticipate and rehearse new living arrangements, new time schedules, new roles.

As we have pointed out earlier, the individual, particularly in urban society, depends on his immediate family almost entirely to satisfy his needs for security. Whether a child will feel emotionally secure depends in the last analysis on his parents' attitude toward him. Furthermore, the emotional security or lack of it that he experiences during childhood will affect, in a significant way, the kind of adult he becomes.

The importance of the family group insofar as a child's development is concerned cannot be overemphasized. The child begins his life in the parental family at a time when he is most plastic, most impressionable. Never again, as he matures, will he be as helpless as during his first days and weeks. Never again, in any subsequent five years of his life, will he learn as much as he

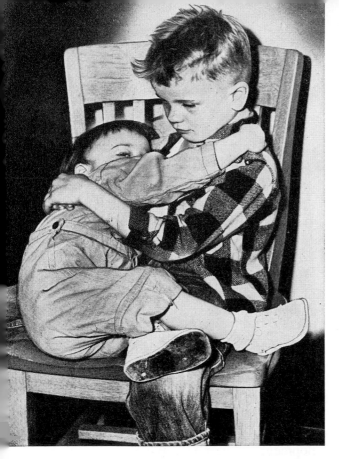

Parental acceptance or rejection will be a vital influence in the development of these children. The children in the top photo were abandoned by their parents. In the bottom photo, an adopted child has found an accepting, loving family.

(*Courtesy the* Los Angeles Mirror.)

has in his first five. What he learns then will determine to a great extent how he will react later.

The importance of a child's early experiences has been recognized, more or less, by many people and for many years, but it was Freud who re-emphasized it. He was the first to call attention to the necessity of examining the early childhood experiences of adult patients in order to understand their problems. Since then the practice has gained general acceptance. In order to understand a person's drives and goals, his attitudes, his generalized emotional reactions, and his specific emotional attachments, it is necessary to examine the home environment he was exposed to as a child.

The family is, first of all, the satisfier of the basic needs of the child. The human animal is more helpless at birth than any other new-born animal. Moreover, the child remains helpless for a relatively longer period than do other animals. Thus, directly or indirectly, the parents, especially the mother, must satisfy the child's physical needs.

However, parental responsibility is not limited to the physical needs of the infant. Clinical evidence indicates that the manner in which these needs are satisfied also is very important to the psychological development of the child. Whether the infant is cared for grudgingly or willingly, with love or hostility, will determine, to a great extent, how emotionally secure he will be as an adolescent and adult.

That this should be so is by no means surprising. The child's concept of himself will be based on the attitudes his parents display toward him. If he feels accepted, he becomes acceptable to himself; if he feels rejected, he learns to look upon himself as lacking those qualities that would make him acceptable.

The relationship established between the child and his parents is significant also for the child's future social development. If his parents have treated him with respect, he will probably be able to approach others with confidence. If his parents have nagged him and found fault with him, he may treat outsiders as though he expects them, too, to nag and criticize him. If his parents have overprotected him, he is likely to lack initiative and to depend too much on others.

It can also happen that parents try to be too many things to their children, to play roles that properly belong to other persons in the child's social world. The father who wants to be a constant playmate to his son may make it difficult for the boy to get along with others his own age.

Usurping roles. "Look, I'm satisfied to have you be my father . . . you don't have to try to be my pal too." (Courtesy Herb Williams and Gordon Steedman.)

The following case study illustrates how a father who "usurped" other roles seriously handicapped the courtship and marriage adjustment of his daughter.

The case of Dorothy M. illustrates some of the personality difficulties that may arise from *over-attachment to the father.* Dorothy's father is a highly successful corporation lawyer. From the time she was a very little girl her father used to spend almost all his spare time with her, and introduced her to a great many intellectual activities. He taught her to read, took her to concerts, to museums, and even to political meetings. Her mother always remained at home, and Dorothy regarded her as a dull, uninteresting person who merely wasted her life in useless activities. She regarded her father as her ideal and at a very early age decided to become a lawyer like him. She considered him handsome, intelligent, cultured, graceful, well-informed, and "socially smooth." She continued this pattern of going out socially with her father through most of high school. Although she occasionally went out on parties with the other boys and girls, she never dated any single boy until her senior year in high school. She felt strongly attracted to this boy and they began going steady. After a few months they decided to become engaged and Dorothy informed her father of this. He became extremely angry, saying she was too young and that she did not know her own mind yet. Dorothy became engaged anyway. A few weeks later, when her fiance placed the engagement ring on her finger, she became greatly disturbed emotionally and had an unexplainable feeling of guilt. She passed this off as "just nerves." The father still continued to object to the engagement and a few months later, when Doro-thy told him that she was getting married, he also violently objected to the marriage. Dorothy's mother, however, was more amenable and decided that Dorothy knew best what was necessary for her own happines. With the mother's permission, Dorothy was married in a simple, civil ceremony. During the ceremony Dorothy looked up at the judge and experienced a feeling very much like the one she felt when the ring was put on her finger: She was nervous, emotionally upset, and somehow felt extremely guilty. Again, she felt this was "just nerves." After the ceremony, the couple immediately left for their honeymoon, but the wedding night was a very unhappy experience for Dorothy. Although she loved her husband very much, and desired physical contact with him, attempts at sexual intercourse aroused in her the now-familiar feeling of guilt and emotional turmoil. After several repetitions of this experience, Dorothy became very concerned and sought psychological help. During the course of psychotherapy, she began to realize the extent of her deep attachment to her father. She also recognized a striking resemblance between her husband and her father—a resemblance that her friends had previously pointed out to her, but that she had insisted did not exist—and the fact that her husband had the same name as her father. She also felt that the engagement ring had been a symbol of her impending marriage, which meant her separation from her father, and that the judge who had married her had reminded her of her father. She now understood why she had felt so guilty on these two occasions. She realized, too, that her original attraction for her husband was based, at least in part, on the fact that he reminded her of her father, and that her feeling of guilt in connection with sexual intercourse arose from her identification of her husband with her father. She gradually came to understand that her husband is *not* her father and that she loves him for many qualities that are uniquely his own. Her relationship with her husband has improved considerably, and she is gradually approaching a happier, more normal, marital adjustment.

The main problem parents face is to strike a balance between extremes of overprotection and neglect, between overauthority and utter lack of guidance, between pushing the child into adult roles too fast and retarding it for too long at certain levels of development. In the remainder of this section, we shall consider various types of interaction between parents and children, and then suggest criteria for good parent-child relationships.

Patterns of parent-child interaction. Parents may show a variety of interactions with a child. Some of the important relationships, whether they occur consistently or intermittently, are discussed below. These relationships determine, in large part, the nature and extent of the psychological satisfactions the child obtains from the parents—and the parents from the child. It determines, also, how the child reacts with other persons.

REJECTION. A child's reaction to rejection by his parents may show itself in many different ways. Parents who are indifferent or hostile, parents who abandon the child, who isolate or seclude him, lock him up in a room or punish him at the slightest provocation, are rejecting their child. Sometimes, parents threaten to send the child away, or to deny him something he wants. But perhaps the most disturbing thing that can happen to a child is to be humiliated by his parents in front of others. We are all familiar with the mother and father who constantly hold up visiting children as examples for their own to follow, or who criticize their own child to friends and relatives while he is in earshot.

Parents rarely admit that they are rejecting their child. They are always ready with elaborate explanations for their actions, often including the remark, "It's for the child's own good." And sometimes, to be sure, there are valid reasons for sending the child to visit his grandparents or leaving him with the neighbor next door. Isolated or occasional instances of such behavior do not mean rejection. But when such behavior occurs repeatedly, and especially when it is done for the convenience of the parents only and not for the pleasure of the child, then the child is almost certain to feel that his parents do not love him or want him.

The rejected child may react in many ways. One of the more common is to resort to attention-getting behavior in an unconscious effort to win his parents' affection. Usually this attempt defeats itself, because in seeking attention the child merely succeeds in annoying his parents even more. A recent study has shown that children who are denied affection fall back on attention-getting behavior more often than do children who are loved and accepted.[17] Sometimes a rejected child will become hostile and rebellious. This hostility of the rejected child may now create new adjustment problems, especially in relation with other persons. Evidence also indicates that rejection may result in physio-

---

[17] G. G. Lafore, "Practices of Parents in Dealing with Preschool Children," *Child Development Monographs #31*. New York, Teachers College, Columbia University, 1945.

logical, mental, and social retardation. Warm parental relationships are essential if a child is to develop adequately.

OVERPROTECTION OR OVERINDULGENCE. At the opposite extreme from rejection is overprotection, although at times overprotection may be a symptom of rejection. Parents may become overprotective when they feel guilty about not wanting the child and so proceed to overprotect it to assure themselves and others that they are not rejecting it.

Overprotection is usually an expression of anxiety on the part of the parents. The child may have become the misplaced target for an anxiety that is in no way related to him. Perhaps another child in the family has died, and the parents are fearful that something may happen to the one who remains. Perhaps the father's job often takes him away from home and the mother, worrying that the child may be injured or hurt in the father's absence, will not let the youngster out of her sight. Or perhaps the father has died, and the mother, seeing her child as "all that she has left" is unwilling to share him with others and thus deprives him of outside contacts. In her fear that she may lose the child, she watches over him; she helps him dress far beyond the time when he needs such help; she accompanies him to school when other children are going by themselves.

As a result of all this, the child is denied the opportunity to learn for himself. When he starts to school he often finds that he is unable to compete on an equal footing with other children. Having become overly dependent, he fails in situations that require initiative and independence. Such failures may discourage him. To avoid further frustrations he may withdraw into the home, and a vicious circle is established. Or, instead of withdrawing, he may become overly aggressive.

Closely related to overprotection is *overindulgence*. The overindulged child frequently becomes the tyrant of the family. All his wishes are granted, if at all possible. Although he appears to control the family, actually he is highly dependent on his parents. He is likely to develop an exaggerated self-regard and an unwillingness to share with others. Accustomed to having his wishes satisfied, he does not develop much tolerance for frustration.

AUTHORITARIANISM AND OVERSTRICTNESS. In contrast to the overindulgent family, the authoritarian family enforces excessive discipline. Parents demand strict obedience and are quick to punish any deviation from prescribed behavior. Frequently the parents set standards for the child that he cannot possibly meet. And as usually happens with the overprotected, overindulged child, the sternly disciplined youngster will become highly dependent on his parents, since all his decisions are made for him and dictated from above. Or, he may grow defiant and aggressive, as the overprotected, overindulged child does.

AMBIVALENCE. There are times when even the most loving parent is irked or fatigued or upset, when he has mixed feelings about his child. It is important for parents to realize that such mixed feelings are normal and understandable. A mixture of positive and negative feelings characterizes all close personal contacts. But because negative feelings regarding children are socially condemned, parents may feel guilty when they discover themselves growing hostile and angry toward their children. Then, feeling guilty, they resort to overprotection and overindulgence in an effort to make amends. Ambivalent feelings express themselves in inconsistent behavior, and the child, unable to predict what his parents' reactions will be to specific situations, becomes anxious and uncertain.

If parents cannot avoid feeling hostile toward their children at times, then it is important that they learn how to control their anger. If parents realize that their children are sure to provoke them, that such provocation is natural and normal, they will cease to be troubled and embarrassed for occasionally regarding their young charges as reckless demons. Nor will they need to resort to overprotection and indulgence in an effort to excuse their doubts and mixed feelings. If, however, their feelings of hostility are constant and excessive, they should seek professional assistance for their problem.

Criteria for satisfactory parent-child relationships. 1. If a child is to achieve emotional security, it is essential that he be accepted *as he is.* His emotional security derives from *unqualified love*— love that is not dependent on how he behaves, love that is not withheld when he is "bad," or awarded only when he is "good."

2. The parents' behavior should be *balanced* between giving the child too much and too little attention, for one of the tasks of socialization is to help the dependent child achieve a degree of independence.

The objective influencing this kind of parental control is based upon the parents' sensitivity to the welfare of their child. The child is taught to do certain things for his own good. He should receive a reasonable explanation for any demands made upon him. He is taught that his health, safety, and growth often depend on his behaving in a certain way. Not only is he discouraged from doing things that may bring bodily harm to himself, but also he is taught to consider the rights and safety of others. He learns the necessity of a give-and-take relationship. His parents, by tactfully guiding him rather than dictating to him, gain his support and avoid arousing his hostility.

3. The home atmosphere should be *permissive,* rather than authoritarian. In a permissive atmosphere, the child can develop his potentialities and learn the necessary motor and social skills without feeling undue pressure. A permissive atmosphere also means that the demands made on the child should be kept in line with his abilities and his level of development, so that he will not become discouraged by failing to achieve what is beyond his capacities.

4. The questions of *praise and punishment* deserves special consideration. Praise and punishment are the *techniques of control* by which the child learns what is expected of him. Ordinarily, parents reward behavior they wish to encourage, and punish behavior they wish to eliminate. But family standards sometimes differ. There are two contrasting objectives that influence the type of control parents exercise. One is the authoritarian or autocratic approach that we have already discussed. Autocratic con-

trol depends entirely on the wishes or values of the person who exercises it. He allows no recourse to any other standard or principle. He demands obedience to him as a person rather than to a principle. Consequently, all the hostility and hate and fear that is aroused in the person being disciplined must be directed toward the individual wielding the authority, rather than toward a principle that he, as a guide, is merely helping to enforce. We have already noted that if the child feels that his father and mother are autocratic and irrational in their demands, he will grow hostile. This hostility he will direct against his parents, either outwardly or inwardly, if he feels that open rebellion will bring severe punishment. But whatever the child's reaction, his parents attitude will make him anxious and uncertain, since the demands they make on him will fluctuate according to their moods.

One further word should be added here concerning the use of punishment and praise. Punishment is almost certain to arouse hostility or resentment in the child. Frequent punishment, therefore, may irreparably damage the parent-child relationship. Punishment has few benefits; it is a risky practice, benefiting little and damaging much. The wise parent will keep punishment at a minimum and try instead to direct the child's undesirable drives into other channels, showing him alternative ways of behaving that satisfy his needs without being destructive or socially taboo.

5. The manner in which parents treat their children reflects the adjustment these parents have made toward the framework of values emphasized by the culture to which they belong. Since the culture establishes different norms for men and women, parents encourage different forms of behavior in boys and girls. The culture also provides theories concerning the original nature of the child. The newborn baby may be regarded as essentially dangerous and sinful, or as harmless and pure, or as amoral, having potentialities in either direction. Whatever theory the parents accept, it will influence the type of treatment the child will receive. In recent years, the trend has been increasingly toward the latter theory, with the result that parents have been recognized

as the agents primarily responsible for the type of personality the child develops.

Specific family problems. Problems arise in any group. Whether they become disruptive or not depends on their severity, on the resources or alternatives available to the persons facing them, and on the persons' interpretation of and attitude toward conflict situations. The problems may stem primarily from external factors, such as unemployment, or from factors lying within the family relationship and influenced by the personalities of its members, such as differences between husband and wife regarding one another's role, or one member's attempt to dominate others.

However, even when the source of the difficulty is related to external or environmental factors, the attempted solutions depend on the personalities of members of the family and on the patterns of family interaction that have been established. When Mr. Jones lost his job, nobody in the family blamed him. A conference was held and everyone pitched in to help out. Mrs. Jones found a part-time job. The older children took care of the younger. Everyone made some sacrifices. As a result, Mr. Jones' self-confidence remained high and in a few months he had found another job just as good as the one he had lost.

Mr. Green lost his job at about the same time Mr. Jones lost his. Almost immediately, he and Mrs. Green began quarreling and she repeatedly called him a failure, sometimes in front of the children. His ego and confidence shattered, Green took to drinking and eventually the family was broken up by divorce.

Some of the problems the family encounters, such as illness, unemployment, and conscription, are temporary, and usually demand only temporary readjustments, although temporary readjustments may at times have more far-reaching effects than the members anticipate. Other problems, such as divorce and death, bring permanent or irrevocable repercussions and require long periods of re-orientation by family members.

UNEMPLOYMENT. Especially when followed by impoverishment, unemployment forces the family to retrench on many fronts

—to move to a poorer neighborhood, to cut ties with old friends, to send the children to a different school. The father, as we have seen previously, traditionally is regarded as the provider, and his failure to maintain his family, regardless of the reasons, often wounds his status both within the family and in the larger community as well. The psychological effects of this loss in status have been described by several persons who have studied the unemployed. Lazarsfeld,[18] for instance, found that the jobless in an Austrian village grew increasingly hopeless and apathetic, and, as unemployment continued, gave up their hobbies and ceased participating in clubs to which they had belonged.

Sometimes the reverse may happen. Sudden financial gain may demand equally tense and prolonged readjustment and bring anxiety and strain to members of a family.

PROLONGED ILLNESS. A family may be affected by prolonged illness in the same way that it is affected by unemployment, especially if attendant medical expenses become a severe economic strain. Even if the family can bear the financial burden fairly well, it means that some individuals within the family will have to take on additional duties until the sick person recovers.

MILITARY CONSCRIPTION. Homes are often broken up because of military conscription, and as a result serious problems are posed for members of the family. In an intensive study, Hill [19] found that the process of adjusting to the crises of war separation and reunion involved (1) disorganization, (2) recovery, and (3) reorganization of the family, a pattern that also characterizes other adjustment processes. A summary of his findings, based on case study material, indicates that where extreme emotional reactions occurred in the family when the husband left, the adjustive process was poor. On the other hand, indifference to his departure promised good adjustment to separation but poor for reunion. The best adjustment to separation was made by families

---

[18] Paul F. Lazarsfeld, *Die Arbeitslosen von Marienthal.* Leipzig, S. Hirzel, 1933.

[19] Hill, *Families under Stress. Adjustment to the Crises of War Separation and Reunion.*

that redistributed the husband's responsibilities among the remaining members and established a warm affectional and companionable relationship with the absent husband.

DIVORCE. Our divorce rate has increased phenomenally since 1867, almost ten times as fast as the population. In 1867, there were 0.3 divorces for every thousand marriages, but by 1946, 18 marriages were being dissolved for every thousand performed.

What kind of marriages end in divorce? Not necessarily the stormiest. Couples who never have gotten along well together

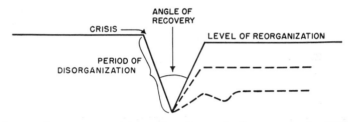

Profile of adjustment to crisis: crisis—disorganization—recovery—reorganization. (From Willard Waller and Reuben Hill, The Family: A Dynamic Interpretation, *rev. ed. New York, The Dryden Press, 1951, p. 465. Reproduced by special permission of the Dryden Press, Inc.)*

may remain married; others who apparently are well matched may suddenly separate.

The increase in divorce rates has to be understood in the context of broader social changes. Before America became predominantly industrialized and urbanized, the family performed many more functions than it does today, functions in which all members participated and from which a sense of cohesiveness and solidarity flowed. Now many of these functions have disappeared and with them have gone much of the cohesiveness and solidarity. Furthermore, in the older society, the relations between the family and the larger community were much more intimate. The community exerted a greater control over family relations and behavior, a moral control that was quite different and much more effective than the political control with which most of us are more familiar today.

Along with these changes, and closely associated with them, has come a more permissive attitude toward divorce. Divorce no longer carries the intense social stigma it once did. We often hear it said that divorce is made too easy, but the fact that this may be so does not indicate that marriages are any less happy now than they were 50 or 100 years ago. In the past, many couples suffered through unhappy marriages because of moral convictions against divorce, or because they feared the disgrace that

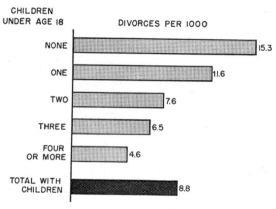

CHILDREN UNDER AGE 18   DIVORCES PER 1000

NONE	15.3
ONE	11.6
TWO	7.6
THREE	6.5
FOUR OR MORE	4.6
TOTAL WITH CHILDREN	8.8

Divorces by 1000 married couples according to size of family, United States, 1948. (From Paul H. Jacobsen, "Differentials in Divorce by Duration of Marriage and Size of Families," American Sociological Review, Vol. 15, 1950, 242.)

divorce might bring to them. But we should note also in this connection that many couples, faced with no other way out, often resolved to try to make the best of their situations and often succeeded in making an unhappy union into a happy one.

But although these changes help to explain the over-all increase in divorce rates, they do not help us understand why certain specific marriages end in divorce and others do not. In general terms, many divorces result from the fact that the emotional needs of one or both partners in the marriage are not met—and since marriage today is expected to serve primarily the psychological needs, where this does not occur, divorce often follows.

Often a marriage will not end in divorce if the partners to the union believe that other considerations may be more important than their own immediate personal happiness. There may be children, and the mother or father or both may hesitate to take a step they believe will bring grief and sadness to the youngsters. Or, a wife may be quite sure that she would retain possession of the children, but still will not be willing to begin divorce proceedings because she quails at the responsibilities that would confront her should she try to bring the children up alone.

There are many other considerations a divorce-seeking couple should keep in mind, considerations that may temper the first flush of relief that goes with anticipated freedom. Daily living habits will have to be reorganized as the divorced couple takes up separate residence. It may become apparent only then that, although both parties are now less anxious and tense, they also miss the many pleasant things they used to do together. And maintaining separate households increases economic burdens. If the children stay with the mother, the husband is usually required to help support both households. If he is unable to meet these obligations, the mother may have to take a job.

This last-mentioned readjustment is one of the more serious that the divorced woman has to make, especially if there are small children and if she has been given custody of them. It means that she has to make arrangements to have the children cared for while she is at work. She also may have difficulty finding a job, especially if she has never worked outside the home before and has not been trained for any particular kind of work.

The couple's social life also will be affected. Undoubtedly both will have had many mutual friends. After the divorce, one or the other may find himself excluded from functions or gatherings they used to attend together. If the couple formerly spent much time with people the husband came to know in his work, the wife may be "left out" after the divorce to avoid any embarrassment or awkwardness to all concerned. Or the two may have been very friendly with relatives who now are likely to take sides in the divorce issue and may ostracize the one they consider "guilty." In some cases, couples separate with little resentment or antagonism and remain friends after the divorce. Under those circumstances, their friends will not hesitate to invite them together. But in most cases, such joint invitations will be avoided and it becomes necessary, then, for one of the divorced couple to seek out new friends.

In addition to reorganizing their daily habits and their financial and social relationships, the divorced couple will be facing psychological repercussions often not anticipated at the beginning of the separation. Sometimes only one of the mates wants the divorce. For the other, the separation may mean rejection, sorrow, and failure. Even if both members want the divorce, they may have become disillusioned because of their failure to attain the happiness they expected when they entered into the marriage.

The severity of these adjustment problems will vary greatly, depending on the individual's needs and resources, both psychological and economic, and on the social support that he receives from others. But even if the problems are severe, they may at times be preferable to the unrelieved tensions of an unhappy marriage.

Many people feel that any advantages that may accrue from a divorce will be small compensation to the couple involved if the separation affects their children adversely. Although more divorces occur in childless families than in families with children, the proportion of the latter is quite high. Forty-two per cent of the divorces granted in 1948 involved minor children. It is pertinent, then, to inquire into the effects of divorce on children. How much the children suffer will depend largely on the nature of the relationship between the parents and between the parents and the child. If the parents are resentful and vindictive toward one another, this may deeply disturb the child. If he has previously identified himself with both parents, he will be torn by his loyalty to them. This feeling often is accentuated when custody is assigned to both parents, each of whom may engage in rivalry for the child's affection. The child, in turn, may exploit this relationship for his own purposes. The child also may be disturbed by the fact

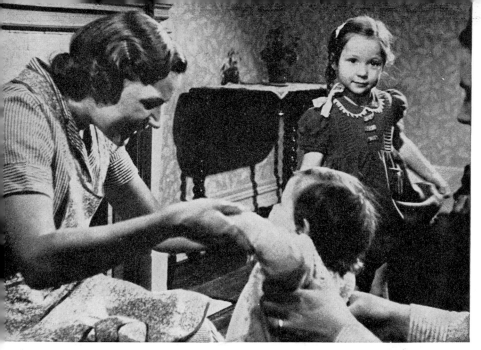

The new baby. (Top) When Margaret was a small child, her parents showered all their affection on her until another child was born. Then the parents transferred their love to the baby, ignoring Margaret and her attempts to win back their attention. (Bottom) No jealousy apparent here. (Top photo is from the film "The Feeling of Rejection," produced by the National Film Board of Canada and used here by permission of the Board. Bottom photo is from the film "Children's Emotions," in the McGraw-Hill text films series and is reproduced by permission of the McGraw-Hill Book Company, Inc.)

that he is now different from many other children, because his father, or mother, no longer lives at home with him. But whatever unfortunate effects a divorce may have on a child, they are probably no worse than the consequences of his being exposed daily to the spectacle of an unhappy marriage. In some cases, the child may actually welcome the divorce for putting an end to the endless bickering, quarreling, and hostility of his parents.

SIBLING RIVALRY. Even for the well-adjusted child, the arrival of a new baby creates some tension and anxiety. These tensions can become quite serious if the older child feels insecure and is maladjusted. Sometimes parents devote their whole attention to a new arrival, thus reinforcing the insecurity and sense of rejection their other child feels. If this happens, the other child will begin to look upon his new brother or sister as a rival with whom he must compete for his parents' affection. The overprotected and overindulged child may become especially disturbed if he suddenly has to share his parents with somebody else. The older child's anxiety and insecurity often prompts him to try to call more and more attention to himself. Often he will regress temporarily and begin to mimic the baby's actions and behavior. He may cry a great deal, crawl on the floor, start wetting himself again, or demand to be fed like the new baby. This is an example of regression, discussed earlier.

An older child should be prepared in advance for the arrival of a new baby and helped to feel the new arrival belongs as much to "him" as to the parents. The new baby should be welcomed as a playmate, not feared and hated as a competitor.

Family adjustment to strains and crises. Although different families respond to crises in different ways, all families usually pass through a series of fairly sharply defined stages in the course of handling a crisis. Hill [20] discusses five main steps. First is the family situation before the crisis appears. What roles do the various members play? Next comes the period of awaiting the crisis. A fam-

[20] Hill, *Families under Stress. Adjustment to the Crises of War Separation and Reunion.*

ily might know, for example, that the father is soon to be conscripted or that the mother is to be hospitalized for a certain length of time. If the family has some advance warning of an impending crisis, members may or may not prepare for it. The third stage is the family's immediate reactions at the time of the crisis. One family may be able to take the crisis in stride, another may be numbed by it, especially if it occurs suddenly. At the height of the emergency's impact, a process of recovery sets in. This may involve long weeks of trial-and-error learning during which the family tries to adjust to its new situation. Out of this period of flux finally comes the new adjustment.

Within this general course of adjustment, a great deal of variation is possible at any one phase. Thus, a family may become demoralized very rapidly; the recovery period may be relatively short or quite prolonged. The level of adjustment that is finally reached does not necessarily correspond to the way things were before the crisis developed. A severe financial setback, for example, may never be recouped or a bitter quarrel may leave lasting scars. On the other hand, the recovery actually may leave the family better off than it was before the crisis developed.

Families may try to solve their own problems, or they may turn to friends and relatives for help or seek professional advice from a clinical psychologist or psychiatrist. Therapy for one member of a family often benefits other members as well. Regardless of where help is sought, three techniques may help in determining what is wrong.

First of all, it is essential that the family be an intimate, friendly unit, in which *good channels of communication exist and are kept open*. If members of a family come and go as they please, using the home as little more than a convenient hotel, sharing few confidences and little talk besides the mere civilities, they will inevitably drift apart. If members of a family cannot talk among one another, there is little hope for progress. An unsolved, undiscussed, problem often stands like a silent barrier between husband and wife, with either one or both refusing to talk about it. Ignoring it, refusing to discuss it, is not likely to solve it.

A second important technique involves *fostering objectivity.* This includes an attempt to understand the problem not only from a personal point of view, but also from the point of view of other members of the family. It also means emphasizing the sources and nature of the problem and how to solve it, rather than blaming someone for it. Objectivity is encouraged when attention is directed from the self (and how to protect one's "rights," "honor," etc.) to the problem and how it is to be solved. A fault-finding attitude constitutes a negative approach; a problem-solving attitude constitutes a positive approach.

Finally, many problems can be eased and more readily solved if they are approached with a *sense of humor.* A sense of humor often helps a person get a new perspective on his problems and reduces disruptive emotions. Humor, however, may often be possible only if a certain objectivity has been attained.

As in other areas, so in marriage and family life, the better prepared we are for it the more likely we are to succeed in it. In recent years, courses for marriage have become increasingly popular. Many colleges now offer them, and other institutions, such as churches and community groups of various kinds, have inaugurated similar programs. Marriage counseling centers have been set up in many cities.

A happy marriage is probably for each of us the most satisfying life experience. Any efforts to understand ourselves, our mate, and our relations to one another, will strengthen the marriage.

For Additional Reading

Ackerman, Nathan W. and Peter B. Neubauer, "Failures in the Psychotherapy of Children," in Paul H. Hoch, ed., *Failures in Psychiatric Treatment.* New York, Grune and Stratton, 1948.

Children of Divorced Parents, *Law and Contemporary Problems,* Vol. 10, No. 5, Summer 1944, 697-866.

Dollard, John, *Caste and Class in a Southern Town.* New Haven, Yale University Press, 1937.

Koos, Earl Lomon, *Families in Trouble.* Morningside Heights, N. Y., King's Crown Press, 1946.

Levy, John and Ruth Munroe, *The Happy Family.* New York, Alfred A. Knopf, Inc., 1947.

Locke, Harvey J., *The Family from Institution to Companionship*. New York, American Book Company, 1945.

Symonds, Percival M., *The Dynamics of Parent-Child Relationships*. New York, Teachers College, Columbia University, 1949.

Terman, Lewis M., *Psychological Factors in Marital Happiness*. New York, McGraw-Hill Book Company, Inc., 1938.

Waller, Willard and Reuben Hill, *The Family. A Dynamic Interpretation*, rev. ed. New York, The Dryden Press, 1951.

Warner, William Lloyd, Allison Davis, Burleigh B. Gardner, and Mary R. Gardner, *Deep South; a Social Anthropological Study of Caste and Class*. Chicago, University of Chicago Press, 1941.

White, Robert W., *Lives in Progress. A Study of the Natural Growth of Personality*. New York, The Dryden Press, 1952.

Winch, Robert F., *The Modern Family*. New York, Henry Holt & Company, Inc., 1952.

Wolfenstein, Martha, "The Emergence of Fun Morality," in Abraham H. Maslow, ed., "American Culture and Personality," *The Journal of Social Issues*, Vol. 7, No. 4, 1951, 15-25.

School

Adjustments

child may find himself rejected by his schoolmates as well as by his parents, a situation that undoubtedly will intensify his aggression and thus set in motion another disturbing cycle. Or the child who is neglected or rejected at home may regard himself as inferior to others. He may be so shy that he will be afraid to meet and mingle with the other children at school, and for this reason he may be overlooked by the others. Thus the child who needs love the most will probably receive the least, either because he is too aggressive or because he is too shy.

Overhearing his parents talk about their own school experiences, listening to them as they tell him what to expect in school, taking too seriously remarks made by other children—all these things may color the child's attitudes toward school. Often the feelings implicit in these comments may be more significant than the actual words used. For instance, a mother who says to her child, "I'll be glad when you start school; maybe then I'll have some peace around here," might give the child the impression that school is a place for people who are not wanted and that attendance at school is, therefore, some sort of a punishment. School thus becomes an undesirable place in the youngster's eyes. Or a mother might say to her child, "You won't be able to do *that* in school. Just wait until the teacher sees you." This may give the child the impression that teachers are tyrants who will bully and badger him from morning till afternoon. Or the mother might complain about how inconvenient it is to have to drive the child to school, or how expensive it is to buy books and clothes, or what a nuisance it is to have to get up so early, and thus arouse other negative emotional feelings in the child.

Often a mother, in her eagerness to instill in the child a favorable attitude toward school, overdoes the job and arouses young hopes and expectations that are unrealistic. When his hopes are not realized, the child may become disappointed and resentful.

Sometimes the mother's initial comments to the teacher on the first day of school may create a problem or erect a barrier between the child and the teacher. For example, an oversolicitous mother may explain to the teacher that the child is "very delicate" and "very sensitive" and that he must be watched carefully, at the same time implying by her tone of voice that she wouldn't trust her child with the teacher for anything if the law didn't require her to do so. In some teachers, such remarks and intimations might arouse feelings of irritation and hostility toward the mother that later will be displaced onto the child. Thus, the mother has inadvertently created an unfavorable climate for her child. There are many other ways in which parents may upset or may callously disregard the feelings of the teacher, as well as those of their child.

It is safe to say, in summary, that a child's school problems are basically home problems. The schoolroom is merely the location in which the child manifests the home problem arising out of the conflicts that may exist between father and mother, or between father, mother, and child. The child who is disturbed at home now brings his problem to school, thus making it a school problem in the sense that teachers and school authorities have to deal with it. The most effective way to treat the problem is, of course, to correct the source of the difficulty in the home. All too frequently, however, the parents are unwilling to accept responsibility for their child's problem and to learn how to solve it.

The following case illustrates how a problem in the home manifested itself in school and how the father failed to accept responsibility for this problem.

Victor was a ten-year-old boy, rather heavy for his age, who had difficulty getting along with other children. He would insult them, often bump into them or push them, or trip them "by accident" when he had the opportunity. In the classroom he was restless, talked a great deal, disrupted other students, and the teacher. He started all kinds of activities but never completed them. In general, he made a nuisance of himself.

When the teacher attempted to restrain him, or to call attention to his disturbances, he would characteristically blame others for what he did—"They made me do it," he would say. Or, "It is their fault." And finally he also accused the teacher of picking on him.

The teacher tried repeatedly to speak with the father or mother but failed. The father took the attitude that this was the school's problem, not his. Finally, the boy had to be sent home as a result of spitting on two girls. The father now called up the school and in great anger accused the school of mistreating his son, that they "always picked on him and had it in for him, that if he spit on a child it must have been that the other child spit first, and that he had advised the boy he need no longer obey the teacher."

The child was transferred to another school, where his behavior continued essentially unchanged. Note that the father's comments reflect not only his attitudes, but also his son's. Both believed that the school was mistreating the boy, that the teachers and principal had it in for him, and that others were to blame for what the youngster did.

This boy's home life, incidentally, was very unhappy. His father and mother quarreled violently and often beat the child. The youngster was not close to either parent, which undoubtedly explains the difficulty he had making friends in school. Before this boy can be helped, his parents must be made to see that their own attitudes and feelings are responsible for his adjustment difficulties and that they must make a determined effort to correct the home environment before their son can derive any benefit from his school experiences.

Often parents who are very anxious to have their children do well in school create more problems than they solve. The following is a case in which the father wanted to help his young daughter to read better but instead prevented her from learning to read at all.

When seen by the psychologist, Lynn, age 10, a bright-eyed, beautiful girl, very popular with all her schoolmates, had not yet learned to read. She was excellent in arithmetic and other school work that did not involve reading. Her reading level was barely that of a second-grader and she had not yet learned to associate the written letter with spoken sounds.

A diagnosis of the reading problem and a history of its origin disclosed that Lynn's father attempted to teach her to read before she started to school. He bought a copy of a beginning reader and would sit down with Lynn to give her a lesson. Invariably the lesson ended with the father becoming violently angry and upset because Lynn did not learn to read as rapidly as he thought she should. By the time she actually started to school, Lynn had grown so emotionally disturbed about reading that she could not accept the guidance of her teachers and keep up with her classmates. The solution of her problem involved reducing her emotional reactions about reading, special remedial procedures, and instructions to her father to refrain from all further efforts to instruct her in reading. Lynn's case, just as Victor's, is an example of a home problem becoming a school problem.

Parents, children, and teachers all might well benefit from a sort of counseling clinic designed to prepare them for a child's entrance into school. Such counseling might help the parents to understand how their attitudes influence the child's approach to school and to realize that the problems that upset him in school are often problems he has brought with him from home. Instruction of the parents might improve the home situation, make the child (and them) happier, and so burden the child with fewer problems to bring to school, thus making the teacher's job easier to teach, and the child's job easier to learn.

Factors in Learning and School Adjustment

Native ability and individual differences. Individual differences, discussed in detail in Chapter 15, are of particular importance insofar as the school setting is concerned because they determine what and how a child learns. These differences include obvious physical differences and differences in abilities,

Individual differences in school learning. In teaching children who are handi-capped in various ways, special methods must be used. (*Courtesy The Nursery School for Visually Handicapped Children, Los Angeles, and the* Los Angeles Mirror.)

interests, personality characteristics, and so on. Success for each of us, whether in school or after school, depends on how we utilize our special abilities.

School work, as we shall see, must be adjusted to children's individual differences. This point was emphasized by John Dewey, who wrote, "an educational aim must be founded upon the intrinsic activities and needs of the given individual to be educated." [1] This statement has three implications: (a) The individual becomes the focal point around which all education must revolve; for this reason the educational philosophy and methods proposed by Dewey and others have been called child-centered education. (b) The educational process must consider the person as a whole, not isolated segments of his personality. (c) Individual differences must be taken into account if education is to be effective.

This child-centered approach has influenced many of our educational practices. The shift from a curriculum of prescribed courses to an elective one is a step in the direction of recognizing that the interests of one individual are different from those of another. With greater freedom for the student to elect courses has also come an increase in the number of courses from which a choice could be made. Many new courses have been introduced into the curriculum during the last 25 years. The introduction of cocurricular programs represents a further attempt to meet the varying needs of students.

One of the most significant developments emphasizing the importance of individual differences was the work carried on by Binet, Terman, and others, in the field of mental testing. (These men and their work are discussed in Chapter 15.) Intelligence testing helped to focus the attention of educators on the extent to which intellectual ability varies. School children no longer progress through the grades in a sort of "lock-step," in which the dullest and the brightest are all expected to perform in the same way, regardless of their mental ability. Much of our educational emphasis today involves discovering and measuring individual dif-

---

[1] John Dewey, *Democracy and Education*. New York, The Macmillan Company, 1937, p. 434.

ferences in order to place the child according to his ability and to guide him according to his capacity to learn.

The importance of considering individual ability when guiding a child in school may be seen from the following case study:

Walter was an only child of nine who lived with his father and mother, both of whom worked. His physical health was good. Walter was referred to the school psychologist because his school work was poor and because he showed extremely poor social adjustment. He was failing in all his courses, all of which he disliked intensely, and when required to do a job, would take an hour for something other students could finish in ten or fifteen minutes. Although Walter was failing in all his subjects, he had a tremendous fund of information about cars, sports, and current events. His vocabulary was good. Walter's teachers believed him to be "stubborn" and perhaps somewhat retarded in intellectual ability, which, they thought, might account for his poor school work. One teacher also remarked that he was "passive and undisturbed about his work at school," which would appear to indicate that she thought Walter did not worry about his low grades. This last opinion most certainly was incorrect. How could a boy fail in all his subjects in school and still not be upset by it? Furthermore, Walter's poor school adjustment might be interpreted as a symptom of his emotional disturbances, and these, in turn, might stem directly from his failure in school work.

Walter was given the Revised Stanford-Binet intelligence test by a psychologist and made a score of 137, indicating very superior intelligence. This would indicate that Walter's failure in school did not stem from inadequate intelligence, but rather that his intelligence was so superior that he found no stimulus or challenge in the work given him. Failure of his teachers to recognize his superiority, and to make allowance for Walter's individual difference in this respect, led to the boy's serious difficulties in both academic work and social adjustment. When a program of education was custom-made for Walter that utilized his superior in-

Feeding is one of the skills the young child must learn. On their first birthdays, the children are messy with their feeding. As they grow older, they learn to feed themselves and others neatly and acceptably. (Top photo courtesy Acme Photo Service. Bottom photo courtesy the Los Angeles Mirror.)

telligence, his entire behavior changed. He took great interest in his work and improved in his social relations.

The measurement of intellectual differences has stimulated the use of measuring devices to assess differences in other areas, such as emotional maturity or special abilities, for example.

The respect for individual differences incorporated into our educational system is, of course, a basic principle of democracy. Democracy stresses that we should all respect one another, regardless of individual differences. Out of the teacher's respect for personality will come for each child, through working with others, a respect for other children.

Motivation and learning. Motives and needs are basic to the learning process. Generally, we learn what we *need to learn.* As we noted earlier, motive initiates, sustains, and directs our activities. We recognize a motive as a want or a need, a driving force behind our behavior. We all have many unsatisfied wants or needs that prompt us to act in many different ways. We can get an idea of the extent and range of our needs by looking at the advertisements in the daily newspaper or glancing at the billboards along the highway or gazing into the windows of a fashionable department store. Advertising is designed to promote wants and thus to stimulate a steady demand for products, i.e., to induce people to buy.

In a sense, the entire learning process has its basis in the dynamic interaction between our needs and their satisfaction. Our behavior is purposive—i.e., it is directed toward the attainment of goals that will satisfy our physiological and psychological drives or needs. Once the satisfaction has been achieved and the tension reduced, motivation is reduced and the organism attains a state of equilibrium. This equilibrium, however, is upset again as old needs reappear or new needs arise. We thus think of learning as an active dynamic adjusting process. We learn by living, and we live by learning.

A child's urge to be active and to explore the world around him is an important factor in his learning. This need to explore, often called curiosity, leads to the acquisition of new skills, new information, and new attitudes. The child, like the adult, wishes to understand what goes on around him. Children are always asking the "how," "what," "why," and "where" of things and events. It is important that these questions be answered for the child in ways he will understand, first by the parents and later by the teacher in school, for these questions play a dominant role in all our lives. They constitute the basis of our quest for knowledge in all fields. Many an adult in pursuing answers to such questions has literally acquired a new motive to learn.

Of the many factors that motivate us to learn both in school and in later life, we may note the following:

1. *Competition.* This is an important stimulant to learning, provided that the competitive situation offers the individual a reasonable chance to succeed or excel. The highly insecure individual will avoid competition because he expects to fail, and failure would merely reinforce his feelings of inadequacy.

2. *Desire for approval.* Another important need that stimulates learning and adjustment is the desire to gain the approval of others. We often tackle a difficult problem merely to please someone else.

3. *Desire for mastery.* This is the need to learn to do things well, to master subjects and skills and to apply them in appropriate ways to achieve specific ends. Related to this need may be such others as the desire for status, for dominance, and so forth.

Related to all these needs is the fact that working or learning in a group often facilitates learning. An example is the student who finds it easier to work in the library with other students than to plug away alone at home. The realization that others are learning stimulates his own desire to learn.

It would be impossible to try to compile a list of all the motives that induce and encourage learning, because different individuals respond to different motives and drives, and motives that are significant for a person at one time in his life may not be important at another time. The motives of a college student are not the same as those of a child in elementary school, for example. And the adult in night school may have motives different from the student in college.

Reward and punishment in school adjustment. When we speak about motivation and its effect on learning, we must also consider the closely related factors of reward and punishment. We,

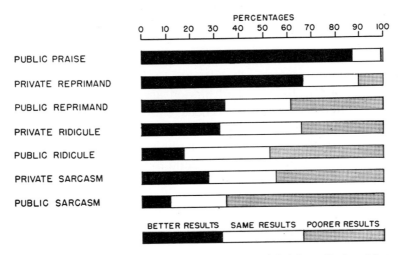

Comparison of positive and negative incentives. (*Modified from Herbert Moore,* Psychology for Business and Industry. *New York, McGraw-Hill Book Company, Inc., 1939, p. 302.)*

as individuals, are motivated *toward* something we wish to attain or *away* from something we wish to avoid, toward rewards and away from punishment. Reward and punishment are the two principal techniques for controlling behavior. They are also the two basic approaches to discipline, discipline here meaning the control methods used in school to encourage an individual to do certain things and to discourage him from doing certain other things. "Old-fashioned" discipline stresses painful punishment, either threatened or applied, to control the behavior of children in school. Such a system may insure obedience but only in a *negative* sense.

The child conforms simply to avoid the pain. Under the constant rain of warnings and intimidations he grows hostile and antagonistic toward the teacher and the entire school situation, and develops marked feelings of inferiority.

Modern discipline, on the other hand, practices the principles of good mental hygiene and is concerned more with guiding, rewarding, and suggesting than with dictating, criticizing, and punishing. Modern discipline is *positive* discipline in that it emphasizes the accomplishments of the child and minimizes his failures and shortcomings, thus making him feel more adequate and secure.

Effective discipline insures not only that a child will behave in a certain desired manner, but also that he will develop wholesome attitudes and feelings toward himself and the entire educational process. In order to be able to behave as he should, the child has to establish effective, long-range self-control. He can do this only if his ego needs are protected while he is being disciplined. Positive methods of discipline help a child to learn. Negative methods hinder the child.

We might note here that all children, regardless of the type of discipline to which they are exposed, inevitably will encounter a certain amount of criticism, and social or group disapproval. Such experiences, however, should not leave a child morose, insecure, or frustrated if he has learned to regard them as normal accompaniments to living and has developed the self-confidence to surmount such temporary setbacks calmly and rationally. Developing the self-confidence that will enable him to endure such experiences without losing faith in himself is an essential part of his education.

Most of our behavior is directed toward seeking success (rewards) and avoiding failure (punishment). In this connection, it might be well to consider briefly the kinds of goals we set for ourselves, or have set for us by others, and how success or failure in reaching these goals affects our behavior. When we are called upon to perform a task, we generally have a fairly good idea about whether or not we can do it. We try to avoid situations in which we expect to fail, and we seek out situations in which we expect to succeed. Furthermore, the quality of our performance in each undertaking will influence our future estimates of our own ability. Expectations regarding future performances we call level of aspiration.

Level of aspiration and level of achievement in learning. The "level of aspiration" refers to the goals we set for ourselves and the plans we make for attaining them. The term "level of achievement" refers to the goals we attain. In school, the level of aspiration primarily involves getting high grades. Sometimes considerable discrepancy exists between level of aspiration and level of achievement; we might, for example, aspire to an "A" and get a "D." By measuring the difference between aspiration and achievement we can determine the extent of our dissatisfaction. How closely our level of achievement approximates our level of aspiration will depend on how high we set our level of aspiration, and whether or not our abilities are adequate to the task confronting us. Let us consider briefly each of these two factors.

Our level of aspiration should be determined by the abilities we possess, by the opportunities presented to us for using these abilities, and by our own physical characteristics as well as by those of our environment, both of which will have some bearing on our achievement. Very often we ignore these factors. For example, the boy with an IQ of 90 who wants to become a doctor is not being realistic, because evidence indicates that an IQ of approximately 120 is the minimum required for a person to be successful in medicine. Likewise, the 120-pound freshman who has his heart set on making the first-string football team will soon learn the hard way that determination and enthusiasm, important though they may be in such a situation, cannot compensate completely for lack of brawn.

One job of a good teacher, and of the guidance services becoming more and more a permanent feature of high schools and colleges, is to help students appraise their abilities realistically and to plan intelligently to achieve goals once these have been set.

Helping a student judge his abilities realistically involves not only that he be prevented from setting his achievement sights too high, but also that he not be allowed to set them too low. A person of high ability often will set a low achievement standard for himself because he feels inadequate and insecure as a result of negative disciplining imposed upon him by his parents or teachers. Or, it may be that his parents have set unrealistically high standards for him and then have criticized and punished him when he has fallen short. This lamentable parental tendency does not apply merely to those who want their son to "do well in school" or to "study engineering like his daddy did." The mother who expects her six-month-old child to acquire proper toilet habits and her three-year-old daughter to display the social skills and manners of an adult is setting ridiculously high standards for her children.

Students sometimes set low goals for themselves solely to insure success. But the student whose goal is too easy to attain may become lazy. Since he *need not* work he *does not* work, and consequently he does not learn *how* to work.

We should set goals for ourselves that we can reach, but only by putting forth our best performance. As noted in Chapter 5, if the goal is set in the future, it is important to intersperse various subgoals along the way. The person striving to become an engineer, for example, will be encouraged as he completes the individual course requirements that indicate he is making steady progress toward his goal.

We see, thus, how serious is the school's responsibility to help children set realistic goals and to plan for their attainment. Interests and aspirations must not be out of proportion to abilities. The goals set must be feasible. A system of positive discipline in the schools can help a child make significant progress in reaching his goals.

Competition vs. cooperation in school. Competition and cooperation are two of the ways in which we interact with other human beings. From earliest infancy on and throughout most of our life, many different influences tend to re-enforce the competitive aspect of our lives. Even before they begin school, brothers and sisters often are pitted against one another, encouraged to outdo one another in tests of strength or skill by their parents. In school, the process is continued. Pupils are constantly contending for the highest grades, for the awards and prizes, for the increased status, that are bestowed on the most successful. Athletic contests reenforce this tendency. It is an alarming emphasis. Competition for grades in college is a source of marked anxiety to many and may become so intense that some students strive not so much to learn as to get certain grades regardless of whether they have to cheat or crib in the process.

Fuller and Baker [2] point out the following consequences of excessive competition among secondary pupils: (1) Slow learners despair and grow discouraged as they begin to fall behind their mates. (2) Average students are under constant strain and stress to keep up their work. (3) The brightest pupils develop exaggerated feelings of superiority. (4) Different students in the various progress brackets develop an attitude of "aggressive noncooperation" toward others in their group in an effort to maintain their relative positions in the group.

On the other hand, when the pupils are placed in situations that call for them to cooperate, the following characteristics in their behavior are observed: (1) The students work together in setting the goal and planning ways of achieving it. (2) They cooperate in all efforts necessary to attain the goal. (3) All share alike in the responsibilities for success or failure. (4) All become more goal-centered rather than self-centered in the pursuit of the task. In the cooperative situation, we see a tendency toward mutual aid and understanding and identification with the group effort, as against the emotional reactions of fear, hostility, and anger so frequently generated in intensively competitive situations.

Language and learning. The very basis of human society is derived from the ability of human beings to communicate with one another through speech and writing. Language not only facili-

---

[2] J. J. Fuller and J. N. Baker, "Competition vs. Cooperation in the Classroom," *Secondary Education*, Vol. 8, 1939, 134-137.

tates communication between people, but also provides the means by which man preserves and passes on knowledge and skills to his contemporaries and to his descendants. By using language symbolically, man is able to select, identify, and manipulate aspects of a situation, generalize about it, express attitudes toward it, relate it to other situations in the past and future, direct the actions of himself and of others accordingly, and evoke in himself and in others similar attitudes and tendencies.

Although words and meanings are arbitrarily connected in any language, a word, to be effective, must carry the same symbolic meaning for all people who know the language. Particular meanings become attached to symbols through usage and social convention. Although the system of symbols used by a person depends on the particular society in which he grows up—German children learn German, Italian children learn Italian—meaning varies even further because each individual within a society will view the connotation of a word in the light of his own particular experience. Many arguments might be avoided if the parties concerned took the trouble to indicate carefully what they mean by the words they are using. Difference of opinion is often a matter of confused wording.

Because language plays such an important role in human relationships, the early acquisition of a good vocabulary and proper speaking habits is a significant factor in helping people to adjust. The school, of course, is concerned with helping students to acquire skill and facility in using language. Language skill is an important asset that, once learned, eases our learning many other things. As we gain skill with language, we become aware of the subtler variations among words and become able to establish finer distinctions, sharper differentiations, and closer relationships between an event and the symbols that describe it. And with each new field of knowledge that we study we acquire a new vocabulary that enables us to describe, relate, and explain accurately the phenomenon involved.

Language, then, provides us with a valuable tool upon which all other learning depends. From the standpoint of personal and social adjustment, therefore, it is wise for us to develop our language skill to the greatest possible extent.

Teacher-child relationships in learning. As we have seen, the teacher plays an important role in a child's intellectual and emotional development. As a parent substitute, the teacher faces many of the same responsibilities that confront parents, but on a much larger scale. The child looks to the teacher, as to the parents, for satisfaction of his needs. Specifically, the child seeks from the teacher clues that will help him understand the world in which he lives and guidance that will enable him to feel secure and safe in his own little part of that world. His personality and his skill will determine how well he succeeds in creating a wholesome social atmosphere in which each child will be permitted to develop his potentialities as fully as possible.

Because personality is so important in teaching, the sole criterion of ability to teach is no longer the number of degrees a person carries after his name. Today's teacher must be scholar, psychologist, counsellor, and guide all rolled into one. In order to understand children, the teacher must first be able to understand himself. He must have an appreciation of his own needs, how he reacts when these needs are frustrated, the kinds of defenses he uses, and the possible influences his unresolved problems may have upon the pupils he teaches. The well-adjusted teacher can help his children to adjust. The maladjusted teacher will probably create new problems for the child or intensify already existing ones. The emotionally healthy teacher who has an appreciation of the psychological principles governing behavior will regard each child as a unique individual whose personal characteristics must be considered in relation to the total learning situation. Such a teacher will be able to help the shy child to grow in confidence, the emotionally starved child to know affection and recognition, or the aggressive child to sublimate or overcome his feelings of hostility.

Democratic versus authoritarian teaching. The kind of leadership a teacher furnishes will be an important determinant of the effectiveness of the learning situation. Some teachers prefer to teach in an authoritarian atmosphere, setting themselves up as the final authority on whatever is said or done, demanding unquestioning obedience, and being quick to resort to strict discipline of the negative type if disobedience appears. The authoritarian teacher is essentially self-oriented rather than student-oriented; he believes that in order to control his class he must appear at all times to be infallible. He displays little understanding or tolerance when children misbehave or go counter to his wishes or advice. His restrictive attitude suppresses the spontaneity and creativity of the children and creates an atmosphere of emotional tension, insecurity, and hostility.

By contrast, the democratic teacher emphasizes the personal value of each student as part of the total social group. Instead of setting himself up as the person who knows it all and who tells others what to do and when and how to do it, the democratic teacher assumes the role of a resourceful leader who is ready to help his students in any way he can. He encourages each pupil to participate in the group, thus stimulating the development of spontaneity and creativity, rather than discouraging them. His methods of discipline involve essentially the positive approach described earlier, thereby inducing desirable behavior while still protecting the feelings of each pupil. The democratic teacher does not feel that his prestige is threatened if he cannot answer a question. He recognizes that students will make mistakes and that they will profit from them. He is careful never to ridicule a student who is slow to learn, recognizing that each of his charges is an individual and adjusting materials and methods to meet the problems created by individual differences.

Aids to better learning. The main job of the student in school is to learn, but all too often he does not know how to learn. Inability to learn well prevents him from taking advantage of his opportunities and so he fails to benefit as much as he might from his school experiences. He will be more effective in school if he modifies his approach by scrutinizing it in the light of the following factors.

1. As indicated in our previous discussion, a person must be motivated to learn. In order to understand how our present activity is related to our goals we need to understand first of all *why* we are in school, why we are studying a particular course or reading a particular book. This implies, of course, that we have a goal, or goals. Without a goal we are not likely to be motivated to study or work in any case. We are probably all familiar with the student who enrolled in a university simply because he didn't know what else to do or because his parents talked him into it. He was not interested in his work and consequently did not learn. On the other hand, the student who has a specific goal in college works hard to attain it and to maintain an excellent scholastic record, even though he may have to sacrifice many comforts and pleasures in order to finance his way through school.

If the subject matter we study is to contribute to the attainment of our goals, we must be able to define those goals. We should also frequently remind ourselves of our goals. A goal that we cannot hope to reach immediately may slip out of sight, and as we lose sight of it, we may lose interest in it. Subgoals, as previously stated, help to forestall this loss of motivation.

2. We must learn to view what we are doing in its own proper perspective. Students sometimes find it difficult to separate the significant from the insignificant. It is always wise to view a problem or a subject in its entirety before trying to break it down into its component parts. If we approach a new book, for example, by reading through the table of contents, we immediately get an over-all view of the subject matter presented and a clear idea of how the chapters are related and how the material progresses from the first chapter through the last. This method of first getting the total picture into focus will facilitate our understanding of each individual chapter.

3. Another aid to learning involves distributing effort. Research indicates that we learn better and retain what we learn longer if

we distribute or space the time we spend on a particular project rather than mass it together. It is better not to try to learn all of a particular project at once but rather to work on it for a reasonable length of time and then to stop and do something else, thereby distributing the learning over a number of short periods instead of trying to master it all at once. This appears to apply equally to motor learning, such as learning to play tennis or golf, as well as to memorizing. The kind of spacing best for the purpose will depend partly on the material and partly on the particular student. Each student must work out his own best method.

4. Another learning aid involves taking an active approach to the study period. This may involve, for example, assuming a "work" position, such as sitting at a desk, rather than lying in bed while trying to read. Another example of an active approach is to take notes, which may involve briefly summarizing the material read, or jotting down ideas and questions suggested by the material studied. Or, to make the material really stick with you, rephrase it in your own words. Still another aspect of the active approach to learning is to compete with yourself, as well as with others, in seeing how much work you can do and how well you can do it. Such competition may motivate you to do your job thoroughly and promptly. Finally, as part of the active work attitude, it is well to set aside a certain time for work and another time for play, thereby avoiding the necessity of deciding every day when to work and when to play. Furthermore, it is important to work hard during the work period and to play hard during the play period. To think of play while you work, or of work while you play, spoils both the work and the play. There should be a definite time for each and you should follow the schedule whenever possible.

5. A further aid to learning, and one of the most important, is to apply the material that you have learned. The conditions under which we learn—in the laboratory, the classroom, or the library —are, of course, quite different from the conditions under which we shall use the information later. Nevertheless, there are many ways to apply the information we have learned in school projects,

in part-time jobs or summer work, or simply in discussing the material with other persons. We learn much better if we can put to daily use the knowledge and skills we acquire while preparing for a profession or occupation.

Applying information in this way is very beneficial. It motivates us to learn more. It makes us more aware of the problems often encountered in attempting to apply to a concrete situation information acquired through intellectual exercise. By fitting such information to a concrete problem, we are able to correct errors and misconceptions in what we have learned. Finally, practical application of our knowledge affords the best test of whether or not the material we are learning is what we really want to learn.

6. Another important aid to learning is to be problem-oriented rather than self-oriented. If we wish to solve a problem, we must focus our attention on the problem itself and not on our own feelings as they relate to the problem. For example, the person confronted with a difficult mathematical problem may become so frustrated and upset, especially if the problem is preventing him from doing something else, that he will have little or no energy left for actually analyzing the problem and solving it. In this case, before he can hope to solve the problem, he must first solve the emotional disorders that it arouses. With these emotions eliminated, a swift solution to the problem may present itself. Frequently in such cases the person simply invites failure by reacting emotionally. Where emotional reactions consistently interfere with the solution of problems, professional assistance in overcoming such emotions may be necessary.

School as a Life Situation

We often hear the remark made that school is a preparation for life. Although this is true in the sense that school is the period of our life during which we devote time to prepare for our life's work, it is not true in the sense that school is only a *preparation* for life. It *is* life. It is a situation in which we find, though perhaps in somewhat milder form, almost all the problems we shall encounter later on in life. In school we do much more than merely learn to live; we are already living.

The way we react to problems encountered in school may serve as a measure of our ability to meet problems that will confront us later on in life. How well do we learn what we need to learn? How well do we adjust to authority and other facets of an organized social activity, such as school? How do we get along with other people—of our own age or class, those younger than we, those older than we, those with similar interests, those with different interests? What kind of close attachments do we form? Can we comfortably give and receive love? All these are questions that confront each of us in school, and for most of our lives after school.

It is well to emphasize again here the importance of "heart training" in addition to "head training" as part of our total education. It is important to master subject matter, to acquire and to remember factual material, to reason, and so forth, but, as already discussed, we live not by our brains alone. Our feelings color almost all our experiences, not only in those situations involving only ourselves, but also in our relations with other people. In fact, our social sensitivity, that is, our feelings toward others, often determines whether or not we shall have the opportunity to use the information and knowledge we have acquired over the years. We need only remind ourselves that about 90 per cent of all persons who lose their jobs do so not because they cannot do the work but because they cannot get along with others, cannot "feel their way" to comfortable social relations. So, too, in school, as we indicated earlier, a child with a high I.Q. may fail in his work, not because he cannot do it, intellectually speaking, but because he cannot do it, emotionally speaking.

School is that time of our life during which we devote most of our time and effort to learning and remembering. However, learning for each of us is a life-long process. The love of learning should find its main stimulation and foundation in our early school years.

For Additional Reading

Anderson, J. E., *The Psychology of Development and Personal Adjustment.* New York, Henry Holt & Company, Inc., 1949.

Bird, Charles and Dorothy M. Bird, *Learning More by Effective Study.* New York, Appleton-Century-Crofts, Inc., 1945.

Buhler, C., Faith Smitter, and Sybil Richardson. *Childhood Problems and the Teacher.* New York, Henry Holt & Company, Inc., 1952.

Bullis, H. E. and E. E. O'Malley, *Human Relations in the Classroom* (Course I and II). Wilmington, Del., The Delaware State Society for Mental Hygiene, 1947.

Cleugh, M. F., *Psychology in the Service of the School.* New York, Philosophical Library, 1951.

Hayakawa, S. I., "Meaning, Symbols and Levels of Abstraction," in T. M. Newcomb and E. L. Hartley, eds., *Readings in Social Psychology.* New York, Henry Holt & Company, Inc., 1947.

Hilgard, E. R., *Theories of Learning.* New York, Appleton-Century-Crofts, Inc., 1948.

Jones, H. E., "Environmental Influences on Mental Development," in L. Carmichael, ed., *Manual of Child Psychology,* 1st ed. New York, John Wiley & Sons, Inc., 1946.

Lewin, K., *et al.,* "Level of Aspiration," in J. McV. Hunt, ed., *Personality and the Behavior Disorders,* Vol. I. New York, The Ronald Press Company, 1944, pp. 333-378.

McCarthy, D., "Language Development in Children," in L. Carmichael, ed., *Manual of Child Psychology,* 2nd ed. New York, John Wiley & Sons, Inc., 1954.

McGeoch, J. A. and A. L. Irion, *The Psychology of Human Learning.* New York, Longmans, Green & Company, Inc., 1952.

Mead, G. H., "Language and the Development of the Self," in T. M. Newcomb & E. L. Hartley, eds., *Readings in Social Psychology.* New York, Henry Holt & Company, Inc., 1947.

Pressey, S. L. and F. P. Robinson, *Psychology and the New Education.* New York, Harper and Brothers, 1944.

Robinson, F. P., *Effective Study.* New York, Harper and Brothers, 1946.

Tilton, J. W., *An Educational Psychology of Learning.* New York, The Macmillan Company, 1951.

Valentine, C. W., *Psychology and Its Bearing on Education.* New York, Philosophical Library, 1951.

Witty, P., ed., *The Gifted Child.* Boston, D. C. Heath & Company, 1951.

Social
Adjustments

CHAPTER 11

Man is born into a group, the family, and his growth is marked at every stage by direct and intimate contact with others. The nature of these contacts with others determines to what extent we will be shy or bold, cooperative or individualistic, boastful or modest, sympathetic or indifferent, and so on. At birth, and for many years thereafter, we depend on others for food, clothing, care, and a variety of other needs; and although we eventually outgrow this dependence, we will, for the rest of our life, be in continuing and close association with other people. Furthermore, our contacts widen as we grow up, a variety of relationships will develop, and the nature of many of our earlier relationships will change.

A child's social horizon expands as playmates and then schoolmates and teachers supplement his early family contacts. Soon he is meeting others—the neighbors, the milkman, the grocer, the minister. As he grows into adolescence and adulthood his circle of acquaintances widens to include co-workers and employers, people in various organizations that he may join, new friends. Dating, courtship, and then marriage become important areas of social interaction, involving a special kind of social adjustment.

The small child at first is apparently non-social; he does not distinguish himself from others. His self-awareness develops as he becomes aware of others, and his awareness of others increases as he learns to distinguish between them. In a comparatively short time the child's behavior begins to show a definite social coloring. He begins to perceive, to remember, to act and to feel with reference to others. As he grows older, he begins to develop understanding, sympathy, greater friendliness, concern, and affection for others. He learns that other people not only are physically different from him, but also that they have feelings, needs, and thoughts that are different from his.

The kind of relationship that is established between the child and his parents is very significant for the child's future social development, for a child learns from his parents certain basic attitudes that will govern his future dealings with other people and other institutions outside the family. The basic emotional patterns and attitudes found by the child in the family will be carried over into his relationships with other people, including eventually the child's own children after he has become an adult.

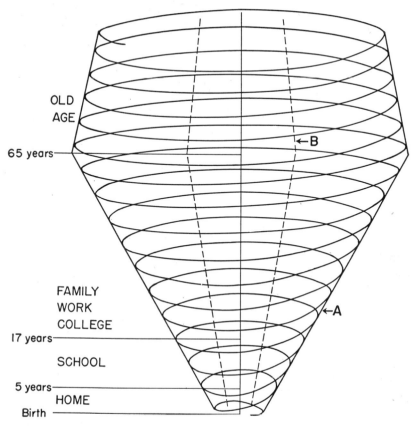

*The widening range of experience in normal development. As the child be-
comes an adolescent and then an adult, his range of experience and contact
with others widens. For some individuals, the increasing range may be a very
wide one (A). For others, the increasing range may be relatively narrow (B).*

For example, the child's reaction toward parental authority will
determine how the child as an adult will adjust to authority, such
as the policeman (representing law), or the teacher (representing
school), or the boss in the work situation.

Being aware of the importance of a child's early family experiences, psychologists emphasize the great importance of child
rearing. Childhood, one might say, is the golden age for preventive mental hygiene. During childhood the foundation of good

mental health is laid upon which we build, as we become older, the complex superstructure of our entire personality—the way we think, feel, and act.

It is probably safe to say that satisfactory and successful adult human relations start in infancy. Whether or not the child feels that he "belongs" to his family will determine to a large extent whether or not he feels that he belongs as an adult in relationships involving friends, acquaintances, co-workers, and other persons with whom he has to deal.

Some Characteristics of Social Relationships

Our social contacts with others differ from person to person. They may be casual or intimate, formal or informal, frequent or infrequent. We may feel very much at ease with one person, and tense with another. A certain acquaintance may always be gloomy and surly; another may always be congenial and charming. We seek out some people and avoid others. Our relationships to others, thus, are colored by all kinds of attitudes and emotional feelings.

But vary though they may, all social relationships are learned. A child learns how to behave towards parents, friends, strangers, and teachers. Indeed, the whole complicated process of living involves learning to adjust to new situations and experiences.

The essence of these social relationships is that they involve not only action and reaction, but also *interaction*. That is, our behavior influences another person's behavior and his behavior in turn influences ours. In conversation, for example, there is a continuous interaction and modification. What we say and do influences what the other person says and does, and this in turn modifies our behavior, to which the other person reacts again; and so we have a situation of mutual stimulation, of interaction. We also speak of this as a "feed-back" situation, in that our behavior is "fed back" to us by the reactions of the other person. The importance of proper feed-back is vividly illustrated when somebody calls you on the telephone and you are unable to identify his voice, although he seems to know you well. You are cautious, hesitant, uncertain, until you recognize who the other party is. Then your words flow more freely and you are more at ease. Or, you may have mistaken the caller for someone else and not realized your error until the end of the conversation. If you have, you may recall the uneasiness this discovery aroused. Even if you said nothing that may have been embarrassing, you still fear that your caller may have been offended by your formality or coolness, familiarity or flippancy, depending on whether you thought your caller was a close friend or a stranger.

The first example, inability to recognize a voice on the phone, is somewhat like meeting a person for the first time. At a party you are introduced to a stranger and then left alone with him. You have no idea what kind of person he is, except that, like you, he was invited to the same party by the same people. Usually you proceed rather cautiously, talking about neutral topics, groping for some common ground, hoping that his responses will provide you with some clues about his interests and attitudes. During this first exploratory meeting, you arrive at certain estimates about the person, sometimes called social expectancies. Sometimes they are correct; sometimes they are wrong, and if wrong, may lead you to make a whole series of mistaken judgments about the person later on.

If our estimates of a person have been incorrect, then obviously the behavior that person shows may surprise us, and we must be able to modify our own behavior in line with the revised estimate we must make of the other person. This does not mean that we should expect to be able to anticipate every gesture another person will make or every word he will say. But we can predict fairly accurately what his attitudes and behavior will be in certain situations. We expect balanced, objective advice from one person, efficient performance from another, grudging compliance from still another, and so on. We base these expectancies upon two main factors: (1) on the basis of past experience we have associated certain traits with certain people and know that each of these traits is relatively stable and enduring; (2) the other person knows what we expect of him; he has learned to anticipate what others expect of him and to act accordingly.

As we have mentioned previously, our expectations are not always realized; some persons disappoint us. Actually, when someone disappoints us, we may be at fault; we have been too generous in our estimate of that person. Some people consistently form a wrong opinion of others, and consequently are always disappointed. On the other hand, many times we are pleasantly surprised by the performance or behavior of someone from whom we expected little.

Once we form an estimate of a person it is difficult to change it. If someone has been inconsiderate to us in the past, we assume that he will be inconsiderate in the future toward us and toward all other people he meets, and this belief will persist even in the face of evidence to the contrary. Sisters and brothers who were hostile and jealous of one another in childhood often carry these attitudes over into their adult life. It often requires a major effort for the person to rid himself of such an emotional bias.

Communication

The learned aspect of social relations, their interactive effect, the expectancies, opinions, and estimates we form about the behavior of others—all are inseparably connected with the process of communication. In the absence of communication, especially communication by way of symbols, social and cultural life would be impossible. Socialization of the child, the transmission of social norms, and the transmission of our cultural heritage all are accomplished through communication.

However much definitions of communication may vary in detail, they all emphasize the interaction that occurs between the communicator—the person who initiates the communication—and the recipient—the person who receives the communication. Communication is a process whereby one person transmits stimuli

Gestures, postures, and facial expressions communicate, as is the case with the tired bakery worker in the top photo and the grief-stricken mother and child in the bottom photo.

(Top photo courtesy Izis Bidermanas. Bottom, World Wide Photos.)

of various kinds, usually verbal stimuli or symbols, designed to modify the behavior of another person or persons.

A few specific situations will illustrate for us the importance of communication. A college student's success or failure depends largely on how well he can communicate with others. It is not enough that he learn an assignment well; he must also be able to speak or write about it, to communicate his knowledge to the instructor. Furthermore, he must be able to communicate his knowledge in a variety of situations. Sometimes the student is quite capable of coaching a fellow student but cannot get the same information across when called upon to recite in class.

Importance of communication is further recognized by the person who finds himself in a country whose language is not familiar to him. He will be compelled to deal mainly only with those people who speak his own language, a very limited and perhaps nonrepresentative group of the country in which he finds himself. To some extent, he may be helped by observing carefully the dress, customs, and habits of the native inhabitants, but he will still be hampered by his inability to speak with them in their own idiom. With communication impaired, the opportunities for interacting are seriously limited.

Language is the main device through which people communicate, but other, nonverbal means are sometimes employed to express moods and attitudes. The shrug of resignation or doubt, the bowed head of despair or defeat, or the frown of anger sometimes are even more expressive than words. Other examples come easily to mind. Dance, sculpture, and painting are highly symbolic examples of communication and often convey very subtle cultural meanings.

But even people who speak the same language sometimes have difficulty communicating. The same words often mean different things to different people; the technique of language permits many different kinds of misunderstandings between communicator and communicatee. We all know that the same words may be interpreted quite differently by different persons because these persons have different experiences as the basis for interpreting these words. Often people who work together or belong to the same club or religious group speak a characteristic language. This will isolate others who do not understand the language and who lack the background of common experiences shared by those who belong to the group.   •

As already mentioned, we frequently communicate with another person because we want to support or modify his behavior. At times this modification may be slight and inconsequential, at others very pronounced. Whenever we try to persuade a person to change his plans or his beliefs we are attempting to modify his behavior. Conversely, whenever someone else tries to convince us to make a similar change, he is attempting to influence our behavior. The technique of communication employed here may vary from person to person and group to group. Advertising, for example, is a technique of mass communication by which hundreds, thousands, even millions of people may be reached, and in recent years advertising and propaganda have been refined to the point where they are very effective in bringing about changes in behavior or social change. Both involve a deliberate effort to control attitudes, either by inducing change or by convincing us not to change, to continue purchasing a certain product or line. The development of such media of communication as television and radio, the movies, and newspapers, has greatly extended the scope of advertising and propaganda.

In summary, we see that in our highly literate society communication plays a tremendously important role in the lives of all of us. Speaking, reading, and writing are our most important tools for interacting with others. It is important, therefore, to master the use of these tools to the best of our ability. Interference with the use of these tools will seriously hinder effective and satisfying social interaction. In many cases, in fact, it leads to almost complete social isolation and withdrawal. Disturbances in ability to communicate with others is also usually one of the first symptoms to appear in neuroses.

Roles of the Individual

The concept of role. Our expectancies regarding another person's behavior—expectancies that he recognizes and accepts —are significant aspects of the role that each person plays in a given situation. As we noted in the preceding chapter, people play a variety of roles every day of their lives. Some of these roles may be freely chosen; others may be forced upon them. A person may experiment with a number of different roles, discarding some, retaining others in accordance with his needs or with changes in his interest, work, place of residence, or friends.

The more roles a person can perform adequately, the better satisfied his ego will be. The woman who is a successful housewife, mother, and social and civic leader probably is happier and better adjusted than a woman who remains tied all day to household chores. But if a person tries to take on too many roles, conflict and confusion may result simply because he does not have enough time to play any of them well.

However, we must not assume from the above that the person who plays many roles is always better adjusted than the person who plays few. The final criterion of sound adjustment is the satisfaction a person gets from each role he plays. A person may be dissatisfied with his position for a number of reasons: (1) He may be forced to play a role that he dislikes because others expect him to play it; social pressure may compel him to assume a role against his will. (2) He may be afraid to play a role, and may, for example, become nervous and panicky if called upon to fill a position of responsibility. (3) He may not know how to play a role. Previous training or background may not have fitted him for the task that now confronts him. (4) His personality may be so rigid or compulsive that it prevents his playing the role called for by the particular situation in which he finds himself.

At times the behavior called for by one role may be quite different from that required by another and may create conflict in the individual. Or a person may have interests that place him in apparently contradictory roles, as would be the case with a clergyman who was also a horse-racing fan. The person who heard him preach on Sunday, playing the role of the minister, might be quite surprised to meet him at the race track on Monday, playing the role of the racing fan.

Contradictory demands of the culture concerning the roles we play create other problems. People going through a period of transition in which old ways of behaving must be discarded in favor of new ways more appropriate to new roles or status often experience conflict. Anyone who has read George Bernard Shaw's *Pygmalion* will never forget the anguish and tribulation that attended the slum-girl's efforts to learn the manners and attitudes of upper-class English society. The situation described in *Pygmalion* is the same that confronts the immigrant who must adapt to a new and alien culture. It also confronts, although to a lesser extent, the child of the immigrant who lives in the hold of "Old World culture" and grows up in the New World with a different culture. Conflict in roles between the home and the new country may provide many emotional problems.

Conflict also occurs when a person is forced to choose between friendship and obligations to a job or to society. He may wish to play at the same time the roles of good friend and impartial employer, with resultant emotional conflict. This type of role conflict is explored by Stauffer and Toby [1] who gave a paper-and-pencil questionnaire to a group of students at Harvard and Radcliffe. The questionnaire consisted of a few short stories and the students checked their responses to them. One of the stories with its responses is as follows:

> You are riding in a car driven by a close friend, and he hits a pedestrian. You know he was going at least 35 miles an hour in a 20 mile an hour speed zone. There are no other witnesses. His lawyer says that if you testify under oath that

[1] Samuel A. Stouffer and Jackson Toby, "Role Conflict and Personality," in Talcott Parsons and Edward A. Shils, eds., *Toward a General Theory of Action*. Cambridge, Mass., Harvard University Press, 1951, pp. 481-496.

the speed was only 20 miles an hour, it may save him from serious consequences.

What right has your friend to expect you to protect him? Check one: My friend has a definite right as a friend to expect me to testify to the lower figure.

He has some right as a friend to expect me to testify to the lower figure.

He has no right as a friend to expect me to testify to the lower figure.

What do you think you'd probably do in view of the obligation of a sworn witness and the obligation to your friend? Check one: Testify that he was going 20 miles an hour.

Not testify that he was going 20 miles an hour.

What decision would you make in this situation? As you may expect, the students gave different answers in line with their personal experiences, their personal values, and how they interpreted their role as friend and their role as a citizen wishing to abide by certain laws and social responsibilities. This and many other similar situations involving value judgments force us to make decisions and so often produce conflicts. The individual may meet these conflicts in a variety of ways. He may repress some of his experiences, rationalize his actions, compartmentalize different beliefs and values. These and other mechanisms to which a person may resort in order to escape from conflict situations that he cannot resolve satisfactorily are discussed in detail in Chapter 6.

Although each one of us plays a variety of different roles, these multiple roles usually display certain characteristics in common. Out of the totality of roles that each one of us plays, and out of the factors that these roles have in common, we develop an image of ourself—our self-concept.

Differences in Social Situations

Although a person may know exactly how to act in some situations, in others he may be less clear about how to proceed.

We face a situation with less anxiety if we have a clear understanding of what is expected of us and what we are to do. Teachers know that if they make vague assignments their students are quick to ask just what is expected of them—how many pages they should turn in, what form they should follow, when it is due, how it will be evaluated, and so on. The students may not like the rigid, detailed assignment, but at least they will know exactly what is expected of them.

There are certain behavior patterns that we call habits of etiquette or of good manners that facilitate social relations. Once we have learned them they save us embarrassment and the trouble of making decisions about a number of relatively minor points of social behavior. Proper manners and conduct often are an index of social status. The person who does not know how to introduce two people to one another, who speaks coarsely or insultingly, who uses his dessert fork during the fish course, clearly does not "belong." Such seemingly minor breaches of etiquette may greatly upset a person who is trying to move a few pegs up the social ladder.

For some persons the formalized behavior of certain manners becomes a protective shell with which they ward off all intimate social relationships. We never get to know them any better than on the day we first met them. They withdraw into formal, polite behavior as into a shell, avoiding any topic of conversation that is not neutral, that calls for some intellectual or emotional commitment. They are like salespeople who have been trained to respond with stereotyped answers to various requests and inquiries. They take their cues from the other person's comment and answer with a prepared statement that best fits the cue. You get the feeling that as far as their conversation is concerned a recording would do just as well.

We find ourselves in many familiar situations in which we know exactly how to act or what to expect. But what about situations that are new to us, unstructured situations for which past experiences provides no behavioral clue? We have previously spoken of the "social fencing" that takes place when we meet a stranger. But here we have at least the framework of polite social intercourse to guide us, so this is one of the least troublesome of the emergencies that arise. How do you behave when you suddenly hear a burglar in your own home? If a fire breaks out what do you do? For the policeman, or the fireman, such questions are not too troublesome because he has been trained to meet such situations. But for us, they are vital, for an emergency often will evoke indecision, anxiety, or even panic.

In organized groups behavior is usually more clearly defined than in small informal groups. The more highly organized the group, the more formal its structure and the more impersonal the reactions of the persons involved. The formal group prescribes and channels activities. On the other hand, the small informal group generally permits freedom and range for interaction. In the formal group, behavior is determined by the group rather than by the individual; in the small group, behavior is determined by the individual rather than by the group.

Individual Differences and Social Contacts

Some people prefer solitude. They may have interests that they can pursue satisfactorily by themselves. Or, if they are insecure or suffer from an inferiority complex, they may fear to meet or mingle with others. Having a low opinion of themselves they fear that others will come to share this low opinion. Therefore, they keep to themselves. At the other extreme are those who constantly seek companionship, as if in so doing they may escape from themselves. They crave sympathy or praise or acceptance from others, but often give very little in return. Because they are unable to give of themselves in social situations, they antagonize others and thus intensify further their need for acceptance.

Reciprocal Gratification in Social Relations

Social interaction is most satisfying if it provides a balanced reciprocal gratification of the needs of the individuals involved. The person who approaches others with the idea of trying to get all he can violates this principle of reciprocity, as does the person who seems to be always giving, who creates in others a sense of obligation because they cannot respond likewise. However, the give and get ratio is not one that we can measure precisely in terms of percentages. In business and politics we can trade work and favors—if you help me paint my house I'll help you put in your lawn, or if you support me in this action I'll see to it that you get that contract. But the more personal and intimate social relations do not lend themselves to bargaining. There are two main reasons for this. First, in a good friendship or happy marriage relation we are so concerned about the welfare and happiness of the other person that his joy and his sorrow are ours. The happiness we give to the other we give to ourselves. The outstanding characteristic of friendship, or of love, is that it is other-oriented, rather than self-oriented. Secondly, where marriage or friendship is involved, you and I become a "we." A community of interests and needs is established, and whatever is given to it is given to both. In this sense, psychologically speaking, a person receives by giving.

Because of his helplessness, the child, in his early years especially, is on the receiving side of the child-parent relationship. He needs physical care and attention and cannot give much in return. But the parents usually are so captivated by the child and get such pleasure from seeing him grow and develop that they are compensated for the time and energy they spend on him. But if a child becomes a burden or a nuisance to his parents, their resentment toward him may take the form of increasingly heavy demands made upon him as he grows up. And each unfulfilled demand may bring forth the familiar cry—"And after all I've done for you!"

Needs Satisfied by Social Interaction

Social interaction is satisfying when it meets some of the needs of the individuals involved; it is unsatisfactory if these needs are thwarted. The question then arises: What are the needs satisfied by social relationships?

Perhaps the outstanding social need of the individual is his need to "belong." We have pointed out previously that in his early life a child's sheer physical survival depends on others. In addition, his emotional security is closely tied in with other people's attitudes toward him. The child who feels rejected, and who out of this rejection develops feelings of hostility and aggressiveness toward others, obviously develops attitudes toward people that are quite different from those of the child who is accepted and loved and who in turn accepts and loves others.

From the family group, the child extends his contacts to the play group. Again the need to belong is the impelling force, and a child is crushed, bewildered, hurt if other children won't play with him. The need to belong to some group is probably one of the motivating factors in the formation of gangs. Adult men and women, trying to satisfy the need to belong, join all kinds of organizations.

To some groups we belong through no choice of our own; we are born into them. Thus we belong to a certain family, a certain state, perhaps a certain minority group. But there are many other groups we join because of affectional bonds, because of common interests, or because of the prestige or status they symbolize. There are also some groups to which we would like to belong, but from which we are excluded, just as there are some groups with which we do not care to be identified.

When an individual belongs to a group he feels that what is important to him is also important to others in the group, and vice versa. Thus the group and the person provide reciprocal support for one another. It is an interacting relationship, imbuing the person with a feeling of acceptance, a reassurance that he belongs.

Group values and personal values may differ. A person may feel uncomfortable in the group. Although he is physically a part of the group, he may be emotionally or psychologically isolated. Noting this isolation, he may withdraw from the group, he may

The child who is re-
jected and ridiculed by
his peers may grow
hostile and aggressive
toward others. The
child who is accepted
and welcomed by his
peers will accept and
welcome others.

(Top photo courtesy Look
Magazine. Bottom, cour-
tesy H. Armstrong Roberts
and American Stock
Photos.)

attempt to change the group in line with his needs, or he may modify his own needs.

If the need to belong is very strong in humans, fear of social isolation is just as potent. Ostracism is often used to rebuke or bring individuals into line. Prison authorities will tell you that many convicts fear solitary confinement above all other forms of punishment. William James has said that "No more fiendish pun-. ishment could be devised, were such a thing physically possible, than that one should be turned loose in society and remain abso- lutely unnoticed by all members thereof."

Homans [2] maintains that:

> If there is one truth that modern psychology has estab- lished, it is that an *isolated* individual is sick. He is sick in mind: he will exhibit disorders of behavior, emotion, and thought; he may, as psychosomatic medicine teaches, be sick in body besides. Perhaps, it is better to say that he will have an impaired capacity for maintaining his personal equilib- rium under the ordinary shocks of life. This does not mean that, for health, he must be a member of any particular group: not every group will be good for him. It does mean that unless he is a fully accepted member of *some* group—a family, a group of friends, a group of fellow workers—he will be in trouble. And perhaps we need not require him to be a fully accepted member of a group at any particular time but only to have been a member at *some* time. A person who has always been isolated may be less able to bear continued isolation than a person who has once known something very different.

> To escape isolation, a person must be able to become a member of a group, and that is not just a problem of finding the group. The capacity for relating one's self to other men and women is not inborn but a result of experience and train- ing, and that experience and training is itself social. It begins early in the family, where the child learns the basic impera- tives of his society.

[2] George C. Homans, *The Human Group*. New York, Harcourt, Brace and Company, Inc., 1950, pp. 313-314.

The isolated person is a sick person. Consider the case of the psychotic. He may be with others and he may be talking to others, but he is not communicating with them. Even the skilled therapist has difficulty in establishing contact with him.

The ability to make friends is therefore a very important skill necessary for good mental health and satisfactory personal adjustment. Where we find a person who cannot make friends, we usually find an unhappy, disturbed individual.

A member of a minority group often becomes frustrated because, although "he belongs," he is prevented by prejudice from reaching some of the goals that he considers worth while. Such frustration may express itself in self-hatred, in hatred for his family, or in hatred for the group. Sociologists and social psy-

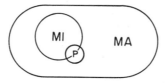

The marginal man is the person, **P,** *standing on the boundary line between the minority group,* **MI,** *and the majority group,* **MA.** *(From Lewin,* Resolving Social Conflicts, *p. 181.)*

chologists speak of the "marginal man," the person who is not sure where he belongs or who is prevented from choosing the group to which he would like to belong. Although the term "marginal man" usually is used to refer to individuals who are members of different cultural groups, it may also be applied to people who are going through a period of transition. The late Kurt Lewin has used these words to describe the conflicts that often confront young people who are passing from childhood into adolescence. An adolescent is standing on the boundary between groups. The adolescent, for example, is no longer a member of the children's group but is not yet fully accepted in the adult group. Or to look at it another way, at one time the adolescent is still regarded as a child, at another time he is expected to be an adult. This obviously creates conflict situations in the adolescent and a confusion of values, some of which are part of the child group, others of the adult group. It is because of this conflict that we find fluctuations of behavior so common in adolescents, such as a swing from overtimidity and shyness to overaggressiveness and hostility.

We have pointed out already that individuals join groups for a variety of reasons. Actually this means that a number of different needs are involved rather than the single need "to belong." Perhaps we should speak of the need to belong as a means by which other needs are satisfied, instead of as a separate need.

Before examining some of the motives that impel people to join various groups, let us first make an analysis of a specific group. You may try to do the same with some group to which you belong. You must remember, however, in analyzing needs that are fulfilled by belonging to a group, that one must make inferences about the needs from the behavior observed; and as we know, the same behavior may express different motivation for different individuals.

The particular group we shall consider consists of 15 people who have been brought together through a common concern about problems of war and peace. It has been in existence for only a short time and has no formal structure or affiliation with other groups, except that a discussion leader is chosen for each meeting and its members are pacifists. Why did the members form this group? In general they feel themselves to be a minority group because of their pacifist beliefs. Being pacifists, they are considered odd by many of the people with whom they work, and even by some members of their own families. Some of them feel isolated in their normal daily activities and seek out others of like mind to reinforce their need for *acceptance*. Among those who share their ideas they do not have to be on guard continually or to defend their beliefs at every turn.

Closely tied in with the need for acceptance is the need for *support*. One person, for example, comments that he wishes some members of the group would go with him to another meeting that he attends regularly. He is the only pacifist in that group and he needs the support of some others once in a while to counter anti-pacifist arguments. Actually, what he means is not so much help in numbers, but emotional support, the feeling that he will not be alone when he takes a stand.

Others have joined the group hoping to improve their ability to discuss and debate current problems. The question frequently heard at the meetings is: What do you *say* to people, how do you answer their arguments?

Many have joined because they are confused by the pace of modern living, by the variety of conflicting demands they are called upon to face daily. Within the confines of their small group they exchange ideas with others, gain a new perspective on their problems, become stimulated to work their way through their un-certainty. For them the group has a *problem-solving* function.

But a person desiring prestige and status would hardly turn to a small, inconspicuous group such as this. If eligible, he would undoubtedly seek admission to a professional organization or honorary society, in part because membership requires a certain amount of intellectual competence and certain academic qualifi-cations, in part because many prominent people belong. Both these considerations make for a certain degree of exclusiveness that adds to the prestige value of the group.

Such organizations also frequently satisfy the individual's need for *recognition*. He may deliver a paper or an address to a con-vention, may become a member of the governing board, may get his work published in a professional journal, may win an award from grateful, appreciative colleagues. Every person must have a sense of personal worth, and in large part this comes from being recognized by others. For some, the greatest punishment is to be ignored.

Some writers believe that the desire for status is the funda-mental principle of social interaction. Thus Jameson [3] writes:

---

[3] Samuel Haig Jameson, "Principles of Social Interaction," *American Socio-logical Review,* Vol. 10, 1944, 6-12.

The desire to gain status, and if found satisfactory, to retain the gained status is universal among the members of the human species and their aggregates. There are no status-less human gatherings; status is the most universal and essential aspect of culture, created by man through his interactions, used by him in his interactions, and transmitted to his contemporaries and successors by means of interaction.

We may or we may not consider the desire for status universal. But we must recognize that much of human behavior is status-motivated and the desire for status influences one person's attitude toward others. This is illustrated by the story about the little southern girl who remarked, after the one Negro family in town had moved away, "Now we don't have anybody to be better than."

To bring this section to a close, let us turn for a moment to some needs that may be satisfied within the intimate family or friendship group. Probably the most important need that can be satisfied through such primary contacts is the *need for love and affection,* and this means essentially an unqualified acceptance that makes a person feel emotionally secure. Unqualified acceptance means that we know that love and affection will be forthcoming regardless of specific behavior. For the child it means that even if he disobeys occasionally he will not lose the love of his parents. Their affection is not something that is given or withheld according to the way he behaves himself. For the child, it also means physical security, and this aspect is not altogether absent in adult relationships.

Thus, when crisis and hardships arise, we are confident that our close friends or family will help out if they can.

The love and affection of a close friend or relative engenders trust and makes it much easier for us to accept criticism from him than from a relative stranger. Often the same sort of trust and confidence marks business partnerships, or partnerships involving creative artists. The partners may differ at times, but their basic relationship is not threatened.

Again, the way in which the need for affection is satisfied initially will have a decisive influence on the individual's later affection for others. In considering how an adult reaches for or expresses affection, it is well to remember the affectional relationship between the child and his mother. From this relationship, the child learns to relate to other members of the family—to the father, to brothers and sisters, or to other near relatives who are frequently part of the family. If the child's relations with his mother are warm and emotionally satisfying, these are the relationships he is likely to have with other persons; if his relationships with his mother are cool and distant, then this is probably the way he will react to other persons. Out of the first affectional relations between mother and child comes the basis for later affectional attachments to playmates, colleagues, and many other adults with whom we have occasion to interact.

None of the needs that we have been discussing can be satisfied in social isolation. They can be fulfilled only through our everyday relations with others.

The Individual as a Group Member

The individual who joins a group does so because he believes that by participating in its activities, by meeting other people, he will be able to satisfy some of his needs. The members of the group, in turn, expect that he will contribute in some way

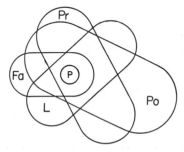

The person as a member of several overlapping groups. P—person; Fa— family; Pr—professional group; L—luncheon club; Po—political party. (From Kurt Lewin, Resolving Social Conflicts. New York, Harper and Brothers, 1948, p. 85.)

to their individual welfare and common goal. It is rather common for someone trying to interest another in a group to which he belongs to say: "I am sure you have a great deal to give to the group, and I think that you would enjoy meeting some of the people in it and taking part in our activities." Discussing group functions as they relate to members' needs, it is well to remember that different members may satisfy different needs through membership in a single group, but in general each member receives satisfactions related to such needs as involve social recognition, protection against threats, satisfaction of sexual pleasures, satisfaction of the need for recognition and prestige, and satisfaction of the need to participate and create something.

It is well, keeping these functions of the group in mind, to evaluate more explicitly those groups to which we belong in order to understand better what we expect from these groups and what we contribute to them. As we know, when an individual becomes conscious of a need or goal, he attempts to satisfy it. Thus, the behavior of groups, comprised of goal-oriented individuals, is goal-directed. Sometimes the goals are explicitly stated and the individual commits himself to them by signing a pledge. At other times, the goals are implicitly understood. But whether the goals are explicitly stated or rather vague, the group always has some direction, some purpose for existing.

Related to their functions, groups develop various kinds of structure. This structure may be quite formal with elected or appointed officers, or it may be merely a loose association of people bound together by common ideas and aims. The formal structure of a group and its psychological structure are not necessarily the same. The person, for example, who is chairman of the group may have less influence on the behavior of the members than somebody who holds no official position. Likewise, somebody who is very popular is not always elected to a position of responsibility. We see thus an interaction of organizational and personal factors in the group influencing the individual members. Initially, the position of different members may be in a state of flux, but as the group develops each person's position becomes more definite.

These positions will generally vary in status and prestige. This is true even in groups that stress equality in membership.

Various criteria may be used in assigning different roles to members of the group—age, sex, social position, particular abilities, or general achievement and competence. Or group roles may be decided in terms of dominance and submission. Some members of the group will gradually assume a dominant role as they lead the discussion or influence the group to take a certain stand or position on certain matters. They make the decisions; they lead the others. The submissive member, on the other hand, is the one who accepts decisions without actually having taken an active part in arriving at them, who does the task assigned to him rather than suggest tasks for others to do. Or the respective positions of group members may depend on the particular situation or activity the group happens to be engaged in. One member may have had long experience in raising funds and will assume the lead in organizing the group's campaign for donations. Another, having been in the theater, will take the lead in organizing the club's annual dramatic presentation, and so on. The status a person has in a group will influence, of course, the amount of weight we attach to his statements, or the amount of influence he can exert upon other persons.

Power in a group may be very unevenly divided. This is especially true of authoritarian groups where power is concentrated in the hands of a few individuals who make all the decisions. Although an individual or individuals may usurp power, it may also be tendered to them by others of the group for whom submission to authority, or escape from freedom, constitutes psychological security, and frees them from the necessity of facing problems and making decisions.

Except in situations of absolute authoritarianism, the relation between the leader and the led is always a social interaction; that is, the action of the leader influences the behavior of the group and his behavior is in turn modified and influenced by the demands of the members of the group.

Many attempts have been made to list the requisites of good

leadership, but this presents a difficult task because they appear to differ according to the kinds of situation or groups in which different leaders function. In a broad sense, of course, the best leader in the group would appear to be the person who serves to satisfy best the needs of the group members. In other words, the person most valued or best followed would be the one who can help each member of the group achieve his goal in the group. A leader thus must know the needs of the group members in order to work for their achievement.

Responsibility and Social Relations

As a member of a group, a person has certain rights and certain responsibilities. The acceptance of *responsibility* is an important characteristic of social relations.

Responsibility involves being able to understand the other person's needs, to be able to put ourself in someone else's place. This type of sensitivity is called empathy. Often, by putting ourselves in another person's place, we come to understand him better, to appreciate his viewpoint, and thus to clarify the problems or conflicts that have sprung up between us. A technique for helping us to get into the other person's place involves taking his part, that is, playing his role as we see it in a particular situation. This role-playing technique is utilized frequently in leadership training programs and involves putting each member of the group into the leadership position and having him play the role of leader as he sees it. The role-playing technique is also utilized in group psychotherapy sessions in which a mother may be asked to play the role of her daughter, or the role of the father. The technique, of course, has its limitations because putting ourselves into the role of someone else is, in the final analysis, not really having to be that person permanently as he is. For example, we might try to play the role of the person who has a speech difficulty and encounter momentarily all the embarrassment and frustration of the stutterer, but knowing that we can stop stuttering when we wish probably makes considerable difference in how we interpret our role as compared with a stutterer who is not able to stop when he wishes.

A socially responsible person also will consider the long-range effects of his behavior. Giving food to a hungry person will satisfy his hunger; it is an act that is essential. But to continue a condition where the person becomes dependent on such handouts, rather than to help him help himself, is irresponsible.

Social responsibility for some persons is confined only to those who are very close to them, such as members of the family and perhaps friends. Others have a sense of responsibility that includes all mankind—people of different nationalities, refugees from disaster, and so on. We see thus that different persons have different ranges of responsibility, or different ranges of empathy, as part of their social behavior.

Social Participation

A sense of responsibility can develop only if an individual feels that he can be effective in his social relations. If he feels that whatever he does his behavior will have little to do with the final outcome, his concern for others will die stillborn. But if he believes that he can influence the outcome of certain events, such as creating a new community facility, or contributing to a new national policy or program, and if he is concerned about or vitally interested in these events, he will then feel it worth his while to participate with others for the achievement of such ends. And the stronger the person feels about the activities in which he engages, the more active and intense is his participation likely to be.

Some people, of course, are appalled at the complexity or modern life and at the bewildering variety of forces that seem to spring up to challenge them every day. They feel often, too, that their efforts may have little or no effect on what goes on around them either at the local level, the state level, the national level, or the international level. It is well to remember, however, that it is our individual decisions and judgments, regardless of the level at which they are made, and those of hundreds and thousands and millions of other persons like us, that bring about the total effect for each of us. It is well, therefore, to remember that we have a responsibility to ourselves and to our fellow man to do what we can, each of us as an individual, to help clarify a problem at the local level, to do what we can to remove prejudice, to help reduce hate, and to help to bring knowledge, understanding, insight, and appreciation into all our activities and social interactions.

For Additional Reading

Allport, Gordon W., "The Psychology of Participation," *Psychological Review,* Vol. 53, 1945, 117-132.
Asch, Solomon, *Social Psychology.* New York, Prentice-Hall, Inc., 1953.
Bales, Robert F., *Interaction Process Analysis.* Cambridge, Mass., Addison-Wesley Press, 1951.
Chisholm, George B., "Social Responsibility," *Journal of Social Issues,* Supplement Series No. 1, December 1948, 6-13.
Hartley, Eugene L. and Ruth E. Hartley, *Fundamentals of Social Psychology.* New York, Alfred A. Knopf, Inc., 1952.
Homans, George C., *The Human Group.* New York, Harcourt, Brace & Company, Inc., 1950.
Hovland, Carl I., "Social Communication," in Bernard Berelson and Morris Janowitz, eds., *Reader in Public Opinion and Communication.* Glencoe, Ill., The Free Press, 1953.
Jameson, Samuel Haig, "Principles of Social Interaction," *American Sociological Review,* Vol. 10, 1944, 6-12.
Kardiner, Abram, *The Psychological Frontiers of Society.* New York, Columbia University Press, 1945.
Katz, Daniel, "Psychological Barriers to Communication," in W. H. Yeager and W. E. Utterback, "Communication and Social Action," *Annals of the American Academy of Political and Social Science,* Philadelphia, 1947.
Katz, Daniel, D. Cartwright, S. Eldersveld, and A. McClung Lee, *Public Opinion and Propaganda.* New York, The Dryden Press, 1954.
Krech, David and Richard S. Crutchfield, *Theory and Problems of Social Psychology.* New York, McGraw-Hill Book Company, Inc., 1948.
Kurt, Lewin, *Field Theory in Social Science,* edited by Dorwin Cartwright. New York, Harper and Brothers, 1951.
Lippitt, Ronald, *Training in Community Relations.* New York, Harper and Brothers, 1949.

Maier, Norman R. F., *Principles of Human Relations.* New York, John Wiley & Sons, Inc., 1952.

Mannheim, Karl, *Freedom, Power and Democratic Planning.* New York, Oxford University Press, 1950.

Marrow, Alfred J., *Living Without Hate. Scientific Approaches to Human Relations.* New York, Harper and Brothers, 1951.

Miller, James G., *Experiments in Social Process—A Symposium on Social Psychology.* New York, McGraw-Hill Book Company, Inc., 1950.

Murphy, Gardner, *An Introduction to Psychology.* New York, Harper and Brothers, 1951.

Newcomb, Theodore M. and Eugene L. Hartley, eds., *Readings in Social Psychology.* New York, Henry Holt & Company, Inc.,1947.

Parsons, Talcott and Edward A. Shils, eds., *Toward a General Theory of Action.* Cambridge, Mass., Harvard University Press, 1951.

Career
and
Job Adjustment

CHAPTER 12

- CHOICE OF A JOB
- TRANSITION FROM SCHOOL TO WORK
- ANXIETY ON THE JOB
- JOB SATISFACTION
- CONDITIONS FOR HIGH MORALE WITHIN A WORK PLANT

Before taking a job, a young person should ask himself two simple questions: "What kind of work do I like?" and "What kind of work can I do well?" These questions are important for several reasons. First of all, we will spend most of our adult life working; and for our own peace of mind, as well as that of others, we should, insofar as possible, settle on a job in which we will be reasonably successful and happy. For if we are frustrated and discontented with our work, we will be irritable and annoyed not only with ourselves, but also with friends, associates, and family.

Also, except for the few of you who will have independent incomes, your livelihood will depend on your job. The kind of job you take will determine your standard of living, the things you will be able to afford beyond the mere necessities of life.

Finally, your work will be an important aspect of your social identity. Frequently one of the first questions we ask about another person is: "What does he do? What is his job?" In our society, occupational status determines to a large extent a person's socio-economic status, the kinds of friends and associates he has, the prestige he carries, the role he plays in his community.

And a person's job is most important to his self-concept, to the image he forms of himself. If he is successful in his work, he will be confident and self-assured. If he is plodding along in a dreary position without hope of promotion, if he sees friends reaching the top while he remains in an occupational rut, he will become defeatist, easily discouraged, and a prey to all sorts of doubts and misgivings about himself.

Our job, then, performs various complex functions in our lives and serves many different needs. Consequently, a person should consider and weigh all factors carefully down to a specific occupation. If possible, he should try a few different jobs in an effort to find one that will satisfy at least some of his needs.

Choice of a Job

Influences orienting us to the world of work. How do we choose a job? What factors affect our choice? These are the first questions we shall consider in some detail.

To begin with, we do not suddenly decide on a particular job without giving the matter any advanced thought. In fact, during our adolescence we have been exposed, through family, school, and friends, not so much perhaps to specific jobs, but to certain attitudes toward work, to certain value judgments about different kinds of work. We have had a chance to discover some of our interests and to explore our abilities. We have found our own preferences and have learned what others expect of us. Many of us, perhaps, have already held part-time jobs during the school year or have worked full-time during the summer vacations. And if these jobs have been varied, we have had a chance to discover some of the things we can or cannot do well, the kind of social relationships we might expect in different jobs, and the sort of frustrations and satisfactions each job has to offer. Through all these influences and experiences we become oriented in the occupational field. By the time we reach the point where we must decide on a full-time job, we may not know exactly which job to choose but we may at least have eliminated those we feel would definitely not suit us.

Developmental aspects of vocational choice. As children, many of us wanted to be firemen, policemen, nurses. During our adolescence, we may have changed our minds and decided to become pilots, teachers, or professional golfers. As adults, we may settle on something entirely different. These changes reflect our growing awareness of ourselves and the world around us. As children, from about six to eleven, we make "fantasy choices." We choose activities that appear pleasurable and attractive, ignoring all other aspects of the occupations of which these activities are a part. In early and late adolescence, we make "tentative choices" in which the question of interest is still paramount, but where we also ask ourselves, "Can I do it?" "Am I suited for it?" By this time, we have had a chance to analyze to some extent and to gain a more realistic picture of what certain occupations demand. Finally, as adults, we make a "realistic choice," in most cases, that is. We consider a job in relation to other preferences and other demands. Perhaps we shall have to weigh our desire to stay in our hometown where job opportunities may be very limited against the necessity of leaving for another part of the country where job opportunities are plentiful. Or, we may have to choose between a job that will fulfill a lifelong ambition to travel or one that will realize our wish to become independent of family support as soon as possible. The job we finally do choose is likely to represent a compromise between various needs and wishes and available opportunities.[1]

---
[1] Eli Ginzberg, Sol W. Ginsburg, Sidney Axelrad, and John L. Herma, *Occupational Choice. An Approach to a General Theory.* New York, Columbia University Press, 1951.

Major factors influencing occupational choice. Choice is, in many respects, a matter of conscious and deliberate decision. However, many of the factors that enter into vocational choice are so subtle that we ourselves are not aware of them and cannot communicate them to others. Motivation is complex and our difficulty in understanding the process of vocational choice is further complicated by the fact that motivational forces influence different people in different ways.

However, three major sets of factors may be distinguished in the process of vocational choice: (1) social-psychological factors, (2) personal factors, and (3) factors characterizing the job itself and the labor market.

SOCIAL-PSYCHOLOGICAL FACTORS. Often a person's vocational plans are influenced by his parents' attitudes. Some parents make the task of choosing a job easier for their children and insure that the children will be happy in the job they do choose by encouraging them to reach their own decisions about which jobs to take and by helping them to appraise their abilities and chances for particular jobs realistically. Other parents, however, may try to dictate the jobs their children take, regardless of any aptitudes or preferences the children show or express. A doctor who looks upon his profession as the finest in the world may try to convince his son to follow in his footsteps, even though the boy may not have the slightest interest in medicine. Or a mother, frightened lest her son become a writer, as he wishes, may try to convince him to become a lawyer because of the social prestige and importance that usually attaches to a career in law. Of course, it sometimes happens that children are happy in careers their parents have chosen for them, but usually not, particularly if they have no interest in the work or can develop none.

Family background influences occupational choice in other ways. The socio-economic position of the family determines, to a considerable extent, the jobs children choose or set their sights on. In his book, *Elmtown's Youth,* Hollingshead queried high-school students about their vocational goals and found that these

CHART 1

VOCATIONAL CHOICES OF ELMTOWN HIGH-SCHOOL STUDENTS FROM THE UPPER-MIDDLE, LOWER-MIDDLE, UPPER-LOWER, AND LOWER-LOWER CLASSES (CLASSES II, III, IV, AND V RESPECTIVELY)

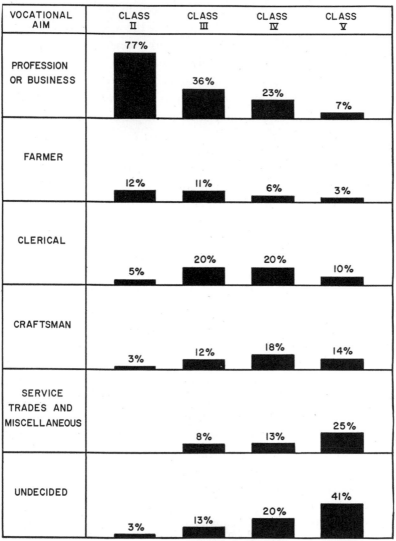

VOCATIONAL AIM	CLASS II	CLASS III	CLASS IV	CLASS V
PROFESSION OR BUSINESS	77%	36%	23%	7%
FARMER	12%	11%	6%	3%
CLERICAL	5%	20%	20%	10%
CRAFTSMAN	3%	12%	18%	14%
SERVICE TRADES AND MISCELLANEOUS		8%	13%	25%
UNDECIDED	3%	13%	20%	41%

(Reprinted with permission from A. B. Hollingshead, Elmtown's Youth, 1949, John Wiley & Sons, Inc., p. 286.)

goals reflected, on the whole, the social class of the parents. Chart
1 depicts the relationship between class and vocational desires.
There is a striking decrease in the choice of professional and business careers from the upper-middle to the lower-lower class, with
77 per cent in the former and 7 per cent in the latter choosing
such careers. What happens here is that the young person is exposed, not to all of society, but only to a certain segment of it.
Within that segment, he hears only about particular kinds of occupations, those typical of his class, and comes to accept almost as a
matter of course that eventually he too will some day be working
at the same kind of job, that such a progression is normal and
inevitable.[2]

It is also interesting to note that as we descend the social scale
in Chart 1, we find more children undecided about their careers.
Only 3 per cent in Class II have not made up their minds, but 41
per cent in Class V are undecided.

We mentioned a few pages back that parents would do well to
help their children appraise their chances for getting particular
jobs. Many young people set their aspirations far beyond what
they can hope to achieve. Miller and Form report a study [3] comparing the occupational choices of male students in their twelfth
year of school with the occupational achievement of students who
graduated six years earlier. Assuming that the aspirations of the
earlier and later graduates were similar, we notice a considerable
discrepancy between choice and achievement. The findings (presented in Table 1) show that although slightly over 50 per cent
of the students still in school aspire to professional jobs, only 14
per cent of the graduates actually hold such jobs. Another disparity is to be found in the clerical jobs. Only about 5 per cent
of the twelfth-graders chose some clerical occupation fields, but
more than 20 per cent of the graduates work in some clerical
capacity. We shall discuss this gap between aspiration and achieve-

---

[2] August B. Hollingshead, *Elmtown's Youth. The Impact of Social Classes on Adolescents.* New York, John Wiley & Sons, Inc., 1949, pp. 284-287.
[3] Delbert C. Miller and William H. Form, *Industrial Sociology.* New York, Harper and Brothers, 1951.

ment more fully later in the chapter when we consider the factors that make for work satisfaction. It is enough to say here that in this gap lies one of the chief causes of occupational frustration and discontent.

TABLE 1

A COMPARISON OF THE OCCUPATIONAL CHOICES OF THE MALES IN THE CLASS OF 1937 WITH THE ACTUAL JOBS ON WHICH THE CLASS OF 1931 IS ENGAGED *

Occupational classification	Occupational choices 12th-year males, 1937 per cent	Occupations of male graduates class of 1931 per cent	Percentage differences between choices and jobs obtained
Professional	52.6	14.1	− 38.5
Public Service	1.9	3.3	+ 1.4
Trade	8.9	19.9	+ 9.0
Clerical	4.8	20.3	+ 15.5
Transport and Communication	5.9	3.8	− 2.1
Manufacturing and Mechanical Industry	22.9	35.7	+ 12.8
Extraction of Minerals	.9	.8	− .1
Agriculture	1.9	.4	− 1.5
Domestic and Personal Service	.2	1.7	+ 1.5
Totals	100.0	100.0	

— indicates excess of choice over fulfillment.
+ indicates excess of jobs secured but not desired by choice.

* Adapted from the Canton, Ohio, High School Survey, 1938, by Delbert C. Miller and William H. Form, *Industrial Sociology*, p. 591.

Usually we approach a job, any job, in terms of the factors that we believe will determine success in that particular occupation. If we believe that sheer ability is all that is required to succeed, and if we are confident that we possess that ability, then we may try to pursue the occupation in spite of social and financial difficulties. If, on the other hand, we believe that ability is of minor importance and that influence and connections are the determining factors, we may try to cultivate the "right" acquaintances and make the correct contacts. Or, we may accept defeat from the start and never give a second thought to that particular profession.

Centers [4] has found some rather striking differences in attitudes toward occupational stratification and success. In a survey of a representative cross-section of the adult white male population, he asked, "Do you think that most people are successful because of ability, luck, pull, or the better opportunities they have had?" Of those interviewed, 45.1 per cent said "ability" without qualification, and another 14 per cent mentioned ability plus luck or pull or opportunity. However, he also found pronounced differences in the attitudes expressed by people in different occupational levels (see Table 2). Among executives of large corporations, 62 per cent said "ability," without qualification, but only 26 per cent of the unskilled laborers approached agreed with the executives. Reading from the bottom to the top occupational levels, we see a steadily increasing number who believe that ability or ability plus is the determining factor in success. At the same time, fewer and fewer say that luck or pull or better opportunities account for success, the percentage decreasing from 5.7 per cent in the semi-skilled group to zero in the executive group.

We are not concerned here with whether these beliefs actually do indicate the factors most responsible for occupational success. Rather, we are interested in the fact that such beliefs do influence our levels of aspiration.

Although all kinds of work are essential to the functioning of our economy, it is also clear that different kinds of work carry different social prestige. When we ask people to rank occupations, we find that they ascribe the highest rank to the professions and to business executive positions, an intermediate rank to the skilled trades, technical occupations, and those in the distribution field, and the lowest rank to the semi-skilled and unskilled occupations.[5] On the whole, the same rank is assigned to these occupations by all members of society, regardless of their position in the occupational hierarchy. However, a few studies have shown that

---

[4] Richard Centers, "Attitude and Belief in Relation to Occupational Stratification," *Journal of Social Psychology,* Vol. 27, 1938, 159-185.

[5] Maethel E. Deeg and D. G. Paterson, "Changes in Social Status of Occupations," *Occupations,* Vol. 25, 1947, 265-268.

TABLE 2

ATTITUDES OF OCCUPATIONAL STRATA: WHY PEOPLE SUCCEED [*]

	N	Ability %	Ability plus other data %	Luck %	Pull %	Better opportunities %	Combination of luck, pull, and opportunities %	Don't know %	For abilities differences are significant between:
National	1,092	45.1	14.4	6.1	7.5	20.3	2.8	3.8	A + B
Urban									
A. All Business, Professional and White Collar	426	52.1	19.2	2.6	6.2	16.4	2.1	1.4	B + A
B. All Manual Workers	413	35.8	12.2	9.4	11.9	21.0	4.1	5.6	1 + 5, 6, 7
1. Large Business	54	62.3	20.8	0.0	0.0	16.9	0.0	0.0	2 + 7
2. Professional	73	46.6	31.5	2.7	5.5	11.0	2.7	0.0	3 + 6, 7
3. Small Business	129	51.9	20.2	3.1	6.2	14.7	1.6	2.3	4 + 6, 7
4. White Collar	171	51.5	12.9	2.9	8.2	19.9	2.9	1.7	5 + 1, 7
5. Skilled Manual	162	41.9	14.8	6.8	10.5	19.1	2.5	4.4	6 + 1, 3, 4
6. Semi-skilled Manual	174	34.5	10.9	8.6	11.5	23.6	5.7	5.2	7 + 1, 2, 3, 4, 5
7. Unskilled Manual	77	25.9	9.1	16.9	15.6	19.5	3.9	9.1	
Rural									
C. Farm Owners and Managers	153	56.2	9.2	5.9	3.3	21.6	1.3	2.5	C + D
D. Farm Tenants and Laborers	69	31.9	8.7	11.6	2.9	36.2	1.4	7.3	D + C

299

[*] Centers, *Journal of Social Psychology*, Vol. 27, 1938, 169.

different jobs are regarded from a different perspective, depending on the person's position. One such investigation showed that manual workers tended to evaluate their own jobs higher than clerical positions, whereas clerical workers gave their jobs a higher rank than manual jobs.[6]

Although some shifts occur, the hierarchical arrangement of occupations is a part of the American tradition. Related to this hierarchy is the culturally induced conviction that a man should better himself, that progress up the occupational ladder is a mark of success.

Family, class, and society do not, as a rule, demand that a young person choose his profession on the basis of his position in society. If he seems to restrict his choice to certain occupations, it is usually because he has accepted the values and norms to which he was exposed as a growing child. Since they have become a part of his own way of thinking they naturally influence his vocational choice. If he fails to live up to these norms, he disappoints not only others, but also himself.

PERSONAL FACTORS. As we noted earlier, the period of tentative choice is characterized by two questions: What am I interested in? and What can I do? Let us now consider these questions by focusing primarily on the individual, his interests and his abilities.

Interest is a dynamic factor in vocational choice because it directs our attention to certain activities, leads us to seek out certain occupations. If interest is strong enough, it can motivate us to study, to seek additional training, and to overcome all sorts of social and financial handicaps. If we have our sights set on a certain job, if we are enthusiastic about the opportunities and challenges the job offers, we will be much more willing to tolerate hardships and delays than if we are only mildly interested in it.

Interest in a certain occupation may spring from the fact that the work involved in it is of intrinsic value to us; i.e., if we like to help people, we choose social work; if we are interested in the

6 William H. Form, "Toward an Occupational Social Psychology," *Journal of Social Psychology,* Vol. 23, August 1946, 85-99.

creative possibilities of children and young people, we may decide to teach; if we are curious about why plants grow well or poorly, we may embark upon a career in biochemistry or experimental agriculture. Our interests, then, center around the nature of the work itself. But our interest in a certain occupation also may issue from such considerations as money, prestige, and status. It is, of course, possible that a job will fulfill both demands.

Interests derive from a number of different sources. Parents may stimulate interest in their children by talking about their jobs at home or by indicating in a number of ways the glamor, prestige, and other rewards that attach to certain occupations. And if a young person shows an ability for one of these positions, his interest will increase that much more. For another person, interest may be a consequence of work well done. If he receives approval and praise for doing certain things well, if his emotional needs are satisfied by the work he does, he is likely to concentrate on these activities. He may learn to enjoy these activities because of the satisfaction he derives from them—the pleasure he gets from solving an intricate mathematical problem or from constructing an elaborate piece of machinery. His interest becomes self-sustained without support from others.

For still others, interests grow out of school and early work experiences. For those in the middle- and upper-income levels, college years are a period for exploring interests and activities. For those in the lower-income groups who may not go on to college, the early years of work serve the same function. During this exploratory period, young people are introduced to new activities and a wider range of job possibilities in which they may discover new interests. They may meet teachers, scientists, doctors, any number of people, who seem to enjoy their work so much that a lasting impression is created in the young person's mind. Or they may meet people who are so disgruntled with their jobs that any interest they may have had in entering such a field will wither and die, unless, of course, something occurs to counteract this influence. These different sources of interest are not mutually exclusive. They may operate simultaneously and reinforce one another.

Interests channel our vocational aspirations in certain directions, but they do not fully determine them. Interest in a job is important, but a person also must display the necessary ability to do well in a particular field. We may, for example, be very interested in painting or in engineering—but may lack artistic talent or mathematical ability. In that case, our interests lead us down a blind alley. It is important, therefore, to consider thoroughly the question of our abilities in relation to our interests.

Extensive studies of many different occupations have given us a good picture of the range of intelligence demanded by various jobs. Table 3 shows the intelligence scores for eight selected occu-

TABLE 3

RELATIONSHIP OF I.Q. AND SELECTED OCCUPATIONS *

Occupation	Mean	Standard deviation
Accountant	128.1	11.7
Teacher	122.8	12.8
Clerk (general)	117.5	13.0
Receiving-shipping clerk	111.3	16.4
Sheet-metal worker	107.5	15.3
Butcher	102.9	17.1
Cook-baker	97.2	20.8
Farmhand	91.4	21.8

* Modified from H. C. Gilhousen and W. Brown, *College Psychology*. New York, Prentice-Hall, Inc., 1950, p. 471.

pations. Both the average or mean scores and the standard deviations are given. Although the mean scores for different occupations may be different, any given occupation will exhibit considerable variation in intelligence scores; and the range indicated by the standard deviation for one occupation may overlap the range for another occupation. Let us take the accountant and teacher as an example. The standard deviation of 11.7 for accountants indicates that 68 per cent of the group fall in the range from 139.8 (128.1 + 11.7) to 116.4 (128.1 − 11.7). Thus, the lower part of the range falls below the mean for the group of teachers.

Approaching the question of intelligence and occupational level in another way, Clark and Gist [7] found that intelligence appears to act as a selective factor in influencing occupational choice. They measured the intelligence of 2,423 students whose median age at the time was 16 years. Thirteen years later they obtained information from these students about the occupations they had entered. Their findings are presented in Table 4. The findings

TABLE 4

PERCENTAGE OF 2,423 PERSONS IN EACH OF THREE I.Q. INTERVALS BY
OCCUPATIONS

| | | | Percentage in each I.Q. interval | | |
Occupational group	No.	Mean	Below 95	95-104	105 and over
Total professional	365	102.82	32.60	33.97	33.43
Clerical	166	100.00	34.34	33.74	31.92
Teachers	207	99.28	38.17	31.40	30.43
Salespeople and proprietors	233	96.61	44.19	32.62	23.19
Skilled workers	131	96.18	45.80	32.83	21.37
Housewives	857	95.44	49.94	30.81	19.25
Semiskilled and unskilled	247	93.28	58.30	27.53	14.17
Farmers	345	92.75	58.84	29.85	11.31
Housekeepers and unemployed	79	91.39	63.29	31.65	5.06

confirm (1) a definite relationship between intelligence test scores and occupational level and (2) a large degree of overlapping of test scores among the various occupational classes. At each level there are some people of above-average intelligence, although in varying proportions.

Knowing the range of intelligence required by different occupations makes it possible to ascertain approximately the occupational level at which a person is most likely to succeed. A job should not strain a person's capacities, yet it should be sufficiently challenging to be stimulating and interesting. If a person scores below the average of the occupational group that he hopes to enter, it does not necessarily mean that he is unable to do the

[7] Carroll D. Clark and Noel P. Gist, "Intelligence as a Factor in Occupational Choice," *American Sociological Review*, Vol. 3, October 1938, 683-694.

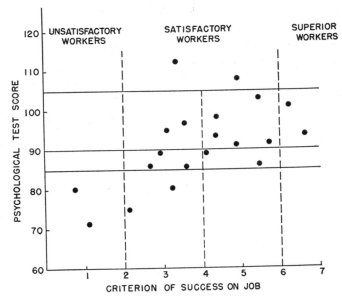

The use of psychological test scores in employee selection. (From Norman R. F. Maier, Psychology in Industry. Boston, Houghton Mifflin Company, 1946, p. 153.)

required work, although he may have to put forth more effort and may need stronger motivation to carry him through.

Intelligence defines the general level of ability called for in various occupations. In many jobs special abilities and aptitudes are also necessary, and many tests have been developed to assess these. Some jobs demand a great deal of mathematical ability or a good perception of spatial relations. Others require special motor skills, involving such factors as speed of reaction, coordination, and fine manipulative proficiency. In still others, resistance to fatigue, good eyesight, or ability to endure extremes of temperature, are essential. Social skills—the ability to meet people easily and to work well with them over long periods of time—are of paramount importance in many occupations. Before we choose an occupation demanding any one or several of these skills and aptitudes, we should determine whether what we can do or can learn to do is adequate for what must be done.

We should also note, however, that the fact that we can do something well does not necessarily mean that we are sufficiently interested in it to consider it as an occupation. It is also possible that we are interested and capable along certain lines but do not see how our interests and abilities relate to vocational choices, how they can be implemented in a specific occupation. This is illustrated in the case of Bill F.

Bill had been referred to the vocational guidance bureau by his advisor in college. He was abandoning pre-medical training in favor of business administration. This was in line with his plan to get into a retail business of some kind because he wanted to be independent and work for himself. He had no qualms about changing his curriculum because he felt he had been more or less forced toward the medical profession by the attitudes and expectations of his parents and teachers. He had no particular trouble in science courses, saying, "they just don't interest me." He had, however, no idea of the kind of courses available in business administration or how they related to his vocational plans. Through interest and aptitude tests, and from reading in the occupational library, Bill was prepared to make a new choice of vocational goal.

We mentioned earlier that emotional factors play a part in the development of vocational interests. We shall now consider in greater detail how these factors bear on vocational choice. Research in this area has yielded less definite results than have studies concerning intelligence and special aptitudes. In part, this lack of definitely established relationships between certain occupations and emotional and personality characteristics results from the fact that many jobs can accommodate equally well the extrovert and the introvert, the shy and the aggressive, the quiet, withdrawn and the talkative, sociable person. Or a given occupation can call into play many diverse personality characteristics. This is especially true in a small business or office where one person has to assume many different functions. Let us look at a specific example:

The director of a sociological field survey has to develop the research design. Although he may discuss the project with colleagues and friends, it is primarily a solitary job, utilizing library facilities and his own experience and knowledge. He must then prepare interview schedules. This involves not only selecting the relevant questions, but also considering format and giving instructions to typists and printers. Next, he must train and supervise interviewers, which calls for quite different skills. With as many as 20 interviewers working over a period of two months, he must be able to get along with people and to be something of a diplomat. During the latter part of the interviewing period, when interviews become more difficult to obtain as the supply of respondents narrows down, the director must be able to handle not only his own problems, but also the annoyances that begin to beset the interviewers who become tense because their work does not go quite so smoothly as it did at the beginning. And, finally, the material must be analyzed and the results interpreted.

This diversity of functions and roles makes it difficult to say that this or that personality characteristic is correlated with a given job. Since little is known about the relationship of personality characteristics to occupations, we cannot look to this field for vocational guidance.

We must consider, instead, more broadly defined emotional factors. Ginzberg and his associates [8] suggest four such factors we must carefully weigh and consider if our occupational choice is to hold promise of satisfaction and success.

The first of these they call "reality testing"; i.e., we must be willing to take a close look at our weaknesses and strengths, to appraise our goals in the light of what we can realistically accomplish, to evaluate what others expect of us in terms of our own resources. If, for example, we choose a demanding job because of its prestige appeal without considering whether we have the necessary ability to handle the work or the kind of temperament required to stand the strain, we may soon become frustrated and have to start all over again.

---

[8] Ginzberg, Ginsburg, Axelrad, and Herma, *Occupational Choice. An Approach to a General Theory.*

The second essential is the development of a time perspective. We must not only take into account what we want to do now, but also must plan ahead for the future. And closely related to this factor is a third one that involves the postponement of gratification, or what we previously have called frustration tolerance. If a person wants to become an actor, for example, he must be willing to begin at the bottom, to spend many years doing bit parts and stand-in roles before he can hope to see his name in lights. In addition to the delay, he may also have to endure hardships and privation.

Finally, a person must be willing to compromise, for it is unlikely that one particular job will satisfy all his needs and wishes. If someone insists on holding out for what he conceives to be "the ideal job," he may never get a job at all, or may find himself constantly moving from one job to another in his will-o'-the-wisp search.

FACTORS CHARACTERIZING THE LABOR MARKET AND THE JOB. Interests, abilities, and aspirations have to be squared with specific jobs. It is necessary, therefore, not only to assess our qualifications and expectations, but also to know something about the labor market, both nationally and regionally or locally.

Over the last few decades, there have been decided shifts in the types of work in which people engage. In 1870, more than 50 per cent of the labor force was employed in agriculture and forestry. Today only 15 per cent are employed in these fields. On the other hand, opportunities have expanded greatly in the manufacturing, distributive, and service fields, as Table 5, which gives a detailed breakdown of the occupations in which Americans were engaged in 1950, very graphically shows.

Within each of the occupational categories listed, there is a high degree of specialization. This is one of the outstanding characteristics of our economic life. The Federal Security Agency lists about 600 occupational fields and approximately 40,000 separate jobs in its *Dictionary of Occupational Titles*. Although many of

CHANGES IN TYPES OF WORK

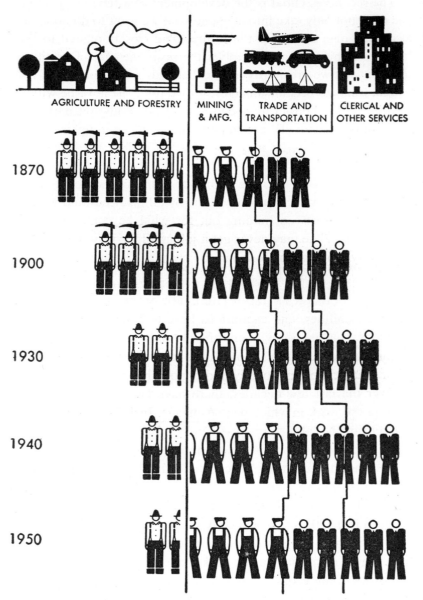

Each symbol represents 10 per cent of all gainful workers

308

TABLE 5

OCCUPATION OF THE EXPERIENCED CIVILIAN LABOR FORCE:
UNITED STATES, 1950 *

For the total population, male and female, 14 years old and over.

Professional, technical and kindred workers	4,988,012
Farmers and farm managers	4,320,576
Managers, officials and proprietors, excl. farm	5,076,436
Clerical and kindred workers	7,070,023
Sales workers	4,044,143
Craftsmen, foremen, and kindred workers	8,152,743
Operatives and kindred workers	11,715,606
Private household workers	1,487,574
Service workers, except private household	4,511,996
Farm laborers and foremen	2,514,780
Laborers, except farm and mine	3,750,990
Occupation not reported	1,366,064
Total	58,998,943

* U.S. Bureau of the Census.

these jobs call for similar interests and abilities, the picture is still highly diverse and offers the individual much freedom of choice.

We should note that the problem of vocational choice exists only in a society where the individual is free to choose an occupation. In a free society, the son need not follow in his father's footsteps, unless he wants to. The laborer who is dissatisfied with his job is free to change it. This does not mean that such a change will not perhaps involve some hardship, or that obligations to his family will not prevent him from making such a change. But it does indicate the absence, in general, of societal restrictions forbidding such changes.

But in the final analysis, freedom of vocational choice is meaningful only if it is possible for *everyone* to choose the job he wishes. A glance at the employment ads in many newspapers will reveal very quickly that not all jobs are equally available to all people, even to people who may be qualified. "For Christian White Only" is a qualifying phrase frequently found in such ads. Although Negroes—to mention our most numerous minority group—do hold professional and managerial positions, they hold far fewer such positions than do white people, the percentages being 1.8 vs. 5.9 respectively for the professional group and 1.3 vs. 10.6

per cent for proprietors, managers, and officials.[9] It seems hardly necessary here to go into the consequences of discrimination, whatever its form. Most of us are all too familiar with the tensions, conflict, and frustration that discrimination breeds. What many people do not immediately grasp, however, is that job discrimination represents a definite loss to society. If a member of a minority group knows that he will be discriminated against in applying for a position he could easily fill, he may prefer to avoid any unpleasantness and instead take a job that is beneath his abilities. But society will be the loser if such a thing occurs, because that individual will not be producing at his full potential. And, as we shall note later in the chapter, the person who does not find his job challenging and stimulating may soon develop adjustment problems.

Since restrictive practices vary in different parts of the country, it is important for a person to study the regional labor market. Fair employment practices laws in some states increase the likelihood that a person will be able to enter certain occupations that are closed to him in other states.

Regional considerations are also important in other respects. In one area there may be a labor shortage, in another, the labor market may be glutted. The hometown may not need another lawyer or another engineer, but there may be many good opportunities for lawyers or engineers in another town.

If we have narrowed our choice to a given occupational field but still are undecided about a specific job, we can turn to a number of sources for information. Many public libraries have books and pamphlets listing and describing many diverse occupations. High schools and colleges often have teachers who are qualified and willing to act as vocational counselors, and many educational institutions maintain vocational guidance bureaus. Or we can often get valuable tips from friends or relatives who work at the jobs we are interested in.

But whatever our sources, there are several questions we need

---

[9] *Sixteenth Census of the United States,* Vol. III, The Labor Force, Part I, Table 64, p. 97.

Different kinds of work situations. Some jobs involve mostly working with things. Some jobs call mostly for working with people. (Top photo courtesy Francis E. Weigel. Bottom photo courtesy Ewing Galloway.)

answered if we want to get as complete a picture of an occupation as possible. It is easy to be misled by the label a job carries and the prestige it suggests. We should make a thorough job analysis of each occupation in which we are interested. The following outline may serve as a guide:

1. *Duties of a person engaged in the occupation:* What kinds of activities are involved? Are these activities connected primarily with people, ideas, or things? Does the job involve indoor or outdoor work? Will there be much traveling connected with it? Are the tasks involved highly repetitive or does the job offer variety?

2. *The conditions of work:* What are the physical conditions at the place of work? Are there any safety hazards? What are the hours of work? Do the hours fall into a set schedule or is the work schedule flexible? What are the provisions for vacation and recreation? How much time does travel to and from work consume?

3. *Payment:* What is the average rate of pay? Can raises be expected in the future? Are there provisions for employee benefits?

4. *Opportunities for advancement:* Is promotion possible within the factory, firm, or institution? What is the basis for advancement? How often is advancement possible? Are there exceptional opportunities for advancement?

5. *Education and training required:* How much general education is necessary? Is trade-school training required? Is there a long period of professional preparation? How much will the training cost? If training takes place on the job, will the employee be paid while he is learning? Is previous work experience necessary?

6. *Personal qualifications:* What special aptitudes and abilities are required? Are there any special physical requirements, such as good eyesight?

7. *Social relations on the job:* What is the status of the person in this job in relation to others in the same professional institution, business, or industrial plant? Does he have to assume a great deal of responsibility for his own work and the work of others

or does he mostly carry out orders and assignments given him by others? Does the job call for teamwork or is it mostly solitary? Are there organizations, such as unions or business and professional groups, to which he can or must belong?

8. *Special advantages:* Is the job an important one in the community? Is there scope for the initiative and special talents of a person?

It is very likely that not all answers to these questions will be satisfactory. Perhaps the job pays less at the start than we had hoped for, but this disadvantage may be compensated by opportunities the job offers for advancement. Perhaps we like most of the working conditions except that we must spend a long time traveling to and from the job or perhaps must even change our place of residence. We have to weigh these different aspects and evaluate the advantages and disadvantages of each.

Transition from School to Work

Adolescence is a period of transition during which we must give up many of the roles and values we acquired as a child and learn those of an adult. Whether a person makes the transition easily or painfully, gradually or abruptly, will depend on the culture of which he is a member.[10]

In our society the transition often is fraught with strain and insecurity. Usually during the last year of high school the young person begins to take action with respect to his own future. He knows that soon he will have to establish a place for himself in the world. This will mean learning to get along without the support of his family, planning for marriage and establishing a family of his own, and preparing for and finally entering an occupation. Sexual, family, and marriage adjustment are discussed in Chapters 9 and 13. Here we shall focus primarily on the adjust-

---

[10] For a review of the writing on adolescence in different cultures and times see Muzafer Sherif and Hadley Cantril, *The Psychology of Ego-Involvements.* New York, John Wiley & Sons, Inc., 1947, Chapters 8 and 9.

ment problems related to the transition from school to work, keeping in mind, however, that all these problems are closely interrelated. The desire to marry and to have a family early, for example, may deter some people from taking jobs that call for long apprenticeships. This is especially true for the young girl who anticipates making an early marriage and sets her job plans accordingly. Other young people may pass up positions requiring long periods of preparation because of financial need or the desire to escape parental domination or dependence.

We mentioned earlier the genetic development from fantasy choice, to tentative choice, to realistic choice. Ginzberg [11] and his associates note three distinct stages during the period of realistic choice, which they identify as exploration, crystallization, and specification. During the exploration stage, the young person tries to acquire background experience and information on which to make his occupational choice by exploring different subjects in college, by talking with teachers and advisors, or by actually trying his hand at different jobs. During the crystallization stage, the job candidate tries to assess the different possibilities open to him and commits himself to a certain occupational field. Finally, in the specification stage the young person reviews the alternatives in a given field and chooses a particular career objective. For example, he may have decided to become a psychologist and now must decide between clinical, industrial, or social psychology, vocational counseling, child guidance, or a host of other specialized divisions.

At whatever point he enters a full-time occupation—after high school, after college, after completing graduate work—the change from school to work brings with it the assumption of new tasks and new responsibilities as well as new rights and freedoms. In order to understand this transition better, let us consider how the school situation differs from the work situation.

First of all, there is a shift from non-monetary to monetary activities. We now get paid for what we do. Although we may have

---

[11] Ginzberg, Ginsburg, Axelrad, and Herma, *Occupational Choice. An Approach to a General Theory.*

worked in part-time jobs before, we usually did not have to pay
for food or rent. Now we become economically self-supporting.
In most cases, we have to learn to manage on what we can earn.

Secondly, provided we had a certain amount of financial support and the necessary mental ability, we had no problem in
being admitted to high school or college. We were not rejected,
for example, because there were too many applicants. But when
we apply for a job, the supply usually will be larger than the demand, and we shall have to compete with others for the position.

Thirdly, although we may have scraped through high school
or college doing mediocre work, we must realize now that the
only way to hold a job is to perform to the very best of our ability.
Inferior work may get us fired from a job. In college, if another
student was smarter than we were, we were not expelled. But if
our employer knows of somebody who promises to fill our job
more satisfactorily and efficiently than we can, we may soon find
ourselves out haunting the employment agencies once again.

Fourth, in high school and college there is a larger peer group
with whom we can associate, all of whom have problems similar
to our own. We can also count on some help and guidance from
our teachers. But in a new job we start generally at the bottom of
the ladder, and even if we find ourselves working with other
people who hold positions similar to our own, we hesitate to discuss problems with them until we have become better oriented to
the whole social set-up of the work plant.

And, finally, the work situation is new to us. We have to learn
new technical as well as new social skills.

This comparison points up some of the difficulties the young
person encounters as he starts on a job. Let us now consider in
more detail these and other adjustment problems that can arise
in the work situation.

Anxiety on the Job

Let us take the case of a young man, a college graduate
and recently married, who has taken his first full-time job as a

salesman in a wholesale company that specializes in small electrical appliances. During summer vacations and on a part-time basis during the last two years, he has worked as a salesman in a large hardware store. It was largely on the basis of this past work record that he got his new position. Still, the new job is different from his old one in many respects. As a full-time salesman, he must have more specialized technical knowledge, and he will be selling to a different group of people, not to customers who come in for relatively small purchases for their own household needs but to businessmen who are likely to have a more expert knowledge of the appliances they buy than most of his previous customers.

How does he respond to these new demands?

He got the job by being selected from a number of other applicants, and that gives him a certain self-confidence. Even so, he may have some doubts about his ability to succeed in the job. Some of the products he is going to sell are complicated and he wonders if he can familiarize himself with them quickly enough. Has his previous selling experience been diversified enough to insure that he will be able to approach and to sell to practical, hard-to-satisfy businessmen? Will he be able to make as good a sales record as the other men in the company? These and many other questions will be on his mind as he takes over his new position.

There are, secondly, his relations to his co-workers and his employers. Most of the other salesmen have been in their jobs for several years. They know one another well. They also have established a definite relationship to their employer; they know when and how to approach him with questions or suggestions. In addition, the older employees are thoroughly familiar with the status relationships in this company. But he is new. Will the other salesmen accept him readily as one of them? Will he be invited to social gatherings outside of work? He is anxious to get along well. But can he be agreeable without appearing submissive? Can he give orders without seeming to be domineering, without antagonizing others? Will he get along with the sales manager and with his employer? Will he make a good impression on the business-men he contacts?

Thirdly, he has to consider not only his own likes and aspira-tions, but also those of his wife. If he brings his associates home, will she get along well with them? Will she be able to manage on the money he earns? Will she be sympathetic to the problems he encounters on the job? Will she support him in his ambitions or, perhaps even more important, will she support him if his job should not work out for him and he should want to change?

Although they have no children so far, both he and his wife want a family. And his anxieties about a family project into the future. Will he be able to provide his children with the kind of home and environment that is best for them? Will he be able to advance in his occupation so that he can give the youngsters a good education?

These are some of the anxieties that plague many of us on the job. They are very frequently a part of normal work experience. They become maladjustive if they overshadow whatever satisfac-tion we derive from our work.

What are the sources of satisfaction in our work? What con-tributes to work satisfaction and what makes us dissatisfied? These are the questions that we shall consider next.

Job Satisfaction

Many different factors contribute to work satisfaction. Some of these factors, such as wages, working hours, employee benefits, and our social relations with our employer and our co-workers, relate directly to the job. Other factors are more closely related to the kind of person we are, i.e., if we are dependent or domineering, if we try to get by with as little effort as possible or if we are a perfectionist, if we are ambitious, and so on. Still other factors derive from our group relationships outside the job—i.e., the satisfaction we get from participating in work-connected groups, such as unions, business organizations, or professional associations; our social standing in the community, our family relations.[12]

We pointed out in the beginning of this chapter that satisfaction or dissatisfaction with our work will be reflected in our adjustment outside of work. The reverse is equally true. People who come to a vocational counseling center ostensibly with vocational problems often have difficulties that lie primarily in other areas of living but which manifest themselves also in their work. The emotionally disturbed person, the person who lacks confidence in himself, who feels insecure in his relations with others, is likely to manifest these characteristics in most situations—on the job and off.

Business and industry have become increasingly concerned with individual work satisfaction and work group morale. For a high labor turnover—too many dissatisfied workers leaving the job— is expensive, especially where prolonged training is required to fill the jobs that have been vacated. And so we find a number of companies and firms who have been willing to cooperate in, or who have initiated, studies of employee satisfaction and morale. Such studies have shown repeatedly that although such things as pay, hours of work, and physical working conditions are important factors in job satisfaction, others that we might call psychological or social factors, such as recognition for good work, a fair hearing for grievances, and congenial co-workers are at least as, if not more, significant in keeping the worker satisfied. The results from a study by Watson [13] are characteristic of many others. They asked workers to report on the most satisfactory job they had held previously and why they considered it so. Their answers are presented in Table 6.

Let us look at a specific example to indicate how social and psychological factors may contribute more importantly to work satisfaction than do physical working conditions.

---

[12] Milton L. Blum, *Industrial Psychology and Its Social Foundations.* New York, Harper and Brothers, 1949, pp. 75-105.

[13] Goodwin Watson, "Work Satisfaction," in George W. Hartmann and Theodore Newcomb, eds., *Industrial Conflict: A Psychological Interpretation.* New York, The Cordon Company, 1940, p. 120.

TABLE 6

REASONS WHY WORKERS PREFERRED ONE JOB RATHER THAN ANOTHER

(In percentages)

Reason	Men	Women
Congenial work conditions, pleasant social contacts	21	38
Responsibility, initiative, prestige	27	23
In line with vocational aspirations	15	13
More variety	15	12
More salary	13	6
Better chance for promotion	6	2
Shorter hours	3	6

An office that has been pleasantly cool all through the summer and fall becomes uncomfortably cold as winter approaches, and there is no way to heat it. One morning the women in the office complain about the chill to their employer as he comes in. But he shrugs off their complaint and does nothing. In this case, the dissatisfaction, stemming from a physical condition, which could easily have been corrected, is greatly aggravated by the employer's attitude.

Congenial relations with our co-workers and our employers, then, contribute significantly to our work satisfaction. A second important source of satisfaction lies in how we perceive our occupational achievement in relation to our aspirations and our abilities. What we hope to be and to do becomes very much a part of ourselves, and our failure to achieve our goal threatens our self-confidence and self-respect. If we have to wait too long for advancement, we shall grow restive and discontented. The same will be true if the job we hold does not challenge our abilities. If we have the intellectual ability and interest required in professional work, we may be satisfied with a clerical job for a short time, but not for long.

We also may find ourselves in a job that is beyond our ability. Because it is too difficult, we never have the satisfaction of doing our work well, and the fear that our deficiencies will become apparent to others hangs like a cloud over our head.

Sometimes we set an unrealistic level of aspiration for ourselves because we have a mistaken conception of the value of our abilities in the labor market. College graduates particularly often try to "sell themselves high." But a prospective employer may not believe that you have something of special value to offer him. Especially in periods of wide unemployment, the labor supply may be much higher than the demand, and our abilities and training will not be as valuable as we expected them to be.

Psychologically, success or failure, satisfaction or dissatisfaction in our work is determined by our level of aspiration. If the gap in either direction between our level of achievement and level of aspiration remains too wide for too long, we shall grow dissatisfied. If, on the other hand, we succeed in reaching one goal, we shall probably raise our ambition a little higher and press with greater persistence and confidence toward further goals.

In summary, if pay, working hours, and physical working conditions are at all acceptable, then psychological and social factors become of paramount importance in work satisfaction. Our social relations with our co-workers, the attitudes of our employers, and the nature of our work in relation to our aspirations and our abilities can make our work an enjoyable and stimulating experience or a dread necessity.

For many who are dissatisfied with their work and see no hope of escape, the job becomes merely a means to an end, without intrinsic value. For some of us, this dissatisfaction may cast a shadow over our home life or our relations with friends, especially if we interpret our dilemma as a personal failure. Others, however, frequently seek achievement outside the job—in active participation in community affairs, in recreational activities, and in hobbies—in an effort to find and savor the satisfactions that they have been unable to find in their work.

Conditions for High Morale
Within a Work Plant

Finally, let us consider the conditions within a work plant that are essential to high morale, which help us feel that we belong and enable us to identify with a work group, or—as Bakke [14] has put it—that make a team out of a crowd. We shall follow his suggestions and speak of five organizational devices or "bonds of organization" that have to be considered if we are to understand why morale is high in some work groups and low in others.

The first of these devices refers to *job specification*. We must clearly understand what our work and the work of our co-workers entails, and our co-workers must know exactly what our responsibilities are as well as their own. Such an understanding is necessary to prevent employees from "passing the buck," to prevent workers from exploiting one another, and to avoid duplication of work. The latter, for example, is not only wasteful, but also discouraging, especially for employees who are interested in their work and try to do their best in everything.

Of course, avoiding duplication of work does not mean that we should not be willing to lend a helping hand if one of our co-workers is taken sick or if the work in our particular department suddenly starts to pile up. Nor does it mean that jobs should be so rigidly defined that individual initiative is stifled.

Usually we are hired for a job because we possess the necessary qualifications that will enable us to accept certain responsibilities, perform certain tasks, and assume particular obligations connected with that job. If, after we have started working, other duties are thrust upon us for which we have neither interest nor ability, tensions are likely to develop that could have been avoided if the job had been more clearly specified.

The second bond of organization involves adequate *communication*. Work may be duplicated, for example, because certain instructions were not properly transmitted. Perhaps the order was vaguely worded, or the person who received the directions did not consider the person who sent them to be sufficiently important to carry out the directive promptly and completely.

Also, communication frequently is incomplete. Although the task itself may be described clearly enough, it is defined too

[14] E. W. Bakke, "Teamwork in Industry," *Scientific Monthly*, Vol. 66, 1948, 213-220.

narrowly—i.e., we do not see how the job fits into the broader work picture, what connection it has with other positions—and we may, therefore, consider the description meaningless.

Morale is improved if communication is a two-way affair, not merely a matter of transmitting instructions and orders from management to worker, but a channel that is open in the other direction as well. The extent to which our constructive suggestions are recognized or our grievances considered will be an important fac- tor in determining whether workers will be satisfied or dissatis- fied.[15]

The third organizational bond refers to the *status system* in an office or factory. All work situations involve hierarchical relation- ships. Different jobs carry different responsibilities and different authority and prestige. Some people can carry authority grace- fully, are tactful, considerate, yet firm when necessary. Such a person has little trouble having his directions followed. Others, however, are stern, inflexible, demanding. Their requests are met with resentment, or perhaps even ignored, especially if they try to lord it over others and to wield influence they don't actually possess.

We all know that it makes a big difference under whom we work. That the quality of immediate supervision is a decisive fac- tor in morale on the job has been demonstrated in a number of studies. In one of these [16] about 8,000 employees in non-super- visory positions in a large utility company were asked to fill out a questionnaire dealing with work satisfaction and morale. On the basis of the results from the questionnaire, 40 groups with high and 40 groups with low morale were selected and compared in their response to the question: In what way does your imme- diate boss supervise you? Table 7 shows the relationship between the type of supervision and high and low morale. Note that the

[15] Richard L. Hull and Arthur Kolstad, "Morale on the Job," in Goodwin Watson, ed., *Civilian Morale*. Boston, Houghton Mifflin Company, 1942, pp. 349-364.

[16] D. Katz, "Morale and Motivation in Industry," in W. Dennis, ed., *Current Trends in Industrial Psychology*. Pittsburgh, University of Pittsburgh Press, 1949, p. 167.

outstanding response differences between the two groups occur in the extent to which the supervisor is interested in the welfare of the employee and in the greater flow of communication between supervisor and employees.

TABLE 7

FUNCTIONS ASCRIBED TO SUPERVISOR IN HIGH AND LOW MORALE GROUPS

The statement that the supervisor	was made in the high morale groups by	was made in the low morale groups by	Difference
Arranges the work and makes work assignments	67%	69%	— 2%
Enforces the rules	54	54	0
Keeps the men supplied with materials and tools	36	41	— 5
Makes recommendations for promotions, transfers, and pay increases	61	22	39
Keeps the men informed on what is happening in the company	47	11	36
Keeps the men posted on how well they are doing	47	12	35
Hears complaints and grievances	65	32	33

A satisfactory system of *rewards and punishments* is the fourth essential for good work morale. The employee who knows his work will be praised and appreciated is much more likely to put forth his best efforts than the employee who knows his work will be ignored or taken for granted. We may know that we have done good work, but it will add to our satisfaction if we find that others also are pleased with what we have done. If, on the other hand, we have made some mistakes in our work, it will make a great deal of difference to us whether we are corrected in a friendly, helpful way or whether we are reprimanded or ridiculed in front of others. If we are criticized in front of our friends and co-workers, the resulting embarrassment and humiliation may well ruin our self-respect.

We have to feel that rewards and punishments are given fairly, and fairly to all. Although it may profit us economically to be singled out for a reward, it is likely that our co-workers will view us with suspicion and hostility if they think such a reward represents a clear case of favoritism. It is demoralizing to a work group if rewards appear to be handed out arbitrarily.

And, finally, Bakke speaks of the *organizational charter* as the fifth bond of organization, what we think about the organization we work for, how we feel toward the people we work with. Do we get along well with our associates, for example, or do petty jealousies and personal likes and dislikes impair the efficiency of the group? Are we pleased to be identified with the firm we work for, or are we forever trying to conceal from others the fact that our organization has a bad name in its field?

Whether these five aspects, then, are present or whether they are absent will determine whether morale on the job will be low or high, whether we will be satisfied members of a work team or disgruntled workers in a crowd.

For Additional Reading

Bakke, E. Wight, *Bonds of Organization: An Appraisal of Corporate Human Relations.* New York, Harper and Brothers, 1950.

Blum, Milton L., *Industrial Psychology and Its Social Foundations.* New York, Harper and Brothers, 1945.

———, *Readings in Experimental Industrial Psychology.* New York, Prentice-Hall, Inc., 1952.

Centers, Richard, *The Psychology of Social Classes.* Princeton, N.J., Princeton University Press, 1949.

Dennis, Wayne, ed., *Current Trends in Industrial Psychology.* Pittsburgh, University of Pittsburgh Press, 1949.

Ginzberg, Eli, Sol W. Ginsburg, Sidney Axelrad, and John L. Herma, *Occupational Choice. An Approach to a General Theory.* New York, Columbia University Press, 1951.

Hollingshead, August B., *Elmtown's Youth. The Impact of Social Classes on Adolescents.* New York, John Wiley & Sons, Inc., 1949.

Hughes, Everett C., "Work and Self," in J. H. Rohrer and M. Sherif, eds., *Social Psychology at the Crossroads.* New York, Harper and Brothers, 1951.

Hull, Richard L. and Arthur Kolstad, "Morale on the Job," in Goodwin Watson, ed., *Civilian Morale.* Boston, Houghton Mifflin Company, 1942.

•

Jacques, Elliott, *The Changing Culture of a Factory*. London, Tavistock Publications Ltd., 1951.

Maier, Norman R. F., *Principles of Human Relations: Applications to Management*. New York, John Wiley & Sons, Inc., 1952.

Miller, Delbert C. and William H. Form, *Industrial Sociology*. New York, Harper and Brothers, 1951.

Morse, Nancy C., *Satisfactions in the White-collar Job*. Ann Arbor, University of Michigan Press, 1953.

Myers, George E., Gladys M. Little, and Sarah A. Robinson, *Planning Your Future*. New York, McGraw-Hill Book Company, Inc., 1953.

Super, Donald E., "Experience, Emotion, and Vocational Choice," in Eugene L. Hartley, Herbert G. Birch, and Ruth E. Hartley, eds., *Outside Readings in Psychology*. New York, Thomas Y. Cromwell Company, 1950.

Tiffin, Joseph, *Industrial Psychology*, 3rd ed. New York, Prentice-Hall Inc., 1952.

The
Psychology of Sexual
Adjustment

CHAPTER 13

- PSYCHOSEXUAL DEVELOPMENT
- FACTORS IN MATE SELECTION
- DATING AND COURTSHIP ADJUSTMENTS
- PSYCHOSEXUAL ADJUSTMENT IN MAR-
  RIAGE

Matters of sex and sexual adjustment are discussed more freely today than they were 50, or even 20, years ago, but they are still surrounded by a great deal of secrecy and misinformation. Students often have difficulty finding good books or classes for supplementing their meager knowledge with reliable information. Many parents and teachers are still reluctant to discuss objectively one of our most important problems. It is strange, is it not, that a topic in which so many persons are interested should be treated with such fear, shame, and confusion.

As a people, we Americans are amazingly inconsistent in our approach to sex. Wherever we turn, at whatever hour of the day and night, sex rushes in upon us, whether it be from the pages of our magazines and newspapers, from paper book covers, from billboards, or from television and radio. We heap adulation and praise upon Hollywood starlets and make lavish productions out of crowning beauty contest winners. Sex has come to be almost an essential ingredient in most of our novels.

Yet most of us are reluctant to discuss the subject frankly, or are willing to do so only if we can be sure that the talk will be kept impersonal and away from particulars. There are even some of us who act as though the whole question of sex was something nasty or unclean, something to be ignored, to be suppressed and hidden.

As a result, many people remain completely ignorant about sex or fall victim to all manner of strange misconceptions or old wives' tales about the subject. Fortunately, in recent years, some progress has been made in disseminating reliable information about sexual matters, but the movement has continued to run afoul of social taboos and misguided opposition. The need for more information is still great. Personal and marital adjustment problems frequently revolve around matters of sex, and we cannot hope to reduce the incidence of these problems by continuing to look upon sex and the dissemination of sexual information as something foreign and somehow evil. In the pages that follow, we shall make an effort to provide concise and factual information on the topic of sex and to study and evaluate some of the romantic, delusional ideas many of us still hold in regard to sex.

Psychosexual Development

Psychosexual development involves interaction between a person's biological functioning, his affections toward others, and his attitudes toward sex and sex roles.

Biological functioning. The sex organs attain full maturity at the end of puberty, which occurs somewhat earlier in girls than in boys. Girls usually pass from puberty around the ages of twelve or thirteen, and boys, around fifteen to seventeen. With full maturity, individuals are ready to mate—but only biologically, not necessarily psychologically.

The male sex gland, the testis, is composed of two types of cells, one producing sperm cells, or spermatozoa, the other acting upon all other cells of the body and producing such secondary male sex characteristics as beard and general hairiness, deep voice, broad shoulders, and so forth.

The spermatozoa are extremely small, being approximately one five-hundredth of an inch in length on the average. In a normal ejaculation, from 200,000,000 to 400,000,000 spermatozoa may be released. The spermatozoa are carried in the semen, which is a fluid ejaculated by the male during the orgasm or sexual climax. The penis is the organ of copulation through which the semen is brought near the opening of the uterus in the female. To transmit the semen and sperm, the penis must become rigid or erect in order to penetrate into the female genital tract. Erection occurs during periods of sexual excitement when the blood supply to the genital organs of both male and female is greatly increased and the vessels and erectile tissue become engorged. The skin surface around the end of the penis contains many sensory nerve endings, thus making the whole genital area very sensitive.

The female sex glands are the ovaries, located in the pelvis on either side of and immediately adjacent to the womb or uterus. The ovaries serve the same double function the testes perform for the male; i.e., they produce the ova or egg cells and cause the appearance of secondary female sex characteristics such as breasts, broader hips, a rounder, softer figure, and the like.

After puberty, the egg cells mature and, under normal conditions, are discharged from the ovary at the rate of one ovum for each menstrual cycle, i.e., approximately every 24 to 28 days. This process is called ovulation and generally occurs about the middle of the menstrual month, which is about twelve to fifteen days after the beginning of the last menstrual period. The discharged ovum is carried along the Fallopian tubes, which are hollow muscular tubes leading to the uterus. In normal reproduction, sperm cells pass through the uterus to the Fallopian tubes, where fertilization ordinarily takes place. The fertilized egg then passes into the uterus, which provides space for its growth throughout the period of gestation. During the development of the egg in the ovaries, changes take place within the uterus and especially in the uterine lining, preparing it to receive the fertilized egg. If the egg is not fertilized, a large part of the uterine lining is sloughed away about every 24 to 28 days; the bleeding that follows constitutes the menstrual flow.

The uterus opens through the cervix into the vagina. The cervix is a canal-like opening through which the spermatozoa enter and through which the menstrual flow leaves the uterus. The vagina, which is a membranous tube or vestibule, is the female organ of copulation. Surrounding the external opening of the vagina is a membranous fold called the hymen. The hymen is almost always ruptured during first sexual intercourse, but may be broken before then in other ways.

The external genital organs of the female are the vulva, which consists of the major and minor lips, and the clitoris. Under sexual excitement the clitoris, analogous to the penis in the male, becomes firm and erect. The clitoris is richly supplied with nerve endings and is, therefore, highly sensitive; it is the chief, though not the only, stimulant of erotic sensation in women.

Although physical contact probably is the most potent stimulus to sexual excitement, it may be initiated by many other stimuli which, through a process of association and conditioning, have become sex-connected symbols. Sexual excitement, once aroused, is kept going chiefly by the autonomic nervous system, resulting in a pleasurable sensation of stimulation. The excitement builds up until an orgasm or climax is reached. In the male, the orgasm is crowned by the ejaculation of semen, in the woman, by a similar climactic response but without ejaculation. The orgasm is followed by a sudden release of tension accompanied by a desire for relaxation and rest.

Affections toward others. Although sexual activity is a universal phenomenon, the particular forms in which it is expressed may vary greatly. As with other physiological drives, expression of the sex drive is socially conditioned and patterned. Man's intelligence, his ability to reason, to memorize, to imagine, and to recognize certain standardized forms of social behavior has greatly modified his sexual activity. His choice of a partner is usually conditioned by his experiences and relationships with others. If an individual has, for example, categorized love and sex into two opposing compartments labeled "good" and "bad," he may avoid sexual relations with anybody whom he loves and respects. Different attitudes toward sexual matters may lead different individuals through the whole gamut of responses from frequent and promiscuous sexual intercourse to total abstinence.

It should be clear, then, that sexual behavior cannot be understood only in terms of physiological processes, but must take into account psychological and social factors as well. It is for this reason that we speak of *psychosexual* development and adjustment.

In describing the physiological processes involved in sexual behavior, we pointed out that an individual reaches biological sexual maturity as he emerges from puberty. However, the manner in which the individual reacts to the biological changes is determined, to a large extent, by his experiences before puberty and during maturation.

The course of development that leads to mature sexual adjustment in our culture may be divided into three phases. The first of these is the *infancy period*. During infancy, most children show an interest in their sexual organs and frequently may be observed touching and examining them. Soon the child becomes curious about the sex function in others, although these early interests and actions of the child have no sexual meaning in and of themselves, as in the adult. Sexual significance is acquired through learning the social meaning of such behavior. Although the child may derive pleasure from his own body, this pleasure may be mitigated by the reaction of others, especially of the mother. An understanding mother who does not become upset over her child's natural curiosity about sex will help the child to develop a favorable atti-

tude toward sex. But the mother who punishes her child for playing with his sex organs or refuses to answer his questions will
cause the child to regard sex as something "unspeakable and un-
touchable."

Infancy gives way to the *latency period*. Latency supposedly is
a neutral period that has little significance for later sex problems.
During this period, a child seems to grow less curious about sex.
It has been pointed out, however, that this is not true of all cultures. The occurrence of this so-called neutral period in our culture may spring primarily from the sex-repressive nature of our
culture. Recently, Kinsey's researches have thrown some doubt on
the assumption that this neutral period really occurs.

During the third, or *puberty period,* the child becomes increasingly interested in sexual activity. Biologically, the organism has
matured, but psychologically and socially the individual has not.
He is learning new ways of behavior and how to fit himself into
new roles. He is in a transition period between childhood and
adulthood. He must cast off his childhood dependency and learn
to become independent. He must assume new responsibilities and
certain of his culture's mores and values.

The following criteria of psychological maturation have been
suggested by Katherine W. Taylor.[1] They are:

> (1) attaining emotional emancipation from one's parents
> and developing genuine self-determination; (2) becoming an
> integral part of a group of one's peers; (3) seeking a satisfac-
> tory hetero-sexual adjustment; and (4) establishing himself
> as a person on his or her own outside the childhood home.
> Until these goals are reached, the person in question can
> scarcely be called a true adult no matter what his chrono-
> logical age may be.

One of the major problems during puberty arises from the fact
that although the individual is biologically mature, social mores
disapprove, generally, of sexual intercourse outside of marriage.
Furthermore, an adolescent is generally expected to remain in

---

[1] In Becker and Hill, eds., *Family, Marriage and Parenthood*, p. 478.

school to complete his education rather than drop out of school to get married and begin work. Many young people are able to solve this dilemma by getting married and continuing their schooling.

In each of the three periods of psychosexual development, a youngster fixes upon certain characteristic love objects. In psychoanalytic terms, the three periods are labeled narcissistic (the infancy period), homosexual (the latency period), and heterosexual (the puberty period). In early childhood, the child finds pleasure primarily in his own body; he is his own primary love object. He is not interested in persons of the opposite sex and shows no particular preference for persons of his own sex; in other words, he does not identify and choose according to sex. As the child grows older, the "gang" stage or homosexual stage emerges. As used here, the word "homosexual" has no connota-

"Do you think it's possible to fall in love with the whole senior class at once?"
(Reproduced by special permission of Consolidated News Features, Inc.)

tions of sex satisfaction; rather, it refers to a person's choice of others of his same sex as associates and playmates. Groups and clubs of the same sex are formed and the opposite sex is avoided. The child is shifting his dependence from the home to outside groups. As the child approaches puberty, as the secondary sex characteristics appear, and as various social-psychological factors begin to make their influence felt, he begins to show an interest in the opposite sex. At first, however, his choices are generalized. That is, the man is interested in women as women and not in any particular woman; the same is true of the girl's interest in men. The tendency to go together in groups and to shift attention to first one and then to another person is characteristic of this stage. But as the individual grows older, this generalized interest in the persons of the opposite sex becomes narrowed down and more and more specific, till he finally settles on one particular person.

The choice he makes will depend, to a considerable extent, on his previous experiences. If, at an earlier date, he suffered some embarrassment or shame or some traumatic experience with someone of the opposite sex, he may be very cautious in his approach to others or may seek out only those people with whom he knows he will be comfortable and at ease. Thus, the personal relationships he has established at each level of his development will be significant factors influencing his psychosexual growth.

Attitudes toward sex and sex roles. The parents' responses to the child's early sex curiosity probably play a major role in determining the child's later attitudes toward sex and sexual expression. Thus they may exert significant influence over the child's eventual marital happiness. The child derives his own attitude toward sex from the attitudes of his parents, and this process can begin while the child is still very young. It develops not only as a result of what they say or do not say, but also—and perhaps primarily—as a result of *how* they say it, the emotional overtones that accompany their answers or instructions. In a sense, there is no such thing as a parent who does *not* give sex education. Even the parent who is embarrassed and who therefore refuses to an-

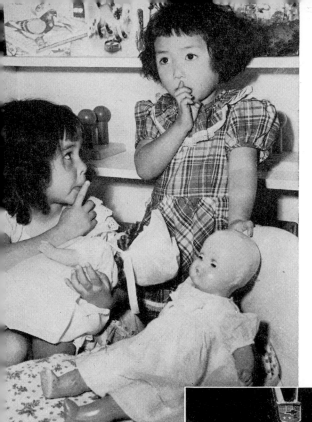

Differential training in sex roles. The two little girls are playing house, learning feminine tasks. The small boy is learning how to handle tools, a masculine task.

(*Top photo courtesy* Los Angeles Mirror. *Bottom photo courtesy* American Stock Photos.)

swer a frank question is contributing to his child's education by conveying the impression that sexual discussions—and therefore sex itself—are humiliating and taboo. Furthermore, the information that has been withheld is likely to be picked up by the child in some other, perhaps less desirable, way.

In addition to learning about sex functions, the growing child and adolescent learn sex roles. Differential training for boys and girls begins in early childhood; boys and girls are given different toys and encouraged to engage in different activities. Moreover, the mother and father serve as examples of typical male and female behavior. In dating, too, boys and girls gain insight into their roles as male or female.

Factors in Mate Selection

As we have already mentioned, the individual, in the final phase of his psychosexual development narrows his attentions down to one person of the opposite sex. However, in this connection we must not overlook the phrase—"in our culture"— for cultural factors, not biological ones, dictate what form the marital relationship will take, whether monogamous, polygamous, or otherwise.

Let us now turn our attention to a consideration of the factors that determine mate selection. These may be grouped into three categories: (1) Impersonal factors, (2) the individual's relationships with others, and (3) the individual's personality needs and characteristics.[2]

Impersonal factors. These pertain to the particular environmental and social conditions in which the individual finds himself. The first is the sex ratio in the area. If it is markedly imbalanced there is less opportunity for either men or women to get married (depending on the direction of the ratio). In general, urban centers have a slight excess of women, rural areas an excess of men,

---

[2] Manford Hinshaw Kuhn, "How Mates are Sorted," in Becker and Hill, eds., *Family, Marriage and Parenthood*, p. 246.

as shown in the following table. This condition may vary, however, for specific areas.

A Comparison of Rural and Urban Sex Ratios

Area	Sex ratio of all classes of the population in each area
United States, 1940	100.7
Urban	95.5
Rural Nonfarm	103.7
Rural Farm	111.7

On the basis of the sex ratio, some states are "good," others "bad," for women or men in terms of their chances of finding a mate. The ten "best" states for women and the ten poorest for men are Wyoming, Montana, Idaho, Washington, Arizona, California, North Dakota, Oregon, South Dakota, and Nevada. The ten poorest states for women and the best for men are Massachusetts, Rhode Island, Connecticut, New Hampshire, New Jersey, New York, Pennsylvania, Ohio, North Carolina, and Missouri.

It is rather surprising to find that in spite of our mobility, residential proximity plays a role in mate selection. The operation of this factor becomes more understandable when we realize that residential proximity does not mean merely physical nearness, but, more significantly, social nearness. That is, people living in the same neighborhood are likely to share a similar economic and social status, to be members of the same neighborhood clubs or organizations, to attend the same churches, and to belong to the same ethnic groups. Since people marry most frequently within their own socio-economic class, and since people living in the same neighborhood generally are of the same class level, we may expect residential proximity to exert an influence on marital choice.

The individual who has many social contacts has, of course, a wider range from which to choose a mate than the person who is relatively isolated and confined. This is reflected in a study made in California by Popenoe,[3] who studied the question of where educated married couples first met. For slightly over 25 per cent of the group, the first meeting took place in educational institutions. The following table shows a detailed breakdown of the places of first meeting.

Places of First Meeting	Number	Per cent
Educational system	2297	25.3
Homes of friends	1656	18.2
Business contacts	1143	12.9
Church and church social organizations	927	10.2
Propinquity	867	9.5
Private recreation	747	8.2
Travel, vacation, resort	638	7.0
Commercial recreation	345	2.7
Miscellaneous	251	2.7
Pick-ups	210	2.3

Although business contacts loom large in this table, we should remember that there are certain jobs in which the chances of meeting eligible persons are very slim. Thus nursing, library work, and social work are some of the areas of work for women where the chances of finding a man are relatively small.

Finally, "cultural permissiveness" with respect to choice of mate should be considered. Cultural stereotypes and prohibitions, if they have been assimilated by the individual, will limit his choice. Incest, for example, is tabooed in most cultures, so strongly, in fact, that the individual does not even consider choosing a mate from within his close family circle. And often intermarriage is frowned upon. "Marrying below one's class" constitutes a more ambiguous situation, being subject to possible social disapproval. However, the very fact of ambiguity may discourage a person from choosing someone outside his own socio-economic level.

The role of interpersonal relationships. Individuals are deeply affected in their choice of mates by the kind of relationships they

---

[3] Paul Popenoe, "Meetings that Lead to Marriage," *Eugenical News,* 1932, Vol. 17, 76-88.

have had with their parents. The emotional intensity of parental attachment, the love or hate or ambivalence that characterized parent-child relations, influences the kind of a person the individual will choose for a mate. If, for instance, a boy has been over-protected by his mother, he may, on growing up, seek a wife who will deal with him in the same way—a mother substitute. Or the opposite may occur. A woman who suffered under the harsh strictures of a domineering father may look for a husband who is gentle, kind, and even-tempered, the exact antithesis of her father.

Similarly, marital choice will be affected by the extent to which relationships outside of the home have been satisfying. One person may be acutely embarrassed or painfully awkward when meeting members of the opposite sex for the first time, which would tend to discourage him from making further approaches. On the other hand, someone who meets people easily, who is perfectly at ease in company, will look forward eagerly to making new friends and acquaintances.

Out of these relationships there usually emerges an image of the prospective spouse that reflects the individual's previous social experience as well as his personality needs. This image, however, is not necessarily consistent. It may vary considerably from period to period. In childhood, for example, the ideal mate image may closely resemble the parent of the opposite sex, as reflected in the child's remark to his mother when he says, "I want to marry you when I get big." This parent image is later modified by images of uncles, cousins, motion-picture stars, athletic heroes, and the like. For some imaginative adolescents the ideal mate image may be strong enough to provide physical as well as personality and social characteristics.

Such ideal mate images may operate as more or less conscious factors in mate selection. The actual choice may correspond rather closely to the ideal, but in most cases the individual probably makes a compromise or finds that other factors are more important.

It is impossible to point to any one factor in an individual's experience as being *the sole* cause for his choosing a particular

person. Many different elements come into play and these vary from person to person.

Personality needs and characteristics of the individual. Actually, we cannot deal with an individual's temperament apart from his interpersonal relationships because the type of person we are depends very much on how well we get along with others. It is only for purposes of analysis that we here deal with them separately.

The individual is not necessarily aware of all of his needs, but the ease or strain he feels in his contacts with different people may indicate that some of his acquaintances meet his conscious or unconscious needs and that others do not.

One of the most important needs operating in mate selection is the need for acceptance and recognition. In a study of psychological factors affecting choice of mate, Strauss [4] reports both men and women as saying that they wanted in their marriage partner somebody who would "show me affection," "understand my moods," "appreciate me just as I am," "make me feel I count for something." Thus, the person who lacks self-confidence may seek out somebody who will encourage and praise him or help him to make decisions.

But marrying someone who we think will satisfy our needs does not necessarily insure that we will become well adjusted. The dominant person, for example, may seek out somebody he feels he can dominate. But all he is really doing is reinforcing his undesirable characteristic, his domineering tendencies, and actually is handicapping himself insofar as his ability to adjust to situations he cannot dominate is concerned. Similarly, a dependent person may become more dependent if he marries someone who protects him and tries to make all his decisions for him. Also, it is possible that two people may try to hide their real selves from one another and may largely succeed because of the idealized, romantic aura that pervades the courtship. A domineering man, for instance, may try to convince his lady love that he

---

[4] Anselm Straus, *A Study of Three Psychological Factors Affecting Choice of Mate.* Ph.D. Thesis, Chicago, University of Chicago Libraries, 1945.

essentially is an easy-going, rather placid type. But the object of his affection may be playing the same game with him, trying to mask her strong will under a cloak of feminine serenity and help-lessness. And invariably, after they are married, a situation will arise where one will refuse to give ground before the other, and both will be at one another's throats. A happy marriage will be one in which both partners are able to satisfy their needs.

Why people do not marry. We may consider the question of why people do not marry within the same frame of reference in which we discussed mate selection.

A person may, first of all, have no opportunity to meet members of the opposite sex. In certain lines of work, as we have already indicated, men and women are relatively isolated from one another. In some parts of the country the sex ratio is de-cidedly unfavorable for one or the other sex. And members of a socially prominent family who are strongly status-conscious may be very restricted in their choice of mates.

Secondly, the particular kind of relationship an individual has had with his parents may make the choice of a mate very difficult for him. Sometimes he develops an excessive identification with his parents. A man may be very close to his mother, for example. Psychologically he has never been weaned and this makes it im-possible for him to find another woman to take his mother's place. Or a person may have been overindulged as a child and so, having had all his wishes catered to, may find it extremely difficult to accept the initiative and responsibilities that go with marriage.

Closely related to the fear of accepting responsibility is the fear of losing one's freedom or independence. The fear of being "tied down" with a "ball and chain" is among the many expressions common to us that imply that getting married is tantamount to losing one's freedom.

Many people do not marry because they set their goals too high. Their ideas of what they want in another person are quite removed from reality. They are in love with a fantasy, an ideal that no real person could ever possibly fit. Often this delusion can be traced to parental influence. A mother, let us say, may be overambitious for her son and daughter and may instill in them the belief that they are much too good for anyone else. In order to avoid quarreling with their mother, the children may give in to her and wait for the "ideal" mate—who, of course, will never materialize.

Frequently the idealized picture of the mate is a defense. The person who has been disappointed in love may now set his goal so high that his chances of becoming involved again, and perhaps of again meeting failure and disappointment, are reduced. The person is afraid of being hurt again and the idealization functions as a protective armor.

Certain other cultural values and pressures may prevent young people from marrying. First, and this is especially characteristic of the middle class, is the demand that young people make a "good marriage." Parents usually prefer that their children marry into economically and socially favorable positions, and they tend to fight against the possibility of a son or daughter's marrying "beneath his or her class."

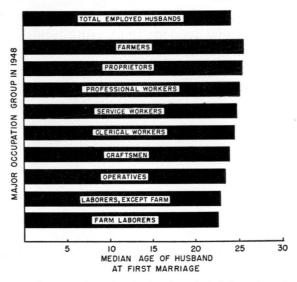

Median age at first marriage for husbands married less than five years, by occupation, in 1948. (From Paul C. Glick and Emanuel Landau, "Age as a Factor in Marriage," American Sociological Review, *Vol. 15, 1950, 528.)*

Secondly, a great deal of pressure is exerted against the idea of marrying too young. Although sexual maturity coincides with adolescence, sexual expression outside of marriage is considered improper. And since few adolescents have the economic means to support a family, marriage is postponed. Therefore, early attachments may be broken up, and these breakups may be very disturbing for the individuals involved.

Often pressures that reflect cultural mores are supplemented by other pressures, reflecting the strong personality needs of the parents. The father, for instance, who prevents his son from marrying the girl he wants to marry may justify his action on the ground that he acted for the boy's own good. Actually, however, the father probably has identified himself strongly with his son and hopes to attain through the boy's success and achievements a little of the glory and adulation he himself was denied, perhaps because he married early and had to support a family. The father regards the marriage as a threat to his hopes. The son, on the other hand, is beset by a conflict of loyalties that may well disturb his relationships both with his father and with the girl he loves.

If a marriage is postponed or a love affair broken off, the individuals concerned may build up defenses against future emotional attachments as a safeguard against being hurt again. On the other hand, it is quite possible for individuals to grow rather than to decline in their capacity to love.

Dating and Courtship Adjustments

Marriages are preceded by a more or less extended period of courtship, and the nature of the courtship affects subsequent marital relations in a significant way. The expectations built up during this period influence marital choice as well as the satisfaction and happiness derived from marriage.

The expectations have to be understood in social terms as well as in terms of the needs and the personality of the individual. The cult of "romantic love" has long flourished in America. Most of the articles of the creed are well known; from childhood on most of us are taught the code. The belief assumes that a perfect mate has been decreed by fate for each of us, that somewhere there is someone exclusively for us and that inevitably we shall meet. Also, love springs into being at first sight, and as long as two people are in love nothing else matters. Winch [5] has pointed out that this emphasis is expressive of cultural values; it functions to support individualism and to give expression to self-realization, and the idealization of the love-object becomes understandable when we consider the feelings of inferiority and insecurity that characterize the adolescent period.

Although this romantic love concept is the stock in trade of movies, much popular fiction, radio serials, and commercial advertising, it is not so all pervasive as might at first be imagined. But regardless of whether the romantic love concept flourished or not, certain individuals would still attribute to their mates characteristics that these mates never actually possessed. And since these idealized projections soon crumble under the harsh realities of everyday married life, strain and conflict result. Young people who accept the romantic illusion often think of love and marriage in terms of impossible perfection. They expect marriage to be a sort of effortless ecstasy, where love conquers all.

On the other hand, young people may try to make it appear that they can "take or leave" a particular person. They may feign indifference; they may keep a neat balance sheet of the other person's good and bad points, which will guard them against loss of status and soften the blow if a relationship is broken off.

The postponement of marriage means, of course, an extension of the dating and courtship period. The courtship period involves much trial-and-error learning. As has been pointed out earlier, when heterosexual contacts are first initiated, they are directed toward members of the opposite sex in general and only gradually do choices become more specific. Waller [6] has pointed out two main functions of the dating and courtship period: (1) It edu-

---

[5] Winch, *The Modern Family*.
[6] Waller and Hill, *The Family. A Dynamic Interpretation*.

was guarded and watched very strictly as a child. So is the adult who is satisfied only when he can dominate somebody else, who has to have his own way. This type of person may have been overly indulged or extremely frustrated as a child. Another great potential source of tension is present if either husband or wife is moody. One mate may never know whether the other is going to be in a good humor or a bad; his moods appear to have nothing to do with what the other has done; incidents that almost anyone else would take in stride either depress or elate him excessively, but it is difficult to anticipate which reaction will materialize. Such "touchiness" in one spouse causes the other spouse to become uncertain, tense, and irritable.

Problems arise in any marriage. In themselves, problems need not be disruptive. More important are the ways in which husband and wife handle and react to them. At times, all of us may fall back on defense mechanisms instead of attempting to solve the problems realistically. But the immature person will utilize defense mechanisms almost constantly. He may rationalize or withdraw or daydream to escape having to face his problems. But such devices merely create new tensions in the individual and the problem remains, to appear again at a later date.

The problem of petting and sexual intercourse often arises to perplex adolescents and young adults during the dating and courtship period. Physiologically the adolescent is quite capable of having sexual relations, but much more than mere biological capacity must be considered here. Our cultural mores forbid sex activity outside of marriage; and although there is often a great discrepancy between prescription and practice, there is a moral issue involved. Each individual must evaluate this moral issue for himself, and many different decisions are possible. Some people reject the moral prohibitions without suffering any resulting psychological disturbances. Others feel guilty and shameful if they yield. Still others observe the prohibitions because they have assimilated the values and mores of the group that frown upon promiscuity. Prohibitions are likely to be especially strong if they involve religious values in which sexual activity is considered sinful. Again, the individual may conform to the mores because he fears pregnancy and all its consequences. Some may have sexual relations with the person to whom they are engaged but not with others.

Different cultures, of course, have different mores. Some societies place relatively few restructions on sexual activity before marriage; others enforce the sexual taboos even more strongly than we do. And the degree to which mores are observed changes. Today, in our culture, we find a wide discrepancy between public and private code, between mores and actual practices, between what people say and what they do.

The frequency with which premarital intercourse takes place depends not only on the over-all cultural mores, but also is influenced by the strictness of childhood training and shows subcultural variations. Subcultural variations become apparent when persons of different educational backgrounds are compared. The Kinsey [8] report shows that by the age of 21, 49 per cent of those with some college education have had premarital intercourse, 77 per cent of the high-school group have indulged, and 84 per cent of the grammar-school group have experimented. Thus, the mores forbidding premarital intercourse operate more effectively among people having advanced educations. However, this trend is reversed regarding other sexual outlets. Masturbation and petting to a climax increase as the educational level increases.

Psychosexual Adjustment in Marriage

The dynamics of marriage and family interaction are discussed in detail in the chapter on family adjustment. We shall here focus on psychosexual factors that are important in marriage.

Clinical case material shows that sexual disharmony and dissatisfaction often is characteristic of marital discord. For this rea-

---

[8] G. M. Gilbert, "Sex on the Campus," in Donald Porter Geddes and Enid Curie, eds., *About the Kinsey Report. Observations by 11 Experts on Sexual Behavior in the Human Male.* New York: New American Library, 1948, pp. 70-74.

son, many people assume that it also is a cause of marital difficulties. However, many writers in this field agree that sexual maladjustment is more often a symptom, rather than a cause, of marital unhappiness. And in cases where it is a cause, it rarely is the only one. Levy and Munroe [9] state this point well when they say:

> Now the appearance of snowstorms is regularly preceded by the dropping of leaves from the trees. Nevertheless we do not consider the fall of leaves responsible for snow. We know very well that the coming of winter produces both these effects. Just so it may be that some fundamental struggle between husband and wife brings about sexual disharmony and the other evidences of discord which make them consider their marriage a failure. Actually the relationship between sexual incompatibility and the failure of marriage is very intricate. I believe that close study of the problem will show us that it is both cause and effect, and also perhaps just an accompaniment, an expression of general lack of harmony.

Once sexual maladjustment arises it may intensify further disturbances in the marital relationship. It is also possible that sexual difficulties will become more and more irritating to the persons involved, since it is more tangible, more clearly recognizable than other more subtle psychological factors. The crucial point to keep in mind is that sexual behavior reflects the personality characteristics and the cultural conditioning of the individual and cannot be understood apart from these. Furthermore, in a happy marriage sexual satisfaction of one partner depends on the satisfaction of the other. Fulfilling the desire of the mate is the condition of satisfaction for the other mate. The husband and wife play complementary, not conflicting roles. We see thus that the sex relation in marriage depends not only on the strength of the sexual need in each person, but also on the fact that the husband and wife are necessary to one another for its satisfaction.

---

[9] Reprinted from *The Happy Family* by John Levy and Ruth Munroe, by permission of Alfred A. Knopf, Inc. Copyright 1947 by Alfred A. Knopf, Inc., p. 109.

Either one or both spouses may be sexually dissatisfied for a number of reasons.

1. It is possible that the sex drive is stronger in one of them and that he or she may desire sexual intercourse more frequently. Terman [10] used the ratio between actual and preferred frequency of intercourse as one of the basic sexual adjustment factors. On the basis of these ratios, he classified the subjects of his study into five categories representing (a) marked hunger, and (b) moderate hunger, when the frequency of preferred intercourse was greater than that of actual intercourse, (c) optimum satisfaction, where the frequencies were the same, and (d) moderate satiety, and (e) marked satiety, where frequency of actual intercourse exceeded frequency of preferred intercourse. He found that in slightly more than half of the wives and husbands optimum satisfaction was obtained, and that, in general, this group had the highest happiness scores. The greater the degree of unsatisfied hunger or of satiety, the lower the general trend of happiness. He found, further, that the happiness of a given spouse depends not only on his own sexual satisfaction, but also on the sexual satisfaction of his mate. Even if the husband enjoys approximately the intercourse frequency that he prefers, he, as well as his wife, will have a moderately low happiness score if his wife suffers marked sex hunger. We should keep in mind that the scores compared are means, and that within each group there is considerable variation.

Frequency of intercourse as such, i.e., whether it takes place once or twice a month or more than ten times, showed only a very slight correlation with marital happiness. A rather high frequency of intercourse was found in unhappy marriages, which may imply that sex is the only type of communion still satisfying to the husband and wife, or that sex is used as a possible means to revive the waning affection between the partners.

2. Another factor in sexual adjustment involves the orgasm. Frequently the man arrives at the point of orgasm more quickly than his wife. Unless he restrains himself, his wife will not find

---

[10] Terman, *Psychological Factors in Marital Happiness.*

the emotional release the orgasm affords. Terman found that the wife's orgasm adequacy was the most important of the sex factors. In the population sample he studied, 66.6 per cent of the wives said that they experienced orgasm usually or always, and 33.4 per cent replied that they experienced it rarely or never. The mean happiness score of wives increases as the frequency of adequate orgasm experience increases; the same is true of the happiness scores of the husbands of these wives.

Again, these are averages; the range of scores in each group shows a high happiness score for some of the wives who never or rarely experience orgasm and a low happiness score for some who always or usually do.

3. Some women who are strongly sexed may have just as much difficulty reaching an orgasm as do women in whom the sex drive may be very weak. Both conditions are included under the term "frigidity." The causes for frigidity are not too well known. Clinical evidence indicates that many factors are involved. Frigidity may stem from biological factors, although endocrine therapy has not generally been successful in effecting a cure. Or, frigidity may be related to the woman's attitudes toward sex, especially if she learned as a child to regard everything related to the sex act with revulsion. Frigidity also may be connected with traumatic experiences. Because of the multiplicity of factors, no one method of treatment can be advocated as being the answer in all cases. Help for some of these women may be obtained from psychotherapy or from instruction in sex techniques. Even those women who are not helped may be able to make a happy adjustment with their husband by reducing the high value they or their husbands may have placed on this sex factor and by emphasizing other values in marriage.

The counterpart to frigidity in women is impotence in men. Impotence may manifest itself in failure to produce an erection or in premature ejaculation, as well as in a very low sexual interest and drive. Clinical evidence indicates that impotence generally is a psychological problem. Often the condition is temporary, caused by general tension and fatigue. Where it is more lasting, it may spring from disturbed emotional relationships with the wife, or personality problems of the husband.

It is clearly apparent from a survey of the work in this field that sexual adjustment and maladjustment are tremendously important problems for millions of couples. A better understanding of the factors that influence the sexual relationship between a man and a woman is needed.

For Additional Reading

Baber, Ray E., *Marriage and the Family.* New York, McGraw-Hill Book Company, Inc., 1939.

Becker, Howard and Reuben Hill, eds., *Family, Marriage, and Parenthood.* Boston, D. C. Heath and Co., 1948.

Bossard, James H. S., "Residential Propinquity as a Factor in Marriage Selection," *American Journal of Sociology,* Vol. 38, 1932, 219-224.

Bowman, Henry A., *Marriage for Moderns.* New York, McGraw-Hill Book Company, Inc., 1948.

Burgess, Ernest W. and Leonard S. Cottrell, *Predicting Success or Failure in Marriage.* New York, Prentice-Hall, Inc., 1939.

———— and Harvey J. Locke, *The Family.* New York, American Book Company, 1945.

———— and Paul Wallin, *Engagement and Marriage.* Chicago, J. B. Lippincott Company, 1953.

Cavan, Ruth Shonle, *The American Family.* New York, Thomas Y. Crowell Company, 1953.

Christensen, Harold T., *Marriage Analysis.* New York, The Ronald Press Company, 1950.

Conn, J. H., "Sexual Curiosity of Children," *American Journal of Diseases in Childhood,* Vol. 40, 1940, 1110-1119.

Duvall, Evelyn Millis and Reuben Hill, *When You Marry,* rev. ed. Boston, D. C. Heath and Company, 1953.

English, O. Spurgeon and Gerald H. J. Pearson, *Emotional Problems of Living. Avoiding the Neurotic Pattern.* New York, W. W. Norton & Company, Inc., 1945.

Geddes, Donald Porter and Enid Curie, eds., *About the Kinsey Report. Observations by 11 Experts on Sexual Behavior in the Human Male.* New York, The New American Library, 1948.

Gorer, Geoffrey, "America's Most Popular Tribal Custom," *Reader's Digest,* January 1950, 34-36.

Kardiner, Abram, *Sex and Morality.* Indianapolis, The Bobbs-Merrill Company, 1954.

Kinsey, Alfred C., Wardell B. Pomeroy, and Clyde E. Martin, *Sexual Behavior in the Human Male.* Philadelphia, W. B. Saunders Company, 1948.

————, *Sexual Behavior in the Human Female.* Philadelphia, W. B. Saunders Company, 1953.

Landis, Judson T. and Mary G. Landis, *Building a Successful Marriage,* 2nd ed. New York, Prentice-Hall, Inc., 1953.

————, *Readings in Marriage and the Family.* New York, Prentice-Hall, Inc., 1952.

Levy, John and Ruth Munroe, *The Happy Family.* New York, Alfred A. Knopf, Inc., 1947.

Locke, Harvey J., *Predicting Adjustment in Marriage.* New York, Henry Holt & Company, Inc., 1951.

Nimkoff, Meyer F., *Marriage and the Family.* Boston, Houghton Mifflin Company, 1947.

Ogburn, William F. and Ernest R. Groves, *American Marriage and Family Relationships.* New York, Henry Holt & Company, Inc., 1932.

Pennington, L. A. and Irwin A. Berg, eds., *An Introduction to Clinical Psychology.* New York, The Ronald Press Company, 1948.

Scheinfeld, Amram, *Women and Men.* New York, Harcourt, Brace & Company, Inc., 1943.

Seward, Georgene H., *Sex and the Social Order.* New York and London, McGraw-Hill Book Company, Inc., 1946.

Terman, Lewis M., *Psychological Factors in Marital Happiness.* New York and London, McGraw-Hill Book Company, Inc., 1938.

Truxal, Andrew G. and Francis E. Merrill, *The Family in American Culture.* New York, Prentice-Hall, Inc., 1947.

Waller, Willard and Reuben Hill, *The Family.* New York, The Dryden Press, 1951.

Winch, Robert F., *The Modern Family.* New York, Henry Holt & Company, Inc., 1952.

Young, Kimball, *Personality and Problems of Adjustment,* 2nd ed., New York, Appleton-Century-Crofts, Inc., 1952.

Old Age
Adjustments

CHAPTER 14

- THE AGING PROCESS
- WAYS OF ADJUSTING TO THE AGING
  PROCESS

In preceding chapters we have discussed the adjustment problems of children, adolescents, and adults. We now turn to consider the problems peculiar to the last period in the life cycle—old age.

Most of us have older relatives and friends. We enjoy the company of some of them, some irk us with their meddlesomeness, and still others bore us with their often repeated stories.

The nature of the aging process and the conditions of our culture create certain problems characteristic of the old-age group. But at the same time there is no "typical" old person, for the process of aging affects different people in different ways, and culturally engendered frustrations and gratifications vary according to the environment. Each person will experience and interpret these frustrations and gratifications according to his own personality, the richness or drabness of his childhood and adult life, and his attitudes toward old age. Thus the prevalence of certain characteristic old-age adjustment problems should not lead us to believe that all old people face the same kind of problems or respond to these problems in the same way. The following two case studies are presented to indicate some of the many differences that can be found in the way elderly people adjust or fail to adjust to their problems.

Mrs. E. has just passed her 85th birthday. She is a handsome woman in good health, although she says that she does not have the energy she had ten years ago. She needs a long night's sleep, and therefore rarely goes out in the evening. But she never complains. She has lived a full life, has traveled a great deal, and always has been very active in community affairs. During the last ten years she has settled down in a small town near San Francisco. She likes the relative quiet there but goes to San Francisco several times a year for special events. She prefers to live by herself because, as she says, she likes to have things her own way at home and is too old to adjust her style of living to someone else's. But she has many friends who come to visit her or with whom she keeps up a lively correspondence. She is still active in community affairs—still is aroused by social injustices and calls on people, writes letters, and works on committees to help remedy what she considers wrong. She reads a great deal and is well informed about national and international politics. Alert and active, she has little time for complaints and boredom.

Mr. S. is approaching eighty. Like Mrs. E. he is in fairly good financial circumstances and lives with his wife and daughter in a comfortable apartment. About ten years ago he retired from a successful import-export business in Brazil and came back to the States. Since then he has gradually deteriorated. He never had any strong interests outside his business, and when he retired from it, he had no resources to fall back on, no interests to keep him going. When he left his business, he also left his acquaintances and friends and did not have the zest to make new ones when he returned to this country. Physically he is still in fairly good health but otherwise he has deteriorated to the point where he is content to sit in a chair all day long, unoccupied, often nodding off to sleep even when there is company. Outside of his immediate family he does not recognize anybody. If he goes out, he soon becomes restless and wants to go home again. His memory for recent events is almost completely gone, and when he talks at all, he fills his conversation with recollections of his childhood days spent on a large farm in Kentucky. To an outsider, his life seems empty, devoid of all interests and meaning.

CHART 1

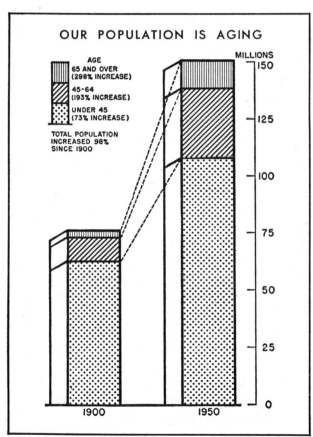

(*From Federal Security Agency,* Fact Book on Aging. *Washington, D.C., Govt. Printing Office,* 1952, p. 5.)

We see in these two examples the tremendous importance that psychological factors play in how we adjust to old age. Some of these psychological factors can be detected while we are still young so that we may better, and earlier, prepare for our old age.

Although old age may seem very remote to most of us, it is a situation we shall all have to face—barring, of course, early death. One in every 12 persons in this country is 65 years old or over, and the proportion is steadily increasing. Chart 1 shows how our population has been aging during the last 50 years. Although the total population has increased 98 per cent from 1900 to 1950, the increase in the 65-year-old age group has been 298 per cent.

Medical advances (especially the rapid strides made in preventive medicine and the control of infectious diseases), improved sanitation, and a general rise in the standard of living have greatly increased our life span. Fewer people die in childhood or their early adult years and more reach their sixties and seventies than was the case 50 years ago. A recent front page news story reports that scientists meeting at the Third Congress of the International Association of Gerontology [1] hope to extend the average life span of man to 100 years within another 50 years.

Through the folklore and mythology of many cultures run themes of a search for the fountain of youth. But scientific research into the problems confronting older people and social planning built around the results of this research are relatively recent developments. One reason for the growing concern with these problems in recent years lies in the fact that more and more people are living to an advanced age. But more important are the social and economic trends that have pinpointed and dramatized the problems of the aged and kindled a social awareness of them. We shall discuss a few of these trends here and the bearing they have on the adjustment problems of the aged.

First, we have become a nation of city dwellers, and living space has become somewhat of a premium. There was, on the whole, more room on the farm than there is in the city apartment,

---

[1] Gerontology is the scientific study of the phenomena of old age. Geriatrics deals more specifically with the clinical problems of the aged.

CHART 2

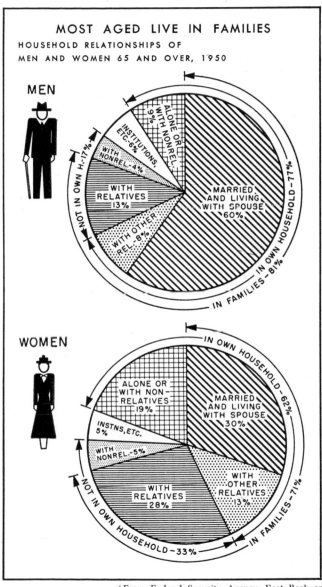

(*From Federal Security Agency*, Fact Book on
Aging, *p. 15.*)

and most rural families—grandparents, parents, and children—
generally lived under the same roof. Even today most older people
live in families; fewer than one-fourth have other living arrangements. Of this one-fourth, 14 per cent live in households of their
own but without relatives, 4 per cent live as roomers or boarders
with non-relatives, and 6 per cent live in hotels, large rooming
houses, and institutions. The household relationships of men and
women 65 years and over are graphically represented in Chart 2.
Although the percentage of older people living in non-family set-
tings is relatively low, in a population of approximately 13 million men and women 65 years old and over this is, in actual numbers, a really sizable group.

Secondly, on the farm there were always chores with which an
older person could busy himself, and these chores usually were in
line with the type of work he had done most of his life. He could
continue to contribute in a meaningful way to the household. City
living, especially in crowded apartments, offers much less opportunity for work of this kind, and the kind of tasks that can be
done usually are different from the work that the man or woman
did when employed. On the farms, responsibilities and functions
gradually decrease and taper off. And usually the small, independent businessmen can ease himself gradually into retirement, showing up at the shop maybe once or twice a week to greet old acquaintances and friends and generally keeping his finger in things.
But in most jobs the break is abrupt—from work to no work.
Generally, the sudden change presents a much greater adjustment
problem than the gradual relinquishing of duties.[2]

Often, the older person is retired when he is still capable and
willing to work. Generally, retirement means that his income will
be reduced and his business and social contacts will shrink. Although many older persons are covered by pension plans of various kinds, the income to be had from such plans is ordinarily
much lower than the income to be had from wages and salaries.
Where the younger person can look forward to advancement and

[2] Talcott Parsons, "Age and Sex in the Social Structure," *American Sociological Review*, Vol. 7, 1942, 604-616.

pay increases in his job, the older person must accept the fact that his days of opportunity are over. At best, he will be allowed to keep his present job and continue at the same level, but it is more likely that he will have to take another position that will involve lowering his standard of living. When we consider further that in 1950, 70 per cent of all women 65 years old and over had lost the benefit of a husband's financial support, and that 59 per cent of the men in that age group were not employed, we realize that a considerable proportion of the aged are financially dependent.

We have already seen that most of the child's and adolescent's problems arise as his contacts expand, as he is forced to adjust to the demands of meeting new people and new and strange situations. Quite the opposite is true for the older person. At retirement, his world begins to shrink. He must face the fact that close business associations will be broken, that the stimulation and challenge that his job offered will soon be gone.

In summary, then, we may say that the shift from rural to urban living, the rise of the conjugal family at the expense of the extended, and the usually sudden retirement from work are among the basic causes of severe adjustment problems for the aged. And the fact that the number of aged in our population is increasing constantly means that more and more people are going to be confronted with these problems.

The problems faced by the older population find their most dramatic expression in the fact that persons 60 years old and over make up approximately one-third of all first admissions to American mental hospitals, and suicide occurs more frequently in the old-age group than in any other. An analysis of admissions to mental hospitals by states and by socio-economic status shows that the rate of admission is highest in the oldest and most urbanized sections of the country—the Middle Atlantic and New England states and in the Pacific area to which large numbers of older people have migrated—and in lower-class dwelling areas.[3] The

---

[3] H. Warren Dunham, "Sociological Aspects of Mental Disorders in Later Life," in Oscar J. Kaplan, ed., *Mental Disorders in Later Life*. Stanford, California, Stanford University Press, 1947, pp. 117-133.

process of aging combined with the frustrations that our culture imposes on the aged may burden the older person to the extent that deterioration and breakdown are inevitable.

We must emphasize at this point that the nature of the adjustment problems that the aged face is not universal for all cultures. Different cultures approach and regard old age and the aging process in different ways, and even within particular cultures we find wide differences in attitudes and beliefs toward the aged. Let us consider some of these different values and attitudes in some detail here.

To begin with, our culture emphasizes youth. Youth we see as a gay, exciting, dynamic period of life. The young person is full of energy, ready to accept all challenges, bold, confident, courageous, pioneering. The world is wide open for him. "Our young people are our most prized possessions, the hope of the future," we say, implying in the same breath that aging is sad and painful, that elderly or beyond-middle-age people are relatively useless and burdensome. This emphasis is quite different from the Japanese tendency, for example, to stress the advantages of old age. Embree [4] reports that in some Japanese villages men and women hold a party when they reach the age of 61, a privileged age that, once attained, henceforth entitles the person to respect and special privileges in recognition of his wisdom.

Further, our society has no clearly established norms concerning the obligation of children to support aged and needy parents. Even if children accept this responsibility, they may do so unwillingly and in the process make the parent feel quite unwanted. In a study of the attitudes of Protestant and Catholic children toward giving an aged parent a home, Dinkel [5] reported that many more students of both faiths accepted than rejected the obligation when the situation presented no special difficulties. But the per-

---

[4] John F. Embree, *Suye Mura: A Japanese Village*. Chicago, University of Chicago Press, 1949, p. 214.

[5] Robert M. Dinkel, "Attitudes of Children toward Supporting Aged Parents," *American Sociological Review*, Vol. 9, 1944, 370-379.

centage of those willing to accept the responsibility decreased rapidly as the hardships or inconveniences connected with such care became more severe (see Table 1). Before proceeding with the test, Dinkel determined whether the students were of rural or urban background. The figures given in Table 1 are for students of urban background. The table also indicates that there are pronounced differences between the attitudes of the Protestant and Catholic students, the obligation of children to support their parents in old age being more firmly established among the Catholics than among the Protestants. But the Catholics by no means accepted the responsibility unconditionally. Children do allow the nature of their personal relationships with their parents to influence their decisions, and this has an important bearing on the psychological security of the parents: they cannot be *sure* that their children will be willing to care for them later on in life.

TABLE 1

ATTITUDES OF CHILDREN TOWARD SUPPORTING AGED PARENTS.
PERCENTAGE OF COLLEGE STUDENTS CHECKING EACH OF SIX STATEMENTS
CONCERNING SUPPORT OF AGED PARENTS UNDER VARYING DEGREES
OF HARDSHIP, ACCORDING TO RELIGION

Statement	Protestant	Catholic
Aged parents who keep getting in the way should not be given a home by their children	21	7
If aged parents are unpleasant, children should not give them a home	25	12
If aged parents are a nuisance in the home, children should refuse to take them in	24	15
Children should not give a home to aged parents who are quarrelsome	34	15
Aged parents who interfere with family affairs should be put out of your home	45	26
Children should not take care of aged parents if it makes for squabbling and turmoil all the time	67	40

And, to cite one more illustration, reports from various industries indicate that, on the whole, workers rarely look forward to their retirement. Surveys made by the Social Security Board of persons receiving old-age benefits show that only 5 per cent have retired while still in good health. By far the largest group has been laid off by their employers, and the rest have retired because of failing health.[6] Although attitudes toward retirement vary among different socio-economic groups, it is true, at least of the industrial worker, that in many cases his retirement is not voluntary. Business and industry place a premium on the young worker, and although most employers seem willing to keep on an older worker who has been with the company for a long time, they do not, as a general rule, hire older employees.

Since retirement, then, is so often not a matter of choice, but is, on the contrary, often resisted, it is not surprising that many older people arrive at retirement age quite unprepared to accept the fact that they are now regarded as surplus, that their hands that heretofore have always been busy and productive must now lie idle. They want to continue working, and their unwillingness or inability to accept their new situation often accentuates the difficulties they face in adjusting to retirement.

The Aging Process

We have discussed in these past pages some of the basic social and economic conditions that create adjustment problems for older people in our society. But we have emphasized at the same time that there is a great deal of variability in the extent to which particular older people are affected by these conditions, and we have pointed out some of the factors that cause this variability.

Now let us consider the physical, mental, psychological, and physiological changes that generally accompany advancing years. We shall find that these changes also vary in extent and severity, depending on the personal characteristics of each individual.

There are two major reasons why these changes vary among

---

[6] Jacob Tuckman and Irving Lorge, *Retirement and the Industrial Worker.* New York, Columbia University, Teachers College, Bureau of Publications, 1953, p. 31.

different people. First, all individuals do not age at the same rate. For example, some people may begin to have trouble with their eyesight or hearing at a relatively early age; others may remain keen-eyed and keen-eared until their seventies or eighties or even later. And we all know or have known some people who seemed old at forty; others who were still alert and "young" at 70. Secondly, various sensory functions do not age at the same rate in the same person. One person may begin to have trouble hearing at age 60 and may be quite deaf by the time he is 65, but his eyesight may remain quite good. Keeping this variability in mind, we can, nevertheless, note certain general trends in the aging process.[7]

With increasing age, vision and hearing steadily decline. A person loses his ability to distinguish between subtle shadings, to match colors, and to focus on close or distant objects; and the extent of his visual field diminishes. These changes spring primarily from changes in the physical characteristics of the eye. Other sight defects, such as the decline in the span and speed of visual perception, probably result from changes that occur in the central nervous system.

The most common hearing defect that afflicts elderly people is an inability to catch high-pitched sounds. This ailment occurs so frequently in older people that it is regarded as a normal result of aging.

It is important to note that the older person often finds it more difficult to adjust to impaired hearing than to defective vision. In a study of older people in Prairie City, a small midwestern town, Havighurst and Albrecht [8] found that 38 per cent of the old-age group reported some degree of visual disability that could not be corrected satisfactorily, and 47 per cent mentioned hearing problems. They also noted, however, that very few people *complained* about poor vision; most of the old people had apparently made

---

[7] For a detailed account of the physiological aspects of aging see Nathan W. Shock, "Physiological Aspects of Mental Disorders in Later Life," in Kaplan, ed., *Mental Disorders in Later Life,* pp. 23-68.

[8] Robert J. Havighurst and Ruth Albrecht, *Older People.* New York, Longmans, Green & Company, 1953.

a satisfactory adjustment to it. But the adjustment to impaired hearing was for many much more difficult. The reason for this lies in the fact that impaired hearing is a much greater social handicap than poor vision. People who are hard of hearing often cannot follow a conversation, cannot understand sales people, and have trouble following stage, screen, and radio dialogue. Some actually feel that other people avoid them because they are hard of hearing, or make fun of them. They find it hard to accept the social isolation that impaired hearing forces upon them.

Very little information is available concerning the relationship between the other sensory functions and advancing age. Although anatomists have found that taste buds and olfactory nerves atrophy with age, they have not actually been able to link these facts to loss of taste and olfactory perception in older people. Nor have researchers been able to prove that the aged are less sensitive to pain than younger people, although some studies have sought to establish this correlation.

Motor abilities decline with advancing years much as do hearing and vision. Decline in reaction time and in speed of muscular movement and muscular coordination begins in the second or third decade of life, but the rate of decline increases toward the end of life. Again, however, there is a wide range of individual differences among older people and much overlapping among age groups.

Reproductive functions decrease with advancing age in both men and women. The cessation of menstrual flow offers a clearly marked end of reproductive capacity in women.

Although the demands made on the physiological functioning of the body are often no greater than those that occur at other age levels, older people have less reserve capacity to meet these demands. Their reduced ability to grow new tissue, for example, means that they recover less quickly from accidents—bones take longer to knit, abrasions are slower to heal, the ravages of cancer, for example, and other degenerative diseases, less easy to throw off. Older people also show less resistance to certain types of infections.

In the minds of many people, chronic disease is associated with old age. Actually chronic illness may set in at any age, and the maximum incidence is found in the 35-50 year-old age group.[9] But impaired health and disability increase progressively from the age of 15 years on, as shown in Chart 3.

CHART 3

Disability Increases With Age

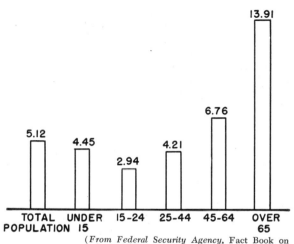

(*From Federal Security Agency*, Fact Book on Aging, p. 39.)

The writers of the *Fact Book on Aging* point out that although these data were, at the time of their writing, some 17 years old, they are the most recent ones we have on the subject, and that they are generally accepted as representative of the current situation. As the chart indicates, on the day of the interview, one in every seven men and women aged 65 years and over was disabled.

Much of the disability in the old-age group arises from disorders that are common in persons 20 years younger. At this earlier age these afflictions are not as yet disabling but they become pro-

[9] *National Health Survey, 1935–1936.* Sickness and Medical Care Series, Bulletin No. 6, National Institute of Health, U.S.P.H.S. Washington, D. C., Government Printing Office, 1939.

gressively so with advancing age. As Shock [10] has pointed out, the sources of old age disability begin in the thirties and forties, and it is during that period that preventive medicine can be most effective.

Intellectual capacity, as measured by our standard intelligence tests, also changes as we grow older. Studies by a number of investigators have shown that rapid gains in intelligence are made during adolescence, reaching a peak around the age of 20. Then a continuous, gradual decline sets in. Intelligence test results, however, actually are composite scores that are derived by testing a number of different abilities and then averaging the results. We can understand the nature of the changes better by studying the scores of particular abilities measured. Such studies reveal that older people do poorly on test items that call for speed of performance and relatively new adjustments. A person's ability to recall digits, work mathematical problems, and reproduce block designs also declines with age. On the other hand, older people do quite well on tests dealing with information, comprehension, and vocabulary. In these, the accumulated knowledge that comes with age is a definite asset.

An individual's ability to learn new material also varies with age. In a series of studies, Ruch [11] has shown that the decline in learning ability that accompanies increasing age varies for different types of material and is most pronounced when the new material to be learned conflicts or interferes with material previously learned. If his subjects merely had to learn a new habit, verbal or motor, the young (12 to 17 years) and the middle-aged (34 to 59 years) groups performed about the same; the older group (60-82 years) needed 20 per cent more time. But when learning a new habit meant that old habits had to be broken down, then the older group required 50 per cent more time.

---

[10] Nathan W. Shock, *Trends in Gerontology*. Stanford, Calif., Stanford University Press, 1951, p. 14.

[11] F. L. Ruch, "The Differential Decline of Learning Ability in the Aged as a Possible Explanation of Their Conservatism," *Journal of Social Psychology*, Vol. 5, 1934, 329-337; and "The Differentiative Effects of Age Upon Human Learning," *Journal of General Psychology*, Vol. 11, 1934, 261-286.

These are the general trends that have been reported concerning the changes in mental ability that occur with the onset of old age. Although there is little doubt that the general trend is one of decline, the results must be evaluated with certain questions and qualifications in mind.

First, there is a great variability within each age group, and considerable overlapping among age groups; many older people actually surpass the average of younger age groups.

Second, most of our intelligence tests, especially speed tests, have been standardized on the basis of young people's responses and may not, therefore, be entirely valid for older persons.

Third, motivation is an important factor in all testing, and we cannot assume that both the younger and the older person are equally motivated. On the whole, the younger person tends to be more responsive to testing situations, the older person more resistant.

And finally, it is difficult to avoid selective sampling. Young people are readily available for testing in our public schools and they are a fairly representative sample of the total population of their age. We do not find older people in such large ready-made groups, except perhaps in some old-age homes, and these are a selective sample. Thus, in evaluating test scores, we always have to ask whether the group studied may be taken as a representative cross-section.

On the whole, functions that depend essentially on physical or physiological factors show an earlier decline than those abilities that are primarily mental.[12] When we inquire into the subjective awareness of aging, we find that older people mention physical characteristics more often than mental ones as symptoms of their growing old. Those who are more highly educated, however, are more likely to mention mental symptoms than those who have had little education.[13]

---

[12] W. R. Miles, "Psychological Aspects of Aging," in E. V. Cowdry, ed., *Problems of Aging,* 2nd ed. Baltimore, Williams and Wilkins, 1942, Chapter 28.

[13] L. W. Jones, "Personality and Age," *Nature,* Vol. 136, 1935, 779-782. 779-782.

A person's attitude toward aging cannot be understood merely as a consequence of physical and physiological deterioration. His feelings will depend on what he still wants to do, on the goals he has set for himself. If these are ambitious, he may fear the onset of old age much more than someone else who has no particular plans for the future. As we have emphasized in other chapters, our behavior and our adjustment must always be understood within the total context of biological and psychological changes and environmental influences and pressures, and in the way a person interprets and responds to these factors.

In measuring intelligence, investigators have gone to great lengths to keep the influence of learning at a minimum. As we have seen, those test items in which accumulative experience is most important—information, comprehension and vocabulary—show least decline with age. It is possible, therefore, that although a person's intellectual capacity may decline with age, this decline may be compensated for by his having perfected many special talents through long practice and by his having accumulated wide knowledge and experience. Thus an older person may still be creative and productive.

In a recent book, Lehman [14] has compiled some well-documented evidence showing the relationship between age and achievement. As one of his criteria of achievement, Lehman has taken the ages at which outstanding figures have most frequently made (or first published) their finest creative contributions. In almost all fields studied—and these include science and mathematics, philosophy, literature, music and painting—the maximum average rate of highly superior production was found to occur in the thirties. For music, for example, the maxima, according to Lehman, are as follows:

Instrumental selections	25-29 years
Vocal solos	30-34
Symphonies	30-34
Chamber music	35-39

[14] Harvey C. Lehman, *Age and Achievement*. Princeton, N. J., Princeton University Press, 1953.

Orchestral music	35-39
Grand opera	35-39
Cantatas	40-44
Light opera and musical comedy	40-44

However, although the highest average output of superior production is in the thirties, the total range for best production extends over several decades. Some of the great philosophers, for
example, were still writing and having their works published after
they had turned 90.

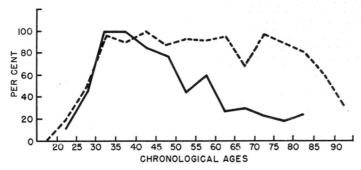

Quantity vs. quality of philosophical output. Solid line, the one best treatise
(as determined by consensus) by each of 182 deceased philosophers. Broken
line, the ages at which these 182 men published 1593 books, an average of
8.75 books per man. (From Harvey C. Lehman, Age and Achievement. Published for the American Philosophical Society by Princeton University Press,
1953, p. 47.)

Many notable creative works are produced in late maturity,
and, as Lehman points out, any stereotyped conception of later
maturity as an unproductive period is quite false. Individual variations exist at each age level and "careful study of the individual
should be the court of last appeal."

Although Lehman is primarily concerned with presenting the
facts concerning age and achievement, he does discuss briefly the
possible causes for the early maxima in creativity. The 16 factors
he lists indicate the great complexity of contributing causes. These
factors include decline in physical vigor and sensory capacity, illness, and glandular changes, as well as psychological and social

factors, such as unhappy marriage and sexual maladjustment, bereavement, preoccupation with practical concerns, less favorable conditions for concentrated work, contentment with early recognition, apathy because of non-recognition and destructive criticism, increasing inflexibility, decrease in motivation leading to weaker intellectual interest and curiosity, a less stimulating social and cultural environment, psychoses, and the cumulative effects of various kinds of dissipation.

The process of aging also leaves its mark on the emotional life and the personality characteristics of the aged. The increasing social isolation and the uncertainty that stalks the lives of many older people lead to emotional instability and anxiety. And as his mental dexterity begins to fade, the older person becomes more and more fixed in his attitudes and interests. He loses his time perspective, becomes preoccupied only with his day-by-day existence and with the past, and has little hope for the future. Add to these the realization that hearing, sight, and reflexes are declining, that status and recognition have been lost through retirement, and it is not difficult to see why old age often is a difficult adjustment hurdle for many to overcome.

When the despair and depression become too great, neurotic behavior patterns may develop.[15] One of the most common of these is an intense preoccupation with bodily functions (hypochondriasis). Lack of motivation and decreased energy may combine to produce periods of chronic fatigue that are usually accompanied by increased irritability. Sometimes fear of reduced sexual potency may lead an older person into excessive eroticism and sexually deviant behavior. Futility may express itself in neurotic depression characterized by self-centeredness and self-disparagement. All these symptoms represent attempts on the part of an older person to find some solutions to the problems confronting him; and they occur, as we have said, when the burdens of adjustment prove too much for him.

---

[15] For a detailed discussion of neuroses, see N. Cameron, "Neuroses of Later Maturity," in Kaplan, ed., *Disorders in Later Life.*

Ways of Adjusting to the Aging Process

As we age, we may find it more difficult to satisfy our psychological needs. The elderly person is confronted with the dilemma of having to find new ways to satisfy his needs at a time when his flexibility and ability to adopt to new experiences and situations have sharply declined.

An individual's well-being hinges upon his ability to satisfy, at least in part, certain fundamental needs. To be sure, some of the needs we regarded as vital in our youth assume less and less importance as we grow older, but they never disappear completely. We have discussed these psychological needs in other chapters. They include the need for some degree of security, for affection, for recognition and status, and for self-esteem. We have shown how older people often are thwarted or frustrated in their attempts to satisfy these needs. We shall now concern ourselves with the question of how new adjustments can be made. What can be done to aid elderly people to adjust? We shall consider the possibilities in the light of the old-age problems we have up to now been discussing.

The sources of the problems facing older people lie partly in social conditions and attitudes, partly in biological and psychological changes, and partly in the kind of person an individual has been—what his outlook on life has been, the kind of life he has led, what his attitude toward old age is. Any approach to satisfactory adjustment, therefore, must take into account all these factors. Often the services of a trained counselor or psychologist are required to pinpoint or isolate complex, intertwined causes of maladjustment and to set the person concerned upon the road to healthy, happy living.

But psychotherapy is not the only recourse. Lack of an income adequate to meet basic needs and failing health are among the major worries of older people. Revised hiring policies in industry and business, adequate pension plans, and provisions for medical care can do much to alleviate these worries. Experience with older workers during World War II led some employers to change their attitudes about hiring older people. Especially in jobs where quality of work was more important than speed or in those positions in which judgment and experience counted heavily, older workers were found to be highly satisfactory.

In recent years the John Hay Whitney Foundation has selected a small group of retired professors each year and arranged for them to teach at various small colleges which could not otherwise have afforded them. Colleges and professors alike have benefited from the experiment. Increased student interest in the subjects taught by these experts has, in some cases, led to the establishment of new departments. Many of the professors have been asked to stay on or have been invited to lecture at other colleges.

In a few communities, job-counseling services for older people have been set up, with very satisfactory results. Of course, the elderly worker will never be in as great demand as the young worker, but developments such as these can do much to influence employers to take advantage of the skills, talents, and productive capacity of older people who still can and want to work.

A consideration of the health needs of older people involves two major approaches. The first centers around the problem of providing facilities and care for the aged who are sick, especially for those who are chronically ill. The second involves preventive geriatrics. As pointed out earlier, many of the disorders of the aged have their genesis in earlier years. Early detection and treatment can do much to arrest the development of serious afflictions. Basic to both approaches is the belief that illness and disorders in old age are not inevitable nor incurable, that the health of older people can be improved, that rehabilitation is possible. Such health programs are valuable not only because of the medical help *per se* that they offer, but also because they imply a changed attitude toward the old person—he is not doomed to live out his days in poor health. And this in turn will affect the concept the aged have of themselves.

Increasing attention also is being given to the living arrangements of the aged, both institutionalized and private. Many older people will continue to live in their own homes, but for many others some form of group living will be desirable or necessary. Recent studies indicate that homes for the aged should not be isolated from the rest of the community. On the contrary, homes should be located in urban or suburban areas where the older people can have access to the larger community and can maintain their contacts with the family and friends.[16]

Another major problem faced by the aged is increasing social isolation. Children grow up, marry, and move away. Many elderly people, especially women, lose their spouse; others lose contact with work associates and friends. Ordinarily, adults function in a variety of social roles—as members of a work group or of various civic, religious, or fraternal organizations; as parents; as friends; and so on. But from the age of about 50 on, people find themselves deprived of many of these roles. Some are prepared to accept this deprivation, to adjust easily and to assume new roles. Others never overcome their loneliness and, falling prey to feelings of self-pity, become demanding or offensive, alienating the few contacts they have left and thereby increasing their isolation. Havighurst and Albrecht found from their study of older people in Prairie City that a wide variety of social roles was positively related to happiness and good social adjustment in old age.[17] Havighurst speaks of "role flexibility" as an important factor in the adjustment of older people and suggests that it would be wise to deliberately cultivate this factor from about the age of 50 on.[18]

Learning a new role may involve choosing new leisure-time activities and joining new groups. Although older people often long to engage in such activities, they may need community support in order to find suitable organizations or groups to associate with. With an increasing social awareness of the problems faced

---

[16] Housing Research Council of Southern California, *The Architect Looks at Housing the Aged.* 1953.

[17] Havighurst and Albrecht, *Older People.*

[18] Robert J. Havighurst, "Flexibility and the Social Roles of the Retired," *American Journal of Sociology,* Vol. 59, January 1954, 309-311.

Old age need not signify the end of constructive living. Many people have enriched their later years by completing interrupted educations, by learning new skills, or by learning new hobbies.

by the aged, more and more communities are establishing recreational, educational, and social day-centers and clubs for the aged. Not all older people need such community support. Many have interests that make their lives stimulating and productive. Some may enjoy visiting with their children and grandchildren. Others may have cultivated a wide circle of friends. Still others may have thrown themselves wholeheartedly into church or civic affairs.

Thus older people react in many different ways to the problems confronting them. Many, recognizing their limited physical capacity, will turn to less strenuous pursuits and enjoy a more leisurely way of life. Some will find retirement an ideal time in which to do many of the things they always wanted to do but never could find time for. And some, insufficiently motivated to seek out new interests or to indulge old dreams, will spend their time reminiscing about the "good old days."

David Riesman,[19] in a recently published study, has distinguished three kinds of reaction to aging—the autonomous, the adjusted, and the anomic—and he characterizes these as follows:

> Some bear within themselves psychological sources of self-renewal; aging brings them accretion of wisdom, with no loss of spontaneity and ability to enjoy life, and they are relatively independent of the strictures and penalties imposed on the aged by the culture. Others, possibly the majority, have no such resources within them but are the beneficiaries of a cultural preservative (derived from work, power, position, and so on) which sustains them, although only so long as the cultural conditions remain stable and protective. A third group, protected neither from within nor from without, simply decays.

In the first, quite small group—the "autonomous"—Riesman includes such people as Bertrand Russell, Toscanini, and Freud. Their lives were not necessarily well-rounded or balanced; they did not necessarily get along well with others. But their lively interests and creative abilities made their old age a rich and satisfying period of life. Instead of accepting the cultural definition of

---

[19] David Riesman, "Some Clinical and Cultural Aspects of Aging," *American Journal of Sociology*, Vol. 49, January 1954, 379-383.

old age as a period when a person should slow down and take it easy, they continued to be alive and productive in spite of advancing years.

In the "adjusted" group, Riesman includes those persons who are kept going primarily by their position and prestige. As long as they can continue to work, the adjusted are able to appear youthful. They are able to carry out the continuous, familiar tasks their environment thrusts upon them, but they are immune to new experiences or new ideas. They are well preserved, but their outward youthfulness actually may mask a stunted psychological growth and inner sterility.

In the "anomic" group, finally, are those people who begin to deteriorate when they lose their physiological vitality and when their cultural environment does not provide them with any support. They are, Riesman suggests, the prematurely weary and resigned, and perhaps they were never young. Whatever their background, they cannot mobilize sufficient inner resources to halt their deterioration.

It is not likely that a rich old age is going to materialize out of an empty, sterile past. Nor is constant activity proof that a person is growing up and maturing. A busy life may prevent us from ever looking at or developing our own resources. Then, if circumstances change and our activities are suddenly curtailed, we may be appalled by the fact that we have so much time on our hands. The level of adjustment maintained by an older person is, to a large extent, an outgrowth of the kind of person he was when he reached later maturity.[20] Preparation for old age should not be postponed until old age has already set in. It should be kept in mind during our entire period of growing and maturity.

For Additional Reading

Cantril, H., *The Psychology of Social Movements*. New York, John Wiley & Sons, Inc., 1941.

---

[20] Raymond G. Kuhlen, "Psychological Trends and Problems in Later Maturity," in L. A. Pennington and Irwin A. Berg, eds., *An Introduction to Clinical Psychology*. New York, The Ronald Press Company, 1948, pp. 218-248.

Cavan, R. S., Ernest W. Burgess, Robert J. Havighurst, and H. Gold-hamer, *Personal Adjustment in Old Age*. Chicago, Science Research Associates, 1949.

Derber, M., ed., *The Aged and Society*. Champaign, Ill., Industrial Relations Research Association, 1950.

Donahue, W. and C. Tibbitts, eds., *Planning the Older Years*. Ann Arbor, University of Michigan Press, 1950.

——, *Growing in the Older Years*. Ann Arbor, University of Michigan Press, 1951.

Federal Security Agency, *Fact Book on Aging*. Washington D. C., Government Printing Office, 1952.

Gilbert, Jeanne G., *Understanding Old Age*. New York, The Ronald Press Company, 1952.

Havighurst, Robert J. and Ruth Albrecht, *Older People*. New York, Longmans, Green & Company, 1953.

Holtzman, Abraham, "Analysis of Old Age Politics in the United States," *Journal of Gerontology*, Vol. 9, 1954, 56-65.

Kaplan, Oscar J., ed., *Mental Disorders in Later Life*. Stanford, Calif., Stanford University Press, 1945.

Lehman, Harvey C., *Age and Achievement*. Princeton, N. J., Princeton University Press, 1953.

Man and His Years. An Account of the First National Conference on Aging. Sponsored by the Federal Security Agency. Raleigh, N. C., Health Publications Institute, 1951.

New York Academy of Science, *The Social and Biological Challenge of Our Aging Population*. New York, Columbia University Press, 1950.

Pennington, L. A. and I. A. Berg, eds., *Introduction to Clinical Psychology*. New York, The Ronald Press Company, 1948.

Pollak, O., *Social Adjustment in Old Age. A Research Planning Report*. New York, Social Science Research Council, 1948, Bulletin 59.

Shock, Nathan W., *Trends in Gerontology*. Stanford, Calif., Stanford University Press, 1951.

Simmons, Leo W., *The Role of the Aged in Primitive Society*. New Haven, Yale University Press, 1945.

Smith, T. Lynn, ed., *Living in the Later Years*. Gainesville, University of Florida Press, 1952.

Tuckman, Jacob and Irving Lorge, *Retirement and the Industrial Worker: Prospect and Reality*. New York, Teachers College, Columbia University, 1953.

Welford, A. T., *Skill and Age: An Experimental Approach*. London and New York, Oxford University Press for the Nuffield Foundation, 1950.

Personal
Differences and
Adjustment

CHAPTER 15

- SIGNIFICANCE OF PERSONAL DIFFER-
ENCES
- SOURCES OF PERSONAL DIFFERENCES
- MEASUREMENT OF INDIVIDUAL DIFFER-
ENCES
- IMPORTANCE OF MEASURING INDI-
VIDUAL DIFFERENCES

No two people are exactly alike. Each person is different in some respect from every other person. However drab and undistinguished he may look in a crowd, however similar to others he may appear in many of his opinions and attitudes, he is a unique person. The particular way in which abilities and traits are organized in him, in which his personality has been shaped by his past experience, in which his behavior is directed toward what he expects from life, makes him an individual different from others.

We have seen in preceding chapters how different people can react in a variety of ways to the same frustrating experience. We have seen how some elderly people regard retirement as a gateway to futility, while others see in it an opportunity to pursue interests previously denied to them by lack of time. We have seen how teachers must be alert to varying degrees of ability and motivation among their students. Now, in considering the matter of individual differences, we might keep two factors in mind: first, that a difference is not a difference unless it makes a difference; second, that the significance of a difference depends on the purpose being pursued.

Significance of Personal Differences

Relevant and irrelevant differences. When we observe the countless ways in which people may differ, we should remember that not all differences are equally important. Adjustment involves the ability to evaluate which differences are significant and which are not. When it comes to choosing between two applicants for a job, for example, the fact that one has blue eyes and the other brown is irrelevant. What is relevant is the degree of training and skill of each applicant.

Differences that loom important in the early phases of a relationship may lose their significance later on. A classic example of this is to be found in Melville's great novel, *Moby Dick.* When Ishmael first catches sight of Queequeg, who is to be his roommate for the night, he is appalled by the man's hideous and utterly foreign appearance—so appalled that he even considers slipping out through the window. But in a very short time, Queequeg's extraordinary consideration and kindness win Ishmael over, and the two become staunch friends.

Physical handicaps especially may prove unimportant. Thus, in recent years, employers have learned that physically handicapped people can fill certain jobs very well. Yet in other situations, in athletic contests, for example, a person with one arm, one leg, or poor eyesight can hardly compete against a perfect physical specimen.

Let us consider this from another viewpoint. We are given a dozen figures of various shapes and sizes, some shaded, some plain. Our concern for their characteristics will depend upon the instructions we receive. If we are asked to sort them according to their shapes, the shading will be irrelevant. If we are instructed to group them according to whether they are shaded or not, the differences in shape will be irrelevant. So it is with individuals and their differences. They must be evaluated in relation to a purpose.

Sometimes characteristics that are actually quite irrelevant assume importance because of the symbolic meaning attached to them. The "boy with green hair" is in no significant way different from other boys, yet the strangeness of his oddly colored hair causes people to *infer* that he must be different and strange in other ways too. If his associates react to this inference, to this symbolic interpretation of a physical characteristic, then the personality and behavior of the "boy with green hair" is likely to be affected. He may even come to see himself as others see him, because the way other people regard him or approach him eventually will influence his attitude toward himself. The initially irrelevant difference will then have become a difference that makes a difference.

Accepting differences in others. Many people are prone to make illogical generalizations on the basis of a quite irrelevant difference. Johnson,[1] in commenting on the dangers of unwarranted generalizations, has this to say:

> . . . A generalization is a statement that asserts that different things are somehow similar, or even identical, and so are to be reacted to or treated alike, or nearly so. Thus not only do we say that all patients who exhibit such and such symptoms are alike in that they have appendicitis, but we also go on to remove the appendixes of all of them. Certain religious sects not only hold that all babies are born "impure" or "in sin," etc., but also proceed to submerge them all in water, or sprinkle them with it, or in some fashion baptize them, all of them. In some countries not only are persons with certain

---

[1] Wendell Johnson, *People in Quandaries.* New York, Harper and Brothers, 1946, p. 27.

pedigrees classified together as Negroes, but they are also all deprived of various privileges and rights. The fact that not all appendicitis patients nor all babies nor all Negroes are alike, even though we say they are, is something that we do not seem able to take into account very easily. The similarities, however slight, impress us much more than do the differences, however great, once we have stressed the similarities by naming them and by generalizing in terms of the name we have given them.

At one time or another we have all heard someone remark, when discussing various ethnic groups, "They are all alike;" or "I can't tell them apart." The social distance that often separates one group from another prevents the members of one group from recognizing the wide range of individual variation that exists among the members of the other group.

This failure to recognize individual differences among the members of a group characterizes the prejudiced person and accentuates intergroup conflict. The prejudiced person sees all Negroes as lazy, all Jews as materialistic, all Irish as irresponsible. A dark skin, a name that sounds Jewish to him, slanted eyes—characteristics that mark a person as a non-Caucasian or a non-Gentile—start the sparks flying in the mind of a prejudiced person and prevent him from seeing that the people who manifest these characteristics are not all alike. He is unable to judge individuals *as* individuals. Instead, he prejudges each individual on the basis of some one distinguishing—and irrelevant—trait, and so reacts to each person of this group as though he is identical to all of the others. His mind is full of stereotypes, preconceived and rigid notions of what all members of another group are like, regardless of their individual characteristics.

Such a person will not permit himself to become involved with another person (or group) until he is sure that the other person (or group) conforms to his own standards. And when he has once developed hostility toward another person (or group) he will resent any implication that he himself resembles that person (or group) in any way. Most of us find it disconcerting, of course, to be told that we resemble someone whom we dislike, especially if we regard that person as somehow inferior. But for the prejudiced person, differences are a threat and are often regarded as justification for hostility.

Failure to recognize individual differences is by no means confined to members of various ethnic groups. The woman who has found that she can get her own way at home by being domineering and overbearing may fail to realize that this same attitude, if directed toward her friends, will alienate them. A mother may be puzzled because two-year-old Johnny does not respond to the same treatment that succeeded with five-year-old Jane. Jane loved to play by herself for hours; Johnny frets and cries unless someone is with him every minute. These two women have failed to realize that different people, because they are different, must be approached in different ways.

Recognition and acceptance of individual differences is a basic requirement for good human relations, whether on the interpersonal, intergroup, or international level. It cannot remedy conflict situations, but it can provide an opening wedge in the direction of adequate resolution. Even so, it cannot guarantee that a resolution will be reached. Often, even when we are fully aware of the nature of the differences between ourselves and others, we still do not know how to approach them or establish a friendly understanding with them.

Accepting differences in ourselves. So far we have talked primarily about our relationships to others as they are influenced by our recognition of—or failure to recognize—individual differences. But we must also realize that the individual difference factor influences our own self-concept as well. It is inevitable that we shall meet people who are better informed than we are on certain questions, people who can write or sing or paint better, people who can make friends more easily. We should not become so blinded by such circumstances that we are able to recognize only such differences as make us appear inferior to others. We must develop our awareness of the things that we ourselves can do well, things for which our friends and acquaintances may have no particular talent. We must learn to accept ourselves in spite of our shortcomings, to utilize our assets to the fullest, and to avoid being handicapped by our liabilities.

On the other hand, self-acceptance should not lead to complacency. Even when we accept ourselves we can continue to try to improve ourselves. But only through self-acceptance can we gain the confidence we need if we are to make full use of our potentialities. And in this process of self-evaluation we can also profit by discovering the idiosyncrasies in ourselves that may irritate others. Some of these we can discard or alter. Others may be so essential to our growth and development that we must retain them as they are or effect some sort of compromise. Here again we must distinguish between relevant and irrelevant differences. Let us look at a specific example.

A young person who feels that his family is "cramping his style" may rebel against his parents, and in this process of rebellion he may take issue with everything that they do—their way of dressing and of serving a meal, their forms of relaxation, their political opinions, their religious beliefs. In his rebellious state everything becomes grist for his mill. He is determined to change it all. But surely not all of these items merit equal scorn or censure, even for his rebellious purposes. Let us grant that some of the issues may be vital to him. They may derive from opposing convictions that he cannot give up without losing his self-respect. But he might learn to modify his attitude toward others—toward habits of eating or dressing, for example—without damaging his integrity.

Just as there are differences, there are also different ways of reacting to differences. Some people will openly rebel, as in the previous example. Some will leave their present surroundings and seek a new social environment in which they can feel less at odds with their associates. Others may withdraw, may isolate themselves from society, thereby relieving themselves of the necessity to adjust to differences. The adjustment each individual will make will depend on how he regards himself and how he is regarded in turn by the group of which he is or has been a part.

Personal differences are an integral part of our life and the basis for the variability we find in every phase of our existence. The personal welfare of each individual depends on his ability to recognize and to use, to modify, or to accentuate his own pattern of differences (in structure, aptitudes, abilities, interests, opportunities—or wherever else they may fall) in order to make what is for him the best possible long-range adjustment.

Sources of Personal Differences

Relationships between individuals are influenced not only by the recognizable characteristics that those individuals display, but also by opinions about the sources of those characteristics. Here we are referring to those basic assumptions that most of us make about the sources of individual differences and that form a part of our philosophy of life. These assumptions reveal themselves in such statements as "He acts that way because he was born with a silver spoon in his mouth," or "She never had a chance—look at the drunk she had for a father." Such assumptions inevitably influence behavior.

The question of whether heredity or environment is more influential in determining particular personality traits or characteristics has long plagued psychologists in their study of personal differences. Those who believed that all individual differences derive mainly from environmental influences have argued that life can be altered or controlled merely by manipulating the environment. Those who believed that all individual differences are inherited have argued that the characteristics we inherit will determine the course of our lives. On the one hand, if mechanical, musical, clerical, or executive ability are *acquired,* then anyone who receives the necessary training should be able to develop these abilities. On the other hand, if such special abilities are *inherited,* the matter of selecting the proper person to function in these capacities becomes more complicated. Again, if individual differences are *acquired,* slum clearance, environmental improvement, and education are the only means of reducing crime. But if individual differences are *inherited,* some authorities have suggested eliminating criminal tendencies by sterilizing all adults who manifest such tendencies.

Three methods have been developed to determine the relative importance of heredity and environment in causing individual differences. These methods are the *genealogical,* the *statistical,* and the *biological.* None of these methods is perfect. Accurate genealogical information is difficult to obtain because the hereditary and environmental influences cannot be clearly separated, especially when the study is carried back many, many years. The statistical method depends on the accuracy of the data under consideration, but the accuracy of such data is not always easy to establish. The biological method is experimental, but since human beings are notoriously reluctant to serve as guinea pigs, whether to test a new recipe or a new vaccine, most of our biological information on the influence of heredity and environment concerns fruit flies, mice, and monkeys, rather than human beings.

Let us look at a specific, though imaginary, case, described by Dunn and Dobzhansky,[2] which illustrates the importance of understanding the sources of individual differences.

> One way in which individuals differ sharply from each other is generally not known to them. To about 70% of all Americans, a weak solution of a chemical substance known as phenyl-thio-carbamide (P.T.C. for short) has an intensely bitter taste; to the other 30% it is tasteless. This difference is inherited, and it is not influenced by any known changes in the environment.
>
> Now imagine that P.T.C. is used as a disinfectant in drinking water in a town in which no one has heard of the difference between "tasters" and "taste blinds." When the first complaints of bad-tasting drinking water are received an inspector is sent to investigate. The investigator, who is taste blind, reports that he can't see what all the fuss is about and

    [2] L. C. Dunn and T. Dobzhansky, *Heredity, Race and Society.* Copyright, 1946, 1952, by The New American Library of World Literature, Inc.

ascribes the complaints to prejudice or "trouble-making." This does not make the water taste any better to those who have complained and gradually two opposed parties emerge, a pro-P.T.C. and an anti-P.T.C. An election puts in the antis, who have a 70% majority, and disinfection with P.T.C. is discontinued.

To the 30% who are pro-P.T.C. (because they can't taste it) the whole procedure has been unreasonable in the extreme. Because of an obstinate majority they have been deprived of protection against infection. If they feel badly enough about this they may rebel and attempt to evade the majority decision in some extralegal way.

This is a train of events which is not only possible but probable where the cause of conflict between two groups rests on a difference between persons which is not known or understood. When it is generally recognized that an inherited influence is at the bottom of it, each side may be expected to understand the position of the other and they may then work together to find an acceptable solution.

In this case the fact that the majority was right was due to the biological accident that the hereditary factor for taste blindness is not very common. The reverse situation is readily imaginable. Although P.T.C. is not used as a disinfectant and the above events are not known to have happened, there is no doubt that many human conflicts have arisen because inborn differences have been ascribed to prejudice and vice versa.

In some characteristics, such as eye color, taste-blindness, and albinism, the hereditary influence is clearly recognizable. In others, environmental influences predominate. The language a person speaks, for example, is due almost entirely to the particular cultural environment in which he grows up. A child of French parents, adopted by an American couple and raised in the United States, will speak English, not French. But in the evolution of other characteristics, heredity and environment interact so closely that isolating one set of influences in order to determine its impact is extremely difficult. Early psychologists were inclined to view heredity and environment as two separate and distinct factors. More recent approaches do not make this sharp distinction, but rather approach the question by asking to what extent heredity is susceptible to manipulation by environmental factors.

A wide range of human variability is, of course, inevitable. Either heredity or environment alone are capable of producing vast differences. Together their influence is that much greater.

Hereditary basis of human variability. When we speak of heredity, we mean biological inheritance. Biological inheritance refers to the handing down of characteristics from one generation to the next. This process is carried on by the genes, microscopically small bodies contained in the chromosomes. Each individual receives half of his chromosomes from his father and half from his mother, 48 altogether. The total number of genes carried by both father and mother is much greater. Geneticists have estimated that one man alone can carry a minimum of 12,000 pairs of genes. Many different combinations of genes are therefore possible, and the chance that brothers and sisters will inherit the same or even similar combinations is negligible, unless they happen to be identical twins, who develop from a single egg and have the same genes. If each parent possesses only ten different genes, the number of possible combinations will be over a thousand. This number grows to more than a million with 20, and to more than a billion with 30 different genes. If such variety is possible in a single family, it is hardly likely that two people from different families will resemble one another to any great extent. This seems reason enough to assert that every human being is unique, without even taking into consideration the *learned* differences that each person acquires.

Geneticists make a distinction between germ cells and body cells. Evidence indicates that modification of the body cells is not transmitted; the germ cells alone provide a starting point for the next generation. Acquired characteristics and behavior are not biologically inherited, although many a folktale about prenatal maternal experiences would have us believe so. A crippled arm or leg, caused by an injury to a parent, cannot be passed on as a deformity to the child.

Another distinction the geneticist makes is between function and structure. Functions include breathing, emotional reactions, changes in metabolism, and glandular activities. Structure refers to the actual construction of the body. Geneticists have concentrated primarily on the study of structure because structure is relatively easy to observe and to manipulate. The study of structural inheritance has led some researchers to assume that certain functions are also inherited. But the lack of definite means for studying functions has thwarted efforts to verify this assumption. Musical and artistic talents, for example, are too elusive and indefinite to lend themselves to this type of interpretation.

Social basis of human variability. Having examined briefly the way in which heredity contributes to human variability, let us consider now how personal differences are influenced by environmental conditions. We have, of course, called attention to these conditions again and again in dealing with work adjustment, psychosexual adjustment, family adjustment, and so on. We shall not repeat this detailed discussion here but instead shall outline some major characteristics of a culture that affect the development of individual differences.

1. A rich and complex culture nourishes personality by affording a variety of challenges and opportunities for putting skills and talents to work. A restricted and limited culture, on the other hand, a culture in which skills and talents are cramped and suppressed, will produce no brilliant citizens, no matter what their innate intelligence may be. A culture that has no use for scientific knowledge, for example, is barren ground for the development of scientific abilities. The greater the opportunities for diverse activities within a culture, the greater will be the range of individual variability within that culture.

We pointed out earlier that each group accepts and supports a certain range of individual differences and that those who fall outside this range are the deviants and misfits. This is true not only of relatively small groups, but also of cultures as a whole. In some societies members have to conform within a relatively narrow range of approved behavior; in others they are permitted a wide leeway of expression. Societies also differ in their treatment of those who fall outside the sanctioned range. One may regard the deviant as silly but harmless. Another may exclude him from certain activities. Still another may punish him severely.

2. One culture may allow a much wider scope of permissive behavior than another. Thus, one society may be permissive politically but strict regarding religious conformity. Or there may be loose controls where sexual activity is concerned but rigid regulation of economic activity. The fact that each society has its own unique set of regulations provides the basis for our ability to distinguish members of one from members of another, even when their physical characteristics seem almost identical.

3. The quality of leadership is an important factor in group life, and the behavior of group members will vary according to the permissiveness or strictness of the leadership to which they are exposed. In one experimental study of leadership and group life, separate groups of children were exposed to democratic, autocratic, or laissez-faire leadership. It was found that the greatest expression of individual differences occurred among children in the democratic group, slightly less was observed in the laissez-faire group, while the range of individuality was much reduced in the autocratic group.[3]

Measurement of Individual Differences

The fact that each individual has his own unique personality does not mean that no laws concerning human personality and human behavior can be established. Although no two human beings are exactly alike, all share certain fundamental needs that

---

[3] Ronald Lippitt and Ralph K. White, "An Experimental Study of Leadership and Group Life," in Newcomb and Hartley, eds., *Readings in Social Psychology.*

must be satisfied for the sake of either survival or psychological well-being or both. Deprivation or frustration will elicit certain predictable responses that differ from those elicited by pleasure and satisfaction. Again, different environmental conditions foster different behavioral tendencies.

In studying any psychological phenomenon, a two-fold approach is possible. We may concern ourselves with the general nature of the phenomenon and attempt to determine the basic processes underlying it and the conditions causing it, or we may focus on the variability of the phenomenon as manifested in specific instances. Thus, we may concentrate on the general principles of personality organization or, by contrast, the particular personality of a given individual. We may consider the laws of perception or, by contrast, the way in which a particular person perceives a situation. We may investigate the principles of learning or, by contrast, the way in which a particular person learns. These two approaches are complementary. A law that explains the regular and the frequent without accounting for individual case peculiarities is inadequate.

The approach dealing with the individual case is known as the *idiographic* approach. Its source material consists of personal documents of various kinds—autobiographies and diaries, letters, and expressive and projective documents such as literary works and various other art forms. Robert W. White's book, *Lives in Progress*,[4] is an example of this approach. In it he describes in great detail the lives of three people—a physician and scientist, a business assistant, and a housewife and social worker. His presentation of these three quite different personalities demonstrates the valuable contribution that such source material (introducing information concerning biological roots, social forces, and psychodynamics of development) can make toward the understanding of personality.

The approach that aims at generalization is called the *nomothetic*. Its source material consists primarily of data collected

---

[4] Robert W. White, *Lives in Progress*. New York: The Dryden Press, 1952.

through questionnaires, standardized interviews, and controlled experiments on large numbers of people This approach may utilize personal documents, but with the intent of discovering statistical generalizations or uniformities of behavior, rather than the concrete nature of a single personal life.[5]

Both approaches are essential to our understanding of human behavior. Both are based on the human difference factor. There would be no need to accumulate comparable data on large numbers of people—as the nomothetic approach does—if all people were alike. One person would do as well as another, and one would be sufficient.

Major trends in the testing movement. Let us now consider in some detail the specific methods that have been used in the study of individual differences.

Strangely enough, the first systematic investigation of individual differences came not from a psychologist but from an astronomer. In 1796, in the observatory at Greenwich, an assistant named Kinnebrook was bent over his telescope busily recording the instant when certain stars crossed his field of vision. At the same time, Maskelyne, the astronomer royal of the observatory, was making a similar record. But when the two men sat down to compare figures, Kinnebrook's times were found to be almost a second later than Maskelyne's. On the assumption that Kinnebrook was incompetent, he was dismissed. Twenty years later, Bessel, an astronomer at Koenigsberg, read about this incident in a history of the Greenwich observatory and began to ask himself if Kinnebrook actually had been incompetent or whether some other factor was responsible for the unfortunate assistant's apparent error. His curiosity aroused, Bessel began to collect data on the records of several trained observers and discovered the same kind of variations that had cropped up at Greenwich 20 years earlier. Continuing his study, he soon arrived at two significant conclusions. The first was that observers' records differed

---

[5] Gordon W. Allport, *The Use of Personal Documents in Psychological Science*. New York, Social Science Research Council, Bulletin No. 49, 1942.

because some reacted more quickly than others—that is, one person could make a reading and translate it onto paper in one half or one quarter the time it took another to do the same thing. The second point was that differences appeared not only among individuals, but also within an individual's own record. Bessel's study is the first published account we have on individual differences—on the psychological factor that has since become known as the *personal equation*.

Since Bessel's time, psychological tests have been devised to measure every conceivable aspect of personality. Before we describe them, let us note some of the major trends in the development of tests.

1. Early investigators in the field of individual differences were concerned almost exclusively with measuring sensory and intellectual functions. Today, testing techniques have been extended to measure emotional characteristics, social behavior, and a wide range of different aptitudes. There has been a definite trend away from the measurement of segmented, isolated aspects of personality to a study of the total personality.

2. The first tests developed were individually administered tests. Such tests, although they helped to establish good rapport between tester and testee and made it easier to observe the person's reactions while he was being tested, hindered the rapid accumulation of data. When large groups were to be tested, individual administration became too time-consuming. Psychologists, therefore, became interested in constructing tests that could be given quickly to large numbers of people. The desire for mass testing of recruits in World War I gave added impetus to their work. Out of World War I emerged such group tests as the Army Alpha, an intelligence test for soldiers who understood English, and the Army Beta, a "non-verbal" intelligence scale for those who were handicapped in the use of the English language, either because of lack of education or because of a home background where English was not spoken.

3. It was one thing to construct a test. It was another to con-

struct a test that would be sure to measure the particular thing it
was supposed to measure. As each new test or technique appeared, it was subjected to close scrutiny and critical examination.
Did an intelligence test actually measure "native" intelligence?
Did a questionnaire of emotional maturity really measure emotional maturity? These were the kinds of questions that were being
raised, and that are being raised today with new test developments. And the checking became more rigorous as more complex
personality traits began to be tested. Today we have scores of
books, monographs, and articles dealing with test construction
and the adequacy of test material. Improvements are constantly
being made as more refined statistical methods and measuring
techniques are developed.

4. The testing movement has been more extensive in this country than anywhere else. In part, this is due to the particular nature
of American society, with its traditional emphasis on individualism and with a population of many diverse backgrounds. The
study of individual and group differences went hand in hand. The
techniques suitable for the study of group differences could often
be used in the study of individual differences as well. In this respect, it is interesting to note that results have demonstrated that
the differences between individuals of the same group are generally much greater than the differences between averages of the
groups as a whole.

5. Although the testing movement was in part a response to
practical demands, it also stemmed from certain significant theoretical developments. In 1869, Galton wrote: "I have no patience with the hypotheses occasionally expressed, and often implied, especially in tales written to teach children to be good, that
babies are born pretty much alike, and that the sole agencies in
creating differences between boy and boy, man and man, are
steady application and moral effort. It is in the most unqualified
manner that I object to pretensions of natural equality." [5] Galton
thus rejected the concept that the mind was a *tabula rasa,* a wax

---

[5] Wayne Dennis, ed., *Readings in the History of Psychology.* New York,
Appleton-Century-Crofts, Inc., 1948, p. 231.

tablet, that merely accumulated facts as it was exposed to them. He stressed the importance of heredity, believing that heredity sets limits to a person's accomplishments. It was this same native or hereditary intellectual ability that Binet, a French psychologist, wanted to measure when he developed his intelligence scales. "Our purpose," he said, "is to evaluate a level of intelligence. It is understood that we here separate natural intelligence and instruction. It is the intelligence alone that we seek to measure, by disregarding, insofar as possible, the degree of instruction which the subject possesses. He should, indeed, be considered by the examiner as a complete ignoramus knowing neither how to read nor write." [6]

We note that Binet said to disregard *insofar as possible* the degree of instruction, indicating that he was aware of the difficulty of separating that which was inherited from that which was acquired.

Standardized measuring techniques. Today, psychological tests are used in many different fields, in schools and colleges, in vocational guidance, in employee selection in business and industry, in the psychological clinic, and in hospitals for the mentally ill. The different tests may be grouped into six major categories: (1) intelligence tests, (2) aptitude tests, (3) achievement tests, (4) interest tests, (5) tests measuring social attitudes, and (6) personality tests.

INTELLIGENCE TESTS. The first widely used intelligence test was developed by Binet when he was asked in 1904 by the French school authorities to assist in the placement of school children. In contrast to earlier psychologists who had tested rather narrow aspects of mental activity, such as reaction time and rote memory, Binet undertook to measure the general level of intelligence, concentrating particularly on the higher mental processes. To judge well, to comprehend well, to reason well—these Binet believed to be the essential ingredients of intelligence.

The best known revision of the Binet test is the *Revised*

---

[6] Dennis, ed., *Readings in the History of Psychology,* p. 416.

Stanford-Binet Tests of Intelligence, constructed by Lewis M. Terman and Maud A. Merrill. The test is scored in terms of IQ or intelligence quotient. The IQ is the ratio of the mental age to the chronological age:

$$IQ = \frac{MA}{CA} (100).$$

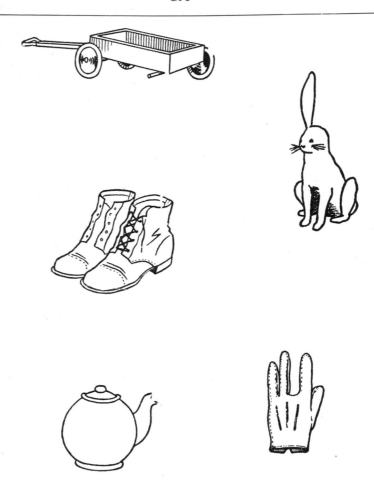

Test item from the Stanford-Binet test. (From Lewis M. Terman and Maud A. Merrill, Revised Stanford-Binet Tests. *Boston, Houghton Mifflin Company, 1937.)*

Thus a person who performs at the 5-year level on the test is given a "mental age" of 5. If his chronological age is also 5, his IQ is 100. If his MA is 10 and his CA is 5, he has an IQ of 200; i.e., he has superior intelligence. If his MA is 5 and his CA is 10, he has an IQ of 50; i.e., he is feebleminded.

The Stanford-Binet test is an individually administered test, primarily of the verbal type—i.e. the person has to be able to use and understand words to take the test. Subsequent developments in intelligence testing have resulted in the construction of group and performance tests. We have already mentioned the *Army*

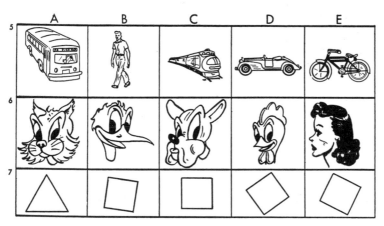

A non-verbal test. Practice item from the SRA Non-Verbal Classification Form, Form AM, prepared by Robert N. McMurry and Dale L. Johnson. (Courtesy Science Research Associates, 1946.)

Alpha and the *Army Beta* developed during World War I. Since then, other intelligence tests, of either the group or individual type, stressing either the verbal or the performance aspects, have been developed.

An individual test that gives both a verbal and performance score and is styled especially for adults is the *Wechsler-Bellevue Intelligence Test*. This test is constructed in such a way that the scoring shows the pattern of an individual's mental functioning, indicating his strengths and weaknesses.

First item of the picture-arrangement subtest of the Wechsler-Bellevue Intelligence Scale. (From David Wechsler, The Wechsler-Bellevue Intelligence Scale. New York, The Psychological Corporation, 1947.)

One major advance development has been the diagnostic mental tests that seek to measure different aspects of intelligence. Thus Thorndike distinguishes between abstract, concrete, and

In the two rows below, mark an X in the box of EVERY figure which is LIKE the first figure in that row. If you wish to change an answer, draw a circle around this box like ⊗. Then mark the new answer in the usual way.

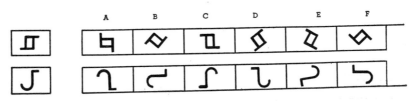

In the first row, you should have marked **A**, **D**, and **F**. In the second row, you should have marked **C** and **F**.

Practice item from the space series of the SRA Primary Mental Abilities Test, prepared by L. L. Thurstone and Thelma Gwinn Thurstone. (Courtesy Science Research Associates, 1947.)

social intelligence. And in his *Tests of Primary Mental Abilities* Thurstone has delineated verbal understanding, word fluency, number facility, space perception, reasoning, and shape recognition as basic intellectual functions. The results from such tests, when expressed graphically, give a profile with high and low points corresponding to the individual's particular fundamental abilities and thus afford a more detailed picture than a single IQ score.

APTITUDE TESTS. Aptitude tests are designed to indicate a person's potential ability to perform a certain kind of activity. Although intelligence tests actually are aptitude tests in a broad sense, the term "aptitude test" usually refers solely to those tests that are used to measure a specialized kind of activity within a narrow range. The two most common forms of aptitude tests are mechanical and clerical. Such aptitudes are often difficult to measure because many different kinds of activity may be called for in a given mechanical or clerical task. This difficulty may be overcome either by using tests that measure different aspects of mechanical aptitude or by including various subtests in a mechanical aptitude test. Thus the *MacQuarrie Test for Mechanical Ability,* a paper-and-pencil test, has seven subtests, some of which measure manual dexterity, others spatial visualization, and one, speed of perception. The *Minnesota Spatial Relations Test* and the *Minnesota Paper Form Board* both measure a person's aptitude to visualize spatial relations. Both require matching of shapes and sizes, but the first requires actual manipulation of the shapes while in the second all the matching must be done mentally.

Some of the aptitude tests are paper-and-pencil tests, while others, such as the *Minnesota Rate of Manipulation Test,* are performance tests, involving motor activities considered essential in various occupations. Still others are actual work samples.

Clerical aptitude, like mechanical aptitude, calls for several abilities. Extensive work in this field, however, indicates that the most important factors in clerical aptitude are perceptual speed and accuracy in checking numerical and verbal symbols. These

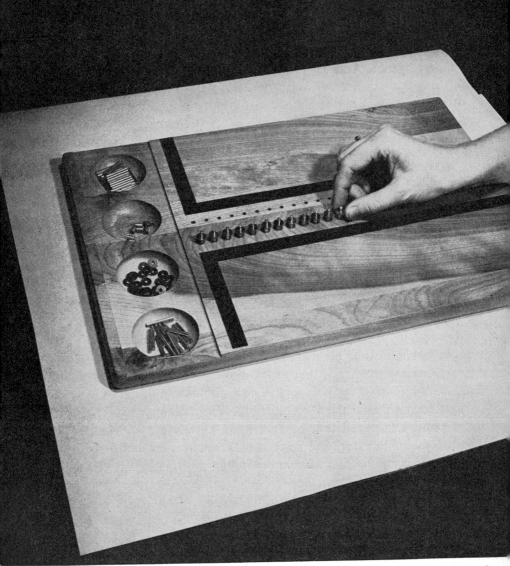

The Purdue Pegboard aptitude test. This test measures certain basic aspects of manipulative dexterity. Separate measurements may be obtained for right hand, left hand, and both hands. The test can be given to ten or more persons simultaneously. (Courtesy Science Research Associates.)

are primarily the factors that the *Minnesota Clerical Test* measures.

In the field of artistic and musical aptitude, the *Seashore Measures of Musical Talent,* the *Meier Art Judgment Test,* and the *Knauber Art Ability Test* are the best known.

Another development in the field of aptitude testing has been the construction of custom-built batteries, or groups of tests, for testing specific occupational aptitudes. Some of these tests are available for general use; others are restricted for use in professional schools. The *Moss Medical Aptitude Test,* the *Ferson-Stoddard Law Aptitude Test,* and the *George Washington University Series of Nursing Tests* are all examples of group tests used to measure occupational aptitude. In recent years, standard batteries have been developed with norms for specific occupations. One of these is the *General Aptitude Test Battery* of the United States Employment Service that gives scores for ten different aptitudes, including intelligence, verbal aptitude, numerical aptitude, spatial aptitude, form perception, clerical perception, eye-hand coordination, motor speed, finger dexterity, and manual dexterity. Another example is the *Differential Aptitude Test* of the Psychological Corporation, New York City, which measures eight different abilities, such as verbal reasoning, language usage, and space relations. The main use of aptitude tests is in vocational guidance and in selecting qualified personnel for various occupations.

ACHIEVEMENT TESTS. An aptitude test measures potential ability; achievement tests measure what and how much a person has learned or how well a person can perform a particular task. However, the dividing line between these two kinds of tests is not always clearly drawn. Aptitude tests measure abilities that have been practiced and developed by the individual; achievement tests, although they measure a person's present knowledge and performance, also may indicate an individual's future potentialities and in that sense are indexes of aptitude.

Achievement tests may be grouped into two main categories:

educational achievement tests and tests of vocational proficiency. Some educational achievement tests measure achievement in a single subject, such as history or arithmetic. Others cover many different areas of school achievement and thus make possible a comparison of a student's knowledge in one field with his ability in other areas. The *Cooperative General Achievement Tests,* the *Metropolitan Achievement Tests,* the *Stanford Achievement Tests,* and the Tests of *General Educational Development* are all examples of this latter type.

Since reading is an essential tool in educational achievement, a great many reading tests have been developed. Many of these indicate not only how well a student can read, but also serve as diagnostic tools that enable a teacher to locate sources of his pupils' reading difficulties. One example of a diagnostic reading test is the *Iowa Silent Reading Test* that reports nine scores from sub-tests on rate of reading, word meaning, and sentence meaning.

Vocational proficiency tests are used mainly to measure a trained candidate's possible success in a job. When a firm is seeking a capable typist or experienced bookkeeper, a proficiency test often will indicate which candidate comes closest to meeting the requirements the job demands. Achievement tests in typewriting, bookkeeping, and stenography are available. In addition, the United States Employment Service is at present working to develop trade questions, designed for measuring ability in various trades. The test for carpenters and plumbers, for example, includes such questions as "What are the two most commonly used methods of testing plumbing systems?" These tests are constructed and scored in such a way that they will distinguish between novices, apprentices, journeymen, and experts. One difficulty connected with drawing up trade questions, however, is that rapid technological changes make it necessary to revise the questions frequently.

MEASUREMENT OF INTERESTS. The main impetus to the development of measures of interest has come from psychologists working in the field of vocational adjustment. *Strong's Vocational*

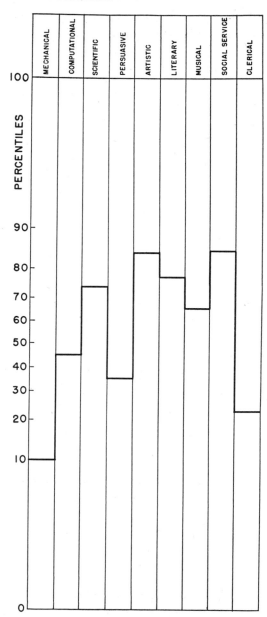

Profile of a college girl on the Kuder Preference Record. Test prepared by G. Frederick Kuder. (Courtesy Science Research Associates, 1942.)

Interest Blank and *Kuder's Preference Record* are the two best known and most widely used measures of interest. These tests enable a person to compare his interests with those of people who have been successful in various occupations that he may be considering. A young man who is interested in becoming an engineer, for example, can compare his interests with those of men who already have been successful in the engineering field. Investigations in this field have succeeded in establishing that people engaged in one particular occupation share characteristic patterns of likes and dislikes that differ from the preferences and interests of people in other occupations.

Measures of interest have also revealed differences between men and women. Using the *Allport-Vernon Study of Values*, it was found that, in general, women are more interested in activities centering around aesthetic, social, and religious values, whereas men prefer activities of theoretical, economic, and political interest. The following question will illustrate the nature of the questions asked in this test: "Would you prefer to hear a series of lectures on (a) the development of child care centers in large cities or (b) contemporary poets?"

As always when we are dealing with group differences, whether it be differences between occupational groups or sex differences, we have to keep in mind that we are dealing with general trends and group averages. Some engineers, some physicians, some teachers do not share the interests that characterize most of their colleagues. Some women are not interested primarily in religious and social activities, and instead favor those things that appeal most frequently to men. There is, in all such measures, a great deal of overlapping among groups.

MEASUREMENT OF ATTITUDES AND OPINIONS. The measurement of beliefs and attitudes has become a major American industry. Almost every day commercial polling agencies publish the results of their latest findings in the daily newspapers or stand ready to make a custom-built attitude survey to meet a particular individual's own business or political needs.

Most measurement of attitudes and opinions is done by means of a questionnaire, consisting of a series of carefully standardized items or propositions. The person being interviewed either rejects or endorses these propositions or indicates to what extent he agrees or disagrees with them. The summation or pattern of responses yields a numerical position along a continuum that extends from one extreme of approval or acceptance to the other extreme of disapproval or rejection.

Attitudes toward a wide range of objects have been investigated. Scales have been developed that measure attitudes toward war, capital punishment, birth control, labor, management, the church, and a variety of other subjects.

One area in particular that has received quite a bit of attention has been people's attitudes toward various national, ethnic, or religious groups. One of the earliest measuring instruments in this field is the *Social Distance Scale,* constructed by Bogardus, in which the individual is asked to express his willingness to accept members of various ethnic groups into social groups to which he belongs—to his family, his club, his neighborhood.

MEASUREMENT OF PERSONALITY. Although intelligence, attitudes, and interests are aspects of personality, we usually focus on the emotional aspects of behavior, on interpersonal relations, on the different kinds of adjustment the individual has made, when we speak of personality tests. There have been two main approaches to the study of personality, the *clinical* approach and the *psychometric* approach. The clinical approach includes interviews and case histories; the psychometric approach, the use of standardized tests, some of which are administered to individuals, others to groups.

Personality questionnaires are widely used. Some measure different areas of adjustment, others various personality traits, still others clinical reaction patterns. The *Bell Adjustment Inventory* is an example of the first, measuring a person's home, health, social, and emotional adjustment. Responses to the *Bernreuter Personality Inventory* are categorized in terms of neuroticism, self-sufficiency, introversion, social dominance, self-confidence, and sociability. The *Guilford-Martin Personnel Inventory* measures cooperativeness as opposed to fault-finding, objectivity as opposed to self-centeredness, and agreeableness as opposed to belligerence. These tests are used in educational and vocational counseling and in personnel selection. The *Minnesota Multiphasic Personality Inventory* was developed as a clinical instrument for use in psychiatric diagnosis and can be scored in terms of nine reaction patterns, such as depression, hysteria, paranoia, and the like. The following questions are characteristic of the kind used in personality questionnaires: Do you feel that your parents have been unduly strict with you? Do you feel tired most of the time? Do you usually enjoy spending an evening alone? Do you try to avoid bossy people?

Another method of studying personality is by behavior sampling. This technique is used particularly where children are being studied. The procedure involves making a close observation of the child's actions, how he reacts toward other children, how he treats his toys, how he responds to discipline, and the like.

One of the most significant developments in the field of personality measurement involves projective techniques. These will be discussed in some detail.

Projective tests. A projective test provides the individual with a stimulus situation into which he can project his own feelings and needs, his particular perceptions and interpretations. A projective test is designed to call forth responses that will reveal the individual's feelings, values, motives, and characteristic modes of adjustment. Through his interpretations and creations he projects the inner aspects of his personality, involuntarily revealing traits of which he is unaware and which would not be elicited in response to the direct questions of a personality questionnaire.

Many projective techniques have been developed, a few of which will be described here. Probably the two most widely used and best known projective tests are the *Rorschach Inkblot Test* and the *Thematic Apperception Test*.

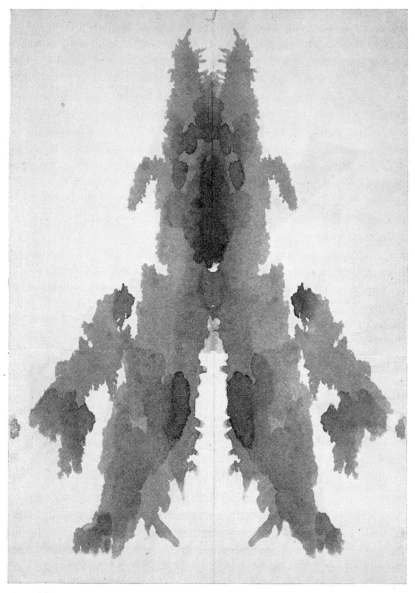

An inkblot. (From Harry W. Hepner, Psychology Applied to Life and Work, 2nd ed. New York, Prentice Hall, Inc., 1950, p. 336.)

The Rorschach Inkblot Test, developed by the Swiss psychologist, Hermann Rorschach, consists of ten cards, each containing one bisymmetrical inkblot. Five of these cards are shaded in black and white; the other five contain varying amounts of color. The cards are presented to the subject one at a time in a prescribed sequence, and he is asked to tell what he sees in the cards. After the subject has seen all ten cards, the person administering the test starts to ask questions in order to learn just what parts or aspects of the blot the subject perceived and responded to, and to give the subject an opportunity to add to or to clarify his original responses. Interpretation of the data thus obtained is a time-consuming task that requires considerable training. But it provides important information about the individual's personality: his intelligence as indicated in part by the originality and complexity of his responses, his emotional control or instability, the nature of his relations to other people, the richness of his imaginative life.

The Thematic Apperception Test was developed by the clinical psychologist, Henry A. Murray. It consists of 20 cards with pictures resembling actual scenes or objects that are still ambiguous enough to allow the individual leeway in interpreting what he sees. As each card is given to the subject, he is asked to tell a story about it—what is happening, what led up to it, and what will be the outcome. Thus some see in the picture of the older and younger woman (see page 411) a story of conflict between them, preceded by many quarrels between the two because the older woman has always sought to dominate the younger one, and ending with the younger woman leaving. Others perceive in the photo a friendly relationship, with the older woman giving sympathetic support to the younger one. Each person sees what he needs to see in the picture. The content of the stories is analyzed in terms of their underlying themes—whether, for example, the plots are happy or tragic, with whom the subject identifies, and the influences in the environment that he takes into account as he tells what is happening to the people.

The Rosenzweig Picture-Frustration Test, another projective test, consists of 24 cartoon-like pictures and is intended to reveal

Thematic Apperception Test, Card 12F. (Courtesy of Dr. Henry A. Murray and the President and Fellows of Harvard College.)

the subject's characteristic responses to common stress-producing or frustrating situations. Each picture shows two persons involved in a common, mildly frustrating situation. The person at the left of each picture is represented as making a statement that either describes the frustration of the second individual or is itself actually frustrating to the second person. The caption box above the person on the right of each picture is blank. The subject is asked to study each picture and then to write in the blank box the first appropriate response that occurs to him. The assumption is that the subject identifies himself, consciously or unconsciously, with the frustrated individual in each situation and that his replies will indicate the way he would act if confronted with a similar situation. The scoring of the responses is based upon (1) the direction of aggression and (2) reaction type. Under direction of aggression, three forms of expression are distinguished: extrapunitiveness, in which the subject blames the environment for his predicament; intrapunitiveness, in which the subject blames himself; and impunitiveness, in which the subject evades aggression or avoids blame. Under reaction type, the following three classes of responses are distinguished: obstacle dominance, in which the subject emphasizes the barrier that stands between him and the solution to his problem; ego-defense, in which the subject's ego predominates and in which he tries to protect his self-esteem; and need-persistence, in which the subject emphasizes the solution of the frustrating problems. (See Chapter 5, p. 107, for sample test item.)

Frustrations are common experiences. The way a person adjusts to them provides significant clues about his behavior and personality organization.

A number of projective techniques have been developed primarily for use with children. Many of these involve manipulation of materials rather than verbalization. Doll-play, building a world (out of a set of toy houses, vehicles, and people), and finger painting are examples of such techniques.

The main difference between personality inventories and questionnaires, on the one hand, and projective techniques on the other are these:

1. A projective technique is much less structured than a personality questionnaire. A personality questionnaire asks the person how he feels or acts in a variety of typical situations that are definitely structured. For example, representative questionnaires

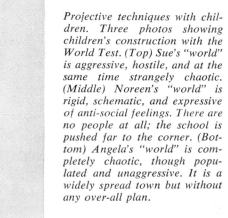

Projective techniques with children. Three photos showing children's construction with the World Test. (Top) Sue's "world" is aggressive, hostile, and at the same time strangely chaotic. (Middle) Noreen's "world" is rigid, schematic, and expressive of anti-social feelings. There are no people at all; the school is pushed far to the corner. (Bottom) Angela's "world" is completely chaotic, though populated and unaggressive. It is a widely spread town but without any over-all plan.

(By permission from Charlotte Buhler, Faith Smitter, Sybil Richardson, and Franklyn Bradshaw, Childhood Problems and the Teacher. New York, Henry Holt and Company, Inc., 1952, pp. 351 and 352.)

pose such questions as, Would you rather be a chemist than an artist? Do you prefer working alone rather than in a group? Projective techniques involve no such specific questions. However, the degree of structuring may vary for different projective techniques. The Thematic Apperception Test, for example, is more structured than the Rorschach.

2. Personality questionnaires generally attempt to portray the individual segmentally, emphasizing what are considered to be the *important segments* of his personality. A projective test, on the other hand, attempts to view and understand the personality as a whole.

3. Projective techniques are usually less obvious in what they attempt to measure and thus can be faked less easily by the subject.

Three basic assumptions underlie the use of projective techniques:

1. All behavior manifestations express the individual's personality. Any aspect of an individual's behavior offers some insight into his personality, his needs, goals, defenses, and the like.

2. The subject will reveal through the answers he gives some aspects of his personality that he either will not or cannot reveal otherwise. Projective tests usually involve the presentation of purposely ambiguous or unstructured material. It is assumed that when the individual attempts to explain these apparently objective bits of material he will disclose his preoccupations, his wishes, his fears, and his aspirations without suspecting that he is doing so. His resistance to disclosing personal and sometimes painful information will, therefore, be substantially diminished.

3. Each response is assumed to have its cause in the psychological make-up of the individual. Many critics of projective techniques have objected to the Thematic Apperception Test, for example, on the grounds that the subject may merely recount the plot of a movie he has seen or the content of a book he has read recently, instead of producing personally meaningful information.

This objection, however, disregards the fact that from all the experiences a person has had, he selects certain ones to remember and to recount, and that these selections in turn have personal meaning.

Importance of Measuring
Individual Differences

When we measure certain characteristics—mechanical aptitude, intelligence, self-sufficiency—in a large group of people, we usually obtain a "normal distribution" of scores. In a graph of such a distribution we find a peak in the center with the frequencies of scores falling off to either side of it. Thus in a test of me-

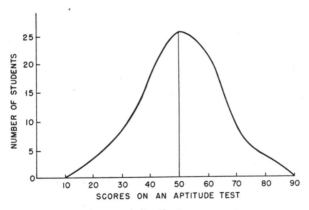

A normal distribution curve.

chanical aptitude, the scores obtained by a group of 100 students may range from 10 points to 90 points. The largest number of students obtain a score of 50, but very few get a score at the extremes—i.e., very few know a great deal and very few know very little.

One conclusion is clearly evident from such a distribution of scores: people do not fall into distinct, separate types. We cannot say that they are either intelligent or not intelligent, self-sufficient or not self-sufficient, that they either exhibit or do not exhibit mechanical aptitude. Rather, they possess the characteristics in varying degrees.

The use we make of the scores obtained on a given test depends on our purpose. Let us look at a few possibilities.

If we are hiring people for jobs that require a certain type of knowledge, we may find it advisable to hire those who fall in the range from 60 to 80 in our distribution. For we know from past experience that those with lower scores cannot perform the tasks well, and that those with the higher scores are too good for the job; they are overtrained and will become dissatisfied because the work is not stimulating enough.

Or let us assume that we are dealing with a group of adults who want to improve their reading proficiency. With the help of tests we can find out how quickly they read and how well they understand what they read. Again we find a normal distribution of scores. In this case we may decide that we can teach them more effectively if we divide them into three groups, putting together the low-scorers, the middle-scorers, and the high-scorers.

The information psychologists have accumulated on individual differences has led to far-reaching changes in our educational procedures at all levels, in personnel practices in business and industry, in civil service, in fact in almost every area of life.

We realize today that we may find high mental ability at any socio-economic level, that children may be brighter than their parents, or that not all bright parents have bright children. And we realize the importance of using an individual's assets to the best possible advantage, both for his own good and for the good of society. As has been said often, our greatest asset is our people —and their *various* abilities. It would indeed be a dull, perhaps unbearable, world if we were all alike, if we all had the same interests, the same likes and dislikes.

The systematic and extensive measurement of individual differences has made a significant contribution to our knowledge of human ability and personality, particularly insofar as diagnosing and predicting human behavior are concerned. The question of individual differences is important not only in vocational guidance, but also in marriage counseling. And the clinical use of tests can help the psychologist to detect instances of unusual or abnormal behavior that may indicate maladjustment, or worse, may be the forerunner of a serious breakdown. Having detected them, he may take steps to prevent further disturbances by helping the person to achieve a better adjustment.

For Additional Reading

Abt, Lawrence Edwin and Leopold Bellak, eds., *Projective Psychology. Clinical Approaches to the Total Personality.* New York, Alfred A. Knopf, Inc., 1950.

Allport, Gordon W., *The Use of Personal Documents in Psychological Science.* New York, Social Science Research Council, Bulletin No. 49, 1942.

Anastasi, Anne, *Psychological Testing.* New York, The Macmillan Company, 1954.

———— and J. P. Foley, Jr., *Differential Psychology,* rev. ed. New York, The Macmillan Company, 1949.

Anderson, H. H. and G. L. Anderson, *Introduction to Projective Techniques.* New York, Prentice-Hall, Inc., 1951.

Benedict, Ruth, *Patterns of Culture.* New York, Penguin Books, Inc., 1947.

Boring, Edwin G., *A History of Experimental Psychology.* New York, The Century Company, 1929.

Cattell, R. B., *Description and Measurement of Personality.* Yonkers, New York, World Book Company, 1946.

Conant, James B., and others, *Prospects for the Scientific Study of Human Relations.* University of Chicago Round Table, 1947.

Cronbach, Lee J., *Essentials of Psychological Testing.* New York, Harper and Brothers, 1949.

Dennis, Wayne, ed., *Readings in the History of Psychology.* New York, Appleton-Century-Crofts, Inc., 1948.

Dewey, John, *Democracy and Education.* New York, The Macmillan Company, 1937.

Dunn, L. D. and Theodosius Dobzhansky, *Heredity, Race and Society,* rev. ed. New York, Penguin Books, Inc., 1952.

English, O. Spurgeon and Gerald H. J. Pearson, *Emotional Problems of Living.* New York, W. W. Norton & Company, Inc., 1945.

Eysenck, H. J., *The Scientific Study of Personality.* New York, The Macmillan Company, 1952.

————, *The Structure of Human Personality.* New York, John Wiley & Sons, Inc., 1953.

Frank, Lawrence K., *Projective Methods.* Springfield, Illinois, Charles C. Thomas, 1948.

Goldstein, Kurt, *The Organism.* New York, American Book Company, 1939.

Goodenough, Florence L., *Mental Testing—Its History, Principles and Applications.* New York, Rinehart & Company, Inc., 1949.

Gulliksen, Harold, *Theory of Mental Tests.* New York, John Wiley & Sons, Inc., 1950.

Johnson, Wendell, *People in Quandaries.* New York, Harper and Brothers, 1946.

Klopfer, Bruno and Douglas M. G. Kelley, *The Rorschach Technique.* Yonkers, New York, World Book Company, 1942.

Krech, David and Richard S. Crutchfield, *Theory and Problems of Social Psychology.* New York, McGraw-Hill Book Company, Inc., 1948.

Lewin, Kurt, *Dynamic Theory of Personality.* New York, McGraw-Hill Book Company, Inc., 1935.

Murphy, Gardner, *An Historical Introduction to Modern Psychology.* New York, Harcourt, Brace & Company, Inc., 1938.

Murray, Henry A., *Explorations in Personality.* New York, Oxford University Press, 1943.

————, *Thematic Apperception Test Manual.* Cambridge, Harvard University Press, 1943.

OSS Assessment Staff, *Assessment of Men.* New York, Rinehart & Company, Inc., 1948.

Practicing the Democratic Way in School. Los Angeles City School Districts, Curriculum Division, *Publ. C-414,* 1950.

Shneidman, Edwin S., *The Make A Picture Story Test.* New York, The Psychological Corporation, 1949.

Terman, Lewis M. and Maud A. Merrill, *Measuring Intelligence.* Boston, Houghton Mifflin Company, 1937.

Tomkins, Silvan S., *The Thematic Apperception Test: The Theory and Technique of Interpretation.* New York, Grune and Stratton, 1947.

Tyler, Leona A., *The Psychology of Human Differences.* New York, D. Appleton-Century Company, Inc., 1947.

Wechsler, D., *The Measurement of Adult Intelligence,* 3rd ed. Baltimore, Williams and Wilkins, 1944.

Some Characteristics
of
Satisfactory Adjustment

CHAPTER 16

- CHARACTERISTICS OF GOOD MENTAL
  HEALTH
- THE MATURE PERSONALITY
- CHARACTERISTICS OF GOOD MENTAL
  HEALTH AND THE GOALS OF PSYCHO-
  THERAPY

To define and discuss mental health and signs of the healthy personality, not merely in terms of the absence of mental disease symptoms, but also by stressing the positive or desirable aspects of good mental health, will be the objective of this chapter. By shifting our attention to the characteristics constituting sound mental health, we emphasize prevention of mental illness rather than merely its cure; for if we know how to strive toward good mental health we may avoid having to cure mental illness. It is not enough to know what to avoid; it is equally important to know what to strive for.

Actually, the problem of mental health or good adjustment is a two-fold one. It involves (1) determining criteria for mental health, and (2) defining and creating the conditions that are conducive to mental health. In this chapter, we shall be concerned primarily with the first aspect; in the succeeding chapter, on psychotherapy, with the second.

Characteristics of Good Mental Health

When we discuss characteristics of mental health, we set up a sort of "ideal" person, because not all of these characteristics are necessarily found in all normal persons, nor is each of the characteristics found in each of us in the same degree. Personality is a complex combination of many characteristics. Psychological maturity, therefore, must be measured not by a single factor, but by how many different characteristics are coordinated and integrated in a person's total personality. Thus we should not be disappointed if we find that we lack some of these characteristics or that friends and acquaintances may seem, on the basis of these criteria, to be better adjusted than we are. We should simply remember that knowing what these characteristics are can help us to attain better mental health. And, finally, we must keep in mind that adjustment is a continuing process, since the demands made on us at various periods of our lives vary and since our abilities, our needs, and our goals change. Neither the problems a child faces nor the resources he possesses to meet these problems are the same as those faced or possessed by the adolescent or by the adult.

The quality of our mental health is reflected in our attitudes toward ourselves and others. Various characteristics provide clues to these attitudes. In the following discussion, we shall consider what these characteristics are and how each affects adjustment.

A sense of individuality. Very early the child learns that he is a person separate and different from others around him; and if his development is a healthy one, this sense of self, of his own individuality or ego-identity, will be continually confirmed. Most of the time he will have a basic insight and understanding into what he is capable of doing, what he is willing to do, and what he will not do. At times, he can yield to others and conform readily to social demands. At other times, he must refuse to compromise or to conform. For if he yields too often, he loses his individuality and becomes "mass-man," psychologically ready to be manipulated and exploited by others. Such loss of individuality may result from blind submission to an authority figure or from over-conforming for the sake of gaining approval. Then individuality becomes diffused and loses its identity.

On the other hand, when we feel our sense of identity threatened, we may over-assert ourselves and grow intolerant of others. This happens frequently during adolescence and must be understood as a defense against loss of identity [1] that the young person may be experiencing because many new demands are being made of him at this time. He may feel isolated from others and tend to forget the common human experiences and needs he shares with others.

Neither blind conformity to others nor rebellious isolation from others are signs of a healthy personality. Rather we may say that what is desirable in terms of good mental health is that a person be capable of conforming to the norms of his society, but also be free to choose whether to conform or not. Riesman [2] has called such a person an autonomous person, aware of others, responsive to them, but capable of making choices in accordance with his own individuality.

A sense of independence. Being capable of making such choices requires a sense of independence, a certain self-sufficiency that permits us to carry out our wishes and to work toward our goals without feeling constantly concerned about what others think or say. A sense of independence permits us to show more initiative, to be more creative, to depend more on our own judgment, and so to show more of the qualities of leadership we may possess. We can set our own goals, work toward them, and attain them—all under our own power. The struggle for independence—or

---

[1] Erik Homburger Erikson, "Growth and Crises of the 'Health Personality,'" in Clyde Kluckhohn and Henry A. Murray, eds., *Personality in Nature, Society, and Culture,* 2nd ed. New York, Alfred A. Knopf, Inc., 1953, pp. 185-225.

[2] David Riesman, *The Lonely Crowd. A Study of the Changing American Character.* New Haven, Yale University Press, 1950.

autonomy, as Erickson calls it—begins early in the child's life, and it is the parents' responsibility to encourage their youngsters' self-expression, to help them to learn to stand on their own feet, to prevent their being ashamed of their first failures or setbacks, to avoid discouraging them and making them doubtful of their own ability. Only in this way can a youngster learn to test his abilities. At the same time, the child must be protected against potential dangers in his environment and against certain of his potentially destructive inner impulses that he has not yet learned to recognize or to control. Without this protection, the child may come to distrust himself and others. Thus parents have to find a delicate balance between protection and autonomy. In this way they can contribute to that independence and self-reliance, coupled with social trust and reasonable consideration for others, that characterize the mature person.

Self-confidence and confidence in others. If we lack confidence in others, our social relationships will be disturbed. If we lack self-confidence, our development will be crippled. The truth of these statements is seen most strikingly in the mentally ill, especially in the paranoic, whose distrust of others and own lack of self-confidence leads him to withdraw into a world of fantasy. One of the first indications of neuroticism in a person is his inability to trust others and to form warm, close relationships with others. It is this sense of basic trust or confidence that Erikson nominates for the first component of a healthy personality, and it should be established very early in the life of the child.

Helping a patient accept himself is an important aim in psychotherapy. Sheerer [3] selected the concept of acceptance of and respect for self as an important one for describing the individual's level of adjustment. She devised a method that allowed her to rate any given psychotherapeutic interview on a scale from 1 to 5 in terms of the amount of self-acceptance shown by the patient during the interview. The number 1 indicated a minimum of self-

---

[3] Elizabeth T. Sheerer, "An Analysis of the Relationship Between Acceptance of and Respect for Self and Acceptance of and Respect for Others in Ten Counselling Cases," *Journal of Consulting Psychology,* Vol. 13, 1949, 169-175.

respect; 5 indicated a high degree of self-acceptance. She applied her scale to seven patients who, according to their therapist, were making good progress. When she compared the first seven interviews with the final seven interviews, she found that the average score had climbed from 2 on the initial interviews to an average of 4.2 on the final interviews, showing that self-acceptance increased as successful therapy proceeded.

Other studies have shown that the number of positive self-references increases in cases of successful therapy, while in unsuccessful cases of therapy the number of negative self-references increases.

The ability to love is rooted in the ability to trust. The two are closely related from earliest infancy on when we learn as children that we can trust, and therefore love, our mother. And just as a child needs to love his mother, so an adult needs a person to love. For most of us this other person is a husband or wife.

And just as the ability to accept love and to give love is a measure of good mental health, so the inability to form close attachments, the inability to give or receive love, is a measure of emotional disturbance and poor mental health. A person whose emotional conditioning is such that he views every other person with suspicion and distrust cannot love them and so must build around himself a wall as protective armor against the attacks he expects from others. Even when others are kind and considerate to him and show him affection, he may be afraid to respond to them because he believes that their feelings are not genuine. The person whose parents neglected or ignored him or the person who has had an unfortunate love affair may assume this kind of attitude as a defense against further serious emotional involvement and possible emotional hurt.

The world is full of people who want to love others and to make friends but are unable to do so. As a result of certain damaging personal experiences that probably occurred in early childhood, they are afraid to break out of the shells they have built around themselves, both consciously and unconsciously, and to give of themselves as required in love. The psychotic represents in the most extreme degree the person unable to love—unable to form a close relationship.

It is well to mention here again that relationships with others are most satisfying when the needs of each of the individuals involved are satisfied. Adjustment requires the ability both to accept love, in the broadest sense of the word, as well as to give it. The absence of this dual ability reflects insecurity and emotional disturbance. Sometimes we find an adult who wants to receive or to get as much love as possible without giving any in return. For the small child, who has little to give until he gets, being on the receiving end rather than on the giving end is normal. But for the adult, such an attitude reflects emotional disturbances. Normally all of us need to give love and affection as much as to receive it.

The insecure person is afraid not only of others, but also of himself. His fear of others leads him to be hesitant and unsure of himself. Plagued by feelings of doubt and distrust, he betrays his emotional turmoil by statements such as, "I know that what I'm doing is wrong, and I know what I *should* be doing, but somehow I cannot bring myself to do it."

It is also likely that such a person will not only miss the experience of pleasure and happiness in his day-to-day activities, but will also "take it out on others." He will make others the victims of his own insecurity.

Emotional security, as we have seen from our earlier discussion, depends first on the acceptance and love we received as a child, and secondly on the degree to which we are able to accept ourselves. Menninger [4] refers to security as "one of the pillars upon which mental health rests." From this security, he points out, comes an inner harmony of the personality that makes the person feel confident and at peace with himself.

A sense of responsibility. Responsibility means (1) being responsible for our own actions, i.e., taking into account the con-

---

[4] William C. Menninger and Munroe Leaf, *You and Psychiatry.* New York, Charles Scribner's Sons, 1948.

sequences of our behavior, and (2) being responsive, or sensitive, to the needs of others. A mother who tells her friends in the presence of her child that "Mary will never be a beauty" is insensitive to the feelings of the child and does not consider the effects that such a remark may have on the youngster. The mother's behavior is irresponsible.

Responsibility also means that we consider more than the immediately apparent effects of our actions. If, as parents, we pamper and protect a child excessively, we may be satisfying our own needs, but at the same time may be making our son or daughter wholly dependent on us, preparing the way for all the difficulties such a situation breeds. This, too, is an example of irresponsible behavior.

Some people are much more responsible than others. One individual may confine his sense of responsibility to those who are very close to him, to members of his family and perhaps to his friends. He shows little concern for community problems, for the people who live on the other side of the track, or even for the neighbor whose child is sick. Others can include in their sphere of sympathy and effective action, i.e., in their field of responsibility, people caught in various types of disasters, suffering people in war-torn countries, even citizens of former enemy nations (as seen in all the *Care* packages shipped to Germany and Japan after World War II). In one sense, socialization is a process whereby we acquire an increased range of social sensitivity and responsibility. Instead of feeling responsible merely for our family or for our own group or community, we feel responsible for our fellow citizens, then for citizens of other countries, and so for all human beings, regardless of race, creed, or color.

A sense of direction and goal orientation. Whether we derive satisfaction and pleasure from our activities depends to a large extent on the goals we have set for ourselves and on how we have channeled our energy and efforts to attain these goals. This sense of direction and goal-directed behavior involves not only occupational goals, but also such other goals as finding a wife or husband, establishing a home, having children, finding financial security, having time for recreational activities, and so on. It involves purposeful striving and a kind of directed productivity and creativity that makes the attainment of goals possible.

The person who has no goals, who doesn't know what to do with himself, or whose goals are so fleeting that he changes them every day, is scattering or wasting his potentialities. Such a person may change jobs every month, or become very excited or enthusiastic about an activity one day only to drop it the next. The jack-of-all-trades and the dilettante are examples of persons who have failed to acquire a consistent, highly motivated goal-orientation. They are like small children who flit from toy to toy, unable to find pleasure or satisfaction in anything for long. Most of us have at times been uncertain about our goals. When we have failed to achieve something we greatly wanted, we may have asked ourselves anxiously, What now? Or even when we have reached the goal we had set ourselves, we may have felt undecided about where to turn next.

The ability to handle frustrations and irritations without becoming upset involves a high degree of goal-orientation, as contrasted to self-orientation. The self-oriented person caught up in a frustrating situation is concerned primarily with protecting his ego. The goal-oriented person, by contrast, is interested primarily in working out his problem and reaching his goal. The goal-oriented person may be baffled by a situation and even succumb to despair for a time, but eventually he will rally his resources and make a new attempt to resolve the conflict.

If we are sure of our goals and of our plan for attaining them, we will be better able to tolerate frustration and tension without becoming emotionally upset—without immediately going to pieces or losing our temper. But if we are not sure of what we want or of how to get it we are not likely to achieve a sense of accomplishing anything.

A sense of time perspective. Many of our more important goals can be reached only in the distant future. Each of us lives in the present, but this present has past and future reference points that influence our present attitudes, actions, and feelings. For the child, the present is narrowly defined because he has few past experiences to draw upon and cannot think far beyond today. But as we grow up our time perspective becomes broader. We can see beyond the immediate demands of the day, can plan ahead, can set our sights on distant goals. In so doing, we can utilize a great many more experiences from our past than can a child. In formulating our reactions to various situations in the present each of us brings into play not only his time perspective but also the emotional attitudes and values that color his time perspective.

As we have previously indicated in other chapters of this book, poor mental health is reflected in an excessive dwelling on the past. Some individuals who are unhappy in the present and for whom the future holds little promise derive their greatest comfort and pleasure from looking back on the "good old days." Memories become their substitute for future plans and actions. Other people, tormented by shame and guilt about past experiences, are unable to live happily and constructively in the present. For these people the present is "wasted," and this wasted present becomes in turn a further source of regret tomorrow. The well-adjusted individual, on the other hand, does not try to blot out the present or future by escaping into the past. He uses his past experiences as guides in planning future courses of action.

If future goals are to continue to have meaning for us in the present, we must be fairly certain that our present activities will help us to reach them. For example, we may set our goals and levels of aspiration so high that they become a source of highly disturbing frustration because we cannot believe we shall ever attain them. We may lose hope and incentive, allow actual accomplishment to give way to dreaming and fantasy. Goals set realistically are indicative of good adjustment. A realistic goal is one that we can feel reasonably sure of attaining if we work hard and faithfully. This *hope* of attainment will stimulate constructive activity and help to reduce the tension that comes from delayed satisfaction. Hope of success increases the amount of frustration we can endure and prevents slackening of efforts. Thus, the person who is looking for a certain job and knows he has the ability to fill such a job successfully will continue his search longer than the person who has in mind a job for which he is not qualified. The first few refusals will have a more damaging effect on the last-mentioned job-seeker. Hope—or we may call it confidence—is, then, an important aspect of time perspective.

Memories of success in the past help to reinforce confidence in present efforts. If we are confident, if we can view our opportunities optimistically, we are much more likely to take temporary setbacks in stride and to continue along the path we have marked out for ourselves.

But there is such a thing as being too cocky and over-confident. We have all seen the swaggering, brash student, for example, whose confidence bordered on conceit, who felt he did not have to prepare for the big exams coming up. Remember how he appeared after the exams—abject and crestfallen? And needlessly so, if he had only taken a more realistic look at his own abilities.

Personal values and a philosophy of life. The values we hold, although they are socially derived, are highly personal and subjective. It is difficult, therefore, to determine and analyze these values objectively. But it is not impossible. Our preferences for wearing certain colors, our choice of friends, our religious beliefs, our political convictions, all these represent values; and the mature person, in order to understand himself and to control his reactions, explores these values. He comes to see them more objectively, i.e., he maintains a problem-solving attitude toward them, and learns that these subjective, and often very important values can be understood and modified. The mature person is able to re-evaluate values acquired as a child, when he was uncritical, and to change and modify his values as he grows intellectually and emotionally.

How can we evaluate our values? Because our values are so highly subjective, many persons believe that we cannot assign a higher or lower rating to them or judge them as valid or invalid, except in terms of the personal meaning they have for us. Is there no objective standard for judging which value is more important? Have we, then, no guide for evaluating values and value judgments? Hartmann [5] has developed certain hypotheses concerning value judgments and has proposed "that we may tentatively adhere to the basic criterion that a good that moves toward a universal involving all people as an upper limit is higher than one that approaches a particular as a lower limit." From this position he derives the following six corollary criteria for rating values:

1. *Inclusiveness.* A value that affects *all* men rather than *some* is, other things being equal, superior. For example, freedom for all is of greater value than freedom for only a few persons.

2. *Permanence.* A value that lasts is higher than a temporary one.

3. *Irrevocability.* A value that is not replaceable or readily created by human effort is higher than one that can be produced easily. For example, the books of brilliant thinkers and the paintings of gifted artists are of more worth than mediocre products.

4. *Congruency.* A value that harmonizes with a person's total pattern of beliefs is superior to one that is inconsistent with the entire structure of integrated behavior.

5. *Cognitive completeness.* A value that is based on full information and broad experience is higher than one resting on partial and fragmentary knowledge.

6. *Survival.* A value that contributes to the maintenance of the individual or the human race is superior to one that leads to the extinction of either.

Another discussion of values and their relation to adjustment is given by R. B. Perry.[6] He suggests evaluating our actions from three points of view:

[5] George W. Hartmann, "Pacifism and Its Opponents in the Light of Value Theory," *Journal of Abnormal and Social Psychology,* Vol. 36, 1941, 164.

[6] R. B. Perry, *General Theory of Value.* New York, Longmans, Green & Company, Inc., 1926.

(1) How *adaptive* is our behavior in helping us to survive? (2) How *adjustive* is it in helping us to experience pleasure and comfort? and (3) How *integrative* is it in helping us to eliminate personal and interpersonal conflicts and to harmonize our various motives. Behavior that helps us to achieve these three goals is more valuable than behavior that helps to achieve only one or two of these goals.

Value judgments are an integral part of our personal philosophy of life. A person's philosophy of life is the system of values by which he lives. It includes, among other things, a person's aims, ideals, and manner of thinking, the principles by which he guides his behavior and conducts his affairs. Many people have built their life philosophies around religious concepts; others have developed humanitarian or materialistic or pragmatic or opportunistic approaches to life.

Whatever the outward form, a philosophy of life will have meaning to a person only as he assigns value to it. Every culture has its basic assumptions and beliefs, and every generation has to re-examine these beliefs in its search for meaning. As we saw in Chapter 3, man has always sought to erect systems of thought that would aid him in understanding more about himself, about the nature of some final reality, about the universe. With these explanations, man is at home in his world; he feels secure. Whether these explanations are "right" or "wrong" is often immaterial to him. The belief that an erupting volcano was caused by a god's sneezing served the same "comforting" psychological function for primitive man that our more scientific explanation does for us.

This does not mean that one belief can serve as well as another to make a person feel secure. The explanations, beliefs, and theories that comprise an individual's philosophy of life must be able to stand the test of reality—i.e., fit the real world and to provide a person some means by which he can predict and control events and direct his behavior. If the system fails in this, disillusionment, anxiety, even panic may result. When our philosophy of life reveals itself to be inadequate or invalid, we feel lost, at sea, desperate to find something with which to replace it. An example of this might be seen in the behavior of many ex-communists who seek solace in religion or some other "system" after the shattering effects of losing their faith in communism. Allport and Kramer,[7] in a study of prejudice that included probing into the philosophical orientation of the persons studied, emphasized the importance of personal philosophy in the following way:

> We are saying that prejudice will be prevented only if the philosophical mould of one's life is sound. A sound mould requires a basic trust of mankind, freedom from the jungle-outlook, from rigid categories, from the paranoid inability to take blame upon oneself or to adopt the point of view of the other fellow. A sound mould requires one to know the extent of one's hostile attitudes, and to feel some shame in having them, and to understand their probable roots in his home environment, in his school, or in his own temperament.

All of us, whether well or poorly adjusted, are faced with frustrations and conflicts all through life, but the well-adjusted person has developed more adequate and more effective ways of dealing with these problems. His approach to problems is characterized by a problem-solving attitude, requiring objectivity, an understanding of cause-and-effect relationships, and flexibility. Let us consider this approach in more detail.

A problem-solving attitude. A problem-solving attitude is the scientific approach as applied to ourselves and our problems. Such an attitude stresses (1) carefully defining and analyzing the problem, (2) evaluating various possible solutions to the problem, and (3) carrying out such solutions in order to solve the conflict or problem.

Just as the scientific method helps us to deal with the physical world, so it can help us to unravel the complexities of human behavior and help us to adjust. The extent of our adjustment is reflected in the amount of satisfaction and pleasure we derive from each day's activities. The greater our success in dealing with our

---

[7] Gordon W. Allport and Bernard M. Kramer, "Some Roots of Prejudice," *Journal of Psychology,* Vol. 22, 1946, 36.

problems, the greater will be the pleasure we experience as we meet and deal with these problems. If we fail, then, like the scientist in his laboratory, we should try another approach until we finally discover one that works. Sometimes, of course, the solution to our problems may require professional help (see Chapter 17). This professional help, as we shall discover later, is designed primarily to help us acquire the habit of approaching all our difficulties with the idea that they can be solved, i.e., to help us cultivate a problem-solving attitude. The problem-solving attitude implies a willingness on our part to change or to modify our behavior in order to meet the particular situation that confronts us, or to learn how to change the situation.

Why is it important to develop a problem-solving attitude? The answer is simply to solve problems. But why solve them? Why is it so important to recognize a problem, analyze it, understand it, solve it? The answer lies in the fact that an unsolved problem acts like a boulder blocking a highway. It prevents us, emotionally, from solving other problems or from accomplishing other aims. We do not "go beyond" an unsolved problem that has deep emotional significance for us. Each problem that arises must therefore be solved so that it can serve as a stepping stone; failure to solve one problem jeopardizes the possibility of solving the next. The neurotic person, as we saw earlier, is one who has failed to identify, analyze, and solve his problems. He has become fixated at that point in his development where he encountered the problem that, for various reasons, he was unable to solve. An unsolved problem may thus have a kind of derailing effect and prevent us from reaching our goals.

The problem-solving attitude involves *self-objectivity*. To be objective about ourselves involves a willingness to see ourselves as others see us, not as we might wish to see ourselves. Objectivity involves a readiness on our part to examine ourselves realistically, to appraise our assets and our liabilities, our strengths and our limitations, our shortcomings and our talents, our *potentialities* for growth. It involves a readiness to accept ourselves as we are, and to analyze our characteristics in order to achieve a better understanding of ourselves. It involves a certain degree of insight into our motivations, our goals, our defenses, and into the way our behavior affects others.

Objectivity also involves a sense of humor. The person who can laugh at himself reveals a certain awareness of his own foibles and idiosyncrasies. A sense of humor prevents us from taking ourselves and our problems too seriously.

Basic to the problem-solving attitude is the assumption of *cause-and-effect relationships*. Without this assumption, any attempt to solve a problem or to attain a goal is meaningless. For if we cannot anticipate the effect of our actions, we cannot distinguish the sensible course of action from the ridiculous; we are unable to predict the consequences of our behavior or to control a situation.

Sometimes when we have acted unwisely, we try to excuse ourselves by insisting that we had no way of knowing what the effects of our behavior would be. A stern parent whose harsh discipline has caused his child to become neurotic often will wring his hands and plead that if he could have foreseen the consequences of his actions, he would have been less tyrannical. It is true that we cannot always anticipate these effects. But the chances are that if we weigh our actions carefully and explore all the ramifications of our decision thoroughly, we shall not go astray so easily, shall not be forced to look back ruefully on what might have been.

A child, as we know, has a very limited understanding of cause-and-effect relationships, and therefore cannot analyze his behavior or predict the results of his actions. Unfortunately, many adults are just as incapable of analyzing their behavior rationally as are children. These adults feel themselves to be in the grip of forces far beyond their control and eventually adopt an attitude of help-lessness and of irresponsibility. We label this kind of irresponsi-bility in an adult as infantile behavior.

Irresponsible and inconsistent behavior by parents may handi-cap a child in learning about cause-and-effect relationships. For instance, if a child is punished for lying on one occasion but not punished if he lies again, he will be unable to anticipate the effects of his actions and so to learn what is and is not acceptable behavior. His parents' behavior will appear erratic rather than predictable, and his own behavior, influenced by the erratic behavior of his parents, will show the same tendency.

Finally, a basic feature of the problem-solving attitude is the ability to be flexible. Flexibility implies the ability to adapt our behavior to the special requirements of a situation, or to learn how to modify the situation. The inflexible person in a changing world is an anachronism. The whole process of living requires constant adjustment, constant change. And the person who is unable or unwilling to adapt to change or who stubbornly persists in a course of action long after such action has proved to be impractical, is neurotic and maladjusted.

Related to adaptability is creativeness, which is directly opposed to rigidity. To see new approaches to a problem, new versions of old facts, new significance in common phenomena (e.g., the laws of gravity in a falling apple), implies a unique and productive flexibility called creativeness. Creativity is the mark of the great artist, writer, scientist, or statesman—but it is something all of us can show in varying degree. The parent in rearing his child can be creative. In fact, fewer children would have fewer problems if parents were more creative in dealing with their youngsters. It is much more creative to explain to a child why he should go to bed, to make him content to go to bed, for example, than it is to drive him off to his room with threats of punishment.

The Mature Personality

Dr. Leon Saul [8] in commenting about the attributes of the mature person, summarizes many of the things we have been talking about in the following description of the mature person.

> The mature adult is both *predominantly* independent and responsible, with little need to regress, and also is giving and productive, although still able to relax and to receive nor-

---

[8] Leon J. Saul, *Emotional Maturity*. Philadelphia, J. B. Lippincott Company, 1947, pp. 16-17.

mally; he is cooperative rather than egotistical and competitive; he is in relative harmony with his conscience, which easily integrates with his mature feelings and behavior; his sexuality is free and integrated with mating and responsible productive activity, both sexual and social; his hostility toward others and toward himself is minimal but is freely available for defense and constructive use; his grasp of reality is clear and unimpaired by the emotional astigmatisms of childhood; and freed from childhood patterns, he is discriminating and highly adaptable. And among the many results of such development, his anxiety is at a minimum.

It cannot be too strongly emphasized that maturity means not merely the *capacity* for such attitudes and functioning— but also the ability to *enjoy* them fully. It means that the individual now derives pleasure from the exercise of his adult powers and not only from his infantile demands. In the neuroses there is typically a protest against the adult productive, responsible activities and guilt and shame over the childish impulses; each vitiates the other.

Characteristics of Good Mental Health and the Goals of Psychotherapy

The characteristics of good mental health, of the mature personality, which we have been discussing would be, for the person who does not have them, the goals of psychotherapy. In the learning situation of psychotherapy, discussed in the next chapter, a person strives to attain these characteristics to the maximal degree possible for him in line with his capacities, experiences, and opportunities for growth. We must remember that what constitutes normality or adjustment for one person may differ markedly from what constitutes normality or adjustment for another. This implies that each of us has a *personal* aim in adjustment, not a *group* aim. Or to put this another way, each of us must aim to achieve personal comfort, creativeness, and happiness in the manner that is best for us, regardless of what the adjustment goals of other persons might be. Adjustment for each of us is a *personally* tailored item, not a socially manufactured product, even though our personal welfare is closely related to the welfare of other people.

For Additional Reading

Allport, Gordon W., *Personality. A Psychological Interpretation*. New York, Henry Holt & Company, Inc., 1937.

———— and Bernard M. Kramer, "Some Roots of Prejudice," *Journal of Psychology*, Vol. 22, 1946, 9-39.

Boettiger, Elizabeth F., *Your Child Meets the World Outside. A Guide to the Children's Attitudes in Democratic Living*. New York, Appleton-Century-Crofts, Inc., 1941.

Carroll, Herbert A., *Mental Hygiene. The Dynamics of Adjustment*. New York, Prentice-Hall, Inc., 1947.

Cole, Luella, *Attaining Maturity*. New York, Rinehart & Company, Inc., 1944.

Erikson, Erik Hamburger, "Growth and Crises of the 'Healthy Personality,'" in Clyde Kluckhohn, Henry A. Murray, and David M. Schneider, eds., *Personality in Nature, Society, and Culture*, rev. ed. New York, Alfred A. Knopf, Inc., 1953.

Frank, Lawrence K., *Nature and Human Nature. Man's New Image of Himself*. New Brunswick, N. J., Rutgers University Press, 1951.

French, Thomas M., *The Integration of Behavior*, Vol. 1, *Basic Postulates*. Chicago, University of Chicago Press, 1952.

Fromm, Erich, *Man for Himself*. New York, Rinehart & Company, Inc., 1947.

Hartley, Eugene, *Problems in Prejudice*. Morningside Heights, New York, King's Crown Press, 1946.

Horney, Karen, *The Neurotic Personality of our Time*. New York, W. W. Norton & Company, Inc., 1939.

Katz, Barney and George F. J. Lehner, *Mental Hygiene in Modern Living*. New York, The Ronald Press Company, 1953.

Lecky, Prescott, *Self-Consistency—A Theory of Personality*. New York, The Island Press, 1945.

Levy, John and Ruth Munroe. *The Happy Family*. New York, Alfred A. Knopf, Inc., 1947.

Mannheim, Karl, *Freedom, Power and Democratic Planning*. New York, Oxford University Press, 1950.

Menninger, William C. and Munroe Leaf. *You and Psychiatry*. New York and London, Charles Scribner's Sons, 1948.

Overstreet, H. A., *The Mature Mind*. New York, W. W. Norton & Company, Inc., 1948.

Saul, Leon J., *Emotional Maturity*. Philadelphia, J. B. Lippincott Company, 1947.

Symonds, Percival M., *The Dynamics of Human Adjustment*. New York, D. Appleton-Century Company, 1946.

——, *The Ego and the Self*. New York, Appleton-Century-Crofts, Inc., 1953.

Thorpe, L. P., *The Psychology of Mental Health*. New York, The Ronald Press Company, 1950.

Warters, Jane, *Achieving Maturity*. New York, McGraw-Hill Book Company, Inc., 1949.

Weinberg, S. K., *Society and Personality Disorders*. New York, Prentice-Hall, Inc., 1952.

White, Robert W., *Lives in Progress: A Study of the Natural Growth of Personality*. New York, The Dryden Press, 1952.

Psychotherapy
and
Adjustment

CHAPTER 17

- PSYCHOTHERAPY AS A LEARNING PROCESS
- RELATIONS BETWEEN THE PATIENT AND THERAPIST
- CHANGES AND GOALS IN THERAPY
- TYPES OF THERAPY
- PSYCHOTHERAPY AND SELF-HELP
- QUALIFICATIONS OF PSYCHOTHERAPISTS

Psychotherapy, as the term indicates, is a process for treating an illness or problem by psychological methods. It is a learning process involving two people that attempts to correct the effects of disruptive emotional experiences or of certain deficiencies in learning. Problems so treated are generally emotional or psychological in nature. Frequently, however, psychological methods are used as an adjunct to physiological treatment when a physiological problem, such as an ulcer, is related to emotional disturbances. Thus, psychotherapy is a process effective mainly in psychogenic, i.e., functional, diseases.

Psychotherapy further implies utilizing methods of treatment that are based on an understanding of psychological dynamics, that is, the knowledge of cause-and-effect relationships as they operate in the area of our feelings, our thoughts, and our general interactions with other persons.

In our earlier discussion about defense mechanisms, the neuroses and the psychoses, we touched on some of the dynamic factors related to psychological disturbances. In the previous chapter, on criteria for satisfactory adjustment and the characteristics of the mature, mentally healthy person, we touched further on dynamic factors related to mental illness. In this chapter, we shall discuss how to improve a person's adjustment to his environment by helping him to alter his thoughts, feelings, and behavior—in short, his personality. Since psychotherapy is a process for changing behavior, it can be thought of as a special kind of learning situation. As we know, we learn in order to change, and in psychotherapy we learn to change in particular ways. This brings us to a consideration of the relationship between psychotherapy and learning.

Psychotherapy as a Learning Process

Our personality develops and we become what we are through a series of experiences in which we learn how to think, feel, and behave. We may learn poor ways to adjust, or we may learn good ways. If we have learned, for example, to react to all situations and problems angrily and aggressively, we have not developed satisfactory techniques for handling our problems. The well-adjusted person has learned to approach his problems calmly and rationally, with a firm belief that he can think them through by applying or modifying lessons he has learned in the past. Of course, not all past solutions will apply to present problems. We must guard against relying so heavily on the "tried-and-true" technique that our approach becomes rigid and unimaginative. Here psychotherapy is important, for it is designed to bring us greater personal satisfaction and happiness in our daily affairs by showing us how to *alter* our behavior. Successful psychotherapy teaches the neurotic person to discard his warped methods of reacting and to replace them with useful, normal, adjustive techniques. Psychotherapy is the process by which the neurotic unlearns old "bad" habits and relearns new "good" ones.

Let us illustrate briefly how a particular experience might produce neurotic behavior and how this neuroticism might be modified by psychotherapy. For the sake of discussion, we shall divide the person's responses into three groups: (1) his observable behavior, (2) his feelings and emotions, and (3) his thoughts and fantasies concerning the experience or event.

Let us consider the case of a child who has been severely frightened by a dog. His *observable behavior* may exhibit the following pattern: He may start avoiding not only this particular dog, but all dogs, thus generalizing from the specific dog that threatened him to all dogs. At the sight of a dog he may run, or begin to cry, or seek comfort and shelter with adults. His *feelings and emotions* may be revealed in the following way: He may tell us that he is afraid, or that his stomach hurts, or that he is tense, anxious, and fearful. An examination of his thoughts and fantasies also shows his fear of dogs. He may imagine that vicious dogs are following him wherever he goes or lying in wait for him around every corner and in every dark cranny. He may spend much of his time "dreaming up" various ways of escaping dogs. His mind may, in fact, be so full of thoughts about dogs that he "sees" dogs in all kinds of places when actually there are none. Psychotherapy in this instance would help the child to see that his fears about all dogs were unfounded, that there are some dogs, perhaps the majority, who are gentle, affectionate, and playful. With psychotherapy the child could relearn and develop a more appropriate, constructive attitude toward dogs.

We also see in this example how certain causes lead to certain behavioral effects. By observing these cause-and-effect relationships, we learn to understand why a particular person behaves in a particular way. Thus, if a patient is afraid of dogs, we assume that at some time in the past he has been frightened by a dog. If a person is tense and distraught before starting off to work in the morning, we assume that perhaps he must make an important decision that day, or that possibly he fears that his superior will rebuke him for having made a mistake in the monthly accounts. Thus, the anxiety the person experiences has its roots not "in the mind" of the person but in the experiences he has had.

The interrelationship between a person's characteristics and his experiences can be illustrated by the case of Mrs. A.

Mrs. A. was born with one leg three inches shorter than the other. This physical handicap involved her in certain experiences that taught her, eventually, to behave in a certain way, to feel a certain way, and to think a certain way. At the commencement of therapy, her behavior was forceful, aggressive, and domineering. She reported that she often felt anxious, fearful, and insecure. She further recounted that certain thoughts and fantasies kept recurring to her in which she saw herself carrying off unusual physical triumphs, such as winning foot races, or beauty contests, or being complimented on her ability to dance gracefully.

Her problem was caused not only by the physical handicap, but also by the humiliating experiences she had suffered as a crippled child in a culture where physical beauty and perfection are highly valued. She had found it impossible, from earliest infancy on, to do what others did, to compete with them, to be accepted by them in certain situations. Thus the interactions between herself and the world had led to the development of certain behavior, certain feelings, and certain thoughts that created a new difficulty in themselves and prompted the need for psychotherapy.

Through psychotherapy, Mrs. A. was able to modify her behavior so that she no longer needed to compensate for her handicap by being dominant and aggressive, or to feel ashamed and rejected when people looked at her. She no longer had to satisfy certain emotional needs by dreaming about athletic victories or dancing contests. The anxiety about her handicap, and her need for defense mechanisms to handle this anxiety were eliminated in therapy by talking about her feelings, what they were related to, and how she might change her reactions. She was freed, so to speak, of her maladjustment. If she had learned as a child, when she first encountered the problems related to her physical handicap, the things that she learned as an adult in psychotherapy, then obviously no adult psychotherapy would have been necessary. Psychotherapy thus may be viewed as a technique that serves to remove the "learning lag" reflected in maladjustment. Or to put it another way, psychotherapy is a technique that helps a person to learn today something he should have learned yesterday, or the day before, or months or years ago.

Let us consider further the effect of environment on what we learn to do or learn not to do as we grow from childhood to adulthood. We are all familiar with the old proverb that the burned child fears the fire. Analyzed psychologically, this adage indicates that a certain action, touching the fire, has been followed by a certain consequence, being burned. The experience of being burned has changed the behavior of the child with respect to fire —he avoids, he dreads, he fears fire. The proverb points out that a certain form of behavior can spring from a single, isolated stimulus in our non-human environment. Actually, as we grow up, thousands of other non-human factors influence our behavior. More important, however, even than these non-human factors are the innumerable human stimuli that modify our behavior— stimuli that come through our dealings with parents, other members of the family, children, teachers in school, friends, "enemies," and adults with whom we work. These endless and varied social interactions provide for each of us many social learning experiences that change us from mere biological organisms at birth into highly socialized, civilized adults. Sometimes this adult is normal. Sometimes he is neurotic.

So complex is the world in which we live, so varied and often bewildering are the demands made upon us, so involved and hectic the problems we face, that it is easily possible for us to fail to learn some of the things we need to know or to mislearn certain other things. Either of these possibilities can lead to maladjustive behavior. When we consider how many things there are to learn, and how many ways there are to learn them, or how many reasons we can find for not learning them, or how many different effects learning or not learning them can produce, it is not surprising to find that some of us have failed to learn something we need to know or have learned it wrong. In view of the fact that most of our learning experiences involve relations with other people, it follows that most of our behavior "disorders" are learned as a consequence of our coming into contact with people.

The function of the psychotherapist is to help us to unlearn disordered behavior patterns. The therapist and the patient work together in a social learning situation. In this setting, the therapist helps the patient to see his deficiencies, to understand their sources, and to work out satisfactory ways of adjusting. Let us, therefore, consider in more detail the relations between patient and therapist.

Relations Between the Patient and Therapist

The relationship between the patient and his therapist is believed to have a decisive influence on the course the therapy will follow and the kind of learning the patient will achieve. The patient-therapist association is a special kind of social relationship encountered nowhere else. It offers the patient, through the behavior and attitudes of the therapist, a unique kind of learning situation. The therapist provides factors conducive to learning. Some characteristics of the psychotherapeutic learning situation as provided or created by the therapist are the following.

Attitude of acceptance. The therapist must be able to accept the patient, to sympathize with him, and, through his behavior and attitudes, to communicate his sympathy and understanding to the patient. The therapist must be able to accept the patient regardless of the problems or characteristics the patient presents.

This acceptance of the patient by the therapist leads to what psychologists call positive *transference*. The patient becomes strongly attached to his therapist. He may view the therapist as the idealized parent, husband, wife, or lover. The patient may also, in cases of negative transference, hate the therapist violently. Or, the patient may love the therapist one moment and hate him the next. And through all his patient's changing moods and attitudes, the therapist must continue to accept him with warmth and understanding. In addition, the therapist must at all times maintain an objective approach to his patient. Failure to do so may create serious new problems for the patient. This is why it is so important for the therapist to be well trained, emotionally stable, and well adjusted in his own right. Otherwise, he may have difficulty maintaining the objective, professional relationship with his patient that is so crucial for successful psychotherapy.

The therapist's acceptance of the patient, then, leads the patient to feel that he is intellectually understood, emotionally accepted, and sympathetically supported in all his reactions during therapy. In other words, the patient feels safe.

In addition, the constant encouragement and support provided by the therapist will encourage the patient to face his problems anew or to meet people again. Even if his problems overwhelm him again or if people still reject him, he knows he still will have the love and support of the therapist.

The permissive atmosphere also leads to *catharsis* for the patient. Catharsis is the process whereby the patient obtains emotional release by being able to unburden himself of feelings that he has hitherto kept "bottled up" inside himself, perhaps for years. Most of us harbor thoughts and feelings that we fear to disclose to others even though they build up tremendous pressures in us. In the protected, permissive atmosphere of therapy, the patient can sit down and talk such feelings over with the therapist, confident in the belief that the therapist will soothe away his doubts and fears.

Freud at first believed that catharsis was enough to cure a patient, but he discovered that it was not enough; catharsis is only one aspect of therapy.

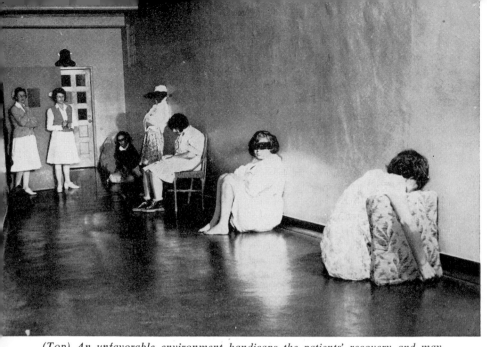

(Top) *An unfavorable environment handicaps the patients' recovery and may even contribute to their further deterioration.* (Bottom) *A favorable environment gives support to the patients by encouraging them to learn new skills and allowing them to engage in pleasant activities.* (Courtesy the Los Angeles Mirror.)

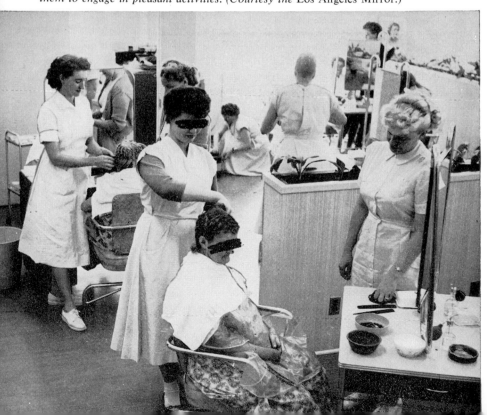

Permissive atmosphere. The therapist must specifically avoid criticizing his patient, must refrain from allowing his own feelings to color a patient's response, must conceal any judgments or shock he experiences at what his patient says, does, or thinks. Instead, the patient must be able to feel that the therapist takes only an objective interest in his disclosures, and that the therapist's only aim is to help him to attain a better understanding of himself. This non-judgmental, non-prejudicial, non-condemning attitude on the part of the therapist, so important in the process of psychotherapy, is almost never present when a person talks to his parents, his marriage partner, his friends, his minister or priest, or other persons in whom he may confide his problems. These persons, because of their particular frame of reference, their values, and their attitudes, may not be in a position to help the patient to understand himself better. Rather, through their personal, opinionated reactions and advice, they may influence the patient to accept *their* particular solution or view of a problem or situation when actually such solutions may have little or no relationship to the needs of the person who is hobbled with the problem.

The therapist, on the other hand, is permissive. He has no ready answers to give. Rather, the therapist listens and gives the patient a chance to talk about all kinds of things that he cannot discuss with anyone else. In talking freely about them to the therapist without fear of criticism or censure, the patient learns what he needs and also extinguishes the fear responses he has associated with some of these verbalizations. The more he talks, the more his confidence returns, the more the patient begins to disclose previously forbidden feelings, thoughts, or concealed behavior. The patient may suddenly find himself talking about things he had forgotten (or repressed) for years.

Feeling of support. To buoy his patient's confidence the therapist generally tries to reassure his patient, to give him carefully selected advice, to suggest and persuade judiciously. Sometimes, the therapist may believe that his patient's environment needs changing and may help him find a new job, make new friends, try to make his home life happier, and help him find new and interesting hobbies and activities.

The therapist may also direct his patient toward certain groups specifically organized to help people in need. Alcoholics Anonymous, or Divorcees Anonymous, or various forms of group therapy may have great therapeutic value. For other patients, participation in religious activities and the support they derive from religious inspiration may provide a valuable adjunct to therapy.

Sheltered reality-testing situation. In a sheltered reality-testing situation, the therapist provides a haven of safety for the patient, a calm harbor, so to speak, where the patient can analyze, explore, and test his ways of thinking and feeling before venturing out into the world. The therapeutic setting is a kind of testing laboratory for the patient in which he may make all kinds of experiments, and perhaps all kinds of errors, as he experiments, without having to experience feelings of failure, shame, or disappointment, as he might in the world outside. In fact, the more he experiments and explores, regardless of his errors, the more "successfully" the patient utilizes the therapeutic situation. Like a child learning to swim, a patient may need to start with a wading pool, then progress to the shelter of a swimming pool, then to a stream or lake, and finally plunge into the ocean. In short, then, the therapeutic situation provides a safe learning situation devoid of the anxiety that everyday contacts and relationships induce.

Opportunities for making new discriminations and avoiding old generalizations. Learning is a process through which we discover labels for objects, events, thoughts, feelings, and behavior. A small child, for example, associates the word "father" with his father, the word "mother" with his mother, and may apply the same label to any other man or woman until he learns, by differentiating his father from other men or his mother from other women, that the label applies only to his own parents. Were the child to continue to regard all men as his father and all women as his mother, he would be making a false generalization that might create serious difficulties for him if he attempted to react to all men or all women as though they were his parents.

Generalization may occur in another manner. A young man's father, for example, may have been an extremely cruel, arbitrary, tyrannical man whom his son feared and disliked. As a result, during his childhood, youth, and early manhood, the young man may have come to regard all men in authority with the same mixed feelings of fear and hatred aroused by his father. Such a generalization, of course, is inappropriate and maladjustive when applied so indiscriminately. We have here again an instance of a maladjustive generalization.

A person beset by such intense emotional reactions thinks in terms of absolutes and "allness" concepts that reflect the kind of emotional spread or generalization we have just mentioned. The young man just mentioned has come to believe that "all" persons in authority are "always" arbitrary and tyrannical and that they "never" understand and appreciate the problems of "anyone" working for them. His attitude toward his superiors may become offensive; he may refuse to cooperate, react to suggestions as though they were threats, constantly complain that he is being bullied and treated unfairly. Thus he invites from his superiors the same kind of behavior he hated and feared in his father. And when his superiors begin to lose patience with him or rebuke him for his attitude, he uses their actions as an excuse to over-generalize about his inability to get along with people in authority. He says to himself, "I can *never* work for *anyone* else." "*I can't get along with anyone.*" Or, worse still, he believes, "*No one* loves me." When we stop to analyze, in a therapeutic relationship, what the patient may mean by the remark, "No one loves me," we may find that he is actually referring to only a few experiences in which he felt rejected but on the basis of which he now generalizes and *feels* that he is rejected by "everyone."

In cases of neurotic over-generalization, the therapist's job is to help the patient make finer and more valid differentiations between persons, events, and experiences. Our young man must learn, for example, that not all people in responsible positions are arbitrary and tyrannical, even though his father was and even though he feels all his superiors are.

The person who over-generalizes also must learn to distinguish between past events and the feelings these past events evoked when he was younger and less experienced and present events that occur amid new situations and circumstances. The neurotic, for example, because of his inability to make the necessary distinctions, reacts to the "present" as though it were the "past." He confuses in his mind the events of yesterday and today and so brings into the present, where they are not appropriate, past feelings he should have discarded.

In addition to differentiating between past and present, it is necessary for the person who over-generalizes to distinguish between childhood conditions and adult status. In the therapeutic situation, the patient must re-evaluate his childhood inadequacy in the light of his adult capacities and accomplishments. In fact, the ability to discriminate between childhood and adult status is a way of seeing that the past is not the present. The adult who says "I was shy as a child," must discover the source of these childhood feelings in order to see that shyness need not continue to plague him as an adult. In like manner, an adult in a therapeutic situation has an opportunity to work through and to re-evaluate all his attitudes, feelings, defenses, and other aspects of his behavior that have prevented him from functioning as creatively and productively as his capacities might allow.

From this description of a neurotic's maladjustive generalizations, we see that the neurotic is his own worst enemy. We often meet neurotic persons who possess all the elements of success and yet cannot succeed. The bright student who fails in school, the beautiful woman who can't get or stay married, the mother who can't love her children, the executive who can't deal with his subordinates—all of them are examples.

The therapist can help his patient to make clearer differentiations by providing him with new names or labels for his disruptive experiences and feelings. This is especially true in the spheres of human relations and emotions. Emotions, as we know, are peculiarly unique phenomena that we all experience but can never fully describe or label, either to ourselves or to others. Only when we can view the overt "emotional response" of others in the light of our own experience can we imagine what their feelings must be. Actually we do not even know if the terms "blue" or "sweet" indicate the same things to others as they do to ourselves. Yet in interpreting responses we assume that other people react to stimuli in the same way we do.

Because much of our feeling is left unlabeled, it is difficult to make adequate discriminations and distinctions between different feelings, or even between the situations that arouse the same feelings. This inability to distinguish our emotions hinders our control of them. If we cannot distinguish and label different animals, we have no control over our reactions to animals, and we are as likely to fear the lapdog as the lion.

The supplying of labels may involve interpretating relationships between events and feelings. When a person thinks in terms of such evaluative words as "good" or "bad," "right" or "wrong," he cannot see people or events as they really are, because people and events rarely fit the extremes of this either-or dichotomy. We should note further that when words like "good" or "bad" are applied to a person they do not tell us what that person did, or when, how, or why he did it, but only how another person *feels* about what was done. To understand what the person meant when he used these words, we must know something about his standards of good or bad.

The process of therapy causes a patient's feelings and attitudes to change. He comes to make fewer broad generalizations, makes finer and clearer distinctions and discriminations, and avoids the the use of "allness" terms and evaluative concepts. These newly acquired abilities further the re-socialization process of psychotherapy, in that the patient learns to react to others in terms of their actual characteristics, rather than in terms of his own biases toward them. Just as the small child learns that not all men are his father, so the neurotic adult learns that not all persons can be lumped into the extremes of his earlier either-or categories. Out of the therapeutic process comes a new process of control and responsible evaluation, free from the emotional distortion and anxiety-produced defenses of the past.

Changes and Goals in Therapy

Psychotherapy becomes necessary when an individual is extremely dissatisfied with his behavior, or when members of his family or his friends note symptoms of trouble and urge him to see a therapist. At first glance, it would seem that the goal of therapy should be simply to change this behavior and thus get rid of the symptoms. But just as a mechanic cannot repair a car merely by tampering with the gauges on the dashboard, so a therapist cannot change behavior merely by "treating" reaction patterns. We don't cure the alcoholic's problem by hiding his whiskey. In order to change behavior, it is necessary to dig into the cause-and-effect relationships that govern a person's behavior, to find out and to understand what makes a certain person act the way he does. A new appreciation of cause-and-effect relationships and how they function in our behavior is one of the major benefits to be derived from psychotherapy.

What changes, then, take place in therapy? These can be classified, for convenience, as: (1) changes in our feelings, (2) changes in our perceptions, (3) changes in our interpretations, (4) changes in our judgments, (5) changes in our motivations, (6) changes in our awareness, and (7) changes in our behavior.

Changes in feelings. During the therapeutic process, the patient describes his behavior—his past behavior and his present behavior. In doing so, he gives vent to his feelings. Usually he is apprehensive at first and gives only superficial, rehearsed information, hoping to stave off a deep, intensive examination of his personality. Gradually, however, he begins to express more and more of his hostile, aggressive feelings. In all this the able therapist guides the patient, trying to clarify and explain these feelings to him. The patient discovers that he can give vent to physical signs of fear, anxiety, and anger as he discusses certain experiences, whereas formerly he may have consciously fought against revealing such feelings, thereby repressing them. Therapy exposes the extent of these repressed feelings, as well as the unexpressed desires that exist in the patient's "unconscious." When these feelings have been uncovered and identified, the patient, with the help of the therapist, can examine them and decide what to do to satisfy them or to banish them. In learning to make such decisions, the

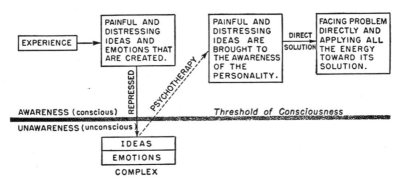

The application and functioning of psychotherapy. (From B. Katz and George F. J. Lehner, Mental Hygiene in Modern Living. *New York, The Ronald Press Company, 1953, p. 492.)*

patient achieves new satisfactions and acquires better control of his behavior.

Changes in perception. Perceiving is a process by which we give "meaning" to our sensations. When we see a red light flashing from a traffic pole, for example, we know that it is not there merely for decoration. It is a signal that means stop. When an individual over-generalizes about one person or a group of people because of experiences he has had with another person, as the young man did a few pages back, then his perception becomes distorted. It is possible, therefore, to perceive objects, persons, or events, including ourselves, correctly and realistically or incorrectly and unrealistically.

Many neurotics have distorted perceptions that lead them into serious difficulty. Because of these distortions, the neurotic reacts to people and to events not as they are but as he "sees" them through his "refracting lenses." These distortions are, of course, related to his needs. In therapy these needs and their effect on a person's perception are laid bare. In the course of treatment the patient learns how his style of perception may tend, for example, to impute guilt or danger into his everyday life, thus filling him with anxiety. It shows him how the fear he projects onto others may be a reflection of his own insecurity, or how the aggressiveness he sees in others is a sign of his own hostility toward them. From this new awareness comes the realization that how he "sees" others is rooted in his own feelings and that his personal subjective perceptions of the world must be modified to fit the realities of the situation. Through therapy, a patient is helped to regain an objective and realistic relationship to his world.

Changes in interpretation. In addition to perceptual changes, therapy can also effect changes in a person's interpretations of events. When the maladjusted individual perceives others as hostile, unfriendly, or threatening, he tends to disregard or distort their friendliness or kindness and consequently cannot interpret their actions correctly. Because of his problems, he is so bound by and limited to a few motives and, consequently, to their overemphasis, that understanding, predicting, or interpreting behavior is impossible for him. Yet he is baffled and puzzled when he fails to predict correctly how other people will react to a certain situation.

We have already spoken about the importance of the multivalued orientation as contrasted with the two-valued orientation, or either-or type of thinking, the disturbed person frequently employs. The emotionally healthy person interprets events through a continuum ranging from black through many, many shades of grey to white, and probably very seldom utilizes the ends of the continuum in his interpretations.

Psychotherapy attempts to change the manner in which we make interpretations and the kind of interpretations we make. The patient is led to examine his motives and the motives of others more closely in order to see how the interpretations he places on things are rooted in his needs. He becomes aware of the infinite number of forces that influence behavior, and he learns to avoid attempting to interpret behavior in the light of a few simple generalizations that, in reality, have little foundation. For example, he no longer believes that the alcoholic lacks will power, or that the person who fails in a certain job is lazy or stupid. All the factors that combine to make a person an alcoholic, another a dreamer, still another shy and retiring, cannot be covered by such terms. These meaningless interpretations must be replaced with significant ones. And when the patient is able to make significant, meaningful interpretations of situations, circumstances, and events, his own behavior as well as the behavior of other people will become more intelligible and predictable to him.

Changes in judgment. Judgment is the process by which, through comparisons and discriminations among events, we make decisions and assign values to persons and experiences. It involves relating persons and events to our own frame of reference, set of values, or philosophy of life. When we judge, in a sense we set ourselves up as authorities. Judgment is a highly subjective process in which we express our personal values. Consequently, if the neurotic has acquired a distorted set of values, his judgments will be distorted. A person who thinks other people are threatening him will probably regard such people as "bad."

Judging implies arriving at a decision, and this step for most persons involves feelings of either approval or disapproval about the event or person judged. Such judgments, particularly in the neurotic, are frequently made on the basis of inadequate information or on the basis of a serious distortion of the available facts. Thus the neurotic's decisions often lead him into further difficulties.

Psychotherapy attempts to help the patient to evaluate the process by which he makes judgments and arrives at decisions. It also attempts to divert his attention from the process of judging to the process of understanding, to substitute objectivity in place of subjectivity. The ability to *suspend* judgment involves an emotional maturity and feeling of security that the neurotic often lacks. He wants a decision, an answer (often he wants a simple "yes" or "no" answer!), even when decisions and answers are impossible.

The neurotic often feels compelled to display his judgments about events or persons, no matter how vague his understanding of the situations judged. He may be hypercritical, always ready to denounce, even when he has no basis for making such denunciations. This tendency is what therapy hopes to change.

Changes in motivation. We have already remarked many times in this book how important it is to understand our own needs. These needs, as we know, determine our goals, our self-conception, and the way we make interpretations or judgments. Suffice it to say here that psychotherapy attempts to help a person to recognize his motives, to let him see where they are leading him, and to understand the central role they play in his behavior. When a person comes to understand his motives, he may relinquish old goals that were unattainable, set his sights upon new goals that are more within his reach, and come to realize the importance of constantly examining and re-examining his goals and his motives in terms of his own needs.

Changes in awareness. Psychotherapy attempts to make a person more aware of all the factors, conscious and unconscious, that affect his behavior. Increased awareness is sometimes called insight and may be related, as we have already indicated, to a better appreciation of how we perceive, interpret, judge, and are motivated. In psychotherapy, much of our improvement in self-awareness comes about through uncovering long-forgotten and suppressed experiences and the thoughts and especially the feelings associated with them. Psychologists sometimes call this process "making the unconscious conscious."

Changes in behavior. The therapist's first objective is to change the behavior of his patient along the lines we have just been discussing. In changing a patient's behavior, the therapist is interested in eliminating not only behavioral symptoms, but also the problems that produced the symptoms. Of course, the compulsive patient who eats or drinks too much, who suffers from phobias and irrational fears of all kinds, who is depressed, or who exhibits physical symptoms without any organic basis, wants first of all to be relieved of his symptoms and the suffering they bring him, regardless of what changes may be made in the source of his problem. He might in fact measure the therapist's proficiency by the success the therapist has in removing these symptoms.

The therapist, however, looks at the situation differently. For him the symptom is important mainly as a sign of a deeper, more basic trouble. In terms of long-range success, the therapist may not even consider it advisable to remove the physical symptoms immediately. He is more interested in the underlying behavior patterns that are causing the symptoms, and he must distinguish between symptomatic treatment (such as giving an aspirin for a headache) and depth treatment (finding the cause of the headache). Changing behavior in therapy, then, involves changes at both the symptom level and the depth level.

In general terms, the goal of therapy is to make the patient feel more secure and to increase his self-esteem, thereby making it easier for him to accept himself, to sharpen his insight, and to lead him into paths of greater spontaneity and creativity. Accomplishing these aims will further the patient's total well-being and remove the barriers that stand in the way of his becoming well adjusted.

Types of Therapy

The differences between the various "schools" of therapy are often less a matter of fundamental divergences than a matter of shift-in-emphasis about certain theoretical formulations. All therapists, for instance, recognize the value of a certain amount of catharsis, but the methods by which they approach it and the theoretical importance they assign to it in their system varies from school to school and from therapist to therapist. Frequently, too, therapists of differing convictions may use very similar methods and concepts. We might say, as a kind of summing up, that therapists often are more easily distinguished by their terminology, by what they say, than by what they do. The factors conducive to learning, mentioned earlier in this chapter, are probably used by all therapists regardless of their theoretical orientation. The effectiveness with which therapists use these factors depends, of course, on their ability, training, and experience. Increasingly, therapists are concerning themselves more and more with the psychodynamics of learning.

We shall differentiate and discuss briefly the following types of therapy:

1. Psychoanalytic therapies—Freud, Jung, Adler
2. Directive psychotherapy
3. Non-directive psychotherapy
4. Relational psychotherapy
5. Group psychotherapy

Psychoanalytic therapies. Psychoanalysis, whether we emphasize the views of Freud, Jung, or Adler, is a theory of personality as well as a method of therapy. Many of the views about personality and the procedures originally developed by Freud, Jung, and Adler have now been absorbed into the body of general psychotherapy. In psychoanalysis, as distinguished from general psychotherapy, we generally find a heavy emphasis on such techniques as free association, dream analysis, and a systematic use of interpretation, catharsis, and emotional re-education. Crucial to the psychoanalytic process is the relationship between the therapist and the patient, involving the so-called "transference," which provides the emotional leverage for therapy, as we saw earlier. In general, the goal of psychoanalysis is to uncover and resolve emotional conflicts of the patient, many of which stem from early childhood experiences.

It should be mentioned, too, that psychoanalysis, since its inception by Freud, has gone through different stages of development. At various times different key concepts have been stressed —catharsis, free association, and the transfer neuroses, for example. Today the tendency is to emphasize emotional re-education (as discussed earlier in this chapter) as a key concept in the therapeutic process. This emphasis is particularly apparent in the recent developments involving so-called "brief" psychoanalysis, which appears to be more similar to re-education than to therapy in the conventional sense. This new approach emphasizes further the close relationship between psychotherapy and the learning process that we discussed earlier.

PSYCHOANALYSIS: FREUD. The most elaborate and systematic attempt to explain the origin, development, and cure of psychological disturbances was made by Sigmund Freud. From his early publications in the 1880s until his death in 1939, he continually examined the psychodynamics of mental disorders, their origins and manifestations, developed and elaborated his theories, and promulgated a method of psychotherapy. He was an acute, sensitive observer of human nature, and his insights into human nature and his ideas, regardless of the controversy they have aroused, have in many ways become a part of our everyday thinking and have exerted a profound influence in many different areas.

Freud believed that all of us, as infants, pass through stages wherein we emphasize certain bodily areas or functions and that at each stage we encounter different social learning problems. First comes the so-called oral-erotic stage, during which the child derives his chief emotional satisfactions from nursing, thumbsucking, biting, and chewing. In this stage the child also encounters his first major psychological frustration—weaning. This weaning frustration provides the child with his first clue that he is a separate person from his mother.

Second comes the anal-erotic stage, during which the child is concerned with the process of controlling the expulsion and retention of feces. The main frustration appearing at this time concerns toilet training. Freud believed that this frustration led to the development of further self-awareness and the beginning of a sense of responsibility, by indicating to the child that he had certain obligations to fulfill and that he must adjust to certain social and physical demands in his pursuit of pleasure.

The third stage Freud called the genital, or phallic stage, during which the child derives emotional pleasure and satisfaction from discovering, exploring, and using his sex organs. Frustrations at this stage arise from infantile masturbation, the suppression of the sexual urges that develop toward the parent of the opposite sex, and the Oedipal situation of the son in love with his mother or the daughter in love with the father. Freud believed that these frustrations help the youngster to develop a sense of self-reliance and responsibility that enables him to become independent of his parents, to stand alone in society, and to form new attachments with other adults, leading to the establishment of a family of his own.

Freud felt that the basic groundwork of a person's personality was laid during his infancy and early childhood. He believed that later breakdowns or maladjustive behavior resulted from a fixation at the oral or anal stage arising from inadequate development.

Freud's emphasis upon childhood experiences explains why his therapy stresses examining the infancy of the patient in order to determine at which stage his development lagged or was diverted from the normal developmental channels. The process by which childhood experiences are retraced is known as *free association*. In free association, the patient is asked to say anything that occurs to him, regardless of how insignificant or irrelevant it may seem or how reluctant he may be to express it. He is asked to assume a detached attitude toward his own thoughts and to exert as little direction and control over his associations and ideas as possible. The ability to free-associate is facilitated for the patient by the permissive atmosphere created by the therapist and by the objectivity with which the therapist approaches everything the patient says.

These free associations sooner or later lead the patient back to his adolescence and infancy and involve, of course, the child's parents and possibly other authority figures. Re-living these infantile experiences may cause the patient to react emotionally to the therapist in the same way he previously reacted to his parents. This is the *transference* situation, mentioned previously, in which the patient comes to project onto the therapist the feelings of love or hatred he formerly felt toward his parents. This transference phenomenon and the strong emotional reactions involved between the patient and therapist constitute an important aspect of the therapeutic process. Through the transference situation, the patient gains new insights into his feelings, attitudes, and behavior.

Another technique that helps the patient to remember and to disclose material about his early life and development is the *analysis of dreams*. In dreams, the patient's feelings, hopes, and wishes visit him in disguise, and the therapist can help him to see through this disguise, to recognize the latent content of the dream, and to understand the dream's real significance. Dreams and the symbolism in which they express themselves are often unconscious efforts at wish fulfillment.

PSYCHOANALYSIS: JUNG. An early co-worker of Freud, and a man who has made important contributions to psychoanalysis, is C. J. Jung, a Swiss psychiatrist. Jung's system of psychoanalysis is known as *analytic psychology*. Jung came to disagree with Freud primarily about the concept of libido, which for Freud meant the total life urge based mainly on love and sex. Jung defined the concept more broadly as a general life urge, not merely sexual in nature, but connected with all pleasures, especially social pleasures.

Jung also differed from Freud in his views about the unconscious. Jung's theory postulated an *individual unconscious,* consisting of repressed personal experiences, and a *collective unconscious,* consisting of inherited predispositions toward archaic ways of thinking. Thus, dreams for Jung involve interpretations related to racial unconscious motives as well as to personal unconscious motives. The concept of the racial unconscious has led Jung to undertake an intensive study of primitive cultures and the folklore and symbolism of various cultures.

Jung places great emphasis upon dream analysis and upon artistic productions of the patient. He also uses free association but has developed specially controlled association techniques in which the therapist provides a word and the patient responds with the first association that occurs to him. Through this use of the controlled association technique, Jung has uncovered so-called "complexes," which are clusters or patterns of emotional ideas and wishes related to certain objects or experiences.

Jung's ideas about personality structure and development involve a pattern of opposite qualities and tendencies, such as thoughts vs. feelings, sensations vs. intuition, and extroversion vs. introversion. In the normal person, all these contradictory poles are integrated and so enable a person to achieve maximum development and to realize his potentialities to the utmost. The neurotic, on the other hand, has allowed one tendency to develop out of all proportion to the others.

Jung, then, believes that analysis can help a person discover which tendency has become over-exaggerated and how he should go about redressing the balance. Jung stresses the wholeness of personality and believes that a person must combine the rational and irrational aspects of his make-up in order to live a happy, well-adjusted life.

PSYCHOANALYSIS: ADLER. Alfred Adler, originally a member of Freud's group of analysts, later broke with Freud and developed his own views, which have come to be called *individual psychology*. Adler rejected Freud's concepts of the unconscious, of repression, and his emphasis upon the psychosexual origin of personality characteristics.

Adler accepted Freud's insistence on psychological determinism, but felt that the source of this determinism for a person was his *will to power* and believed that this was the primary motive of man. Adler saw the will to excel in social, economic, and sexual competition as the paramount consideration in our lives. Failure to excel in these basic areas, Adler asserted, led to an *inferiority complex,* which, in turn was responsible for our manifold efforts to compensate for our defects. These compensatory efforts, Adler believed, restricted a person's personality growth.

According to Adler, personality development progressed along a road paved with evidence of either personal superiority or inferiority. From infancy onward, the advantages of size, beauty, and strength, are emphasized both within the family and by society as a whole. As an infant, small, helpless, inexperienced, we are especially subject to the whims of others and vulnerable to inferiority feelings.

As we grow older, there develops in us a continual see-sawing conflict between our attempts, wishes, and dreams for superiority and the social realities that may make us feel inferior. This striving for prestige, which Adler called the "masculine protest," occupies a place in his theory similar to the niche that the Oedipus situation occupies in Freudian theory. An individual develops into either a normal adult or into a neurotic or psychotic personality according to how this struggle between the masculine protest and social reality develops.

In Adlerian therapy, which differs considerably from either the Jungian or orthodox Freudian therapy, no distinction is made between so-called conscious and unconscious material. The Adlerian analyst, for example, uses dreams to discover the "style of life" of the patient in order to determine the type of defenses he utilizes in trying to establish his superiority. The therapist tries to analyze the inferiority feelings that stem from personal deficiencies, particularly so-called organ deficiencies, or from organic inferiority, which everyone is supposed to possess. Next the analyst proceeds to examine the patient's marital, vocational, and social adjustments. The therapist dwells upon the way in which the patient has maintained or achieved superiority in each of these three major areas of life and examines the type of inferiority feelings that plague the patient in these areas. A primary goal of Adlerian therapy is to demonstrate the over-compensations and defensive patterns that the patient has acquired and to help him to find better ways of successfully competing in these three areas.

Child-guidance clinics give help to parents by providing opportunities for them to talk over their problems with other parents under the direction of a psychologist. (Courtesy the Southern California Society for Mental Hygiene and Hal Adams, photographer.)

apist is to get the process of growth going again by removing these troublesome blocks. Since he has the natural growth forces of a person's personality for allies, the therapist can restrict himself to a subservient passive role. By his permissive and accepting attitude, he encourages the patient to unburden himself of suppressed feelings, and through the technique of reflection (mirroring the patient's own feelings), the therapist helps the patient to recognize, clarify, and accept these feelings, and, finally, to develop new insight. By striving to keep his own personality unobtrusively in the background, the counselor minimizes the danger of forcing the patient's growth in the wrong direction.

Rogers holds that non-directive therapy, when skillfully applied, leads to an orderly and predictable sequence of development, the major therapeutic steps being the expression of feelings, the recognition of feelings, and the initiation of new positive steps. As this latter stage is reached, the client begins to feel less and less dependent on the counselor. He begins to realize, at first timidly and then with fewer qualms, that the therapeutic relationship eventually must end. The initiative in making the final break is left to the patient. Since this step is frequently accompanied by a new upsurge of anxiety, the client is assured in the final interview that he may come back if he should feel the need to do so.

Relationship therapy. All the above-mentioned therapies recognize the importance of the interaction between the patient and the therapist, and between the patient and his social surroundings. Relationship therapy stresses this interaction even more emphatically. In effect, relationship therapy claims that the social relations of the patient—his dealings with parents, children, friends, and the like—are responsible for his maladjustment. The therapist, therefore, tries to rectify these errors by assuming the roles of these other people in the hope that the patient will identify with the therapist and assume the therapist's more successful defenses and adjustments.

An important tool in relationship therapy is psychodrama. In psychodrama, the therapist suggests a social situation that appears important to the patient and has him act out the various parts of the different individuals involved. This produces a catharsis and helps to lessen the patient's social deficiencies. The patient acquires the habit of picturing the reactions and attitudes of others to his behavior, and in this way learns which habits or traits to discard and which to retain and develop.

Group psychotherapy. An important recent development in psychotherapy is the use of group treatment. A group, selected by the therapist, usually consists of six to eight patients, sometimes more, who have disorders and complaints that are neither too different nor too similar in nature. The group meets for about one and a half hours one to three times a week. Group therapy, its advocates believe, has certain advantages over individual psychotherapy insofar as the patients are concerned. Group participation reduces the artificiality of the therapeutic situation, providing a more natural, everyday setting than does the individual patient-therapist relationship. The group provides a certain social support for each member, a "we" feeling that may reduce the patient's anxiety about his own problems.

The group provides a special social "testing situation" in which each person can learn how to improve his social relations, test his methods of dealing with others, identify himself with other persons and their problems, and obtain comfort through mutually sharing problems. The patient, becoming aware that other people suffer from problems similar to his own, is apt to lose much of his own sense of social rejection and isolation. As he looks around at other members of the group, he begins to realize that they too have problems just as he does—some even worse, in fact. Thus the patient's courage is bolstered and new hope is found.

Through group discussion, the patient's resistance is overcome. Hearing others talk about their problems often encourages the more inhibited patient to do the same. Powerful emotional currents of positive and negative transference may begin to flow.

Group therapy is frequently used in combination with individual therapy. The patients have one or two hours of individual therapy and one group session per week. Many group therapists use the individual sessions to acquire information that can later be used to guide the group discussion. The individual sessions, for example, may be used primarily to get at the root of neurotic conflict while the group study may serve mainly for exploratory purposes and as a medium in which to try out new forms of behavior associated with the neurotic conflict. The new therapy appears to have been successful in the treatment of fairly severe neurosis of the obsessional or anxiety type. It has appeared to be less valuable in the treatment of hysteria, hysterical disturbances, and in working with manic-depressive patients. Group therapy is currently the object of much research, and it seems fairly certain that the technique will be used more and more as time goes on.

Psychotherapy and Self-help

The student may well be wondering at this point, "How can I help myself? Can I myself eliminate anxiety, a phobia, a compulsion, or other maladjustive symptoms? The answer to these questions may be either yes or no, depending on what is implied in the questions. To the extent that we will modify our behavior through learning, it must follow that we can bring about many changes in ourselves without the specific help of a therapist. And often many other persons besides a therapist can help us with our problems—parents, teachers, clergymen, counselors, coaches, and friends, for example.

In the light of what we have already said about psychotherapy, it might be argued, too, that therapy primarily is a method of helping the individual to help himself by creating an atmosphere conducive to learning. Since the individual is the only one who has the power to change himself, any improvement in his behavior is essentially self-improvement. Even with the help of the best therapist, successful therapy is still in a sense a "self-cure."

Perhaps the question we should ask ourselves is this: Can we help ourselves or provide self-therapy when our behavior shows excess emotion or psychological maladjustments that are expressed in certain symptoms? Have we any evidence to help us answer this question? One of the most comprehensive discussions of self-therapy is contained in the book *Self-Analysis,* by Karen Horney, which is listed in the recommended readings at the end of this chapter. She believes that self-analysis is possible in many cases and discusses the theoretical and practical aspects of the process in her book. Another interesting discussion of self-analysis is given by the biologist E. T. Farrow in his book, *Analyze Yourself,* also listed in the recommended readings. He indicates that after two-hundred hours of analysis under two different systems of analysis he decided to try to analyze himself. His book describes in detail the progress of his self-analysis, the techniques he evolved, and the results he obtained. It might be mentioned in passing that Freud also analyzed his own dreams, although his theoretical orientation in psychoanalysis and his emphasis on the transference phenomenon as a tool for successful psychotherapy deny the feasibility of self-analysis. Farrow adapted the method utilized by Freud in analyzing his dreams, namely, writing down everything that came to his mind during specified periods, and maintained that he was able to recreate the emotional experiences of incidences as early in his life as six months of age. Following this recreation of his emotional crises, an improvement in his health and sense of well-being occurred.

Horney discusses various difficulties in self-analysis, such as the difficulty of maintaining high motivation without a therapist, or of stopping too soon with self-analysis after removing a few difficulties or blocks and then arranging one's life to fit the remainder of the neurosis that was not worked through. Furthermore, the patient in self-analysis may not find it possible to deal with the problems he uncovers.

Even if we accept the theoretical possibility of self-therapy, there are many persons in need of psychotherapy who would be unable to follow through on self-analysis. Some of these persons, such as psychotics, would not even be aware that they needed psychotherapy or self-help, no matter how obvious their mental and emotional predicament might be to others. Still others might be aware of the existence of a problem but might completely misinterpret its nature. For example, a person suffering from conversion symptoms, such as colitis, an ulcer, or certain kinds of asthma or allergy, would recognize his symptoms but attribute them to an organic cause and not even realize that actually they stemmed from psychological causes. To suggest psychological self-analysis to such a person would strike him as ridiculous.

Still another person might be aware that a problem of psychological origin exists and yet lack confidence in the ability of his organism to cure itself, just as it lacked the ability to "cure" or avoid the symptoms of the problem in the first place. Neurotic symptoms indicate that the organism has been unable to handle a problem, so how, he reasons, can he hope now to work through the problem that led to the symptoms.

Finally, there are persons who have a problem, recognize its psychological nature, analyze the difficulties, and work through their own psychological dynamics to provide solutions for their difficulties. Into this class would fall the generally well-adjusted individual who suddenly developed a specific problem in a special situation and discovered his own methods for working the problem out.

We have already spoken about the importance of obtaining "insight" in psychotherapy. If such insight appears to result from the interactions of the patient and therapist, we might conclude that if the patient had, without help, developed this insight earlier, he would not have developed his present neurotic symptoms. His symptoms, in other words, indicate that he was not able to achieve this insight alone. We might even carry this reasoning a step further and say that if insight is the key to curing one's psychological difficulties, then it must also be the key to solving any problem that arises, thereby preventing symptoms from developing. This raises a related question, discussed earlier, "Why do psychological difficulties arise?" Or, in other words, "Why does one person develop psychological symptoms while another person does not, when both are confronted with the same situation?" The answer lies in the fact that we don't always have sufficient insight to handle our problems.

Qualifications of Psychotherapists

As we have emphasized before, the person who is emotionally disturbed and who seeks help for his problems has to unlearn old ways of behaving and learn new ones. But in order to do this he needs the help of someone who understands the psychodynamics underlying maladjustment. To whom can he turn for help? Or to whom can those who are concerned about him turn for help, for in some cases of severe disturbances or disorganization, the person himself may not be aware that anything is wrong and others have to assume responsibility for affecting his cure.

In some cases, emotional disturbances are temporary, surface phenomena, just as are many physical ailments, and the help and care of family and friends may be all that the person needs to recover from them. But if such disturbance occurs repeatedly or if it is severe, then expert help is called for, and one of the following three specialists in personality disorders should be consulted—a psychiatrist, a psychoanalyst, or a clinical psychologist.

The *psychiatrist* is a physician with special training in the diagnosis and treatment of mental illness. He is thus equipped to determine both the organic and the psychological basis of personality disorders. Frequently an illness that manifests itself primarily in physical symptoms, such as headaches or excessive fatigue, may be aggravated by or be caused primarily by emotional disturbances. Or, a patient who shows symptoms of emotional disturbance may be suffering from some organic injury, such as brain damage. The psychiatrist has been trained to detect both kinds of symptoms and to recognize what they mean.

The psychiatrist who has specialized in the function of the nervous system is called a neuropsychiatrist. Or if he has been trained especially in operations on the brain and the spinal cord, he is a neurosurgeon. Ordinarily psychiatrists are members of the American Psychiatric Association, and the American Orthopsychiatric Association. Neuropsychiatrists usually also belong to the American Neurological Association.

The *psychoanalyst* is a psychiatrist with special training in psychoanalysis. He may practice psychoanalysis exclusively or he may use other methods of treatment. The training of the psychoanalyst requires that he himself undergo psychoanalysis by a recognized psychoanalyst. The two main methods that the psychoanalyst uses are free association and dream analysis. Usually the psychoanalyst belongs to the American Psychoanalytic Association.

The *clinical psychologist* is a specialist whose training has been at an accredited university, who has a Ph.D. in clinical psychol-

Psychosurgery has been employed successfully in many cases of mental illness. The photos show how one patient appeared before and after prefontal lobotomy. (From W. Freeman and J. W. Watts, Psychosurgery, *2nd ed. Springfield, Illinois, Charles C. Thomas, 1950, pp. 413-414.)*

ogy, and who has had at least a year's internship at a mental hospital or a clinic. The clinical psychologist, like the psychoanalyst, has in many cases also been psychoanalyzed. Because so much of psychotherapy involves the dynamics of the learning process, the clinical psychologist receives extensive training in this area, as well as in diagnosis and research techniques. Efforts are now being made in many states to obtain licensing for qualified clinical psychologists in order to guard against quacks infiltrating the profession.

The clinical psychologist is generally a member of the American Psychological Association and an increasing number are Diplomates in Clinical Psychology, American Board of Examiners in Professional Psychology. The clinical psychologist usually works in close cooperation with physicians to be sure all medical aspects of a case are carefully covered.

The team approach. In recent years an increasing number of clinics have been set up that maintain teams of professionally trained people. The minimum staff of such a team consists of a psychiatrist, a clinical psychologist, and a psychiatric social worker. Such teams are widely used today in child-guidance clinics, in neuropsychiatric out-patient clinics, in prisons, and in student counseling agencies.

In addition to the specialists in the field of mental illness—the psychiatrist, the psychoanalyst, the clinical psychologist—there are others who are sufficiently trained to help a person with his adjustment problems, or rather, to prevent the problem from appearing in the first place. People such as your pastor, school psychologist, vocation counselor, and others usually are ready and willing to lend a sympathetic ear to whatever may be troubling you and to offer helpful advice when they can.

But some people, aware of their problem and knowing the type of treatment they require, do not know where to find competent psychologists and psychiatrists. Here are some suggestions:

Call or write to the psychology department at the university nearest to you. The faculty will be able to refer you to qualified clinicians. Or contact the local office of the American Medical Association or ask your doctor. In many cities you will find a branch of the National Association for Mental Health. These local organizations ordinarily maintain an information and referral service, and although they will not recommend any one specific person, they will give you a list of qualified people in the area in which you live, from which you can choose. The American Medical Association follows the same procedure. Some communities have compiled a directory of psychiatric and psychological clinics, especially for persons in the low-income bracket. Finally, the states maintain mental hygiene clinics that will send you an application blank on request and schedule an appointment for you.

For Additional Reading

Adler, A., *The Practice and Theory of Individual Psychology,* translated by P. Radin. London, Kegan Paul, Trench, Trubner and Company, 1929.

Alexander, Franz and Thomas M. French, *Psychoanalytic Therapy.* New York, The Ronald Press Company, 1946.

Axline, Virginia M., *Play Therapy.* Boston, Houghton Mifflin Company, 1947.

Bach, George R., *Intensive Group Psychotherapy*. New York, The Ronald Press Company, 1954.

Brill, A. A., ed., *The Basic Writings of Sigmund Freud*. New York, The Modern Library, 1938.

Colbry, Kenneth M., *A Primer for Psychotherapists*. New York, The Ronald Press Company, 1951.

Dollard, J. and Neal E. Miller, *Personality and Psychotherapy*. New York, McGraw-Hill Book Company, Inc., 1950.

Farrow, E. P., *Analyze Yourself*. New York, International Universities Press, 1945.

Fenichel, Otto, *The Psychoanalytic Theory of the Neuroses*. New York, W. W. Norton & Company, Inc., 1945.

Freud, Sigmund, *A General Introduction to Psychoanalysis*. New York, Garden City Publishing Company, Inc., 1938.

————, *Collected Papers*, Vols, I-IV. London, The Hogarth Press, 1949.

Fromm-Reichmann, Frieda, *Principles of Intensive Psychotherapy*. Chicago, The University of Chicago Press, 1950.

Horney, Karen, *Self-Analysis*. New York, W. W. Norton & Company, Inc., 1942.

Ingham, Harrington V. and Leonore R. Love, *The Process of Psychotherapy*. New York, McGraw-Hill Book Company, Inc., 1954.

Jung, C. G., *Psychological Types*. New York, Harcourt, Brace & Company, Inc., 1923.

————, *The Integration of the Personality*. New York, Farrar and Rinehart, Inc., 1939.

Kubie, Lawrence S., *Practical and Theoretical Aspects of Psychoanalysis*. New York, International Universities Press, Inc., 1950.

Lief, Alfred, ed., *The Commonsense Psychiatry of Dr. Adolf Meyer*. New York, McGraw-Hill Book Company, Inc., 1948.

Masserman, Jules H., *Principles of Dynamic Psychiatry*. Philadelphia, W. B. Saunders Company, 1946.

Mowrer, O. Hobart, *Learning Theory and Personality Dynamics*. New York, The Ronald Press Company, 1950.

————, *Psychotherapy—Theory and Research*. New York, The Ronald Press Company, 1953.

Reik, T., *Listening with the Third Ear*. New York, Farrar, Strauss and Company, 1949.

Rogers, C. R., *Client-centered Therapy*. Boston, Houghton Mifflin Company, 1951.

————, *Counseling and Psychotherapy*. Boston, Houghton Mifflin Company, 1942.

Rotter, Julian B., *Social Learning and Clinical Psychology*. New York, Prentice-Hall, Inc., 1954.

Slavson, S. R., *Analytic Group Psychotherapy*. New York, Columbia University Press, 1950.

Snygg, D. and A. W. Combs, *Individual Behavior*. New York, Harper and Brothers, 1949.

Steiner, Lee R., *Where Do People Take Their Troubles?* Boston, Houghton Mifflin Company, 1945.

Sullivan, Harry Stack, *The Interpersonal Theory of Psychiatry*. New York, W. W. Norton & Company, Inc., 1953.

Index